# OFFICIAL HISTORY

## OF THE

# OPERATIONS IN SOMALILAND
# 1901–04

## VOL. II

*General Staff, War Office*
1907

The Naval & Military Press Ltd

Published by
**The Naval & Military Press Ltd**
5 Riverside, Brambleside, Bellbrook
Industrial Estate, Uckfield, East Sussex,
TN22 1QQ England

Tel: +44 (0) 1825 749494
Fax: +44 (0) 1825 765701
www.naval-military-press.com

*In reprinting in facsimile from the original, any imperfections are inevitably reproduced and the quality may fall short of modern type and cartographic standards.*

# CONTENTS.

## VOL. II.

| Chapter | | Page |
|---|---|---|
| IX.—Organization of Commands and Staffs.—Field States | | 335 |
| X.—Organization of Lines of Communication and Bases | | 347 |
| XI.—Staff Duties | | 367 |
| XII.—Local Levies and Mounted Troops | | 417 |
| XIII.—Artillery | | 445 |
| XIV.—Services and Departments— | | |
|     1. Engineer Services, including Water Supply | | 452 |
|     2. Telegraph, Signalling and Postal Services | | 477 |
|     3. Supply and Land Transport | | 489 |
|     4. Marine Transport, Disembarkations and Re-embarkations | | 529 |
|     5. Medical and Sanitary Services | | 578 |
|     6. Veterinary Department | | 583 |
|     7. Remount Department | | 586 |
|     8. Ordnance Department | | 595 |
|     9. Accounts Department | | 600 |
| XV.—Demobilization | | 603 |
|   Index | | 617 |

# LIST OF PLATES.

## VOL. II.

| No. of Plate. | Title. | To face Page |
|---|---|---|
| 16. | Three Sowars of the Somali Camel Corps | 417 |
| 17. | Ponies grazing | 420 |
| 18. | Bikanir Camel Corps—Embarking Camels | ⎫ |
| 19. | ,, Review Order | ⎪ |
| 20. | ,, Full Dress | ⎬ 428 |
| 21. | ,, Indian and Arab Camels | ⎪ |
| 22. | ,, Heavy Marching Order | ⎪ |
| 23. | ,, Maxim Gun Detachment | ⎭ |
| 24. | K.A.R. Camel Battery—Draught Equipment | ⎫ |
| 25. | ,, Draught Equipment | ⎪ |
| 26. | ,, Camel in draught and loaded | ⎪ |
| 27. | ,, Section ready to march and on the march.. | ⎬ 448 |
| 28. | ,, Camel in Draught and Camels kneeling for "Action" | ⎪ |
| 29. | ,, "In Action" | ⎭ |
| 30. | Dam at Upper Sheikh | ⎫ |
| 31. | ,, | ⎬ 456 |
| 32. | Details of the Dam at Upper Sheikh.. | ⎭ |
| 33. | Sketch of Well at Shimber Berris, with method of carrying water | ⎫ |
| 34. | Water Supply—Wadamago | ⎬ 457 |
| 35. | Section of Well at Wadamago | ⎭ |
| 36. | Bohotle Fort | ⎫ |
| 37. | Blockhouse, Dubar | ⎪ |
| 38. | Ber Defensible Post | ⎬ 472 |
| 39 40. | Burao Defences | ⎪ |
| 41. | Upper Sheikh Post | ⎭ |
| 42. | Upper Sheikh Redoubt | 473 |
| 43. | Berbera | 473 |
| 44. | Kirrit Post | 474 |
| 45. | Ain Abo Post | 474 |
| 46. | Halin Post | ⎫ |
| 47. | Las Khorai Post | ⎬ 475 |
| 48. | Las Khorai. Plan of Coast | ⎭ |
| 49. | Plan of Somali and Field Force Telegraphs—15/1/04 to 31/1/04 | 482 |
| 50. | Plan of Somaliland Field Force Telegraphs on 22/3/04 | 482 |
| 51. | Somali Pony | 590 |

The Coloured Plates in this reprint Are Placed at the End

## CHAPTER IX.
### ORGANIZATION OF COMMANDS AND STAFFS.
### FIELD STATES.

ORGANIZATION OF COMMANDS AND STAFFS.*

FOR the period of command of Colonel E. J. Swayne in 1901–1902, no documents appear to be available from which the organization of the forces employed in the first and second expeditions can be recorded. Such organization as existed is described in the narrative of these expeditions given in Chapter III and IV. First and second expeditions.

After the action at Erigo and the retirement of the British forces to Bohotle, Brig.-General W. H. Manning was appointed to the command of the troops in Somaliland, and in accordance with his plan of campaign the troops were constituted as the Somaliland Field Force, and separated into two parts in January, 1903 (see Chapter V). The commands and staffs were:— Third expedition.

| | |
|---|---|
| General Officer Commanding | Lieut.-Colonel (local Brig.-General) W. H. Manning, Indian Army (with Obbia force). |

**OBBIA FORCE.**

| | |
|---|---|
| Chief Staff Officer | Major (local Lieut.-Col.) G. T. Forestier-Walker, Royal Field Artillery. |
| D.A.A.G | Major C. L. Petrie, D.S.O., Manchester Regiment. |
| D.A.Q.M.G. for I. | Major E. M. Woodward, Leicestershire Regiment. |
| Principal Medical Officer | Lieut.-Colonel J. F. Williamson, C.M.G., Royal Army Medical Corps. |

---

\* The distribution of officers to some appointments and of troops to commands varied from time to time.

| | |
|---|---|
| C.R.E. .. .. .. | Captain W. B. Lesslie, R.E. |
| Chief Transport Officer | Captain M. L. Hornby, D.S.O., 56th Infantry. |
| Chief Supply and Transport Officer | Captain H. de B. Codrington, Supply and Transport Corps, Indian Army. |
| Inspecting Veterinary Officer | Major A. F. Appleton, Army Veterinary Department. |
| Superintendent, Post Office | Mr. C. W. Wynch. |
| Commanding lines of communication and base | Major W. H. Rycroft, 11th Hussars. |
| Staff Officer .. .. | Brevet-Major A. R. Hoskins, D.S.O., North Staffordshire Regiment. |

*Troops.*

28th Mountain Battery (one section).
One company British Mounted Infantry, King's Royal Rifles.
Burgher Contingent.
Bikanir Camel Corps.
One company Punjab Mounted Infantry.
No. 17 Company, 3rd Sappers and Miners.
52nd Sikhs.
No. 15 British Field Hospital (one section).
No. 69 Native Field Hospital.
1st King's African Rifles.
3rd King's African Rifles (detachment).
5th King's African Rifles.

together with detachments of the following corps, services and departments :—

| | |
|---|---|
| Wireless Telegraph. | Army Ordnance. |
| Marine Transport. | Survey. |
| Medical. | Army Pay. |
| Supply and Transport. | Remount. |
| Army Veterinary. | Field Post Office. |

### Berbera Bohotle Force.

| | |
|---|---|
| Commanding Berbera–Bohotle lines of communication and base | Lieut.-Colonel J. C. Swann, 101st Grenadiers. |
| D.A.A.G. .. .. | Captain J. H. W. Pollard, Royal Scots Fusiliers. |
| Intelligence Officer .. | Captain G. M. Rolland, Indian Army. |
| Senior Medical Officer | Major W. S. P. Ricketts, Indian Medical Service. |
| Chief Ordnance Officer | Captain H. A. Anley, Army Ordnance Department. |
| Supply and Transport Officer | Captain L. M. R. Deas, Supply and Transport Corps, Indian Army. |
| Chief Transport Officer | Brevet-Major C. Ballard, Norfolk Regiment. |
| In charge of telegraphs | Captain G. B. Roberts, Royal Engineers. |
| Inspecting Veterinary Officer | Lieutenant H. M. Lenox-Conyngham, Army Veterinary Department. |

*Troops.*

Telegraph Section, R.E.
3rd Sappers and Miners (detachment).
101st Grenadiers (half battalion).
107th Pioneers.
No. 65 Native Field Hospital.
2nd King's African Rifles.
Indian Contingent, British Central Africa.

Camel Corps .. ⎫
Mounted Infantry ⎬ 6th King's African Rifles and Somali Levies.
Infantry .. .. ⎭

together with detachments of the administrative services and departments.

The principal change made by General Manning from the normal Indian organization was that he separated the Supply and Transport Services, placing Supply and Transport under separate heads. From the time of General Manning's assumption of command a regular staff was instituted, lines of communication and bases were established, and services and departments were organized. Regular returns were rendered (the Adjutant-General having made a request for a monthly return on 3rd January), and staff diaries were kept. In this matter the task of the Commander was made considerably easier by the arrival of officers from Great Britain, India and South Africa. Officers of the Supply and Transport Corps and Accounts Department came from India and of the Army Ordnance Corps from England, while the personnel of the medical, veterinary and engineer services was largely increased.

Lieut.-Colonel Swann, though nominally Officer Commanding Lines of Communication, Berbera–Bohotle, was actually, under General Manning, in command of all troops on that side, including flying columns. All combined operations, however, were undertaken by the orders of General Manning, and were, as far as possible, under his direction. When, in June, 1903, the Obbia force was transferred to Bohotle, Colonel Swann became Officer Commanding Lines of Communication only; a position which he continued to occupy until the end of the fourth expedition. On the Obbia side a separate Officer Commanding Lines of Communication existed until the rolling up of that line in April-May, 1903, while there was a separate base and Base Commandant; though, as will have been seen above, the offices of Officer Commanding Lines of Communication and Base Commandant were combined in one officer.

Fourth expedition.
When Major-General Sir Charles Egerton assumed command of the forces in Somaliland, he was accompanied by an Assistant Adjutant-General and a Deputy Assistant Quartermaster-General together with a Divisional Headquarter Staff Office, which was mobilized in India.

General Egerton submitted for the sanction of Government a scheme of re-organization of the Field Force, based on the Indian Field Service Manual and Regulations, for a division of all arms.

339

In the absence of the formal sanction of Government, the force was provisionally organized from the 16th July, according to the proposed scheme, viz. :—

Headquarters of a division with divisional troops.
Two infantry brigades.
One "lines of communication."
(Subsequently, on the 8th October, the mounted troops were brigaded and formed a fourth command.)

The commands and staffs were, however, eventually constituted as follows :—

| | |
|---|---|
| General Officer Commanding | Major-General Sir C. C. Egerton, K.C.B., D.S.O. |
| A.D.C. | Captain R. G. Munn, 36th Sikhs. |
| | Lieutenant J. B. Egerton, 23rd Cavalry |
| C.S.O. | Major H. E. Stanton, D.S.O., Royal Artillery. |
| D.A.A.G. | Major R. G. Brooke, D.S.O., 7th Hussars. |
| D.A.Q.M.G. | Major C. O. Swanston, D.S.O., 18th Tiwana Lancers. |
| A.Q.M.G.(I.) | Major (local Lieut.-Colonel) G. T. Forestier-Walker, Royal Field Artillery. |
| Intelligence Officers | Captain R. W. C. Blair, 123rd Outram's Rifles. |
| | Major F. Cunliffe Owen, Royal Artillery. |
| | Lieutenant I. S. C. Rose, King's Royal Rifle Corps. |
| | Captain A. W. H. Lee, 10th Gurkha Rifles. |
| | Captain G. H. Bell, 27th Punjabis. |
| | Lieutenant R. D. Marjoribanks, 107th Pioneers. |

| | |
|---|---|
| C.R.E. | Major R. F. Allen, Royal Engineers. |
| Adjutant R.E. | Captain W. B. Lesslie, Royal Engineers. |
| Superintendent Army Signalling | Captain H. B. Protheroe Smith, 21st Lancers. |
| Provost Marshal | Commander E. S. Carey, Royal Navy. |
| Principal Medical Officer | Lieut.-Colonel J. F. Williamson, C.M.G., Royal Army Medical Corps. |
| Inspecting Veterinary Officer | Captain C. B. M. Harris, Army Veterinary Department. |
| Assistant to Inspecting Veterinary Officer | Captain W. A. Wood, Army Veterinary Department. |
| Director Supply and Transport | Lieut.-Colonel W. R. Yeilding, C.I.E., D.S.O., Supply and Transport Corps, Indian Army. |
| Assistant to D.S. and T. | Captain H. de B. Codrington, Indian Army. |
| Principal Ordnance Officer | Captain E. P. Carter, Royal Artillery. |
| Survey Officer.. | Captain G. A. Beazeley, Royal Engineers. |
| Field Controller | Major T. H. Henderson, Military Accounts Department, Indian Army. |

## MOUNTED TROOPS.

| | |
|---|---|
| Officer Commanding | Major (local Lieut.-Colonel) P. A. Kenna, V.C., D.S.O., 21st Lancers. |
| Staff Officer, Mounted Troops | Captain A. Skeen, Indian Army. |

341

*Troops.*

| | |
|---|---|
| No. I Corps | 1st Company British Mounted Infantry.<br>2nd Company British Mounted Infantry.<br>3rd Company British Mounted Infantry.<br>4th Company Somali Mounted Infantry.<br>5th Company Somali Mounted Infantry. |
| No. II Corps. | 6th Company Poona Mounted Infantry.<br>7th Company Umballa Mounted Infantry.<br>Bikanir Camel Corps. |
| No. III Corps .. | Tribal Horse. |
| No. IV Corps .. | Gadabursi Horse. |

1st Brigade.

| | |
|---|---|
| G.O.C. .. | Lieut.-Colonel (local Brig.-General) W. H. Manning, C.B., Indian Army. |
| A.D.C. .. | Lieutenant H. W. Peebles, Reserve of Officers. |
| D.A.A. and Q.M.G. .. | Captain J. H. Lloyd, 6th Gurkha Rifles. |
| Signalling Officer .. | Captain H. S. Hammond, Dorset Regiment. |
| Brigade Supply and Transport Officer | Lieutenant J. A. Longridge, Supply and Transport Corps, Indian Army. |

*Troops.*

King's African Rifles Camel Battery.
No. 4 Company (Somali) Mounted Infantry.
No. 5 Company (Somali) Mounted Infantry.
Indian Contingent, British Central Africa.
1st Battalion, King's African Rifles.
2nd Battalion, King's African Rifles.
3rd Battalion, King's African Rifles.
5th Battalion, King's African Rifles.
Somali Levies.

## 2ND BRIGADE.

| | |
|---|---|
| G.O.C. .. .. .. | Lieut.-Colonel (local Brig.-General) C. G. M. Fasken, 52nd Sikhs. |
| D.A.A. and Q.M.G. .. | Captain P. C. Eliott-Lockhart, Corps of Guides. |
| Signalling Officer . | Lieutenant A. W. H. M. Moens, 52nd Sikhs. |
| Brigade Supply and Transport Officer | Captain D. G. Bryce, 76th Punjabis. |

*Troops.*

28th Mountain Battery.
1st Battalion, Hampshire Regiment (half battalion).
27th Punjabis.   52nd Sikhs.

## LINES OF COMMUNICATION.

| | |
|---|---|
| Officer Commanding .. | Lieut.-Colonel (local Colonel) J. C. Swann, Indian Army. |
| D.A.A.G. .. .. | Captain J. H. W. Pollard, Royal Scots Fusiliers. |
| D.A.Q.M.G. .. .. | Capt. G. M. Molloy, 34th Poona Horse. |
| Section Staff Officers.. | Capt. W. F. B. R. Dugmore, D.S.O., North Staffordshire Regiment. |
| | Brevet-Major A. R. Hoskins, North Staffordshire Regiment |
| | Brevet-Major A. W. S. Ewing, North Staffordshire Regiment. |
| | Lieutenant E. C. W. Conway-Gordon, 3rd Skinner's Horse. |

| | |
|---|---|
| Director of Telegraphs | Captain G. B. Roberts, Royal Engineers. |
| Provost Marshal .. | Brevet-Major A. G. Maxwell, 6th Cavalry. |
| Senior Medical Officer | Lieut.-Colonel J. W. Rodgers, Indian Medical Service. |
| Veterinary Inspector.. | Captain H. M. Lenox-Conyngham, Army Veterinary Department. |
| Post Commandants .. | Lieut.-Colonel P. J. H. Aplin, 107th Pioneers.<br>Brevet Lieut.-Colonel C. J. Melliss, V.C., 109th Infantry.<br>Major A. P. A. Elphinstone, 106th Hazara Pioneers.<br>Captain P. C. R. Barclay, 120th Rajputana Infantry. |
| Base Commandant .. | Major E. M. Woodward, Leicester Regiment. |
| Base Staff Officer .. | Lieutenant W. B. Roberts, 101st Grenadiers. |
| Base Medical Officer .. | Major F. W. Gee, Indian Medical Service. |
| Base Supply and Transport Officer. | Captain F. W. Hallowes, Supply and Transport Corps, Indian Army. |
| Advanced Base Supply and Transport Officer | Captain A. R. Burlton, Supply and Transport Corps, Indian Army. |
| Marine Transport Officers | Commander C. J. C. Kendall, Royal Indian Marine.<br>Lieutenant E. W. Huddleston, Royal Indian Marine. |
| Remount Officer .. | Captain Hon. T. Lister, 10th Hussars. |
| Adjutant and Quartermaster Military Base Depôt | Captain C. R. Kelly, Royal Garrison Artillery. |

*Troops.*

No. 17 Company, 3rd Sappers and Miners.
No. 19 Company, 3rd Sappers and Miners.
101st Grenadiers.     107th Pioneers.

together with detachments of the following corps, services and departments :—

| | |
|---|---|
| Telegraph Section, R.E. | Provost. |
| Field Park, R.E. | Military Accounts. |
| Survey. | Veterinary. |
| Marine Transport. | Remount. |
| Supply and Transport Corps (including Army Service Corps). | Indian Ordnance. Protectorate Paymaster. Water Boring Establishment. |
| Medical. | |
| Postal. | |

### Field States.

As previously stated no strength returns seem to have been rendered during Colonel Swayne's period of command and therefore no summary of the states can be given. The approximate strength has, however, been given in Chapters III and IV. More detailed tables are given with reference to the strength of the forces under Brig.-General Manning and Major-General Egerton.

Table I shows the strength during four periods of General Manning's command, the information being taken from the returns rendered to the War Office. Owing to the fact that the original states sent in by General Manning differ in some respects from those sent in by General Egerton, the first table differs slightly in the headings from the second, the principal difference being that hospitals and hospital assistants are shown under non-combatants in the first table, while in the second table hospitals are shown under native troops and hospital assistants are shown separately.

Table II gives the strength at three periods of General Egerton's command. Demobilization took place in May and June, 1904.

345

I.—STRENGTH of the Field Force under Brigadier-General Manning at Various Dates compiled from the Monthly States rendered to the War Office.

| Date and Name of Unit. | British Officers. | Rank and File (Combatants). | | Non-Combatants (includes Hospitals). | Guns. | | | | Animals. | | | |
|---|---|---|---|---|---|---|---|---|---|---|---|---|
| | | British and Burghers. | African and Indian. | | 9-Prs. | 7-Prs. | 2·5 | Maxims. | Riding Camels. | Horses and Ponies. | Mules and Donkeys. | Transport Camels. |
| 11th November, 1902, Whole Force* | 54 | 3 | 2,560 | 200 | 6 | 4 | — | 10 | 155 | 353 | 88 | 780 |
| 1st February, 1903, Obbia Force† | 86 | 265 | 1,955 | 909 | 2 | 2 | — | 8 | 246 | 745 | 766 | 250 |
| 4th February, 1903, Berbera-Bohotle | 79 | 86 | 2,788 | 901 | 4 | 4 | — | 7 | 150 | 205 | 326 | 963 |
| Total, Whole Force, February 1st‡ | 165 | 351 | 4,743 | 1,810 | 6 | 6 | — | 15 | 396 | 950 | 1,092 | 1,213 |
| 1st April, 1903, Obbia Force § | 101 | 282 | 1,963 | 2,246 | — | 2 | — | 8 | 259 | 788 | 872 | 1,819 |
| 4th April, 1903, Berbera-Bohotle | 74 | 122 | 2,172 | 997 | 6 | 2 | — | 7 | 159 | 128 | 555 | 1,260 |
| Total, Whole Force, April 1st‡ | 175 | 404 | 4,135 | 3,243 | 6 | 4 | — | 15 | 418 | 916 | 1,427 | 3,079 |
| 1st May, 1903, Obbia Force ‖ | 86 | 228 | 1,864 | 1,967 | — | 4 | — | 6 | 137 | 632 | 645 | 2,136 |
| 2nd May, 1903, Berbera-Bohotle | 91 | 146 | 2,420 | 1,244 | 6 | 2 | — | 7 | 229 | 125 | 546 | 2,123 |
| Total, Whole Force, May 1st‡ | 177 | 374 | 4,284 | 3,211 | 6 | 6 | — | 13 | 366 | 757 | 1,191 | 4,259 |
| 4th June, 1903, Obbia Force | 55 | 66 | 1,243 | 1,406 | — | — | — | 5 | 113 | 238 | 156 | 2,030 |
| 6th June, 1903, Berbera-Bohotle | 142 | 301 | 3,035 | 1,834 | 6 | 4 | 2 | 8 | 263 | 481 | 870 | 1,224 |
| Total, Whole Force, June 4th‡ | 197 | 367 | 4,278 | 3,240 | 6 | 4 | 2 | 13 | 376 | 719 | 1,026 | 3,254 |

\* Manning's first state. † First monthly state after separation of Force. ‡ Approximate.
§ Last monthly state before Gumburu. ‖ First monthly state after Gumburu.

## II.—STRENGTH of the Field Force under Major-General Egerton at various dates, compiled from the Monthly State rendered to the War Office.

| Date and Name of Unit. | British Officers. | British Troops. Warrant Officers, Sergeants, Rank and File. | Native Troops. African & Indian Officers and (includes Native Hospitals). | Assistant Surgeons and Hospital Assistants. | Civilian Agents. | Followers (including Kahars). | Guns. 8-pounders. | Guns. 7-pounders. | Guns. 2.5. | Guns. Maxims. | Animals. Camels (Riding). | Animals. Camels (Baggage). | Animals. Horses and Ponies. | Animals. Mules and Donkeys. | Vehicles. Tongas. | Vehicles. Carts. | Vehicles. Buck Wagons. | Vehicles. Water Carts. | Vehicles. Ekkas. |
|---|---|---|---|---|---|---|---|---|---|---|---|---|---|---|---|---|---|---|---|
| **November 3rd, 1903\*—** | | | | | | | | | | | | | | | | | | | |
| i. Headquarters | 17 | 5 | — | — | — | 27 | — | — | — | — | 12 | 19 | 419 | 3 | — | — | — | — | — |
| ii. 1st Brigade | 37 | 4 | 368 | — | — | 285 | — | — | — | — | 14 | — | 385 | 44 | — | — | — | — | — |
| iii. 2nd Brigade | 38 | 290 | 1,806 | — | — | 294 | — | — | — | — | 6 | — | 73 | 207 | — | — | — | — | — |
| iv. Mounted Troops | 30 | 370 | 1,532 | — | — | 244 | — | — | — | — | 317 | — | 850 | 24 | — | — | — | — | — |
| v. Lines of Communication | 41 | 8 | 533 | — | — | 363 | — | — | — | — | 13 | — | 41 | 273 | — | — | — | — | — |
| vi. Departments | 120 | 313 | 1,574 | 80 | 97 | 8,447 | — | — | — | — | 164 | 9,474 | 1,959 | 2,385 | 61 | 200 | — | — | 1,104 |
| Total Force | 283 | 990 | 6,303 | 80 | 97 | 9,660 | — | — | — | — | 526 | 9,493 | 3,727 | 2,936 | 61 | 200 | — | — | 1,104 |
| **December 31st, 1903†—** | | | | | | | | | | | | | | | | | | | |
| i. Headquarters | 21 | 5 | 1,432 | — | — | 55 | — | — | — | — | 35 | — | 1,107 | 327 | — | — | — | — | — |
| ii. 1st Brigade | 43 | 2 | 1,460 | — | — | 241 | — | — | — | — | 8 | — | 383 | 16 | — | — | — | — | — |
| iii. 2nd Brigade | 39 | 303 | 1,470 | — | — | 314 | — | — | — | — | 6 | — | 68 | 160 | — | — | — | — | — |
| iv. Mounted Troops | 30 | 370 | 525 | — | — | 256 | — | — | — | — | 306 | — | 827 | 32 | — | — | — | — | — |
| v. Lines of Communication | 46 | 8 | 1,677 | — | — | 362 | — | — | — | — | 13 | — | 45 | 84 | — | — | — | — | — |
| vi. Departments | 130 | 315 | 503 | 76 | 111 | 9,186 | — | — | — | — | 223 | 10,422 | 2,070 | 2,567 | 20 | 119 | — | — | 995 |
| Total Force | 309 | 1,003 | 7,067 | 76 | 111 | 10,414 | — | — | — | — | 591 | 10,422 | 4,500 | 3,186 | 20 | 119 | — | — | 995 |
| **May 1st, 1904‡—** | | | | | | | | | | | | | | | | | | | |
| i. Headquarters | 15 | 5 | 382 | — | — | 25 | — | — | — | — | 12 | — | 279 | 3 | — | — | — | — | — |
| ii. 1st Brigade | 44 | 1 | 1,370 | — | — | 247 | — | — | — | — | 10 | — | 360 | 41 | — | — | — | — | — |
| iii. 2nd Brigade | 42 | 291 | 1,495 | — | — | 340 | — | — | — | — | 6 | — | 58 | 54 | — | — | — | — | — |
| iv. Mounted Troops | 33 | 347 | 524 | — | — | 227 | — | — | — | — | 281 | — | 669 | 43 | — | — | — | — | — |
| v. Lines of Communication | 41 | 8 | 1,228 | — | — | 309 | — | — | — | — | 12 | — | 41 | 111 | — | — | — | — | — |
| vi. Tribal Horse | 2 | — | 100 | — | — | 14 | — | — | — | — | — | — | 109 | 12 | — | — | — | — | — |
| vii. Departments | 133 | 311 | 500 | 79 | 114 | 8,549 | §6 | §4 | §2 | 21 | 159 | 6,911 | 1,556 | 2,617 | 20 | 126 | 80 | 4 | 941 |
| Total Force | 310 | 963 | 6,099 | 79 | 114 | 9,711 | §6 | §4 | §2 | 21 | 480 | 6,911 | 3,072 | 2,881 | 20 | 126 | 80 | 4 | 941 |

First state, showing the Force as reorganized into brigades, &c.   † Last state before Jidbali action and about the greatest strength.
Last state before demobilization.   § Not shown on original states but believed to be the same as under General Manning.

## CHAPTER X.

### ORGANIZATION OF LINES OF COMMUNICATION AND BASES.*

During the expeditions under Colonel Swayne the lines of communication extended to Burao in 1901 and were subsequently prolonged to Bohotle. Posts were established as follows :— First and Second expeditions.

At Sheikh.—A small masonry blockhouse in charge of police and levies.
At Burao.—A strong entrenched post with two 9-prs., in charge of a detachment of levies.
At Burdab.—A post of observation of 50 Somali rifles.
At Bohotle.—A strong masonry blockhouse with two 9-prs., a maxim with a detachment of Somali levies.

There was also a blockhouse at Las Dureh held by a detachment of levies, but this was off the lines of communication proper.

In the first expedition the "advanced base" was at Burao, and during the second the "advanced base" was first at Burao and subsequently at Bohotle. It must be understood that during Swayne's operations in the Eastern Nogal, he cut himself adrift from his lines of communication and carried a certain quantity of supplies with him, depending, however, largely upon captures and the resources of the country for the supply of his native troops. There was at this time no regular organization of the lines of communica-

---

* For the detailed organization of Services and Departments, see Chapter XIV.

tion under a commander, the number of officers available not allowing of this, nor was such an organization apparently considered necessary for the requirements of the expedition. As far as they went the lines of communication seem to have fulfilled their purpose of protecting Swayne's communications with Berbera, and of enabling supplies to be forwarded when necessary, as for example, on the return of the expedition to Bohotle in 1901.

Third expedition.
But in 1902-03 the larger numbers of the expedition under General Manning, as well as the conditions under which this expedition was conducted, rendered a more complete organization necessary. He therefore constituted two separate lines of communication—one for the Berbera-Bohotle force and one for the Obbia force.

*The Obbia Force.*—Obbia was made a base in January, 1903, and Lieut.-Colonel W. H. Rycroft, 11th Hussars, was appointed base commandant, which appointment was extended on January 26th, 1903, to that of Officer Commanding Base and Lines of Communication. The staff under Lieut.-Colonel Rycroft consisted of three officers with a supply and transport officer and an inspecting medical officer.

Subsequently, on the 7th March, the lines of communication was divided into three sections, as follows :—

Obbia to Lodobal, under Lieut.-Colonel Rycroft.
El Dibber to Inideenli, under Major Hoskins.
Rhakn to Galkayu, under Major Brooke.

Lieut.-Colonel Rycroft still remaining Officer Commanding the whole line.

The lines of communication consisted of a series of posts pushed from time to time further forward towards Galkayu, troops being sent to the front as required to reconnoitre, seize wells, improve water supply and fortify posts. After the occupation of Galkayu the principal work consisted in sending supplies to the front.

Posts were established at :—

> Gabarwein.
> Lodobal.
> El Dibber.
> Dibit.
> Inideenli.
> Rhakn.
> Wargallo.
> Galkayu.
> Bera.
> Dudub.
> Galadi

This line was finally rolled up during April-May, 1903, and all lines of communication troops proceeded with the main column to Bohotle during June.

*Berbera–Bohotle Force.*—This line, as well as the movable column was under Lieut.-Colonel J. C. Swann, 101st Grenadiers, who was allotted the following staff :—

> 1 Deputy Assistant Adjutant General.
> 1 Intelligence Officer.
> 1 Base Staff Officer.
> 1 Base Supply and Transport Officer.
> 1 Principal Medical Officer.
> 1 Inspecting Veterinary Officer.
> 1 Chief Ordnance Officer.
> 1 Chief Transport Officer.
> 1 Supply and Transport Officer.

Posts and garrisons were established at :—

| | | |
|---|---|---|
| Berbera | .. | 60 men, 101st Grenadiers. |
| Hargeisa | .. | 50 men, 101st Grenadiers. |
| Burao .. | .. | 53 men, 101st Grenadiers. |
| Bohotle | .. | 100 men, 101st Grenadiers. |
| Shimber Berris | | 26 men, 101st Grenadiers. |

and the flying column consisted of :—
  2nd Battalion, King's African Rifles.
  Detachment, Indian Contingent British Central Africa.
  Somali Mounted Infantry.
  Somali Camel Corps.

The total length of the lines of communication from Berbera to Bohotle was 210 miles, along which there existed nothing except a camel track, which had been roughly improved up the Sheikh Pass. The further improvement of the track was not possible on the then existing alignment, and it became, therefore, necessary to survey a fresh alignment. This work was effected by the Pioneers.

The provisioning of the posts was carried out chiefly by hired caravans.

After the Obbia line had been rolled up, the Berbera–Bohotle line became the only lines of communication, and eventually, in June, 1903 (see Chapter V), the whole of General Manning's force retired on to this line, when, pending the arrival of General Egerton and his decision as to future operations, the posts on lines of communication were garrisoned as follows :—

*Bohotle.*
1 Company Sappers and Miners.
101st Grenadiers.
3rd Battalion King's African Rifles.
5th Battalion King's African Rifles.
Indian Contingent British Central Africa.

*Garrero.*
2nd Battalion King's African Rifles.
50 Somali Mounted Infantry.

*Burao.*
1st Battalion King's African Rifles.

*Lower Sheikh.*
52nd Sikhs.

The standing orders of the Obbia lines of communication were as follows:—

When thorn bush is available zaribas of not less than 15 feet in breadth and interlaced with barbed wire, with a defensible wall inside, will be formed, a strong guard being always kept inside, while at night each man will sleep at his accustomed place near the defensible wall with rifle beside him; one quarter of the total garrison always sleeping in a central point as an inlying picquet, rifles beside them. *No. 1, Zaribas.*

As the Mullah has a large force of horsemen, said to be capable of moving from 50 to 70 miles in a day, special precautions against sudden attack must always be taken and garrisons be invariably under arms half an hour before daybreak.

A separate zariba capable of holding 1,000 camels will be made, and if ground permits be arranged as below:— *No. 2, Camel Zariba.*

Guard.

Animal Zariba.

Troops.

A zariba capable of holding these must, if square, have each face 75 yards long.

This zariba should, if possible, be placed to leeward of the camp.

Men while employed on fatigues outside the zariba will carry their rifles unless a perfectly clear view of the surrounding country is obtainable, but in any case a proportion of them will always be under arms and on the alert. Arms never will be piled. *No. 3, Fatigues.*

(a) The greatest care must be taken to see that the surroundings of the camp are sanitary, latrines for day use being to leeward and not too near the camp. These should be moved frequently to fresh sites, and all places where latrines have been placed should be marked to avoid the chance of troops camping over them. *No. 4, Sanitation.*

All offal should be burnt, and dead animals dragged half a mile to leeward, disembowelled and carcases burnt with dry grass.

(b) Night latrines will be formed outside, but near, and to leeward of the zariba, and men going out to these will invariably take their arms and warn the sentry over the entrance to the zariba.

On occupying a post, wells will be baled out before the water is used in order to get rid of stagnant water, which may be impregnated with sulphuretted hydrogen, the presence of which causes diarrhœa. Wells will *No. 5, Wells.*

also be improved, but should not be sunk much deeper, as if so water bearing stratum may be passed through and water let out.

If wells are in rock or hard ground they should be hollowed at bottom like an inverted mushroom.

Wells should be fenced in, and, where a sufficient number are available, told off respectively for British officers and troops, Mohammedans, Hindoos, horses, mules, and camels, and sentries posted.

Whenever possible reservoirs of water stored in sunken tarpaulins will be formed, and troughs made for animals to drink out of.

Leather buckets will only be used in wells set apart for animals.

**No. 6, Division of lines of communication.** The lines of communication will be divided into sections, the sphere of each section being notified from time to time, while the sections will, if necessary, be subdivided into sub-sections.

**No. 7, Commanders of sections to facilitate communication.** Commanders of sections will have sketches made of their section and copies of same will be given to each post commander, and shown and explained to all officers and others passing through, with all information about the road to the next post, its compass bearing, &c.

Wherever possible the road will be marked out by (*a*) heaps of stones (*b*) posts or branches (*c*) blazing of bushes, &c., according to local requirements; while at points where the road can be shortened or improved by ramping nullahs, &c., this should be done. If possible signalling communication will be established between posts.

**No. 8, Executive command.** Officers in executive command of posts on the lines of communication will not be superseded in command of posts by Transport or other officers who may be senior to them who are merely passing through.

**No. 9, Firewood.** Officers commanding posts will collect and store a considerable quantity of firewood, both as a reserve for themselves and for use by troops marching through.

**No. 10, Responsibility of O.C. posts for ordnance and other material.** Officers in command of sections or posts will keep a record of all Ordnance and other material, and be responsible for the same.

**No. 11, Diary to be kept by O.C. posts** A concise diary will be kept by officers commanding posts and handed over to successor, the duplicates being sent weekly to officer commanding lines of communication. Entries in diary to chronicle :—

(*a*) Letters received and dispatched,
(*b*) Arrivals and departures of troops,
(*c*) Weekly statement of supplies,
(*d*) Statement showing expenditure on guides, purchase of live stock, &c.,
(*e*) Any unusual occurrence.

**No. 12, Issue of limejuice.** All troops will receive two issues of limejuice per week at scale of 2 ozs. per issue. Officers commanding posts will see that it is drunk.

**No. 13, Escorts.** Officers commanding posts will arrange, in conjunction with Transport Officer, so that troops detailed to move forward act as escort to convoys. This will greatly relieve the permanent garrisons of posts.

**No. 14, Shepherds.** A proportion of native shepherds who have been sent up country in charge of live stock will be retained at each post to look after stock.

Chaguls will be invariably kept filled with water. Some solution of permanganate of potash is being sent up to different posts. Officers commanding posts will arrange for all chaguls be'ng washed out with water to which a small quantity of the solution has been added. — No. 15, Chaguls

Officers commanding posts will always forward letters which are marked "very urgent" with the greatest despatch, viz., by camel orderly, runner or spare horse, vide lines of communication Order No. 61 of 12th February; other letters are to be forwarded by first available opportunity. The only persons authorised to forward "very urgent" letters are:— — No. 16, Very urgent letters, mode of dispatch.

(1) G.O.C., or C.S.O.,
(2) Officer commanding lines of communication,
(3) Major Brooke, D.S.O.,
(4) Major Hoskins,
(5) Officers commanding posts.

Great care should be taken of all washers for water fantasses, which, if lost, should be at once replaced by new ones made from goat skin or string. Also it must be remembered that a full water tank rides well on a camel, whereas a partly full one is a shifting, and therefore very bad, load. — No. 17, Water fantasses.

When Somali prisoners are being sent to the base, or from one station to another on the lines of communication they must invariably be supplied with rations for journey. — No. 18, Somali prisoners.

All Government horses which are located at posts on lines of communication are liable at discretion of officers commanding posts to be used for carrying despatches, &c., at times when officers or others in whose charge they are are not using them for military purposes. — No. 19, Government horses on lines of communication.

Two filters will be issued to each post on lines of communication. Wherever there is a portion of a hospital the medical officer or assistant will be in charge of and detail hospital followers to work the same; while at other posts, officers commanding will see that men are specially told off and instructed in method of working and cleaning the filters. — No. 20, Filters.

(a) The officer commanding base and lines of communication will, under instructions from the Chief Staff Officer, decide what material is to be forwarded from time to time, and will instruct officers commanding posts on this point. — No. 21, Procedure re forwarding supplies to front.

(b) The Chief Transport Officer, Local Transport Officer, or Non-commissioned Officer will settle the number of animals available.

(c) The frequency of convoys and the hours of starting will be settled by officers commanding posts in conjunction with the local Transport Officers who are responsible that due regard is given to the rest and grazing of animals.

Officers commanding posts are responsible for the provision of escorts of proper strength.

(d) At posts where there is no Supply Officer, Non-commissioned Officer or Agent, the British Non-commissioned Officer in charge of the transport of convoys will make out the waybills, see that the loads billed are put on the transport animals, and check and hand them over to the supply representative at the post to which they are billed, or in the absence of a supply representative, to the officer commanding the post.

**No. 22, Pay of guides, runners, &c.**
Guides permanently engaged by officers commanding posts will receive 12 rupees per month (or equivalent), 1 tobe, and rations.
Guide for one march, 2 rupees or equivalent.
Runners and spies, according to work done.
When carrying messages, an individual runner should cover the ground at the rate of 5 miles per hour up to 20 miles, and 4 miles per hour up to 30 miles. Should they cover any distance at a quicker rate, they are to be rewarded at rate of 2 lbs. of rice or dates for every additional mile per hour. For instance, the ordinary time allowed between El Dibber, and Dibit (15 miles) would be three hours. Should the distance however be covered at rate of 6 miles per hour, viz., in 2½ hours, bearer would receive the above reward.

**No. 23, Prices of transport and supplies and table of equivalents.**
All transport and supplies bought from this date should be paid for in cash or equivalent to the men who produce them.
The following prices have been approved:—

| | |
|---|---|
| Camels .. .. .. .. .. | 40 rupees. |
| H rios .. .. .. .. .. | 5 ,, |
| Goats' .. .. .. .. .. | 4 ,, |
| Sheep .. .. .. .. .. | 4 ,, |
| Cattle .. .. .. .. .. | 30 ,, |
| Camel-load of wood .. .. .. .. | 2 ,, |

The comparative value of animals and articles of trade is as follows:—
1 tobe, American, which is 10 yards of white cotton, equals 2 rupees.
3 tobes equal 1 than, viz., 6 rupees.
Ghee, per lb., equals 10 annas.
Dates, per lb., equals 2 annas.
Rice, per lb., equals 2 annas.
20 sheep or goats (small or large) equal a good baggage camel.
2 cows or bullocks (small or large) equal a good baggage camel.
20 tobes equal a good baggage camel.
2 good milch cows equal three good baggage camels.
Herios, viz., Somali camel mats, complete with ropes, &c., equal 5 rupees or its equivalent.

These equivalents are only intended as a general guide, and are founded on the usual current rates of exchange at Obbia. Up country, a tobe is of greater value, while at present the value to us of burden camels is relatively greater than milch camels.

**No. 24, Retail supply depôts.**
In due course a retail supply depôt will be opened in each section of the lines of communication. Supplies for these depôts will be separately waybilled and stored on arrival. All troops in the section will draw rations from their respective depôt, while any troops moving from the base or from one station to another must be provided with last ration certificate.

**No. 25, Convoys.**
If the country is unsettled, convoys should leave at irregular times and the route be occasionally somewhat varied.

Where sandbags are available, blockhouses can be rapidly built of same, 2,000 being required for a blockhouse 10 feet square (outside measurment) and 10 feet high.

**No. 26, Blockhouses.**

Each blockhouse will be equipped with :—
    2 water fantasses.
    Reserve ammunition (200 rounds per signaller).
    7 days' reserve of rations.
    2 hatchets.
    2 spades.
    1 pickaxe.

None but the most urgent messages should be sent through signal posts on the lines of communication, as communication is difficult and slow.

**No. 27, Signalling.**

All messages will be handed in on Indian forms (India A.F. X 356). If no Indian forms are available the British forms may be used and filled in as below :—

    To.................... From ....................
    Message .........................................

All messages, if to be sent by native signallers, should be written in block letters.

All messages must be signed.

Message books should be inspected by Officers Commanding as often as possible, and rendered in the order in which messages were received and sent to the Signalling Officer, lines of communication, who will notify his whereabouts at the end of each month.

Any message which for any reason is not sent by helio should be taken to the officer commanding post in the evening. He will then decide whether it is to be sent on by road or helio on the following day.

Signallers will invariably carry rifles except when actually inside the posts.

Midday halts are necessary to permit the camels to graze. Strong mounted and foot picquets will always be detailed to accompany them when grazing.

**No. 28, Formation of troops on march.**

In the thick bush country the advance will invariably be in square formation, with the transport and all followers in the centre. The front and rear faces of the square will move in lines of sections at deploying intervals.

This formation must be practised before entering bush country in order to accustom troops to keep correct intervals between sections, and to deploy rapidly into line.

Whenever a halt is made the force will halt invariably in square, transport in the centre. Strong picquets will be thrown out to the front, rear, and both flanks. Arms will never be piled. In open country the order of march can be modified as required for such conditions.

No natives on any pretence whatever should be allowed to enter a camp or to come within the line of picquets when halted.

| | |
|---|---|
| No 29, Order on march. | No Somali is to be allowed to carry firearms on the line of march. All public and private followers will march immediately behind the transport column.<br>Men falling out on the line of march will invariably be accompanied by a comrade.<br>Hospitals will march at the head of the transport column. |
| No. 30, Transport on march. | Transport animals will march in several lines. The number of lines necessary will be determined when in square formation by the number of troops available to form the side faces of the square, which, when halted, should be able to completely protect the transport animals in the centre.<br>Separate orders will be issued by the Chief Transport Officer as to the positions of transport officers with transport.<br>Should a square or column be attacked, however, all transport officers non-commissioned officers, and armed assistants will at once proceed to the head of the transport column and await orders. |
| No. 31, Scale of baggage. | The following will be the scale of baggage allowed for all transport officers and troops proceeding to the front :— |

British officers .. .. .. .. .. 150 lbs.
British warrant and N.C.O.'s .. .. .. 100 „
British and Burgher troops .. .. .. 15 „
Native officers and hospital assistants .. .. 25 „
Native troops and followers .. .. .. 12½ „

Rations for officers' chargers will be carried by Supply Department.
Transport for the carriage of mess utensils, cooking pots, &c., will be allowed as follows :—

Officers .. .. .. .. .. .. 15 lbs.
Rank and file .. .. .. .. .. 2 „

This will be termed the " Light scale."

| | |
|---|---|
| No. 32, Tents. | No tents will accompany the advance force except hospital tents, of which a sufficient number for actual requirements only will be taken. |
| No. 33, Ammunition. | All troops moving out will take with them 100 rounds in pouch and 200 rounds in reserve ; maxims, 1,500 rounds per gun.<br>All other ammunition in excess of this amount will be handed over to the Ordnance Department at the base. |
| No. 34, Surplus baggage, storage of. | All units before leaving the base, Obbia, will store their tents and surplus baggage in the base camp. Every package must be clearly marked with the name of the unit. Any baggage which is likely to be required again at Obbia or at Berbera before the force returns to the coast should be separated from baggage which will not be required again in order that it may be got at quickly. |
| No. 35, Telegraphic address of O.C. lines of communication. | The telegraphic address of the officer commanding lines of communication is " Chowder." |

|  Post. | Maximum. | Minimum. |
|---|---|---|
| Berbera | 457 | 144* |
| Dubar | 14 | 14 |
| Kalgumrah | 14 | 4 |
| Bihendula | 30 | 26 |
| Galoka | 14 | 14 |
| Wagon's Rust | 30 | 14 |
| Lower Sheikh | 68 | 15 |
| Sheikh | 286 | 21* |
| Dubbar | 42 | 14 |
| Gololi | 50 | 6 |
| Waran | 50 | 0† |
| Hopesprings | 12 | 6 |
| Burao | 343 | 22* |
| Elkadalanleh | 54 | 25 |
| Olesan | 25 | 25 |
| Kirrit | 167 | 29 |
| Garrero | 75 | 75 |
| Wadamago | 102 | 30* |
| Eil Dab | 100 | 51* |
| Ain Abo | 25 | 25 |
| Bohotle | 104 | 3* |
| Las Dureh | 50 | 50 |
| Las Adey | 54 | 0† |
| Hagal | 20 | 0† |
| Beyi | 25 | 12 |
| Hargeisa | 150‡ | 50 |
| Shimber Berris | 52 | 25 |

\* Also garrisoned at this time by troops of 1st or 2nd Brigades.
† Abandoned.
‡ Includes 100 Somali Levies.

NOTE.—Strong parties of Pioneers who were road-making in the vicinity of posts, but did not, strictly speaking, form a portion of the garrison, have been omitted from this table.

From the 21st July, 1903, to the 29th October, 1903, the posts south of Burao were occupied by the 1st Brigade troops, and the General Officer Commanding 1st Brigade commanded the communications from Burao south. Ain Abo and Eil Dab were under the General Officer Commanding 2nd Brigade up to the 16th December, 1903, when Colonel Swann took these posts under his command.

The following staff was allotted to the lines of communication:— *Organization.*

Orderly Officer.
Deputy Assistant Adjutant-General and Quartermaster-General.
On 24th December a Deputy Assistant Adjutant-General was appointed and the Deputy Assistant Adjutant and Quartermaster-General became Deputy Assistant Quartermaster-General.
Two Section Staff Officers, subsequently (January 16th, 1904) three.
Base Commandant, with Base Staff Officer, and Officer Commanding Base Military Depôt, with Adjutant
Commanding Royal Engineer.
Remount Officer
Senior Medical Officer.
Inspecting Veterinary Officer.
Provost Marshal.

The line was divided into two sections, each administered by a Section Staff Officer :—

(1) The Sheikh Section, from Bihendula to Elkadalanleh.
(2) The Kirrit Section, from Elkadalanleh to Eil Dab, and from Kirrit to Bohotle.

To these was added for operations of the Las Dureh column towards Jid Ali and Gebi :—

(3) The Las Dureh Section, including the following posts from Berbera :—
  Beyi.
  Hagal.
  Las Dureh.
  Las Adey.
  And the Wagon's Rust, Las Dureh road, upon which it was unnecessary to place posts.

Upon the line east of Las Dureh being rolled up, Las Adey

was evacuated on the 17th April, 1904, and Hagal on the 23rd April, 1904, and the Section Staff Officers of that section returned to Berbera for employment at Las Khorai.

*Troops.*  The troops placed at the disposal of Colonel Swann for garrisons on the lines of communication were : —

101st Grenadiers.
107th Pioneers.
Depôt 52nd Sikhs.
Depôt 27th Punjab Infantry.
Depôt African troops of 1st Brigade.
400 Somali levies. These were disbanded on and after 17th October, 1903 (Memo. 1026 S.A., dated 27th October, 1903), 50 only being retained for lines of communication work.

*Defence of posts.*  All posts were placed in a state of defence (for details see Chapter XIV).

*Roads.*  The construction of the road from Berbera to Bohotle, begun during the previous phase, was pushed forward to completion, and the Kal Gumri-Bihendula section was opened on the 5th September, 1903, thus giving access to Wagon's Rust for wheeled traffic. The upper section of the Sheikh Pass road was opened on 9th August, 1903, cutting off the worst part of the old road, and the whole pass road was open and ready for two-wheeled vehicles and pack transport on the 1st October, 1903. Roads were also cut through the bush from Kirrit to Olesan and Kirrit to Wadamago.

On the decision to advance viâ Las Dureh the track from Wagon's Rust to Las Dureh, which for the first 20 miles runs through rough stony ground, intersected by nullahs with steep banks, was improved from an indifferent mule into a generally fair camel path, though the time was too short to avoid leaving places which were still trying to camels.

*Water Supply.*  South of Sheikh, as far as Wadamago, the water supply was a source of constant anxiety, and it was only by unceasing labour in the development of the wells, and maintaining the storage in tanks, and the strictest supervision in the distribution that it was possible to provide for the needs of troops and convoys passing along the line.

The digging of the wells, construction of storage tanks and pumping arrangements were in the hands of the Commanding Royal Engineer, the distribution and the control of traffic rested with the lines of communication Staff, and it became one of the most important duties of the Section Staff Officers to watch the storage and daily output, and so to arrange the timing of convoys and troops moving on the line that no undue strain should be put on any one post at the same time.

Fatigue parties were supplied by garrisons both for digging and pumping, the latter frequently demanding day and night work continuously, involving a heavy strain on the troops in addition to guard and escort work. As time went on and the Commanding Royal Engineer had more Arab labour available, the strain on the garrisons relaxed, but throughout the operations the lines of communication troops at all posts had hard and continuous work.

That cases of dissatisfaction with the arrangements for distribution occurred was only what might be expected. *Distribution of Water.* The individual transport officer, anxious, and rightly so, to maintain the efficiency of his own corps, did not like to pass a place where water was stored, and find that he was told off to water his camels at the next march, and could only draw for his men. Not knowing what other movements were in progress it seemed to him hard that he should have to leave so much water untouched, yet had he been allowed to water his camels, the next corps to arrive, probably a day or two days longer without water than his, would have suffered. In one case it would have been a luxury, in the other it was a necessity.

Apart, however, from a few cases of this kind the water arrangements worked smoothly. All requirements of mounted troops, infantry, remounts, mules, ekka trains, and camels were met, and a reserve kept in hand to meet any sudden movement of troops, which might be ordered to meet an unforeseen emergency (for details of distribution see Chapter XIV).

**Prisoners of** Prisoners of war were received over at the advanced posts of the lines of communication, and transferred down the line to the base at Berbera.

Specially strong zaribas were constructed at each post for their accommodation en route, and a strong enclosure of barbed wire, with suitable shelter, provided for their reception at the base.

**Captured stock.** Major G. W. Rawlins, 30th Lancers, was appointed to superintend the reception, and tending of captured stock, pending distribution or sale. Sales were effected at Eil Dab, Wadamago, Bohotle, Burao, and Berbera, under officers specially detailed for the purpose.

The condition of the animals varied much in different lots, and with it both the percentage of loss en route to the market, and the ultimate prices realized.

**Gardens.** The greatest benefit was derived by the troops on the lines of communication when vegetables were grown at some posts, and it was considered that a Government issue of vegetable seeds should always be made on future occasions at the commencement of a campaign.

The cost would be small, difficulty of transport nil, and the saving in the better health and efficiency of the troops great. This would especially be the case in a country like Somaliland where the inhabitants are non-agricultural, and raise no crops of any sort.

The general deficiency of water, of course, militated against gardens being started at any but a few favoured spots. Indian troops are generally drawn from the agricultural classes, and where water was available there was no difficulty in raising vegetables for the supply of the garrison and the hospitals. Burao, on a small scale, Sheikh, Lower Sheikh, and Dubar (supplying the base hospital at Berbera) were able to keep gardens going sufficient for their needs, and the issue of fresh vegetables was much appreciated by the scorbutic patients invalided from the operating column.

There was no political officer attached to the lines of communication staff. Cases which would have fallen within his purview were referred to the Consul, Berbera. Political officer.

The advanced depot was first formed at Kirrit, but subsequently (1st January, 1904) moved to Wadamago. Advanced depôt.

The extent of the lines of communication (400 miles) and the long distances between water supplies (*e.g.*, 45 miles from Elkadalanleh to Kirrit and 50 miles from Wadamago to Bohotle) would have entailed the use of a much larger force than two regiments for the protection of the communications, but for the following reasons :— Protection and escorts.

> The exposed (eastern) flank of the line was protected at first by a movable column and latterly by the operating columns.
>
> Want of enterprise on the part of the enemy.
>
> The fact that the tribes on the line were either friendly, or at least content to wait the issue of events before displaying any overt animosity.

No attempt was made to molest our convoys passing up or down. The utmost vigilance had, however, to be exercised to prevent thefts of camels whilst grazing. As, however, camel raiding is the national pastime of Somaliland, this cannot be regarded as any proof of partizanship.

Cases of interruptions to telegraph line were not infrequent, sometimes doubtless due to karias moving at night and gurgi poles on their camels becoming entangled in the wires, but often malicious or mischievous. The latter generally occurred soon after construction through a fresh district and yielded to measures concerted with the civil authorities or political officer.

The base at Berbera was organized under the Officer Commanding Lines of Communication, and was provided with the following staff :— Base organization.

1 commandant.
1 staff officer.
1 senior medical officer.
1 base supply and transport officer
1 assistant for transport.
1 remount officer.

A plan of the base at Berbera is inserted which shows fully the arrangements made and the general plan of accommodation.*

Defence.
The plan alluded to above shows also the defence organization, and the defence works are described in detail under the heading engineering works. These defence works were rendered necessary by the fact that the camp was situated, within a few hundred yards of the native town which contained a considerable population, said at one time to amount to 25,000 and described as "seething with discontent." It was therefore, necessary to take all possible precautions to protect the large accumulation of transport animals and Government stores from the danger of being raided by parties of hostile natives from the town.

Police.
At first no police establishment was sanctioned, but afterwards a provost marshal, lines of communication, was appointed with an establishment of :—

2 British.
5 Indians.
5 Somalis.

The Base Commandant considered this insufficient and recommended that :—

- A provost marshal should be appointed in the first instance for duty solely at the base.
- A special police force, in the proportion of at least 10 men to every 1,000 natives in military employ at the base should be provided at the outset.

Prison.
A prison was constructed in December, 1903, for the

---
* See page 473.

receptions of prisoners of war. It consisted of an enclosure 100 yards by 50 yards with a shelter and space for kitchens, infirmary, &c.

The administration of the base was considerably affected by the curious congeries of races there collected. At Berbera there were always to be found representatives drawn from nearly every part of India, besides Kaffirs, Zulus, Arabs, Abyssinians, Yaos, Soudanese, Swahilis, and Somalis. *Racial feeling.*

With such an admixture of races, all speaking different languages, and representing so many types of humanity, differing widely in customs, religion, and interests, it was not to be expected that a certain amount of friction would not be engendered. The Somalis were the more troublesome to manage than any other race, owing no doubt to their utter ignorance of discipline and to their ingrained independence, and quarrels occurred at intervals between Somalis and Arabs, Somalis and Abyssinians, and Somalis and Kaffirs. The Base Commandant remarked as a curious fact that the Hindu got on better with the Somali than the Indian Mahommedan did.

In any place, such as a base camp, where large numbers of Somalis, Arabs, Indians and Abyssinians were necessarily collected within a limited area, it was advisable to keep the Somalis as much as possible together, and at any rate to separate them from Arabs and Abyssinians.

The trench systems of latrines was adopted at Berbera, the soil, however, is practically all coral and very hard, which made digging difficult. *Sanitation.*

A large incinerator was established for the destruction of carcases of animals, and was kept going night and day.

The Base Commandant found that sufficient allowance at the outset had not been made for possible expansion of the camp, which rendered considerable areas of ground useless for camping purposes when additional troops began to arrive. He considered that from the very beginning the strictest measures should have been taken for compelling the men to

On the 4th July, 1903, the lines of communication ex-  Fourth
tended from Berbera to Bohotle, and comprised the following expedition.
stations :—

>Berbera.
>Bihendula.
>Lower Sheikh
>Upper Sheikh.
>Burao.
>Elkadalanleh.
>Garrero and Olesan.
>Bohotle,

in the direct line, with Las Dureh and Shimber Berris on the east flank, and Hargeisa on the west.

To these were subsequently added :—

Kirrit.—As the centre point of concentration area and advanced base.

Wadamago, Eil Dab, Ain Abo.—Working out eastwards towards the Nogal.

Dubar.—For protection of the Berbera water supply.

Kalgumrah.—Water post for use of buck wagons 14 miles south of Berbera.

Wagon's Rust.—Terminal station for buck wagons at the entrance to the Sheikh Nullah.

Dubbar, Gololi, Waran.—Intermediate watering stations between Sheikh and Burao.

Ber, near Elkadalanleh, was occupied during October while the water supply was being developed and water stored, but evacuated after the tribal horse had gone forward.

The garrisons originally allotted were reduced as the necessity for strong escorts diminished with the advance of the operating troops. The following table shows maximum and minimum garrisons at each post :—

conform to regulations for sanitation, and that the position of all latrines, refuse pits, &c., should be marked.

<small>Military Base Depôt.</small>
A military base depôt was established, which relieved the Base Staff Officer of an immense amount of detail, and the Commandant considered that without the depôt it would have been quite impossible to cope with the large amount of clerical work at the base.

Some difficulty was experienced, owing to the large number and the variety of race and language of the component parts of the force, in always identifying men who came to the depôt. Men frequently lost their service books, and it was recommended that the books should be of a stouter pattern.

<small>General remarks.</small>
The appointment of a camp quartermaster would have been a great advantage in a large camp such as existed at Berbera, where units were constantly arriving and leaving for the front. The duties of marking out camps and roads, of meeting units on arrival, and conducting them to their respective camping grounds, of arranging for the distribution of the water supply, an important item in Somaliland, and of generally supervising the camping grounds to ensure their being kept in a clean condition, entailed a considerable amount of work. A portion of these duties was carried out by the Provost Marshal, but they do not fall properly within this officer's sphere of jurisdiction.

## CHAPTER XI.

### STAFF DUTIES.

In Chapters IX and X an account is given of the organization of the staffs and commands of the forces which took part in the four expeditions. In this chapter it is proposed to explain briefly the working and distribution of the duties of the staff as they were conducted at the headquarters of Sir Charles Egerton's command. This period is preferably selected because the organization which previously existed was not adaptable to the Field Force as reconstituted for the fourth expedition, owing to the varied staff and departmental requirements consequent on its increased strength. Moreover, as the scheme of organization was based on the Indian Field Service Regulations for a "Division of all arms" and a "Lines of Communication," it affords a suitable illustration of the working in the field of the staff system which obtained at the time in the Indian Army.

Briefly described, this system included three kinds of staff appointments, which may be classified as the Personal Staff, General Staff* and the Technical Staff.

The General Staff, which included a separate branch for intelligence duties, consisted of officers holding the appointments of A.A.G. (Chief Staff Officer), D.A.A.G., A.Q.M.G. and D.A.Q.M.G., and section staff officers on the lines of communication.

The Technical Staff consisted of heads of services and departments with their assistants, and officers holding special appointments, such as Provost Marshal, Chaplains, &c., most

---

\* This term should not be confused with the "General Staff" referred to in the King's Regulations.

of whom were generally employed on the lines of communication in connection with the administration and maintenance of the force.

The following extracts from a report of Lieut.-Colonel H. E. Stanton, D.S.O., who was Chief Staff Officer of the Somaliland Field Force from July, 1903, to May, 1904, explain the working and distribution of duties of the staff :—

*Staff organization.* As regards the organization of the staff, its object was to provide the means for Commanders to deal with the principle and policy of maintenance and to directly control the employment of the troops of their commands.

The employment of officers trained to staff duties in India and the simple adaption of the Indian system ensured homogeneity throughout, and resulted in smooth working.

The peculiarity of the situation in July, 1903, as regards the work of the Headquarters Staff was that the force, consisting for the most part of unbrigaded reinforcements, had no sanctioned organization, nor had it any authorised mission, nor was it provided with the appliances or material to enable it to maintain its position, much less to take the field.

Until October, 1903, while the former matters were under the consideration of the Government, the multifarious requirements of the Field Force were, of necessity, dealt with in detail by the General Officer Commanding in direct communication with the War Office. During this period the inactivity of the enemy simplified the questions connected with the immediate employment of the force, but the task of the General Commanding in connection with its maintenance was abnormal.

Subsequent to October, 1903, the receipt of Government sanction enabled the Officer Commanding Lines of Communication to carry out the details of maintenance in direct communication with the sources of supply, and the General Officer Commanding was enabled to devote his whole attention to the conduct of operations and such matters of principle and policy of maintenance as affected the mission of the Field Force.

At the outset the situation was that of a mobilization on an over-sea theatre of war. This was practically undisturbed by the enemy, but, owing to the want of a sanctioned organization and mission for the force, and to the absence of local resources, it was subject to the delays arising from the incompleted cable communication with army headquarters and from the length of the sea journeys between the bases of supply (England and India) and the base of operations (Berbera).

Commanding and Staff Officers, both general and departmental, were provisionally detailed from the available officers present in the country to fill such appointments as were indispensable. Special attention was paid to the organization of the Intelligence, the Lines of Communication, the Base, the Supply and Transport, and the Remount Departments.

As all departments, except the Ordnance, and the large majority of the units were from the Indian establishment, which, besides requiring Indian patterns of stores, had their accounts audited on the Indian system, it was found that the relief of the Army Ordnance Department by the Indian Ordnance and Indian Engineer Field Park and the Indian Supply and Transport (already in the country) was desirable upon economic grounds; this was accordingly recommended and eventually carried out.

The equipment of the force to enable it to take the field was at once commenced by all staffs and departments.

The great value of the Indian Field Service Manual was much appreciated during the period of organization. It provides, in a portable form, details of organization and instructions for the co-ordination of all duties of staffs and departments under a system of mobilization and administration, which, besides being specially applicable to campaigns in uncivilised countries, has been constantly tested and brought up to date in recent years. No difficulty was experienced in adapting its provisions to the special circumstances of the Field Force and the theatre of operations, or in the application of its system of administration to the various component parts of the Field Force which were not from the Indian Establishment. *A field service manual.*

A difficulty arose as to the precedence "inter se" of officers holding local rank granted by the King, viz., whether officers recorded in the Army List as holding local rank whilst with the King's African Rifles were entitled to the advantages of precedence and command, outside "the command" of the King's African Rifles, which was of itself only an integral portion of the Somaliland Field Force. To obviate the possibility of any doubt as to precedence in such cases, it appears desirable that either the wording of King's Regulations, paragraph 9 (1), should be amended, or that the Army List should define in each case whether the limits, within which local rank has effect, are confined to "a command" or "a country."* *Precedence of local rank.*

The difference in system of payment of special service officers under the Allowance Regulations, and of special service or staff officers paid according to Indian Regulations, was found to operate to the disadvantage of officers of the Indian Establishment, pending the formal sanction to the scheme of organization of the Field Force; no staff pay is available for them till this sanction is received, whereas the grade pay of special service officers of the Home Establishment is available in whatever position they are employed. *Special service and staff officers.*

The Indian system has the advantage that the rate of staff pay is fixed according to the responsibility and importance of each appointment, but has a great disadvantage in the restriction it imposes on the employment of an officer for various duties according to the exigencies of active service, in that he is liable to suffer pecuniary loss unless he is performing the duties of an appointment already included in the sanctioned establishment of the Field Force.

---

\* This point has now been rectified.

Staff duties.

This and other anomalies would be avoided were all officers, sent for extra-regimental duty from the Indian Establishment, appointed special service officers, with graded pay at rates fixed on the analogy of the grading under the Allowance Regulations.

The distribution of staff duties was made on the system prevailing in India at the time of mobilization. Pending the receipt of general sanction for the organization of the force and the scheme of operations, all proposals and requisitions were, of necessity, dealt with by the Headquarters Staff, and, in addition to the Chief Staff Officer, separate staff officers were required to deal with Adjutant-General's subjects and Quartermaster-General's subjects.

When the general sanction had been received, a considerable proportion of these duties became routine, and were accordingly transferred to the Officer Commanding Lines of Communication, thus enabling the services of a Deputy Assistant Adjutant-General on the Headquarters Staff to be dispensed with, but necessitating a second General Staff Officer on the Lines of Communication Staff, and a special distribution of subjects between the Chief Staff Officer and the Deputy Assistant Quartermaster-General. These two officers sufficed during operations for the Adjutant-General's and Quartermaster-General's duties of the Headquarters Staff.

On return from operations there was additional work connected with bringing outstanding cases up to date, preparing confidential reports, and making perparations for demobilization, which again necessitated the appointment of a Deputy Assistant Adjutant-General.

The sphere of operations was partly within and partly without territory administered under the Foreign Office. It was, therefore, of importance that the Headquarters Staff should include a Political Officer with local knowledge and experience of the local administration. Captain H. E. S. Cordeaux, C.M.G., Consul of Berbera, was appointed on the 19th October, 1903. All duties connected with the civil administration devolved on him when, on return from operations, the General Officer Commanding was directed to assume the duties of Consul-General of the Protectorate on the 8th March, 1904.

The office memoranda distributing and redistributing the staff duties are attached, Appendices A, B, C and D.

Two General Staff Officers for the Headquarters of the Lines of Communication, and one for each brigade and independent command met all requirements.

Equipment of staff offices.

The equipment and clerical establishment of staff offices for the Field Army in India were mobilised according to the requirements of the Field Force, and proved satisfactory in every way.

The means of equipping staff offices were not in the country when the re-organization of the force took place. Pending the arrival of the additional mobilised offices from India, the various staff officers laboured under considerable disadvantages, being dependent on a very limited supply of stationery in Army Ordnance charge.

Typewriters were found to be portable and invaluable both in standing camps and on operations.

A printing press was mobilised from India and was fully employed to great advantage both in saving clerical labour and ensuring a suitable circulation of important orders. It is an important adjunct to the headquarters and lines of communication of an expeditionary force.

The clerks were, for the most part, trained men from the Indian staff of military clerks, and performed excellent servvice. The Headquarters Office had the advantage of two clerks from the permanent establishment of the Indian Army Headquarters, and one clerk from an Indian Command Headquarters.

## *Appendix* A.

ORGANIZATION and Procedure of Somaliland Field Force, Headquarters Offices, as approved by the General Officer Commanding, 30th July, 1903.

Establishment.

### C.S.O.

1. Disposes of all requisitions and correspondence (both staff and departmental) for higher authority and for other authority outside the Field Force .. ..
2. Disposes of all non-departmental questions which affect more than one staff officer .. .. .. ..
3. Issues Standing Orders, Orders of the Day and Operation Orders .. .. .. .. .. ..
4. Deals with :—
    Discipline—officers .. .. .. .. ..
    Appointments—staff .. .. .. ..
    Confidential reports.. .. .. .. ..

Head clerk and one assistant to deal with the general services of the office.

### D.A.Q.M.G.

Deals with (B) subjects and returns .. .. .. 1 clerk.

### D.A.A.G.

Deals with (A) subjects and returns, also artillery, and the preparation and distribution of orders .. .. 1 clerk.

### A.Q.M.G.—I.

Deals with intelligence, interpreters, and Press Censor's duties .. .. .. .. .. .. .. } Intelligence Establishment.

(8927A) 2 A 2

## Appendix B.

ORGANIZATION and Procedure of the Somaliland Field Force Headquarters Staff Offices, with effect from the 23rd October, 1903, and in supersession of Memorandum dated 30th July, 1903. (Dated 23rd October, 1903.)

Establishment.

### C.S.O.

I.—(1) Takes G.O.C.'s orders on all general questions which affect the duties of more than one staff officer
(2) Disposes of all the G.O.C.'s correspondence (both staff and departmental) for higher authority, and for other authority outside the Field Force
(3) Keeps the Staff Diary
(4) Issues Standing Orders, Orders of the Day and Operation Orders
(5) Deals with A.G.'s subjects, except as shown in D.A.Q.M.G.'s duties

} Head clerk and one assistant for general services of the office.

### D.A.Q.M.G.

II.—Deals with Q.M.G.'s subjects and the following A.G.'s subjects:—
Armament of defences, clothing as supplied by the Supply and Transport, horses, provost, signalling and telegraphy

} 1 clerk.

### A.Q.M.G.—I.

III.—Deals with intelligence, interpreters, Press Censor's duties, and surveys

} Intelligence Establishment.

## Appendix C.

ORGANIZATION and Procedure of the Somaliland Field Force Headquarters Staff Offices, with effect from 29th February, 1904, and in supersession of Memorandum dated 23rd October, 1903. (Dated 3rd March, 1904.)

Establishment.

### C.S.O.

I.—(1) Takes G.O.C.'s orders on all general questions which affect the duties of more than one staff officer
(2) Disposes of all G.O.C.'s correspondence, both staff and departmental, for higher authority, and for other authority outside the Field Force
(3) Keeps the Staff Diary
(4) Issues Field Force Standing Orders, Orders of the Day and Operation Orders
(5) Deals with:—
    Discipline—officers
    Appointments—officers
    Confidential reports
    Captured stock

} Head clerk.

Establishment.

#### D.A.A.G.

II.—Deals with A.G.'s subjects other than those shown as dealt with by C.S.O. and D.A.Q.M.G. .. .. 1 clerk.

#### D.A.Q.M.G.

III.—Deals with Q.M.G.'s subjects and the following ⎫
    A.G.'s subjects :— ⎪
        Armament of defences, clothing as supplied by ⎬ 1 clerk.
        the Supply and Transport Corps, horses, ⎪
        provost, signalling and telegraphy .. .. ⎭

#### A.Q.M.G.—I.

IV.—Deals with intelligence, interpreters, Press Censor's ⎫ Intelligence
    duties, and surveys .. .. .. .. .. ⎭ Establishment.

## Appendix D.

ORGANIZATION and Procedure of the Somaliland Field Force Headquarters Staff Offices, with effect from the 18th March, 1904, and in supersession of Memorandum, dated 3rd March, 1904 (Dated 19th March, 1904)

Establishment.

#### C.S.O.

I.—(a) Takes G.O.C.'s orders on all general questions ⎫
       which affect the duties of more than one staff officer ⎪
  (b) Disposes of all G.O.C.'s correspondence (both staff and ⎪
       departmental) for higher authority, and for other ⎪
       authority outside the Field Force, except as in ⎪
       paragraph V. .. .. .. .. .. .. ⎬ Head clerk.
  (c) Keeps the Staff Diary .. .. .. .. .. ⎪
  (d) Issues Field Force Standing Orders, Orders of the Day ⎪
       and Operation Orders .. .. .. .. ⎪
  (e) Deals with :— ⎪
      Discipline—officers .. .. .. .. ⎪
      Appointments—officers .. .. .. .. ⎪
      Confidential reports .. .. .. .. ⎪
      Captured stock .. .. .. .. .. ⎭

#### D.A.A.G.

II.—Deals with A.G.'s subjects, other than those shown as dealt with by C.S.O. and D.A.Q.M.G. .. .. 1 clerk.

#### D.A.Q.M.G.

III.—Deals with Q.M.G.'s subjects and the following ⎫
    A.G.'s subjects :— ⎪
        Armament of defences, clothing as supplied by ⎬ 1 clerk.
        Supply and Transport Corps, horses, provost, ⎪
        signalling and telegraphy .. .. .. ⎭

#### A.Q.M.G.—I.

IV.—Deals with intelligence, interpreters, Press Censors ⎫ Intelligence
    and surveys .. .. .. .. .. .. ⎭ Establishment.

## POLITICAL OFFICER.

V.—(*a*) Deals with all matters connected with the civil administration on behalf of the G.O.C. and in his name.

(*b*) He will, in the first instance, refer through the C.S.O. all matters on which the G.O.C. will need to be advised by staff officers other than himself, and, with the exception of routine matters, he will refer these cases, with the observations of the responsible staff officer, for the personal orders of the G.O.C. before disposal.

(*c*) The C.S.O. and A.Q.M.G.—I. will keep the Political Officer informed of the progress of operations and intelligence matters respectively.

(*d*) Copies of important correspondence will be exchanged between the Political Officer and the C.S.O.

(*e*) The G.O.C.'s decisions will be communicated by memorandum between the Political Officer and members of the General Staff. Other communications will be in the form of office notes, to be available for reference in the office of origin.

VI.*—General and Departmental Staff Officers will take the G.O.C.'s orders direct on all matters which affect their own subjects only, and will keep the C.S.O. informed on all important orders received, or decisions taken, and of general progress.

A weekly Field Force Progress Report is cabled home from the C.S.O.'s office by the Indian mail steamer.

VII.*—All papers put up to the G.O.C. will be either taken personally or attested by the initials of the responsible staff officer.

The working and distribution of the staff duties adopted at the headquarters offices of the Field Force were followed, so far as they applied, by the staffs of brigades and other organizations. The following extracts illustrate the nature of the diaries, routine standing orders, Field Force orders and orders of the day, the preparation of which formed an important part of the work of the staff:—

---

* These instructions were also included in the preceding memoranda—Appendices A, B and C.

CONFIDENTIAL.

## EXTRACT FROM HEADQUARTERS STAFF DIARY

### SOMALILAND FIELD FORCE.

### FROM 25TH DECEMBER, 1903, TO 1ST JANUARY, 1904.

*Summary of Staff Diary, Headquarters.  (For the period ending 1st January, 1904.)*

Operations.—Secret orders have been issued for the future action of the Galadi garrison when joined by Major O'Bryen's convoy escort.

Convoy.—The convoy, under Major O'Bryen, left Bohotle for Galadi on the 29th December.

Operations.—Orders issued for the completion of the concentration for operations in the Nogal—

    The 1st Brigade, under Brigadier-General Manning, in the southern Nogal.

    The 2nd Brigade, under Brigadier-General Fasken, in the southern Nogal.

    A movable column to be formed at Eil Dab (the advanced base).

    Reconnaissance of Jidbali report its reinforcement by the enemy.

    Reconnaissance of Tug Der Valley, east of Bur Dab range, met no traces of the enemy.

Political.—The Consul-General is raising Musa Abukr levies to form a nucleus of resistance to raids in the north-east of the Protectorate.

Diaries.—Staff Diary, Mounted Troops, for the period ending 31st December, 1903; Staff Diary, 1st Brigade, for the period ending 26th December, 1903; Staff Diary, 2nd Brigade, for the period ending 2nd January, 1904; *Progress Report, Royal Engineer Works, for the week ending 19th December, 1903; and Meteorological Report of Upper Sheikh, for the period ending 28th December, 1903, are attached, and marked A, B, C, D and E respectively.

H. E. STANTON, Major.<br>
Chief Staff Officer.

2nd January, 1904.

| Source and Date of Intelligence. | Intelligence. |
| --- | --- |
| 25th December | Concentration.—Orders issued for the following :— <br>    To Bohotle from Wadamago, No. 5 Company, Somali Mounted Infantry. <br>    To Eil Dab from Burao, Waran and Lower Sheikh, 52nd Sikhs. |

* Not printed.

| Source and Date of Intelligence. | Intelligence. |
|---|---|
| 25th December—*cont.* | To Eil Dab from Lower Sheikh, one section, 28th Mountain Battery. (*See* diary, 21st December.) Co-operation of northern tribes.—The Consul-General was asked what he could arrange to prepare the northern tribes to resist raids and attack fugitives. |
| 26th December | Operations.—Secret orders issued for future action of Galadi garrison and Major O'Bryen's convoy escort. (Diary, 24th December.) Reconnoitring party of Tribal Horse returned on the 25th to Badwein after spending the night of the 24th in the neighbourhood of Jidbali. Report force there considerably strengthened and zariba extending to Chidan, 1½ miles south. Also that Nur Hedig's raiding party from the north has joined them. Galadi.—Report from Galadi, all well. Messages received from Munn. Ali Yusuf's men were found at Galkayu by Illalos. Naval.—Senior Naval Officer given general news, and requested to occupy Illig about the 10th January. |
| 27th December | Co-operation of northern tribes.—Orders issued sanctioning the raising of foot levies to former strength of 400. The 350 new levies to be at the disposal of the Consul-General. The Consul-General will take 50 men and rations for 350 for 1 month to Ankor by sea, and arrange for establishment of fort by the Musa Abukr at Dubbatad to south-east and half-way to Wirrig, remainder of new levy to be raised at once. He considers this will enable Musa Abukr to hold their own and induce Ali Naleya to refrain from joining the Mullah. Lieut.-Colonel Melliss, V.C., the 101st Grenadiers, placed at the disposal of the Consul-General for the Musa Abukr levy. (Diary, 25th December). Italians.—(Diary, 23rd December.) Intelligence news from Obbia reports that, beside Galkayu and Douilli, Ali Yusuf holds Badwein, 44 spearmen and detachments at Rohr. Also reports abandonment of Illig by Mullah, and confirms Italian report of Osman Mahmud having moved inland in force ostensibly to harass the Mullah. Operations.—The General Officer Commanding, 1st Brigade, reports Illalo reconnaissance is at Damot till the 31st, to cover O'Bryen's advance to Galadi. |

| Source and Date of Intelligence. | Intelligence. |
|---|---|
| 28th December | Concentration.—Headquarters Staff established at Eil Dab.<br>Two companies, 52nd Sikhs; one company, 27th Punjabis, reach Eil Dab.<br>Gadabursi Horse reconnaissance from Ber, viâ Shimber Berris, Waridad and Arregir reaches Badwein. (Diary, 21st December.)<br>Consul-General proceeds in H.M.S. "Perseus" to Ankor. (Diary, 27th December.)<br>Operations.—Report received of gallantry of Lieutenant H. A. Carter (117th Mahrattas), No. 6 Company, Poona Mounted Infantry; and Subadar Bhairo Gujar (119th Mooltan Regiment), No. 6 Company, Poona Mounted Infantry, at Jidballi on the 19th December. |
| 29th December | Operations.—The Gadabursi Horse reconnaissance to the north and east of Bur Dab reached Badwein without encountering the enemy.<br>A party of Ogaden (Ali Wenak) are due at Wadamago to take over the camels recovered from raiders at Lasakante by General Manning. Money compensation is ready for them for camels and flocks which have been purchased by the Supply and Transport Corps. |
| 30th December | Operations.—Report received at Bohotle from convoy camp, 15 miles south, all well.<br>Gadabursi Horse concentrated at Ain Abo.<br>Major O'Bryen informed of raiding party of dervishes said to be sending in captured stock, viâ Lasakante and Damot, to the Nogal, having raided them from Aidagalla section of Habr Yunis, near Gonda Liba.<br>The report states that the main body of the raiders has remained out to continue raids. (Headquarters at Hodayuwein.)<br>Report from Major O'Bryen camp, 15 miles south of Bohotle, all well.<br>Orders issued for (1) 1st Brigade to operate in the southern Nogal, leaving Bohotle, viâ Lassader, on the 5th January.<br>From Bohotle :—<br>  Somali Mounted Infantry, 125 rifles.<br>  King's African Rifles, Infantry, 550 rifles.<br>  Ilalos, 150 rifles.<br>From Eil Dab, viâ Yaguri :—<br>  27th Punjabis, 200 rifles.<br>  Gadabursi Horse, 550 rifles.<br>  Illalos, 50 rifles.<br>(2) For the 2nd Brigade to operate in the southern Nogal, leaving Eil Dab on the 7th January, Badwein 8th January. |

| Source and Date of Intelligence. | Intelligence. |
|---|---|
| December—*cont.* | Headquarters staff :—<br>Mounted troops—<br>                       Rifles.<br> Nos. 1 and 3 Cos., British Mounted Infantry 201<br> Nos. 6 and 7 Cos., Indian Mounted Infantry 262<br> Bikanir Camel Corps..  ..  ..  ..  183<br> Tribal Horse ..  ..  ..  ..  ..  454<br> Ilalos ..  ..  ..  ..  ..  ..  80<br>                        1,180<br>Artillery.—28th Mountain Battery, 2 guns.<br>Infantry—<br>                       Rifles.<br> Hampshire Regiment  ..  ..  ..  237<br> Sappers and Miners ..  ..  ..  ..  100<br> 27th Punjabis..  ..  ..  ..  ..  307<br> 52nd Sikhs ..  ..  ..  ..  ..  578<br>                        1,222<br>(3) A movable column to be formed at Eil Dab. |
| 31st December | Raids.—The Consul-General reports enemy at Dagar in some force, after raid on Protectorate tribes. Also refers to raid on Aidagalla to the west. He has been informed that present concentration for immediate operations appears the most efficacious and only possible action at present.<br>Reconnaissance.—Report from the Officer Commanding, Mounted Troops, that Major Beresford, with 250 Gadabursi Horse, reconnoitred from Ber Shimber Berris, Areged, Gosawein to Badwein, between the 24th and 28th December, covering 95 miles. Water only obtained at Shimber Berris, 4 gallons per animal. 100 ponies suffered severely. 150 mules seem very little the worse.<br>No sign of the enemy. (Diary, 30th December.)<br>Convoy.—Major O'Bryen reports all well from Lasakante. |
| 1st January, 1904 | Inspections.—The General Officer Commanding visited Badwein and Aya Selaleh. Inspected the tribal Horse.<br>Convoy.—At Dalaat. All well.<br>Galadi.—Report received. No news.<br>Navy.—The Rear-Admiral Commander-in-Chief, East Indies, does not sanction Senior Naval Officer's proposal to land a force at Illig owing |

| Source and Date of Intelligence. | Intelligence. |
|---|---|
| 1st January, 1904—*cont.* | to the surf and unsuitable state of the sea. Sanctions demonstration, which the Senior Naval Officer is arranging.<br>Distribution.—One company of Mounted Infantry at Badwein is to be relieved by one company of 27th Punjabis from Eil Dab.<br>Operations.—A party of the Tribal Horse on Mayo Hill report that they saw the glow of the dervish camp fires at Jidbali last night.<br>Jidbali is being watched by our Illalos. |

A.—*Staff Diary, Mounted Troops, Somaliland Field Force.*

| Source and Date of Intelligence. | Intelligence. |
|---|---|
| WADAMAGO | No. 5 Company, Somali Mounted Infantry, arrived from Bohotle. |
| Saturday, 12th Dec.<br>Sunday, 13th Dec.<br>Monday, 14th Dec.<br>Tuesday, 15th Dec. | Halt. |
| Wednesday, 16th Dec. | Officer Commanding Mounted Troops left for Eil Dab to take command of Badwein Column. |
| Thursday, 17th Dec. | 100 rifles, No. 3 Company, British Mounted Infantry; 100 rifles, No. 6 Company, Indian Mounted Infantry; 50 rifles, Bikanir Camel Corps, left for Badwein with column. |
| Friday, 18th Dec. | Above party left Badwein with 200 of Tribal Horse. |
| Saturday, 19th Dec. | Above party engaged the enemy at Jidbali.<br>Casualties.—3 Tribal Horse killed, 1 Mounted Infantry horse killed ; 2 British soldiers, 4 horses and 1 camel wounded.<br>Retired on column and marched towards Badwein. |
| Sunday, 20th Dec. | Mounted troops, with Badwein Column, arrived Badwein and halted. No. 7628 Private J. Rose, 1st Bn. Warwickshire Regiment, reported missing ; strayed from line of march. |
| Monday, 21st Dec.<br>Tuesday, 22nd Dec. | Halt. |
| Wednesday, 23rd Dec. | No. 1 Company, British Mounted Infantry, arrived Eil Dab from Wadamago. |
| Thursday, 24th Dec.<br>Friday, 25th Dec.<br>Saturday, 26th Dec.<br>Sunday, 27th Dec. | Halt. |

A.—*Staff Diary, Mounted Troops, Somaliland Field Force*—cont.

| Source and Date of Intelligence. | Intelligence. |
|---|---|
| Monday, 28th Dec. | A reconnaissance in which 100 Tribal Horse, 50 British Mounted Infantry, 50 Indian Mounted Infantry, and 10 Bikanir Camel Corps took part went out from Badwein to meet 280 of the Gadabursi Horse arriving from Shimber Berris, meeting them near Gosaweina, about 2 miles to the south-west of it. |
| Tuesday, 29th Dec. | The Gadabursi Horse moved to Ain Abo. |
| Wednesday, 30th Dec. | Headquarters, Mounted Troops; No. 3 Company, British Mounted Infantry, and detachment, Bikanir Camel Corps, moved to Eil Dab. |
| Thursday, 31st Dec. | Halt. |

P. A. KENNA, *Lieut.-Colonel,*
*Commanding Mounted Troops,*
*Somaliland Field Force.*

B.—*Staff Diary, 1st Brigade, Somaliland Field Force.*

| Source and Date of Intelligence. | Intelligence. |
|---|---|
| Sunday, 20th Dec. | 1. Water storage:—<br>1,397 large tins,<br>57 small tins, and<br>14,800 gallons stored in tanks. |
| Monday, 21st Dec. | 2. Work at wells continued, 1,300 gallons being added to the tanks, giving now total storage of 16,100 gallons. |
| Tuesday, 22nd Dec. | 3. Wells showing a decrease in their yield, only 900 gallons being stored to-day, and additional wells had to be handed over to 4th Somali Mounted Infantry for their daily requirements, which will further reduce storage. |
| Wednesday, 23rd Dec. | 4. 800 gallons stored to-day. Total up to date:—<br>1,434 large tins, and<br>17,800 gallons stored in tanks. |
| Thursday, 24th Dec. | 5. Storage to-day, 700 gallons only, and an additional 10 large tins. |
| Friday, 25th Dec. | 6. Letters received from Galadi:—<br>Major Marsh reports that his Illalos visited Galkayu on the 19th instant and found the fort occupied. Bodies of riflemen were located at Bera and Talaad.<br>He had received news from Captain Munn, who wrote from Harradigit on the 10th instant. |

B.—*Staff Diary, 1st Brigade, Somaliland Field Force.*—cont.

| Source and Date of Intelligence. | Intelligence. |
|---|---|
| Friday, 25th Dec.—*cont.* | Munn had heard that Colonel Rochfort was in the vicinity of Sesebani with the Abyssinian force.<br>The messengers passed through Gumburu, where there had been a little rain, and they reported good grazing between Galadi and Gumburu, and plenty of water at Wardair.<br>Major Marsh reports the health of the garrison as good, but all ponies in very poor condition. He had received no news from Obbia.<br>7. Troops in Bohotle had a holiday, being Christmas Day. |
| Saturday, 26th Dec. .. | 8. Mail received in Bohotle.<br>9. Party of Illalos left for Damot with orders to remain there till the morning of the 31st instant, when they will return to Bohotle.<br>10. A party of Ogaden (Ali Wenak) arrived in Bohotle to take over the camels recovered from the Mullah's raiding party on the 22nd November.<br>The party leaves this evening for Wadamago with a letter to Officer Commanding of that post to hand over the camels to them, and then send on representatives to Kirrit to receive the money due to them for sheep and burden camels taken over by the Supply and Transport Corps.<br>11. Water storage up to date as follows :—<br>    1,432 large tins,<br>    22 small tins, and<br>    19,800 gallons stored in tanks.<br>12. Messengers to Galadi leave this evening. |

W. H. MANNING, *Brigadier-General,*
*General Officer Commanding, 1st Brigade,*
*Somaliland Field Force.*

Bohotle, *26th December,* 1903.

C.—*Staff Diary, 2nd Brigade, Somaliland Field Force.*

| Source and Date of Intelligence. | Intelligence. |
|---|---|
| EIL DAB 27th December. | Nil. |
| 28th December | Reconnaissance went out from Badwein round northern foot of Bur Dab to meet Gadabursi Horse coming from Shimber Berris. The whole returned to Badwein in afternoon.<br>One double company, 52nd Sikhs, arrived Eil Dab from Burao. |
| 29th December | The whole of the Gadabursi Horse concentrated at Ainaba. |
| 30th December | Headquarters, Mounted Troops; No. 3 Company, British Mounted Infantry, and 50 Bikanirs returned from Badwein to Eil Dab. |
| 31st December | No. 3 Company, Sappers and Miners, left Eil Dab for Badwein to develop the water supply at that place. |
| 1st January, 1904 | Nil. |
| 2nd January | 100 rifles, 27th Punjabis, proceeded to Badwein, and No. 6 Company, Indian Mounted Infantry, was ordered to return from Badwein to Eil Dab. |

C. FASKEN, *Brigadier-General,*
*Commanding, 2nd Brigade,*
*Somaliland Field Force.*

E.—*Meteorological Report of Upper Sheikh for period ending 28th December, 1903.*

| Date. | Maximum (in Shade). | Minimum (in Shade). | Rainfall. | | Direction of Wind. | Remarks. |
|---|---|---|---|---|---|---|
| | | | Inches. | Cents. | | |
| 14th December | Degrees. 80 | Degrees. 40 | .. | .. | N.W. | Heavy clouds in evening in north and west |
| 15th December | 83 | 46 | .. | .. | S.W. in morning, N.E. in afternoon | Heavy mist in morning, very cloudy in afternoon |
| 16th December | 84 | 44 | .. | .. | S.W. in morning, N.E. in afternoon | Heavy mist in morning, very cloudy in afternoon |
| 17th December | 83 | 44 | .. | .. | S.W. in morning, N.E. in afternoon | Heavy mist in morning, very cloudy in afternoon |
| 18th December | 82 | 47 | .. | .. | S.W. in morning, N.E. in afternoon | Heavy mist in morning, very cloudy in afternoon |
| 19th December | 81 | 43 | .. | .. | N.E. | Very cloudy in evening in N.E.; a very slight drizzle |
| 20th December | 75 | 45 | .. | .. | N.N.W. in morning, N.E. in day | Very cloudy in morning and evening in N.E. |
| 21st December | 74 | 41 | .. | .. | N.W. | Cold wind blowing all day |
| 22nd December | 73 | 42 | .. | .. | ,, | ,, ,, ,, |
| 23rd December | 74 | 40 | .. | .. | N.N.W. | Cloudy in the evening, cold wind |
| 24th December | 76 | 41 | .. | .. | N.W. | ,, ,, ,, |
| 25th December | 76 | 42 | .. | .. | ,, | ,, ,, ,, |
| 26th December | 74 | 43 | .. | .. | ,, | Very foggy morning, cloudy and cold all day |
| 27th December | 76 | 45 | .. | .. | ,, | Very foggy morning, cloudy in afternoon |

J. W. RODGERS, *Lieut.-Colonel, I.M.S.,*
*Commanding, No. 1 Native General Hospital.*

Upper Sheikh, *28th December,* 1903.

## EXTRACT FROM FIELD FORCE ORDERS.

1015. **Supplies.**—On the recommendation of P.M.O., S.F.F., the following issues are sanctioned for one month from 22nd September, 1903 :—

*For British Troops of all ranks.*

Scale per man.

| | | |
|---|---|---|
| Rum, 25 per cent. U.P. .. | 1 dram | Two issues weekly— |
| Lime juice .. .. .. | 1 oz. | Wednesday and |
| Sugar .. .. .. .. | ½ oz. | Saturday |

*For Indian and African Troops and Followers.*

| | | |
|---|---|---|
| Rum, 25 per cent. U.P. .. | ½ dram | Two issues weekly— |
| For abstainers in lieu of rum— | | Wednesday and |
| Tea .. .. .. .. | ¼ oz. | Saturday. |
| Sugar .. .. .. | ½ oz. | |
| Lime juice .. .. .. | 1 oz. | Three issues weekly— |
| Goor .. .. .. .. | ½ oz. | Monday, Wednesday and Saturday. |

1025. **Horses.**—Field Force Orders Nos. 947, 974 and 979 are superseded, and the following substituted :—

(1) Under the authority of the Secretary of State for War, No. 476, dated 2nd September, 1903, the following free issues will be made during operations in Somaliland :—

Dismounted Officers—
   1 Riding animal (pony or camel).
   1 Set of line gear.
   1 Set of saddlery.
   1 Attendant, with the same clothing as for transport drivers, with the exception of 1 blouse, 1 fez and 1 Somali axe. Pay, 12 rs. per mensem.

Mounted Officers —Officers of the General and Personal Staff of Headquarters, Brigades and Lines of Communication, including Section Staff Officers and Officers of Mounted Units, are entitled to—
   2 Riding animals (pony or camel).
   1 Set of line gear per animal.
   1 Set of saddlery.
   1 Attendant.
Except as stated below.

No officer in receipt of horse allowance, or of pay which includes horse allowance, or who is entitled to draw forage in kind (or compensation in lieu), may draw an animal from the Remount Department, when by doing so the number of animals in his possession (including free issues and his private property) in excess of two would exceed the number for which he draws horse allowance, or forage in kind.

(2) Officers in receipt of horse allowance, or of pay which includes horse allowance, will not be provided with an attendant at the public expense, except for animals drawn in excess of the number for which they draw horse allowance.

Officers drawing servant's allowance may provide themselves with an attendant at the public expense for each animal drawn as a free issue, less the number of grooms for which servant allowance is admissible.

(3) Animals and attendants provided free, as authorised above, will be rationed at the public expense.

(4) Animals and saddlery, &c., will be drawn from Departments of Supply concerned on the authority of Lines of Communication Orders.

(5) Attendants will be entertained regimentally.

(6) All Government animals, saddlery and line gear will be returned to the departments from which they were received on the break up of the Field Force, or before the officers in charge of the animals and equipment leave the country.

1031. Discipline.—(a) The Transport Officer in charge of a convoy, when senior in rank to the Officer Commanding the escort, will issue all orders as to time and duration of marches, halts, pace and arrangements for grazing and watering.

(b) The Officer Commanding the escort will issue all orders for the protection of the convoy and disposition of the escort, both when halted and on the line of march.

(c) In cases where the Officer Commanding the escort is senior to the Transport Officer in charge of the convoy, the former officer will issue all orders, vide clauses (a) and (b) connected with the convoy and its protection, but will seek the advice and, as far as possible, act on the recommendations of the Transport Officer as regards the matters dealt with in clause (a).

1084. Correspondence.—With effect from the 26th October, 1903, the Officer Commanding Lines of Communication will deal with the following subjects :—

(1) The supply of Royal Engineer stores.
(2) ,, ,, Ordnance stores.
(3) ,, ,, Medical stores.
(4) ,, ,, Veterinary stores.
(5) ,, ,, Supply and Transport stores.
(6) ,, ,, Transport remounts.
(7) ,, ,, Remounts.
(8) ,, ,, Stationery.
(9) Marine Transport.
(10) Maintenance of Postal Department.

2. All correspondence on these subjects should be addressed accordingly from General Officers Commanding Brigades, Officer Commanding Mounted Troops and heads of departments.

3. All demands for the increase of establishments of the Field Force will continue to be dealt with at Field Force Headquarters.

1089. **Supplies.**—The following will be the daily scale of rations for Somali prisoners of war :—1 lb. rice, ½ lb. dates.

If rations in kind are not drawn subsistence allowance at the following rates will be allowed :—

At Upper Sheikh and at posts to the north at 2 annas per diem.
At posts south of Upper Sheikh at 3 annas per diem.

The issue of rations in kind, or subsistence allowance in lieu. is discretional with the officer in whose charge the prisoners are. Sums required for the payment of subsistence allowance may be drawn from the Supply and Transport Agent at the post or the nearest Treasure Chest Officer on a contingent bill, in which details should be given showing the number of men and the period for which the allowance is drawn. The contingent bill should be accompanied by the usual receipts for the amount required.

(2) The case of refugees will be referred to the Political Officer, Somaliland Field Force, for disposal.

## EXTRACT FROM ORDERS OF THE DAY.

1096. **Undesirables.**—Heads of departments and General Officers Commanding Brigades and individual officers having undesirables to report should do so direct to the officer Commanding Lines of Communication, who will publish a list from time to time for the information of all officers, warrant officers and non-commissioned officers, to ensure these men not obtaining employment with the force either publicly or privately.

1134. **Reports and Returns.**—General Officers Commanding Brigades, and other Officers Commanding Columns or Units, should invariably submit when leaving the lines of communication for operating zone, to Head. quarters, S.F.F., by telegram, a marching out state, which should show the numbers of the following :—

(1) Officers, including medical officers.
(2) British rank and file by corps, including Supply and Transport subordinates and assistant surgeons.
(3) Native officers, rank and file by corps, including hospital assistants.
(4) Followers, public.
(5) Followers, private.
(6) Horses and ponies.
(7) Mules.
(8) Riding camels.
(9) Burden camels.
(10) Ordnance and machine guns.
(11) Ammunition per rifle.
(12) Rounds per gun.
(13) Ammunition per maxim.
(14) Water tanks.

1139. **Discipline.**—No sentence of death passed on a prisoner of war may be carried into effect without the confirmation of the G.O.C., S.F.F., unless the officer in immediate command, being out of immediate communication with superior authority, is satisfied that the execution of the sentence is an immediate military necessity and in accordance with the customs of war.

1157. **Water storage.**—An R.E. officer, or, in his absence, the Post or Camp Commandant, will be in charge of the main water storage tanks, pumps, hose and syphoning arrangements. He will regulate the supply of water to the expense tanks, according to the quantity available. The Provost Establishment will furnish the officer in charge with a statement giving the water rations required to be delivered into the expense tanks, and will be responsible for discipline at the watering places and for the issue of water from the expense tanks and from water tins on the line of march.

(This order to be substituted for for Operation Standing Order No. 12, Water.)

1248. **Captured stock.**—(1) All captures of stock from the enemy will be reported by earliest opportunity to the C.S.O., S.F.F., and Major G. W. Rawlins, 12th Cavalry, Eil Dab.

(2) Captured stock retained for the use of the troops will be accounted for by receipts countersigned by the officer authorizing the issue; that otherwise disposed of by a report signed by the officer authorizing the disposal.

(3) All stock not disposed of under paragraph (2) will be sent with the vouchers in paragraph (2) to Major Rawlins on the lines of communication.

(4) Major Rawlins will account for all captured stock. One-third will be kept in kind and the rest disposed of under Major Rawlins' orders, in communication with Captain Cordeaux, Political Officer.

(5) Major Rawlins will be under the orders of the Officer Commanding Lines of Communication.

Besides the report to the C.S.O., all other communications from the Field Force on the subject of captured stock will be addressed to Major Rawlins direct.

(6) On receipt of this order, General Officer Commanding Brigades and Officer Commanding Mounted Troops and Lines of Communication will report (as in paragraphs (1), (2) and (3)), all captures since 1st January, 1904, to date and their disposal.

1306. **Transport.**—Officers who have to distribute transport to units should bear in mind that Silladar Camel Corps, Baluch Camel Corps and Indian Mule Corps do not appreciably suffer by being detached from the head quarters of their corps or by being split up, as their organizations admit of this, though, of course, it is desirable to keep each unit together as far as possible. On the other hand, Somali Camel Corps, Arab Camel Corps and Camel Cart Train soon go to pieces when split up and withdrawn from the supervision of their British personnel, so these units should be kept complete where it may be possible to do so. Details of any of these units should be attached to another unit when employed on detached duties and where it may be possible to do so.

## Intelligence.

During the first and second expeditions no definite system of field intelligence as forming an organized part of the duties of the staff existed. It was left to Colonel Swayne to improvise, with the assistance of the local civil authorities, such arrangements for the acquisition of information about the enemy and the country as the limited means at his disposal and the composition of his force would allow.

In addition to the agents employed by the Consul-General in Somaliland and the other measures taken by the civil authorities in Abyssinia and Egypt for gaining information about the plans and movements of the Mullah, the immediate source of intelligence upon which Swayne had to depend upon for his information were native spies, patrols, and friendly tribes. The patrols and tribal scouting work was placed mainly in the hands of one of his native officers, Risaldar Musa Farah, who, owing to his intimate knowledge of Somali customs and his influence with the tribes, was found a suitable agent for intelligence services. In addition to his own arrangements, Swayne and his officers relied also on captured prisoners, and on the native caravans which traded between the coast ports and the interior of the country. As regards maps, little was known previous to the operations of the topography of the country for military purposes, and recourse was had to the plans and reports of explorers and travellers who had visited that part of Africa, supplemented by sketches and notes made by Swayne and his officers during the course of the campaign.

During the early part of General Manning's operations in 1902, the Intelligence Service was generally conducted upon the lines adopted by Swayne, but it was not until January, 1903, that sufficient officers had arrived from England and India to enable the work to be placed on a proper footing. In February, 1903, when the headquarters of the Field Force was at Obbia, the establishment of the intelligence department consisted approximately of one staff captain,

80 Illalos (native scouts, of which about 40 were mounted), and 20 interpreters. An intelligence officer was appointed to the Berbera-Bohotle force, whilst another was engaged in similar work up country near Dibit. Majors E. M. Woodward Leicestershire Regiment, and G. T. Forestier-Walker, R.A. joined the force from England, and the former was placed in charge of the department, while Risaldar Musa Farah was retained as special intelligence agent at the headquarters of the Field Force during the operations. A small survey party was also sent from India and accompanied the troops for topographical purposes. In addition to the work performed by this party, the Intelligence Department managed to collect a large amount of information regarding the topography and principal routes within the theatre of operations by means of Somalis. The following method of obtaining information with respect to the routes was sometimes adopted and found useful.

The Somali being thoroughly accustomed to wander through the bush guided by the sun and stars, was able to give a fairly accurate idea of the general direction of one place with regard to another. Two places a considerable distance apart were therefore selected, *e.g.*, Galkayu and Walwal. Large stones were then placed on the ground as nearly as possible in their relative positions, as regards direction, to represent the two places. This was explained to the Somali, who was then asked to show with a small stone the position of the first place at which he would halt after leaving Galkayu and so on for all the intervening places between Galkayu (starting point) and the ultimate destination. The respective distances were roughly obtained by questioning the native as to the respective positions of the sun at starting and when arriving at the next halting place. The majority of course had no idea of measuring time by hours.

The bearings of the different stones from each other were taken by prismatic compass and, in this way, a network of routes was gradually built up over the whole country between the Haud and Webi Shebeli. A great many natives were examined in this way and cross checks taken in every direction. Some of the routes from Galkayu were prepared in the above manner, and when the Field Intelligence Department moved up country from Obbia, the opportunity was taken of testing their accuracy.

As regards the collection and distribution of information, each intelligence officer maintained a diary, a copy of which was forwarded weekly to headquarters, where the information, together with that received from other sources, was collated into an intelligence report.

On Major-General Sir C. Egerton assuming command of the Field Force for the fourth expedition, further measures were taken to enlarge and develop the duties and organization of the Intelligence Department. The number of officers was increased and the department was represented by a specially selected officer with each brigade or column, and at all important posts on the coast or lines of communication, as occasion required.

The following extracts from the report of Lieut.-Colonel G. T. Forestier-Walker, who was Assistant Quartermaster-General for Intelligence from 17th July, 1903, to 23rd May, 1904, give an interesting and instructive account of the organization and work of the Field Intelligence Department during the fourth campaign :—

Duties.    In addition to administering the usual field intelligence duties I was directed to superintend the following :—

    (a) Entertainment, classification and distribution of interpreters for the whole force.
    (b) Press censorship.
    (c) Distribution to the force of general information in addition to that coming under the heading of " Intelligence of the Enemy."
    (d) I was also directed to act as staff officer dealing with survey section questions.

Establishment.    On July 17th, 1903, the Intelligence Establishment was as follows :—
    Staff-Captain, Captain R. W. C. Blair, 123rd Rifles, Indian Army.
    Illalos, 150, armed with various weapons.

Ponies, 66.
Interpreters, 39 for the whole force.

The establishment sanctioned shortly after the assumption of the command by Major-General Sir C. Egerton was as follows :—

    Assistant Quartermaster-General, 1.
    Intelligence officers (special service), 3.
    Illalos, all mounted, 350.
    Interpreters.

This establishment was increased in September, 1903, by the addition of a clerk and office. In addition to the 350 Illalos sanctioned above I was permitted, in October, 1903, to enrol 100 men for employment as guides and messengers. In February, 1904, I was granted an additional intelligence officer as a temporary measure, owing to officers having been set free by the disbandment of the Tribal Horse. I thus had four special service intelligence officers, in addition to Captain Everett, 6th King's African Rifles, who had been detailed as an intelligence officer without special service grading.

Intelligence as to the movements, numbers, plans, &c., of the enemy can be gained in Somaliland, as elsewhere, by scouts, spies and deserters.

*Notes on the country, and methods adopted for gaining intelligence.*

*Reconnaissance in Force.*—Owing to the mobility of the enemy, the lack of water in the country and the want of precise geographical knowledge of the theatre of campaign, that source of information which is usually the most successful, viz., reconnaissance in strength, carried out by regular troops, had, of necessity, to be sparingly employed.

Indeed, with the single exception of Colonel Kenna's reconnaissance to Jidbali in the latter half of December last, the only reconnaissances in force which were undertaken were to reconnoitre routes by which it was proposed to move the force, with a view to the water supply being adequately tested. The whole of the work of gaining intelligence of the enemy therefore devolved on the natives of the country.

*Illalos.*—Somali scouts, or "Illalos" as they are termed, are, within certain well defined limits, very satisfactory intelligence agents, but they have their idiosyncrasies :—

(a) They are practically useless, except working in tracts of country with which they are thoroughly familiar.

    As only certain tribes and sub-tribes inhabit specified places it is, therefore, necessary that the Illalos employed should be of the tribes (and usually of the sub-tribes) which ordinarily frequent those districts.

(b) Illalos are useless unless worked in large numbers, that is to say, in parties which are strong enough, or which they themselves consider to be strong enough to successfully engage any opposing raiding parties which they may meet, or, at the worst, to provide for their own safe retirement.

In fact, Illalo patrols are practically entirely reconnaissances in strength conducted by native irregulars and unaccompanied by British officers. The usual business of scouts, in the generally accepted meaning of the term, is not understood by Somalis. Attempts to send out two or three Illalos to any distance in order to gain intelligence always proved unsatisfactory. The men will not move boldly and will not go beyond a certain short radius, On the other hand, Illalos working in parties of from 25 to 50 frequently displayed considerable dash and initiative, when the waterless state of the country, involving possible difficulties of return, is taken into consideration.

As an example of their work, I may mention that a party of 40 mounted Illalos left Bohotle in August, 1903, brushed through a fairly strong party of Dervish Illalos in the vicinity of the Dehjeuner and reconnoitred to about 10 miles east of Beretabli, a distance of 140 miles, the first 80 of which were waterless. The Mullah and Haroun were at that time at or near Gerrowei, but the Illalos managed to penetrate well within the circle of Dervish karias (or Nomad villages), and succeeded in securing two most useful prisoners, returning with the loss of one man only, having covered a distance of 300 miles in nine days.

*Spies and Secret Agents.*—Though undeterred by any ethical scruples, the Somali does not make a good spy, and the occupation is congenitally uncongenial to him. Women and Midgans (an outcast and probably indigenous race) are practically the only spies who can be employed, and neither are satisfactory. It is seldom enough that spies can be trusted under any circumstances, but in this country of double dealing it is practically impossible to get a man sufficiently loyal to make his report valuable, who is not so well known for it as to make his detection by the enemy a matter of ease. Secret agents are difficult to procure. Somalis sufficiently educated to be able to write an intelligent letter in any language are extremely rare, and it is rarer still to find one who is intelligent enough to weigh evidence and to separate the grain of really important information from the mass of useless chaff in which it is invariably hidden.

*Deserters.*—Deserters and refugees often gave information, but chiefly of the corroborative order, and, of course, they could not be depended upon to come in with sufficient regularity to keep up a sustained history of the Mullah's doings. In addition, very few of the Mullah's real fighting men came into us (only four men, bringing rifles, deserted), and those who did come in were nearly all karia, or poor people, who were not in a position to give really valuable information.

*Summary.*—From the above remarks it will be inferred that the Illalos proved to be the backbone of our intelligence system. Though I must admit that they occasionally failed us, and more than once at important moments, their work was, on the whole, most satisfactory, and they kept us throughout in very fairly close touch with the enemy. When they did badly the cause was nearly always either that they had got into a tract of country with which they were unacquainted or else they were not used by the officer commanding the column in parties of sufficient strength.

*Intelligence Officers.*—Although alluded to last, by far the most important factor in all intelligence work is the intelligence officer, and upon his capability and zeal all information hangs. I confess to a deep feeling of gratitude for the liberal manner in which all my requests for intelligence officers have been met. Considering the number of troops employed, the establishment of intelligence officers was on a most liberal scale, but I think the results achieved fully justified their employment. Intelligence duties demand great tact and discernment, considerable ability in the art of judging character, much energy and capacity for hard work under the most trying conditions, and (what I found to be the rarest gift of all) the patience of a Job combined with the cheerfulness of a Mark Tapley. An officer who can perform a long and trying march, and then sit down, as nearly all have frequently had to do, to examine and cross-examine stupid or obstinate prisoners for perhaps five hours at a stretch, through the medium of an indifferent interpreter, without losing his temper, in order to gain one small but important piece of information, shows remarkable endurance and self control. To unhesitatingly separate the grain of accurate information from the mass of lies and irrelevance in the midst of which it is buried is a very rare gift in itself.

Scouting work and general results.

From July to December, 1903, Bohotle proved to be the most satisfactory base from which to work Illalos, and, consequently, from the beginning, Lieutenant Marjoribanks, 107th Pioneers, the intelligence officer at Bohotle, had the largest establishment of Illalos and, on the whole, the pick of the ponies. It would appear from the map that Illalos might have been more easily worked from Olesan or Kirrit and later on from Eil Dab, but the character of the country through which they would have to scout was much against their useful employment, being particularly bare and open, and it was found to be more satisfactory to establish the principal reconnoitring base at Bohotle, from which place Illalos were able to work through the thick bush as far as the Dehjeuner country, and then move through the foothills between the Nogal plain and the Haud without heralding their approach from a great distance, as would have been unavoidable had they operated from the Ain district. In addition to the Bohotle centre, Las Dureh was made an Illalo base, and a party of 25 Illalos was constantly worked from there by Lieutenant Balderston, attached to the 101st Grenadiers, with most useful results. The grazing at Las Dureh proved, however, to be so poor that the Illalo ponies had to be eventually withdrawn, and, in consequence, the radius of reconnaissance was considerably reduced.

It was not until October, 1903, that the enrolment and equipment of Illalos had sufficiently progressed to allow of a body being stationed at the Kirrit–Garrero–Olesan centre, capable of achieving more than the local scouting necessary for the safety of the line of communications. By this time, however, Eil Dab and Badwein had been occupied by us, and 80 Illalos, all mounted, were collected there, with the idea of reconnoitring the eastern Nogal and especially its northern limits from that base.

I must confess, however, that until the new year the Illalo work here was most disappointing. The chief reason for this was, I believe, the unfortunate necessity at this juncture of having to employ a number of Ishak men not conversant with the country.

The matter was the more unfortunate in that when the Mullah, towards the end of November, moved from Adadero to Haisamo and pushed out to Jidbali the force which was some six weeks later defeated at that place, we had to depend for our information on the somewhat belated news brought by the Bohotle Illalos. This was fortunately supplemented by some excellent reconnaissance work executed by No. III Tribal Horse, under the direction of Major Bridges.

On the arrival of headquarters at Eil Dab at the end of December, the Illalos there were used for the first time in large parties, and the result at once proved satisfactory, for although 50 of the men who had been concentrated there for some time without any useful results were sent away to strengthen the Illalo detachment of the 1st Brigade, nevertheless the balance of 110, which had by that time been concentrated, working in two parties, nightly visited the Jidbali position some 50 miles distant, at considerable risk, and brought in daily most valuable information.

In addition to the two large groups of Illalos working from Bohotle and Eil Dab, and the smaller one reconnoitring from Las Dureh, small parties of Illalos were attached to every post on the lines of communication, for the purpose of local reconnaissance and for guide and messenger duties.

A certain number of Illalos at Bohotle and Garrero were trained to mend the telegraph wire when cut, as it several times was, between those places, and proved themselves most useful. Instead of having to send out a linesman with a comparatively strong escort, a small party of mounted Illalos, with the necessary mending material, would be at once despatched, and on two occasions a cut 20 miles distant was located and mended within four hours of its occurrence.

Illalos at these posts also proved themselves of great use in tracking and bringing in individual soldiers and parties who had lost their way while travelling between posts. A small party of 12 Illalos was enlisted at Hargeisa for the purpose of collecting information as to the attitude of the Ogaden tribes to the south and south-west, and did some useful work.

After the fight at Jidbali, close touch with the Mullah was lost, and the direction given to the movements of our two columns made it at first difficult to again get into touch. In fact, it was not until the columns arrived at Gaolo and Halin respectively that information from captured prisoners enabled us to know that the Mullah had started some three days previously to cross the Northern Haud to the north. At this juncture touch was again lost, and for a short time there was some doubt whether the Mullah had gone to Baran near Mijjarten-Warsangli border, or to the Jid Ali district. On the 4th February, reliable information was received that the Mullah was near Jid Ali. From that date until he crossed the Mijjarten frontier on the 27th March, early and accurate information was received of his movements.

As soon as the Mullah crossed into Italian territory the difficulty of obtaining information became very great. It was no longer possible to use the method which had been so successfully employed when the Haroun was in the Jid Ali district, and until it crossed the frontier. The method alluded to was to post an intelligence officer with a scout establishment at the coast port nearest to the Mullah's position. Thus Hais, and later Las Khorai, were made bases of information, and finally a military intelligence officer was taken on board one of His Majesty's ships, and collected intelligence at all landing places in British territory to the east of Las Khorai, and occasionally visited the Mijjerten (Italian) port of Bosaso (or Bandar Kasim). Something more, however, than occasional visits to Bosaso was requisite, but, under the circumstances, it was impossible to station an intelligence officer at that place. Secret agents, entering Mijjarten territory from Las Khorai, proved to be the best means of gaining intelligence, but the delay caused by their having to move backwards and forwards between the two places militated seriously against the freshness of their news, which was, however, very correct on the whole.

Since the Mullah recrossed the Northern Haud to the south we have practically completely lost touch of him, and the withdrawal of the 1st Brigade from Halin makes the distance of his present whereabouts too great to be traversed by Illalos. Information will, however, come in from time to time by refugees and deserters, and Ali Yusuf, of Obbia, should have ample news of the Mullah's movements.

Summing up the results achieved, it may be said shortly that, from July to the end of November, we were never for more than a day or two, without fairly accurate information of the Mullah's whereabouts and movements eight days previously. As the average distance of the Haroun from our chief intelligence centre during this period was some 160 miles, this is a good record. For eight days before the Jidbali fight the Dervish position was visited nightly by scouts and reported upon. During the operations in the Nogal, from January 14 to February 10th, the enemy was undoubtedly lost touch of by the scouts, who, however, did good work in securing stock. The intelligence officers at Hais and Las Khorai quickly took up the running after the Mullah reached Jid Ali, and until he crossed into Italian territory very close touch was kept with him.

Great trouble was taken to the end that all information of the enemy, which might be collected, should be fully appreciated and made use of by officers concerned.

*Dissemination of information.*

*The Intelligence Diary.*—The headquarter intelligence diary for each day was prepared and placed before the General Officer Commanding on the following morning. The Consul-General was also supplied with a daily copy. The week's budget, with a short summary, was sent to the War Office by each mail, together with the weekly intelligence diaries of each individual intelligence officer.

*Summary of Information for Intelligence Officers.*—Each week a summary of information has been prepared, a copy of which has been forwarded to each intelligence officer, and to each officer performing intelligence duties. These summaries have been compiled from the headquarter staff intelligence diary. They have usually been a fairly literal transcript of the intelligence diary, avoiding repetition, and political or international matters have been deleted. These summaries have been regularly forwarded to the Naval Commander-in-Chief, to the Senior Naval Officer on the station, to Colonel Rochfort, to the Officer Commanding Lines of Communication, and to occasional commanding officers who were unprovided with intelligence officers. Thus, every week some 15 copies of the summary had to be made, and, despite the invaluable aid of the cyclostyle, very heavy clerical labour in the headquarter office was incurred.

*Telegraphic Information.*—In cases where the telegraph was available, all important information was, in addition, telegraphed between intelligence officers and headquarters, as well as directly by intelligence officers to any commanding officer whom the information might affect.

*News Bulletins for the Force.*—Such information about the enemy as could be made known to the force generally, was circulated by means of news bulletins, and the same bulletins were made the medium of transmitting other items of information which would not appear in orders and which would prove interesting to the force.

Intelligence officers.

*Employment.*—One of these officers (Captain Blair) was continuously employed for two months in settling claims for rewards and pay incurred during the previous phase of the campaign, and in making up the accounts for that period. He was then appointed intelligence officer at Burao. One officer, Lieutenant Rose, I was obliged to keep back at headquarters, when enrolment and equipment of Illalos and interpreters was being commenced. The remaining officer, Lieutenant Marjoribanks, was appointed intelligence officer at Bohotle.

In August I was given the services of Lieutenant Evans, R.E., and I despatched him to Hais to organize an intelligence centre at that place. Hais, though a considerable distance from the Mullah's whereabouts at that time was an important news centre, and a good deal of valuable information of the corroborative order was obtained there. When the failure of the Abyssinians made it necessary to call on Ali Yusuf for substantial help, Lieutenant Evans was transferred from Hais to Obbia.

Officers for intelligence duties, *i.e.*, regimental officers doing intelligence work in addition to their own duties, were appointed at Berbera, Hargeisa, Las Dureh and Garrero, and subsequently at Wadamago and Eil Dab. Thus, during the long phase before active operations commenced, a line of intelligence officers stretched from Berbera to Bohotle, with outposts at Hargeisa, Las Dureh, Hais, and, later on, Obbia. The value of such an arrangement was very great. Information collected at one point was quickly corroborated or contradicted through a perfectly independent channel, and few men could leave the Mullah and enter our lines without surrendering what information they had to an intelligence officer. After operations commenced, special service intelligence officers were attached to each brigade and to mounted troops; their places at the various posts being filled by officers for intelligence duties. During the last phase, when General Fasken's column operated between Las Dureh and Las Khorai, an additional intelligence officer was provided and sent first to Hais and then to cruise along the coast in one of His Majesty's ships of war.

*Instruction.*—The want of a handbook for intelligence duties in the field was much felt. No handbook can, of course, legislate for campaigns under every conceivable circumstance, but there are many broad principles which do not change, and much valuable help might be given to the examination of prisoners, co-ordination of information, keeping accounts, &c.

I drew up a set of instructions* for intelligence officers, which embodied the chief points on which information was required by them. These instructions had to be hurriedly produced in the pressure of much work, and were very incomplete, but they more or less served the purpose for which they were intended.

*Cyphers.*—Intelligence officers were provided with two cyphers; one a cypher on the Playfair model for really secret use, the other a plain transposition cypher on the well-known South African model, to be used when it was inadvisable to mention the names of certain places of people *en clair*.

*Establishment.*—The original intention, prior to commencement of operations, contemplated the enlistment of 350 mounted Illalos (including the 100 " scouts " remaining over from the former force). Subsequently sanction was given to increase this number to 450 for various reasons, which will be stated. Towards the end of October, 20 Illalos, with their arms, ammunition and ponies deserted to the enemy. These men were of various sub-tribes, but were all Dolbahantas except four, who were Habr Yunis (Saad Yunis). At that period our Illalos were composed mainly of Dolbahantas in proportion of some 85 per cent. (sub-tribes Barkat and Jama S:ad predominating). Dolbahantas had been specially enlisted as Illalos, on account of their superior value as Illalos to Ishak men generally, and their knowledge of the country in which it was proposed to operate. As a result, however, of these desertions it was decided, with certain exceptions, to replace the Dolbahanta by Ishak, and to select such Ishak men from the Habr Toljaala mostly, Saad Yunis being subjected to careful scrutiny.

Illalos, guides and messengers.

The exceptions alluded to consisted of :—

(i) Men who were known to have a blood feud with the Mullah ;

(ii) Men who had recognized guarantees in the shape of relations of property in our sphere ; and

(iii) A somewhat large percentage which the intelligence officer at Bohotle was permitted to retain, in view of the intimate knowledge he had of the Bohotle men who had been with him for some time back.

When these changes were carried out, the proportion showed about six Ishak to four Dolbahantas.

In October, 1903, sanction was given to increase the number of Illalos

---

* See Appendix I, page 404.

to 450, the extra 100 men coming under the heading of "guides" and "messengers." The reasons for this increase were as follows:—

(a) A somewhat large messenger establishment at Hargeisa, hitherto under the Officer Commanding Lines of Communication, was transferred to the Field Intelligence Department.

(b) At the same time a number of Ogaden (Ibrahim) men had to be enlisted for work in the Ogaden country, namely, for work from Bohotle, in connection with the Galadi column, Colonel Rochfort and the Abyssinian force and Captain Munn. All these men were classed as Illalos, but many were simply utilised as messengers and runners, and no extra establishment of ponies were drawn for them.

(c) At the commencement of actual operations it was found absolutely necessary for guide work and also for the general efficiency of the Illalos, to re-engage Dolbahantas, and no further desertions having occurred, some 50 men of this class were added to the establishment for work with the second brigade and mounted troops.

For the later operations in the north-east further changes occurred Advantage was taken to get rid of a large number of the Habr Toljaala men, who had been enlisted during the Dolbahanta scare, and they were replaced by Naleya Ahmed, Saad Yunis, and others with local knowledge of this area. Local Illalos were raised concurrently in the same manner for Las Khorai and Hais.* While these changes were taking place the necessity of engaging men before others were discharged caused the number of Illalos, guides and messengers to rise for a short time to 530.

Illalos worked mounted where possible, but as the number of men was augmented without corresponding increase in ponies, a good deal of foot work was done, and really great distances were covered in this manner. The men are good "riders," but not "horsemen" in any sense. Unless watched carefully they invariably give their ponies sore backs, either from galloping about barebacked to water or grazing, not using saddle blankets, substituting Somali saddles for the proper ones, or not girthing up the animal. They also try to substitute the Somali bit for the Government one, with the usual result of a sore mouth. A great partiality is shown for extracting throat lash and any other small straps possible. When any saddlery is brought in the former is, without exception, missing.

The Illalo, like other Somalis, is not a hard worker in the ordinary sense of the word. He can, however, be started off to work at a moment's notice, can cover comparatively enormous distances, and has some considerable endurance.

*Arms and Clothing.*—Practically all men were armed with Martini-Henry weapon, with bandolier for 30 to 40 rounds. Clothing issued as for

---

* There had been a few men previously at Hais for work under the intelligence officer, who was there in the latter part of 1903.

interpreters, except that the idea was, in the case of an Illalo, to associate the blanket with the pony for saddle purposes, and not with the man. The men, as a rule, took great care of their firearms, but not so of their other things which might be discarded in any moment of excitability.

*Pay.*—Rate of pay was 20 rs.; headmen 10 rs. extra. The original intention limited headmen to proportion of 1 per 20 Illalos, but the number of headmen had to be eventually increased, owing to the necessity for charge of detached parties.* In addition to ordinary pay, rewards were given up to a limit of 100 rs. for obtaining valuable information and for special work incurring risk.

*Enlistment and Miscellaneous.*—There was little difficulty in obtaining Illalos, the pay being good and the service popular. Enlistments were made, as a rule, through some principal men. This had drawbacks, as, for instance, it cannot be doubted but that some considerable " dustoorie " was brought into play; but it is the only practicable method at any rate at present and produces men who can be known and vouched for. The two men through whom the largest number of enlistments were made were Hersi Isa (Rer Wais Adan), retained as a sort of principal headman to the whole Illalo establishment, and Ali Bulali (a Burkat Achil). As in the case of interpreters some trouble was caused through want of back records, but what is being done for interpreters in the way of making lists for future guidance is also being carried out for Illalos, and Illalos are not given to disappearing in the aggravating manner referred to in the case of interpreters.

There are two reasons, I think :—

(i) They do not usually hold property to the extent of the interpreter class;

(ii) Being " fighting " men they have more sense of responsibility in regard to their engagement of service.

The amount of punishment necessary was, I think, on the whole, small. There was a somewhat serious demand for higher rewards at Bohotle on one occasion, leading to court-martial punishment for eight ringleaders; but fines and such like, except for loss of clothing, were very fairly inconspicuous.

*Establishment and Casualties.*—The bulk of the Illalo ponies were Ponies. practically hard at work from August or September onwards.

The authorised establishment of ponies allowed 350, plus 10 per cent. spare, equals 385. As a matter of fact, this number was at first exceeded, but the balance were ponies supplied in such wretched condition that they were returned after a while to the Remount Department without having been taken up for use. Counting from middle of October, when the establishment was about completed, the wastage down to the beginning of January (just prior to the Jidbali advance) works out at 30 per cent. (three

---

* It has been mentioned previously that Illalos were generally congregated in large detachments. Various small parties, however, had to be detached from time to time for lines of communication work.

months). Subsequently down to the Las Dureh advance (beginning of January to beginning of March), 135 fresh remounts were drawn, and the wastage from the beginning of March to April 30th, was 56 per cent. (four months). Total average per month, over the seven months, something over 12 per cent.

Some 20 to 30 of the total number of animals were purchased direct from owners by the Field Intelligence Department. The rest* were all supplied by the Remount Department. All the ponies, except one lot of 20, were Somali or Abyssinian.

*Rations.*—The ration per pony was at first but 3 lbs. grain, in addition to grazing. The grain was later, when the grazing became scarce, increased to 6 lbs., and cut grass was issued in some cases. On the increased ration and cut grass, ponies, with rest and supervision, improved.

*Equipment in General.*—All Ordnance stores, arms, ammunition, saddlery and camp equipment were obtainable on simple vouchers.

Of the arms supplied to Illalos, 85 per cent. were Martini-Henry carbines. The remaining men had Martini-Henry rifles, except a few men here and there who retained Martini-Enfield weapons formerly in use.

The saddlery, yeomanry pattern, with blanket and panel, portmouth bit with single rein but two bars. Very serviceable except that :—

(i) The sizes of bridles were mostly too large for the ponies ;

(ii) Some sort of means should be supplied for carrying up two to three days' corn ration, which the nosebag cannot do.

*Clothing and Rations in General.*—Practically every Illalo was supplied in the six to eight months with two issues of the authorized clothing ("first," and "replacing" issue). In transactions with the supply and transport corps (both clothing and rations) there appear, in comparison with the Ordnance Department, and having regard to a state of active service, some numerous details and forms necessary to fill in before demands are met, Clothing was also not obtainable from the supply and transport corps. even with early notice. This was, however, due, in all probability, to the necessity of utilising transport for more urgent demands.

Spies and secret agents. *Spies.*—As mentioned in a previous paragraph, it is difficult to get good spies in Somaliland. Neither the political officer, who, until November, had exclusive charge of the spy department, nor I, when I started to try my hand at it after that date, had much success. On three occasions men were induced by large rewards to penetrate into the Haroun. One was discovered and killed, and two returned safely with useful intelligence, but neither brought news of really first importance. Somalis themselves chiefly use women for this business, but though I despatched many women to spy, most of them never returned, and the remainder obviously had never been where they pretended that they had. The fact is that, for this style of

---

\* Except a batch of 60 odd, which were purchased before formation of Remount Department, by special purchasing officers detailed for the force.

work, the advice and assistance of a native of high influence, experience and intelligence is absolutely essential.

*Secret Agents.*—Suitable secret agents are also rare birds in Somaliland.

*Establishment.*—The Field Intelligence Department was responsible for the supply of interpreters to the force. At the period of the constitution of the present force, there were 39 interpreters serving, the bulk of whom had been supplied by the Political Resident, Aden. To meet increased needs the above numbers had to be largely augmented, and the supply from Aden giving out early in September, the balance had to be found from that time by engagements in the country itself. The first fixed establishment for the present force comprised a total of 142. Subsequent additions, with replacement of casualties, brought the number of men who have been supplied up to a total of 208 (including those left over from previous operations).

Interpreters.

*Engagement.*—Interpreters were either engaged directly by the Field Intelligence Department or engaged by units subject to following sanction by the Field Intelligence Department. In engaging or giving sanction, the two chief points for consideration were (apart from question of capability) :—

(i) Whether the man had previously served at any time and there were any reasons against his re-engagement.

(ii) Whether he was of suitable tribe.

As regards (i) there was some considerable difficulty. Former records were very scanty, and it is feared some undesirable individuals were re-engaged. It is hoped that this will be avoided in future, because very complete lists have now been compiled of every interpreter employed with the present force; these lists giving full description, with what unit or units employed, if discharged, reasons for discharge, and so on. In this connection it should be observed that, apart from any other faults, a very frequent habit of a man of the Somali interpreter or servant class is to quit his situation at will; in many cases fully intending to return when it suits him, but go he will, with or without leave. Many of such men have hitherto escaped scot free, and have even been re-employed for want of records. Putting aside any other punishment it is now pretty generally understood that no man who has left his employment in the above circumstances will be employed again, and this understanding, coupled with the knowledge that back records are now preserved, is already having an effect. As regards the question of tribe, there were few cases for rejection, as few men of the interpreter class come from the principal tribes favourable to the Mullah.

To turn to the question of capability, the Somali has certainly a linguistic turn, and there are many men engaged as interpreters who have a knowledge of four or five languages. On the other hand, there are a very limited number who can put down as really efficient and first rate English interpreters. Of those who can be classed in this category, the majority are usually engaged by shooting or private parties in and around Somaliland, the civil authorities and His Majesty's ships.

At the latter period of the operations the limit of resources was practically reached of even the quite inferior men, and to meet demands, we had perforce to engage, at the high interpreter standard of wages, individuals who had to a great extent merely the English patter of the Aden cook-boy, gharry-wallah or boat-boy.

*Pay.*—As quoted above, the standard of wages (which was 60 rs. higher rate and 40 rs. lower rate) may be classed as "high." We have practically more than doubled former military rates, and have also rather disturbed the supply of any even moderate speaking English servants for officers (except mere "Chokras") at moderate wages. On the other hand, however, the standard which obtains was probably unavoidable in the circumstances, and it must be remembered that the employers mentioned in last paragraph have all along given considerably higher pay than military rate at any time, a fact which has secured them the best men. In apportioning the two rates of 60 rs. and 40 rs., our theoretical practice was to only grant the higher rate for "efficient English understood and spoken" the 40 rs. rate being allotted to Hindustani speakers and men of inferior English to that considered necessary for the higher rate. Our theory had however, to be considerably modified latterly.* In addition to their monthly pay, interpreters also received free African rations and the usual clothing of tobe, pair of shoes, blanket and Chagul.

Topography.   *Existing Maps at the end of July*, 1903.—The Somaliland maps existing at that time were the "four sheet map," and I.D. Nos. 1,636 and 1,636A, compiled from the four sheets, with corrections embodying the survey work executed in the previous portion of the year, from Obbia to Galadi and Bohotle. All these maps were on the $\frac{1}{1000000}$ scale. A small scale map ($\frac{1}{3000000}$) was also provided and was much appreciated, as it gave an idea of Somaliland in relation to other countries.

All demands for maps were met with great promptitude, and, in the case of the three Nogal maps, which were compiled in the field and sent home for reproduction, less than a month elapsed between the departure from headquarters of the original and the receipt of from 100 to 200 copies, mounted on linen, a good proportion also being mounted to fold. As the actual time of transit is 24 days, I call that a capital performance.

*Map Compilation in the Field.*—It was obvious from the first that the main operations would be conducted in the Nogal district. This tract of country was very badly and inaccurately shown on existing maps.

After the operations of Colonel Swayne, which concluded with Erigo in October, 1902, Captains Everett and Howard had compiled a map from the sketches which they had executed in 1901 and 1902; and from it, with the addition of some native information (afterwards found to be very inaccurate) Nogal No. 1 was compiled in the field and sent home for rapid production.

Very shortly afterwards another excellent sketch map by Captain O'Neill turned up. As this map gave a good deal of information lacking in

---

* Now in process of being again possible.

the Everett-Howard map, and as I had got possession of a sun print of Major Beynon's 1901 map, I had Nogal No. 2 compiled from all the above sources, with the addition of Wellby's route, which had been accidentally omitted from No. 1.

But the best information of all was still unavailable. This was the work executed by Colonel Swayne in 1901 and 1902. Directly Colonel Swayne arrived in the country, I got his notes and sketches (which had been lying at Berbera since he went home in November, 1902), and had a fresh map compiled. As Colonel Swayne is an exceedingly good military sketcher of great experience, besides being a trained surveyor, I had no hesitation in making his work the basis of the new map, Nogal No. 3, and the work previously compiled in No. 2 was fitted on to it.

Luckily the promptitude with which the reproduction was carried out by the Intelligence Division, allowed the force to take the field with this map.

As regards the accuracy of the map itself, as proved by our better knowledge now, I consider it to be wonderful. When it is remembered that it is entirely a compass sketch, often executed at night, and with distances always judged by time and rate of marching, I cannot imagine how it could have been as accurate as it turned out to be.

Colonel Swayne also lent me his notes and field books relating to his 1903 expedition from Las Dureh to the east, and his work was plotted out and put aside. It became, of course, of great value during the last phase of the operations. Most of this compilation work was excellently done by Lieutenant Davis, 107th Pioneers, who was specially attached to my department for that purpose.

*Native Information Sketches.*—In addition to the above four principal compilations, numerous small sketches, chiefly from native information, were made of tracts of country about to be or likely to be traversed, which were a blank on existing maps. These sketches hardly ever turned out to be accurate, but they proved to be a great deal better than nothing, and fully repaid the time and trouble which their compilation cost. One sketch in particular, made at Eil Dab, of the country north the Eil Dab-Gaolo line, proved to be most useful and really very accurate. Finally the best maps of the period were always kept up to date by the information which was being duly collected.

*Map Reproduction in the Field.*—The want of some handy reproducing plant was severely felt, in order that the information which was being collected might be made immediately available to the force. Ultimately I tried the cyclostyle as an experiment, and, though of course the work turned out was very rough, it nearly answered all the purposes which I required. The cyclostyle was also found extremely useful in keeping maps up to date.

*Material for future Compilations.*—A good deal of material for future compilation has been collected. It includes all the stuff used for the field compilations which were naturally not as accurately executed as would be possible at home.

Intelligence officers submitted their accounts to the Field Controller Finance. through the Assistant Quartermaster-General for Intelligence, and money for disbursement was similarly drawn. Considerable delay was experienced in receiving the first observations on intelligence accounts, and those for the preceding July were received in December last. Accounts of payments of individual Illalos proved a great source of trouble. Owing, however, to the necessity of frequently transferring Illalos from one centre to another, and also to the fact that at any time the clerical labour of keeping the accounts of from 100 to 150 men is very severe, officers have frequently found it impossible to submit all these details.

Office.

The intelligence office was provided from India. It was exceedingly well equipped with nearly everything which was required, and proved to be a great boon. It was, however, only equipped for one officer, and consequently additional compasses, drawing materials, &c., had to be demanded, in order to provide intelligence officers with what they required.

Survey section.

It is not necessary to do more than mention that I was staff officer dealing with survey questions. The survey section was not under me in any way, and the officer commanding it renders a separate report.*

## APPENDIX I.

INSTRUCTIONS TO INTELLIGENCE OFFICERS, SOMALILAND FIELD FORCE.

### 1. *Duties.*

(*a*) *General Duties.*—Intelligence officers will collect and collate, as far as possible, all important information received from prisoners, spies, deserters and others as to the position, movements, doings and intentions of the enemy. They will collect and collate, as far as possible, all available information regarding ethnography, topography and geography of the theatre of war. They will collect and report all general information of interest.

(*b*) *Duties as regards the Commanding Officer.*—The first and immediate duty of an intelligence officer is to keep his Commanding Officer as fully informed as possible as to the movements of the enemy in or towards his vicinity. He will give him all the information obtainable regarding the topography of the country in his vicinity. He will also give him all the details which he may wish to have of the wider information enumerated under (*a*).

(*c*) *Duties as regards the Assistant Quartermaster-General for Intelligence at Headquarters.*—He will send all information enumerated under (*a*) which he may have collected, to the Assistant Quartermaster-General for Intelligence, in the manner indicated in para. 2. He will copy and forward direct all route reports and sketches executed by officers in the same command. Intelligence officers will communicate directly with the Assistant Quartermaster-General at headquarters, but telegrams and other reports so submitted can only be sent with the knowledge and consent of the Commanding Officer.

\* See page 416.

2. *Collection and Transmission of Information.*

(*a*) *Telegraphic Messages.*—All important information should be telegraphed direct (with the Commanding Officer's approval) to the Assistant Quartermaster-General. Such information would include news as to the enemy's position, movements and intentions, positions of his Karias and scouts, estimates of armament and information about the importation of arms. Important movements of our own Illalos should also be telegraphed.

(*b*) *The Intelligence Diary.*—Each intelligence officer will keep a diary, in which he will enter all the news received in full (notwithstanding that he will have already telegraphed the more important items). All topographical information gained will be added in the form of appendices. A copy of this diary will be submitted weekly to the Assistant Quartermaster-General at headquarters, in such time as to reach him by Saturday.*

(*c*) *Transmission to other Commands of Information.*—When news is received which affects the dispositions or safety of other posts or commands, it is the duty of the intelligence officer to wire the information to the intelligence officer of the post or command concerned. The fact that he has done so should be invariably recorded on the telegram to the Assistant Quartermaster-General for Intelligence.

(*d*) *Arrangement of Headings.*—The diary of the Assistant Quartermaster-General, compiled from the reports and diaries of the various intelligence officers and other sources, is arranged under the following headings :—

1. Position of the Mullah and Haroun.
2. ,, ,, Mullah's Karias.
3. ,, ,, Mullah's Illalos.
4. The Mullah's intentions.
5. Numbers of his force.
6. His armament.
6A. Condition and morale of Mullah's followers.
7. Number and condition of his ponies and stock.
7A. Attitude of the tribes.
8. Importation of arms. (All information which can be collected as to amounts imported, by whom, and to what ports, and by whom consigned.)
9. Geographical and topographical particulars, not coming under 12.
10. Miscellaneous information (not coming under the above headings).
11. Ancient history. (Fresh information as to details of fights, &c., in the previous phase of the campaign.)
12. Appendices. These include :—
    Diaries of intelligence officers.
    Route reports.
    Reports on localities.

---

* For a specimen copy see Appendix II page 409

In order to render the task of collating reports as simple as possible, intelligence officers will please arrange their reports, telegraphic or otherwise, under the same headings, prefacing them with a short account how the news was obtained, and the degree of reliability to be attached to it. In the case of a reconnaissance by Illalos, a short statement of their doings should be added to the preface.

### 3. *Illalos.*

(*a*) *Control.*—Intelligence officers have charge of the Illalos attached to their post or command, for discipline, interior economy, and for employment according to the general directions issued by the Assistant Quartermaster-General for Intelligence, and the detailed directions issued by, or approved by, the immediate Commanding Officer.

(*b*) *Ponies.*—Special attention must be paid to the condition of the ponies. Practically the whole of our intelligence depends on ponies, and if once allowed to get out of condition, they take a long time to recover, and are very difficult to replace. Illalos should never be sent mounted on jobs which men on foot can do equally well.

(*c*) *Pay.*—Illalos are paid 20 rs. a month. Headmen, in the proportion of about 1 to 20, may be appointed by the intelligence officers, if not already appointed by the Assistant Quartermaster-General for Intelligence, and will be paid an extra 10 rs. a month.

(*d*) *Clothing and Equipment.*—Each Illalo should receive :—
1 tobe.
1 pair of Somali shoes.
1 Martini-Henry carbine and 40 to 50 rounds, according to the capacity of his bandolier.
1 bandolier.
1 Chagul.
1 bridle, saddle and saddle blanket.
1 pony.

(*e*) Intelligence officers should see that a reserve of 150 rounds is kept at their post or with their detachment.

(*f*) *Rewards.*—In addition to the monthly pay as given above, Illalos should be rewarded for special services of a dangerous nature. Intelligence officers will take the greatest care not to be imposed on, and will generally require some evidence of a circumstantial nature before promising rewards for dangers said to have been incurred.

The details of such rewards must be left to the judgment of the intelligence officer, but the following rough rules give a guide :—

1. No risk, no reward.
2. For a well-executed reconnaissance, well up to the enemy, resulting in a fight in which useful prisoners have been captured, and one or more of our own men wounded, a reward up to 30 rs. may be granted each man.

3. For special service, such as carrying urgent messages through country in the occupation of the enemy, special rewards may be given.
4. Wounded men will be specially rewarded.
5. Rewards for any service which, in the opinion of the intelligence officer should exceed 50 rs. per man, must be specially sanctioned by the Assistant Quartermaster-General for Intelligence.

(*g*) *Entertainment and Discharge.*—As the total number of 350 Illalos sanctioned for the force must not be exceeded, intelligence officers should not entertain fresh Illalos without the authority of the Assistant Quartermaster-General. They should, however, always report when good men present themselves. Illalos are well paid; their occupation is looked up to, and there is no difficulty in recruiting any number of men. Consequently, intelligence officers will take care to weed out any men not absolutely first-class. It is impossible to gauge the characters of men when enlisting them, and many indifferent men are sure to be taken on at the first, therefore the earliest opportunity should be taken of testing their grit, and lazy, cowardly or troublesome men should be discharged at once. The names of the men so discharged should be reported to the Assistant Quartermaster-General for Intelligence, so that they may be taken off the general list of Illalos kept at headquarters.

### 5. *Accounts.*

" Intelligence officers will submit their monthly accounts to the Assistant Quartermaster-General for Intelligence as soon after the first of each month as possible. These accounts will include a statement of all moneys received from the field treasury chest officer or other sources for intelligence purposes, and statements of disbursements on account of payment of Illalos and interpreters, rewards, &c. A proper cash account should be made out, and important disbursements supported by vouchers when possible. Illalos and interpreters, though drawing monthly pay, should only be paid at stated intervals, such as the termination of the campaign, or at the end of a distinct phase of the operations, or on discharge.

### 6. *Returns.*

Intelligence officers will submit by telegraph every Saturday a weekly statement showing:—

Number of British officers.
,, British non-commissioned officers and men.
,, native officers.
,, native non-commissioned officers and men.
,, Illalos.
,, interpreters of Field Intelligence Department (*i.e.*, not on the pay list of a unit or post).

Number of public followers (other than Illalos and interpreters).
,, private followers.
,, horses or ponies (other than Illalo ponies). These may be described telegraphically as "staff ponies."

Number of Illalo ponies.
„ mules, riding camels and burden camels.
„ rifles and nature.
„ rounds and nature.

7. *Notes on the Preparation of Reports and Diaries.*

The spelling of names of localities should be in accordance with that of the latest map. (The Nogal Sketch Map, F. 3527, is the latest for that part of the country.)

If places mentioned in the report or diary cannot be identified on the map, the fact should be brought to notice by the word "unidentified," or their position with respect to some place on the map should be explained.

Road reports should be drawn up on, or transferred to, the following model (imaginary) :—

ROAD REPORT.

*Bohotle to Damot.*

(Captain Jones, S.M.I. July, 1903.)

| Place. | Distance in Miles. | | Remarks. |
|---|---|---|---|
| | Inter. | Total. | |
| Bohotle .. | 0 | 0 | Road, bearing , through thick bush, with open patches, and for the last 3 miles over stony ground to |
| Damot .. | 40 | 40 | Four wells, all of small capacity, giving a total daily supply of gallons. Good grazing and camping ground |

Opposite to each place should be the description of the place, and remarks on water, grazing, camping grounds, &c., in the vicinity.

Then on a fresh line, the description of the road to the next place. It is a good plan to end up the description of the road with the word "to," as in the model given, in order that there can be no doubt as to which part of the route is being described. In nine out of ten road reports it is almost impossible to discover between what two places the portion of the road described lies.

(Signed) G. T. FORESTIER-WALKER, *Lieut.-Colonel,*
*Assistant Quartermaster-General for Intelligence.*

Sheikh, August, 1903.

MEMORANDUM.

ADDENDUM to "INSTRUCTIONS TO INTELLIGENCE OFFICERS," F.I.D. 10–49, of 22nd August, 1903.

*Preparation of Intelligence Diary.*

1. The diary, when sent to the Assistant Quartermaster-General for Intelligence, should be headed as follows :—

DIARY OF INTELLIGENCE OFFICER.

(Officer performing Intelligence Duties.)

At

From           to           1903.

2. Each date should be entered, and if no informations has been received on any date the fact should be recorded, "No information received."

3. The diary should be posted so as to reach me by every Saturday.

4. Information under each date should be arranged so far as possible under the headings given in para. 2 of the "Instructions to Intelligence Officers."

(Signed) G. T. F. W.
*Assistant Quartermaster-General for Intelligence.*

Sheikh, 24th September, 1903.

---

APPENDIX II.

DIARY OF INTELLIGENCE OFFICER, BOHOTLE.

(26th July to 8th August, 1903.)

27th July.—Our Illalos returned from Damot. The place had apparently been occupied by some poor people for some few days, but these had all left for the Nogal about the 20th inst.

The houses, barbed wire, &c., were all as we had left them.

31st July.—30 Illalos left for the Nogal at dawn. They will be away for about 20 days, and will go through Waylahed, pass close to Gubli, and try to get as far as Gaolo.

2nd August.—A deserter, named Gal Bihyet (Dolbahanta, Samkab Ahmed), came into Bohotle. States that he came from Walwal where many poor people, left behind by the Mullah, are living in a state of miserable poverty. The Ba Cari have gone to Hundoo, which is unidentified, but appears to be near the Webi, and to be cultivated, jowari being grown there. (N.B.—This man seems to be one of the lot who escaped from Bali Do-oly, when attacked by our Illalos last month. He stoutly denies this, but prisoners who were captured at that time say that he was with them.)

4th August.—A deserter from the Mullah, named Abbas Isman (Ibrahim), came into Bohotle at 5.30 A.M. His story is as follows :—

He was captured by the Mullah during the raid on the Ibrahim on the occasion when Sultan Abdi was killed. He had a French rifle at the time, which was taken away from him. He then became a spearman and lived chiefly with the Haroun.

He left the Haroun at Gaolo on the 1st August in the early morning before daylight, accompanied by three other Ibrahim men who had arranged to desert with him. After going some way the other three men became afraid of being overtaken by the Mullah's scouts and caught attempting to desert, so they turned back.

He then came along by himself, travelling very rapidly and passing through Dijano and Bali Aat, to Bohotle, where he heard that there were men of his tribe in Government employment.

The Haroun was to leave Gaolo on the 1st August, to go to Kobo, which he believes to be 30 miles south-east of Halin, though he has never been there. All ponies and any camels were grazing at Halin.

Before he left the Haroun an Ali Gheri man reported to the Mullah that there were 30 Ali Gheri, Rer Gerad, Karias grazing at Myra and Las Uban.

After staying a few days at Kobo, the Mullah proposes to move further east, going close to Illig.

The Mullah never stays more than four or five days in one place, as he fears that the British may get to hear of his whereabouts and send men to attack him.

Up to the time Abbas left, the Haroun had only 30 rifles and very little ammunition has been received from Nur Isman at Bosaso. This was brought by the Isa Mahmud, also called Isa Rioli, owing to the fact that they possess many goats. The Mullah sent for the headman of this tribe some time ago, and asked them whether they would help him or whether he would have to make them help him by first punishing them. They replied that they would do what he wished if only he would not loot them. They have since then brought him caravans of from 20 to 40 camels every three or four days, laden with clothes, food and all kinds of stores.

The Isa Mahmud and Osman Mahmud act as merchants and receive full payment, in camels or skins, for whatever they may bring. None of the latter tribe are with the Mullah, and only get at the coast and inland whatever he may require.

Rifles are brought from Jibuti to Bosaso in dhows, being concealed outside the boats, underneath the gunwale, extra planks being nailed over the top to conceal them from view and to protect them from the sea water.

The Mullah has plenty of rifles, and informant estimates them at 4,000. The following are the various kinds of rifles :—

| English Name. | Somali Name. |
|---|---|
| French carbine | Mare. |
| French rifle | Jikri. |
| Martini-Enfield carbine | Sumu. |
| Martini-Enfield rifle | Sumu. |
| Lee-Enfield magazine rifle | Sumu. |
| Italian rifle | Italian banduk. |
| Rifle loading through right side (? Remington or Winchester) | Mescot. |
| Muzzle loading rifle | Shoais. |

Muzzle loaders are given to Midgans, and only used for guard purposes. The Italian rifle is said to have a very large bullet.

The Mullah has very little ammunition, and what he has is ·303, captured at Gumburu. Some men have 50 rounds each, but the majority have between 10 and 30 rounds each. The other rifles are useless, as there is no ammunition for them.

As far as Abbas knows, ammunition has only been received through Bosaso, and he has never heard of any coming through Lugh or any other place.

The Mullah was terribly afraid of being attacked when he crossed our line of communications and was at Bali Aat. Since going to the Nogal his only thoughts have been to get food, clothes, ammunition and good grazing for his animals.

He has always horsemen out to watch lest anyone deserts. If any man is caught attempting to desert he is immediately killed and his property confiscated. He has been putting to death a daily average of 8 to 10 men who have displeased him by giving him discouraging news, or whom he suspects of disloyalty. He has killed close on 400 men since going to the Nogal. In consequence, his men are very much afraid of him and many are eager to leave him but are afraid to do so. The tribes which he favours most are the Ali Gheri and the Ba Ararsama. He has no prisoners whatever, having killed any he may have had.

Haji Sudi is still his trusted adviser.

Sultan Nur still lives with the Mullah, but no longer is keen to help him.

Abbas was with the Mullah at Wardair during the fight. When the fight was over a horseman galloped to Wardair and announced that the English had been wiped out. The Mullah immediately mounted his pony, "Dodimer," and rode hard to the field of battle.

Abbas never heard of the bodies of any British officers being mutilated but he was not at the fight itself.

He was at the fight at Daratoleh, being a spearman there. A man came to the Haroun some days after the fight and told the Mullah that he had discovered the grave of a British officer at Dub Dor, which is half way between Daratoleh and Damot. He said that he had dug up the body, and produced some cartridges and a bag (probably a haversack) which he had taken off the body. (NOTE.—This cannot be true, as the two officers killed were buried at Damot.)

There were several dead Sikh bodies found near the scene of the fight in the jungle; their heads were cut off.

Informant estimates the Mullah's losses at Gumburu at about 1,000 and at Daratoleh at about 300; but none counted the dead by order of the Mullah.

Nur Hedig (Ali Naleya, Yusuf Ali) visited the Mullah at Gaolo, and brought him a present of 10 ponies. He promised that he and his own followers should throw in their lot with the Mullah, but Abbas cannot tell what the remainder of the Ali Naleya will do.

The following Ogadens are with the Mullah :—

| Tribe. | Number.* | Headmen. |
| --- | --- | --- |
| Habr Ali | 600 | Mahomed Ali Cora and Jofi Ali Godi |
| Ibrahim | 100 | Abdul Eimi |
| Ba Geri | 30 | Ali Nur Abdi and Wersia Atia |
| Ali Wanaak | 10 | Abdi Horsi |

* About.

### Notes on the above Intelligence.

There are no karias at Myra or near Lasuban, as our Illalos have lately returned from those places and report having seen no signs or tracks of anyone having been there since the Mullah crossed our lines of communication in June.

The following Mijjarten tribes seem to be most friendly with the Mullah: Isa Mahmud, Osman Mahmud and Ceshisha.

The following four Dervishes go to Bosaso, to arrange for rifles and ammunition to be brought to the Mullah :—

Abdullah Shahri (Habr Toljaala, Adan Marleba).
Mahmud Narash (Ogaden Abayunia).
Abdi Alis (Cadain ?).
Ao Omar (Ogaden, Ali Wanash).

Bohotle, 4th August, 1903.

8th August.—The 30 Illalos sent to the Nogal on the 31st July, returned at 3 P.M. They went to Gumburu (see Nogal sketch), and from there sent out scouts to El Kuron which appears to be about 12 miles south of a point half way between Las Anod and Heli Madu. (NOTE.—This is not quite plain from the sketch.—G. F. W.)

The scouts discovered eight men there, opened fire, captured four, the rest escaping. The remainder of the Illalos then arrived, questioned the prisoners and found that they were the advanced scouts of a party of 128 of the Mullah's scouts, mostly spearmen.

They then tied up their camels (the prisoners' camels ?), tied the prisoners to trees, removed their superfluous clothing and prepared for a fight.

They were in medium bush and the enemy emerged from thick bush. They fought for two hours, the enemy losing many men killed and wounded, the exact number not being known ; the enemy dragged their wounded and dead away. One of our men was wounded through the fleshy part of the thigh. Eventually the enemy retired into the thick part of the bush and waited for our men to come on. They, being comparatively few and running short of ammunition, did not follow up, nor did the enemy attack them again.

After the fight they found that the prisoners whom they had tied up had escaped, taking with them some clothes and two camels.

They searched the bush for the camels, and captured one of the enemy's camels loaded up with hans and also found one of their own.

They lost all their rations.

During the fight one of the Mullah's men named Jama Hassen (Dolbahanta, Ayak), a brother of Illalo Mohamed Hassan, recognised his brother, speared the headman of the Mullah's Illalos and deserted to our side. He gives the following news :—

On the 29th July, the Mullah sent out three parties of Illalos, one of 50 men, one of 45 men and one of 33 men. They had orders to look for parties of English scouts and to bring back any karias found in the Haud, which had not yet joined up with the Mullah.

The Haroun was at Gaolo. The horses and camels were at Dumbai, some six miles west of Halin. The karias were scattered about at Gerrowei Kobo (said to be about 18 miles north of Gerrowei on the direct line to Halin—there is another Kobo also known as Sorl, said to be north of Halin), Halin, Dalolo (about 12 miles west of Halin). and Haisimo (a large district about 14 miles west of Gaolo).

There is plenty of green grass everywhere, much rain having fallen about six weeks ago. Consequently animals are fit again, and the people are happy and contented.

A caravan which left Galadi some four months ago for the east under Abdulla Shahri and Sangoya, a Mijjarten, in order to get arms and ammunition from Bosaso, reached the Mullah shortly after he arrived in the Nogal, bringing 160 French rifles, both "Mare" and "Jikri" (*i.e.*, carbines and rifles), and 14 boxes of ammunition.

On the 27th, the day this man left the Haroun, another caravan of 300 camels arrived, bringing great quantities of rifles and ammunition. He, himself, did not see this caravan but heard the news.

Morning and night caravans keep coming in from the Mijjarten with clothes and food, and morning and night they leave, returning empty to Bosaso.

When the Mullah first went to the Nogal, 36 camels were loaded daily with the reserve and spare ammunition.

The Mullah has four machine guns and three big guns. The former are never used and one of the latter is useless, having been damaged at the time when Yusuf Ali's fort was captured, at Galkayu.

The Isa Mahmud tribe, better known at the Isa Riola, were looted by the Mullah, who took all their camels, ponies, and 50 rifles, leaving them their goats. Their headmen appealed against being looted, and the Mullah finally gave them back all their camels but kept the ponies and rifles. They have now promised to join him and help him in any way they can.

The Osman Mahmud trade with the Mullah, sending him rifles, ammunition and stores. They have, however, refused to join him, and have threatened that, if he moves into their country, they will go and fight him.

Islam and the Omar Mahmud are in no way helping the Mullah, who has, in consequence, threatened to send a party to raid them.

The Ali Naleya are not with the Mullah at present. They are living near Guban. (? The Guban or Maritime Plain.—G. T. F. W.) Nur Hodig, with 30 men paid a visit to the Mullah at Gaolo, to come to terms with him, nothing further is known about him.

The Dolbahanta, Mahmud Gerad, Nur Ahmed, moved into the Mijjarten country when the Mullah first went into the Nogal. They are living with the Osman Mahmud and have not joined the Mullah.

The Mullah sent a letter to Fara Hashi, who seems to be a sort of Quartermaster to Nur Isman. On reading it, these two men became very angry, cut it up with a knife, and wrote back ordering the Mullah not to come into their country, and telling him that they would not join him. They also sent round to all the Mijjarten tribes saying that the Mullah would only fool them, and telling them not to join him. All seem, however, willing to trade with him and get for him what he wishes.

The Mullah has now plenty of rifles and ammunition, and is quite ready for a fight. He does not intend to do anything until he receives replies to letters which he has sent to the following tribes :—

    Dolbahanta, Mahmud Gerad, Nur Ahmed.
    Dolbahanta, Mahmud Gerad, Ali Naleya.
    Dolbahanta, Hassan Ugaz.
    Dolbahanta, Omar Wais.
    Mijjarten, Osman Mahmud.
    Warsangli.

An Arab named Naashdone, has been a prisoner with the Mullah for three years. His brother arrived in Gaolo on the 26th July, in company with some prisoners who had escaped from Berbera. The Arab had a camel and a mule, both carrying loads. He brought many letters to the Mullah. He said that he had gone through Burao, and had been given a chit by a British officer there.

On their way back our Illalos met two old men who had been left behind by the British force at Badwein. They said that Islam and the Omar Mahmud had been at Mudug wells, grazing their animals there. A woman had gone to them, telling them of the Mullah being in the Nogal.

They then immediately moved to Golol and Jeriban, between Galkayu and Obbia.

Ali Yusuf has built a stone fort at Talaat, between Badwein and Galkayu.

The Illalos brought back 10 shields, 25 spears, and a blue jersey which had evidently been taken off a dead Yao. They say that several of the enemy were wearing blue jerseys, probably those captured at Gumburu.

The Illalos report that several of the Mullah's karias are at Ana Horigli, guarded by about 200 spearmen and from 13 to 15 rifles.

They say that if they were a few more they would stand a good chance of raiding these karias, and that 30 men is not enough.

Bohotle, 8th August, 1903.

## Censorship.

Complete freedom of the Press being incompatible with a state of war in Somaliland, as it is in any other country under like conditions, it was necessary to establish a censorship over the communications of newsagents and Press correspondents who were permitted to enter the theatre of operations. It was not, however, until December, 1902, when Press correspondents first accompanied the force at Obbia, that the General Officer Commanding was obliged to establish a censorship over Press communications. This was effected by appointing officers as censors at Berbera and Obbia respectively. Subsequently the officer in charge of the Intelligence Department was also appointed Press censor at the headquarters of the Field Force, with one assistant upon the lines of communication and another at the base.

Instructions were also issued to prevent any person, soldier or civilian, from proceeding to the Protectorate during the operations unless in possession of an order to join the command.

## Press Correspondents.

During the third and fourth expeditions a limited number of news agencies and papers were permitted, with the concurrence of the General Officer Commanding, to be represented in the theatre of operations by correspondents. The conditions upon which licences were issued were that correspondents pledged themselves to transmit all their communications for the Press through a Press censor. These conditions were, as a rule, observed by most of the correspondents who accompanied the troops or were permitted to reside in the country. A few cases, however, occurred of serious irregularities being committed by Press correspondents, which resulted in the licences of the offenders being cancelled or suspended.

### Survey Section.

During the third expedition the Obbia force was accompanied by a survey section, which was despatched from India and consisted of three native surveyors and 30 Khalasis, under the command of Captain G. A. Beazeley, R.E. This party was subsequently reorganized in October, 1903, and consisted of :—

    Captain G. A. Beazeley, R.E. (in command).
    Captain C. G. W. Hunter, R.E., Assistant Survey Officer.
    3 sub-surveyors.
    21 Khalasis.
    15 porter coolies.

During the operations in the Nogal Valley in the fourth expedition, the party was divided into two sections, one of which accompanied the 1st Brigade and the other the 2nd Brigade. When the Las Dureh column was formed, Captain Hunter proceeded with it, while Captain Beazeley continued the triangulation and detail survey from Berbera eastwards until the close of the campaign.

PLATE 16.

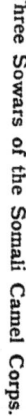

Three Sowars of the Somali Camel Corps.

(*To face page* 417.)

# CHAPTER XII.

## LOCAL LEVIES AND MOUNTED TROOPS.

### LOCAL LEVIES.

As considerable use was made of local levies throughout the operations, indeed, during the first and second expeditions Colonel Swayne depended almost entirely on these irregular troops, it is necessary to give a short account of the measures which were taken to raise them. The tribal horsemen from whom the levies were usually recruited were found particularly useful for co-operating with the regular troops, and for protecting our tribes from the Mullah's raiding parties. They possessed great mobility, and it was by no means uncommon for a Somali horseman, while on a raid, to cover 60 or 70 miles a day, and a man on foot to cover 50 miles.

The system of enlistment, organization, and training of the local levies raised by Colonel Swayne is sufficiently described in Chapter III, and need not be referred to again.

During General Manning's operations, the greater portion of the Somali levies engaged by Colonel Swayne were disbanded at Berbera, while the remainder were reorganized into mounted and dismounted companies, and were mainly employed as garrisons of posts upon the lines of communication.

During July, 1903, the Mounted Infantry of the 6th Battalion King's African Rifles was increased from 150 to 300. These were subsequently organized into two companies of Somali Mounted Infantry.

### *The Tribal and Gadabursi Horse.*

During the fourth expedition two corps of mounted levies were raised in October, 1903, and placed under the orders of the Officer Commanding Mounted Troops. They consisted of :—

No. III, *Tribal Horse*, recruited from the Dolbahanta, Ba Idris, Habr Yunis, and Midgan tribes, and No. IV, *Gadabursi Horse*, recruited almost entirely from Gadabursi men. The strength of each corps was 500 horsemen, 550 horses or mules, and 50 foot levies. Each man was supplied with a rifle, bandolier, blanket, saddle, water-bottle, and one horse or mule. A red tobe* was also issued as a distinguishing badge. The term of enlistment was for three months from the date of commencement of the operations. Pay was at the rate of 30 rs. for headmen, and 15 rs. for others, per month.

Blood money was also granted at the rate of 300 rs., paid to the next-of-kin of men killed in action or dying from wounds.

The organization was based on tribal sections, each section being commanded by its own Akil or headman.

Men who brought their own ponies, with saddle and bridle, received 30 rs. per month, and 100 rs. on termination of their engagement. Those who engaged without bringing their own ponies were supplied with mounts by the Remount Department.

The following British personnel served with the corps :—

### No. III Corps.—*Tribal Horse.*

Commandant : Major G. T. M. Bridges, Royal Artillery.

Assistant Commandant : Captain N. Malcolm, D.S.O., Argyll and Sutherland Highlanders.

Assistant Commandant : Lieutenant J. W. C. Kirk, King's African Rifles.

Medical Officer : Lieutenant J. H. Horton, Indian Medical Staff.

### No. IV Corps.—*Gadabursi Horse.*

Commandant : Major Hon. J. G. H. H. Beresford, 7th Hussars.

---

* Cloth worn as a turban.

Assistant Commandant : Captain H. W. B. Thorpe, King's Own Yorkshire Light Infantry.

Assistant Commandant : Lieutenant Hon. A. A. G. Hore-Ruthven, V.C., Cameron Highlanders.

Medical Officer : Captain H. E. M. Douglas, V.C., Royal Army Medical Corps.

Supply and Transport Officer: Staff-Sergeant J. Humphries, Supply and Transport Corps.

After the battle of Jidbali, both corps were amalgamated and called the Tribal Horse, their combined strength being reduced to 750 men. Of these, 250 picked men were taken for operations with the Mounted Troops, the remaining 500 returned to Ain Abo and Eil Dab, where they were utilised for raiding parties, &c.

During February, 1904, the corps was paid off, and the men discharged at Burao on their arrival there from Eil Dab, except 100 who took part in the operations of the Las Dureh column.

An officer who served with the corps makes the following remarks about these irregular troops :—

Unquestionably the best men as regards fighting and horsemanship are the Dolbahanta, Habr Yunis and Ba Idris tribes. The Gadabursi are very inferior horsemen, more jungly in their ways, and possess a smaller idea of fighting and, in consequence, are more inclined to bolt when under fire. Some of the Midgans proved very useful.

As regards the fighting power of the Somali, I think he has plenty of pluck, but when used in large numbers the Somali gets so frightfully excited that he hardly knows what he is doing. At the first fight at Jidbali some of them were very highly tried, and, after their horses were stampeded, it is not to be wondered at that they bolted from an infuriated mob of riflemen and spearmen. In smaller numbers where they can be controlled, I think they do very well; and latterly when they had a small fight at Madero, they did exceedingly good work. Their knowledge of the country and of the ways of the enemy's fighting is a very strong point; they have wonderful sight, and at night, if they want, are very alert; and, if they know their officers, will take very good care of them, and I don't think they would leave the latter in case of danger.

In February, 1904, to enable the tribe to hold their own and make a "stop" to the north-west of the haroun,

General Egerton sanctioned the raising by the civil authorities of a corps of foot levies for service in the Musa Abukr country. This corps was placed under the command of Lieut.-Colonel C. J. Melliss, V.C. The following extract from Somaliland Field Force Orders explains the organization, &c., of the corps :—

*Organization Levies.*—In lieu of the 350 Somali levies discharged, the General Officer Commanding sanctions the raising of 280 foot levies as under :—

(1) *Composition.*—Three companies, made up of 10 sections as under—

1 havildar.
1 naick.
2 lance naicks.
23 men.
—
Total 27    (27 × 10 = 270).

Native officers, colour havildars and ration naicks to be appointed in the proportion obtaining in the former levy, viz. :—

2 jemadars.
4 colour havildars.
3 ration naicks.
—
Total 9

And one interpreter at 40 rs. per mensem.

(2) *Conditions of Service.*—The same as for the discharged levies, except that the rates of pay will be increased 3 rs. (three) per mensem for all ranks.

(3) *Period of Engagement.*—To be for the present operations.

(4) *Arms.*—·303 calibre, 100 rounds and 1 bandolier per rifle.

(5) *Administration.*—The levy will be raised and maintained under the orders of the Consul-General.

(6) *Officers.*—The services of Lieut.-Colonel C. J. Melliss, V.C., were placed at the disposal of the Consul-General for this purpose, with effect from the 28th December, 1903.

(7) *Finance.*—The accounts of these levies will be dealt with by the Protectorate's Paymaster. Funds will be drawn from the nearest Treasure Chest Officer.

(8) *Equipment and Supply.*—Departments of the Field Force will comply with requisitions on account of these levies.

## MOUNTED TROOPS.

The regular Mounted Troops during the operations in 1903–04 consisted of the Burgher Contingent from South

PLATE 17.

Ponies grazing.

(*To face page* 420.)

Africa, British and Indian Mounted Infantry, and the Bikanir Camel Corps.

### *The Burgher Contingent.*

This corps was raised during the first fortnight in January, 1903, at Pretoria, for service in Somaliland.

The establishment included :—

        3 British Officers.
        4 Boer Officers.
        9 British soldiers.
        93 Boer rank and file.

The organization was :—

Commanding Officer : Captain W. Bonham, D.S.O., 1st Essex Regiment (with temporary rank of Major).
Second in Command : Captain A. A. McHardy, D.S.O., Royal Garrison Artillery.
Adjutant : Captain W. L. Foster, Royal Field Artillery.
Acting Sergeant-Major : E. May, Bloemfontein Commando.
Quartermaster Sergeant : R. W. Smyth, Leinster Regiment.
*No. 1 Section, Pretoria Commando.*—1 sergeant, 2 corporals, 20 rank and file, under Lieutenant Jisager.
*No. 2 Section, Pretoria Commando.*—1 sergeant, 2 corporals, 20 rank and file, under Lieutenant Cronje.
*No. 3 Section, Christiana Commando.*—1 sergeant, 2 corporals, 20 rank and file, under Lieutenant Scott-Harden.
*No. 4 Section, Bloemfontein Commando.*—1 sergeant, 2 corporals, 20 rank and file, under Lieutenant Scott.

In addition, there were 8 British soldiers, consisting of :—

1 lance corporal ⎫ 7th Dragoon Guards ⎫
1 private       ⎬                               ⎬ Signallers
2 privates     .. West Yorks.     ⎭
1 shoeing smith .. Royal Field Artillery
1 gunner     ⎫                             ⎫ Officers'
1 driver      ⎬ Royal Field Artillery   ⎬ servants
1 private    .. Royal Lancaster Regiment ⎭

making a total of 109 all ranks, with 150 cobs (South African, Walers, Argentines, and Russian).

The term of enlistment was six months, or, if operations concluded before expiration of that period, until the conclusion of operations.

The rates of pay were :—British officers (3) graded as Special Service officers; Boer officers (4), £1 per diem; quartermaster-sergeant (1), 10*s.* per diem; sergeant-major, (1), 10*s.* per diem; sergeants (4), 7*s.* per diem; corporals (8), 6*s.* per diem; privates (80), 5*s.* per diem; British soldiers (8), 5*s.* per diem.

Each man was provided with small pay book (Army Book 64) in which entries of each payment were made. All accounts were kept by the Chief Paymaster, Cape Town, to whom pay rolls were sent monthly.

*Equipment.*—Each man was equipped on the same scale as for British mounted infantrymen in South Africa, except that, in addition, 1 extra bandolier per man (carried round horse's neck), 1 British warm and 1 mackintosh cape per man (no cloaks), 1 revolver and 1 carbine per officer were issued.

*Saddlery.*—Indian Cavalry pattern, no wallets, 1 saddle-bag (Mexican pattern) carried on near side of saddle. Rifle-bucket (Mounted Infantry pattern) hitched close up to off-side of saddle, with outer top half of bucket cut away.

*Signalling Gear.*—2 helios and 2 lamps complete.

One ·303 maxim gun, with tripod stand, and pack saddle equipment.

One light Field Service forge, with pack saddle equipment.

Ordinary camp equipment with tents.

*Ammunition.*—30 boxes small arms ammunition, 1,100 rounds per box.

*Transport.*—Provided locally in Somaliland as required from time to time, sometimes camel, at others mules.

The contingent embarked at Durban on January 15th,

1903, on the steamship "Gaul," and disembarked at Obbia, on January 25th and 26th, having suffered no casualties on the voyage amongst men or horses.

The men and stores were landed in boats, the horses swam ashore. On arrival at Obbia the contingent was brigaded with the 1st British Company Mounted Infantry, Punjab Mounted Infantry, and Bikanir Camel Corps.

During the operations the contingent suffered the following casualties :—1 man lost in the bush ; 1 died in hospital ; 1 man accidentally shot ; 1 man wounded near Gumburu ; 56 horses killed or died.

The following remarks are extracted from a report on the contingent :—

The time given (14 days) in which to raise and equip a contingent of 100 Boers from various parts of the Transvaal and Orange River Colony for service in a foreign country was insufficient. Consequently no choice of men could be made, and the first 93 men who presented themselves and passed the medical examination were enlisted. The contingent was not collected together till the day of the embarkation at Durban, January 15th. All personal clothing and equipment was served out to the men, and the unit properly organised during the voyage from Durban to Obbia. During the disembarkation at Obbia, the Boers were usefully employed in assisting to land the horses and stores. The month spent at Obbia was occupied in constant drill. Each man was allowed 100 rounds of ammunition with which to get thoroughly acquainted with his rifle ; buck shooting afforded excellent practice. Except for the skirmishes whilst with Colonel Cobbe's column on April 14th and 16th, the contingent saw no fighting. The few men who were fortunate enough to come into contact with the enemy behaved well, especially on April 16th, when the patrol of which they formed part was surrounded and nearly cut up. The men, however, were not good shots at close ranges of 40 yards to 70 yards, and did not inflict the losses they should have done on the enemy that day. A few chief points noted with regard to the men were :—

The remarkable way they stood the hardships of intense heat, very short rations of food and water, and long rides through the heat of the day. The percentage of sick was very small.

The knack of finding their way in a flat, featureless country, full of thick bushes, by taking the sun as their guide.

The somewhat surprising difficulty of making the men take proper care of their horses ; the fact that the horses did not belong to them may have been the reason for this.

The aversion each man had to exchanging, even temporarily, his rifle for one he was not thoroughly acquainted with.

In conclusion, it may be stated that the men volunteered for a further period of service in the country, but owing to the difficulty at the time of sufficient transport for supplies for mounted troops, and also to there being no immediate prospect of further operations, it was not deemed advisable to accept their offer.

*Mounted Infantry.*

In August, 1903, the Mounted Infantry were organized into two corps, as follows :—

I Corps.

Officer Commanding : Lieut.-Colonel P. A. Kenna, V.C., D.S.O., 21st Lancers.

Adjutant : Captain A. Skeen, 24th Punjabis.

1st Company, British Mounted Infantry.—Officer Commanding : Captain G. C. Shakerley, King's Royal Rifles.

2nd Company, British Mounted Infantry.—Officer Commanding : Captain M. G. E. Bell, Rifle Brigade.

3rd Company, British Mounted Infantry.—Officer Commanding : Brevet-Major J. R. M. Marsh, Lincoln Regiment.

4th Company, Somali Mounted Infantry.—Officer Commanding : Captain T. N. Howard, 4th King's African Rifles.

5th Company, Somali Mounted Infantry (in course of formation.)—Officer Commanding : Major P. Osborn, D.S.O., 3rd King's African Rifles.

II Corps.

Officer Commanding : Brevet-Major J. E. Gough,* Rifle Brigade.

Adjutant : Captain C. G. Woodhouse, 126th Baluchistan Infantry.

6th Company, Poona Mounted Infantry.—Officer Commanding : Captain W. Mitchell, 124th Baluchistan Infantry.

---

* Major Gough was succeeded by Major R. Brooke who commanded the 2nd Corps until it was disbanded in May, 1903.

7th Company, Umballa Mounted Infantry.—Officer Commanding: Captain H. B. Ford, 31st Punjabis.

Bikanir Camel Corps.—Officer Commanding: Captain W. G. Walker, V.C., 1st Battalion 4th Gurkha Rifles.

No. 1 Company, British Mounted Infantry, King's Royal Rifles, landed in Somaliland as a complete and well seasoned unit, having been in the field during the war in South Africa.

No. 2 Company, British Mounted Infantry, was mobilised at Fatigarh, India, and landed in Somaliland in July, 1903. It comprised detachments from three British regiments.

No. 3 Company, British Mounted Infantry, mainly consisted of officers and men who had just completed a course of instruction at Bangalore.

No. 6 (Poona) and 7 (Umballa) Companies, Indian Mounted Infantry, were composed of six and eight detachments respectively of various native infantry regiments.

The Punjab Mounted Infantry, which landed at Berbera in 1902, was composed of two regiments of two castes, Sikhs and Dogras.

### *Bikanir Camel Corps.*

In 1889 the offer of the Bikanir Durbar to raise a camel corps of 500 Rahtor Rajputs as Imperial Service troops was accepted by the Indian Government and its organization commenced. The services of two British officers were lent to the State to supervise the raising, training, and equipment of the corps.

In India, it is organized in six companies and officered entirely by officers of the Bikanir State; 75 per cent. of the men are Rahtor Rajputs, and the balance are Rajputs of other clans and a few Sikhs and Mahomedans (Kaimkhani), all recruited in Bikanir territory.

The services of the corps (dismounted) were accepted for the China expedition, where they remained from September, 1900, to May, 1901. In December, 1902, the corps was ordered to hold itself in readiness for service in Somaliland.

It embarked at Bombay on the 10th January, 1903, and was on continuous service in Somaliland until the end of June, 1904, when it sailed from Berbera, having served with much distinction and proved of the greatest value on the waterless stretches on the interior.

*Organization.*—The corps is maintained on the Silladar system. Recruits can either bring their own camels or purchase from the Chanda fund, paying in instalments. The camel price is 110 rs. Service in the corps is very popular in the State, and consequently it gets a class of recruit which does not willingly enlist in the Indian Army.

The terms of enlistment, rules for discharge with gratuity and pension, family pension, &c., are drawn up on the lines of the regulations for the Indian Army, from which they differ only in small particulars. The scale of pay is also very similar to that of a Sepoy of the Indian Army, with this exception, that an extra 10 rs. per mensem is allowed to each man for the feed of the camel.

## Establishment.

|  | Number. | | |
|---|---|---|---|
|  | Service. | Depot. | Total. |
| **Fighting men:—** | | | |
| *Mounted Officers—* | | | |
| Commandant | 1 | .. | 1 |
| Assistant Commandants.. | 2 | .. | 2 |
| Adjutant .. | 1 | .. | 1 |
| Assistant Surgeon | 1 | .. | 1 |
| *Company Officers—* | | | |
| Subadars .. | 6 | .. | 6 |
| Jemadars .. | 5 | 1 | 6 |
| Hospital assistant | 1 | .. | 1 |
| *N.C.O.'s and Men—* | | | |
| Havildar Major .. | 1 | .. | 1 |
| Quartermaster Havildar.. | 1 | .. | 1 |
| Kote Havildars .. | 6 | .. | 6 |
| Havildars .. | 21 | 3 | 24 |
| Naicks | 21 | 3 | 24 |
| Lance Naicks | 27 | 3 | 30 |
| Sepoys | 345 | 38 | 383 |
| Armourers | 2 | .. | 2 |
| Salutris | 2 | 1 | 3 |
| Buglers | 10 | 2 | 12 |
| Total.. | 453 | 51 | 504* |
| **Public followers:—** | | | |
| Gomashta | 1 | 1 | 2 |
| Pundit | .. | 1 | 1 |
| Mochis | 2 | 1 | 3 |
| Bhisties | 12 | 2† | 14 |
| Cooks.. | 12 | 2† | 14 |
| Sweepers | 6 | 2† | 8 |
| Chowdry | 1 | .. | 1 |
| Kahars | 6 | .. | 6 |
| Ward Orderly | 1 | .. | 1 |
| Barbers | 4 | 2† | 6 |
| Total.. | 45 | 11 | 56 |
| **Private followers:—** | | | |
| Officers' personal servants .. | 11 | .. | .. |
| Hospital Assistant's personal servants | 1 | .. | .. |
| Syces (mounted officers) .. | 2 | .. | .. |
| Total.. | 14 | .. | .. |

\* Organized in 6 Companies.

† Additional entertained on mobilization.

*Transport.*—The following scale is laid down in the Field Service equipment tables of the corps. The followers are all mounted.

Transport is not kept up for the corps, but can be raised at a few hours' notice.

| Details. | Camels. | Followers. |
|---|---|---|
| 425 rifles at 80 rounds per rifle, 57 boxes .. | 29 | 12 bhisties and 3 servants |
| Spare arm kajawahs .. | 1 | 1 bearer |
| Treasure chest .. | 1 | Gomashta |
| Hospital and veterinary equipment .. | 6 | 1 hospital assistant, 1 ward orderly, 2 salutris, 2 bearers |
| Office equipment .. | 1 | 1 writer |
| Signalling equipment .. | 1 | 1 bearer |
| Entrenching tools .. | 4 | (Led) |
| Quartermaster's stores and armourer's tools .. | 2 | 2 mochies |
| 4 guard and office tents (160 lbs.) .. | 2 | |
| 10 officers' tents (80 lbs) | 3 | 11 servants and 2 bearers |
| 37 N.C.O.'s and men's tents (160 lbs.) | 19 | |
| Company cooking pots .. | 6 | 2 cooks to each camel |
| Spare camels .. | 6 | 6 sweepers |
| Total .. | 81 | |

Kits are carried on riding camels.

*Equipment.*—The corps is armed and equipped from Government arsenals in the same manner as the Indian Army. At present they are armed with the M.L.E. Mark II rifle.

The *Full Dress* consists of red turban, with "tura"; white serge "Kurta," red collar and facings; red "cummerbund"; white drill pantaloons, Jodhpur pattern; ankle boots; black putties.

*Khaki Uniform.*—Khaki turban, coat, pantaloons, and putties with ankle boots. Brown accoutrements.

*Camel Gear.*—(a) Drill order :—

*Headstall*—"Mora"—passes over the ears and round the jaws just in front of the eyes and is finished off with one turn of the headstall rope and knotted under the neck. A leather headstall would be more useful.

## BIKANIR CAMEL CORPS.

### Embarking Camels.

(*To face page* 428.)

## BIKANIR CAMEL CORPS.

### Review Order.

(*To follow Plate* 18.)

PLATE 20.

## BIKANIR CAMEL CORPS.

Full Dress, Cowrie Necklet and Headstall.

*(To follow Plate 19.)*

PLATE 21.

## BIKANIR CAMEL CORPS.

Indian Camel.  Arab Camel.

(To follow Plate 20.)

## BIKANIR CAMEL CORPS.

### Heavy Marching Order.

(*To follow Plate* 21.)

## BIKANIR CAMEL CORPS.

### Maxim Gun Detachment.

*(To follow Plate 22.)*

*Necklet—*" Kodala "—full dress only—should be just touching the headstall rope and hang about 12 inches below the point of the skull, usually made of cowrie shells, the buckle of the necklet should be on the top and in the centre of the neck.

*Breast-piece—*" Gorband "—of red webbing, is crossed and buckled to the pommel of the saddle, and should be of such a length that the rosette rests on the breastbone between the fore legs.

*Girth Ends—*" Loomba "—44 inches long, red webbing, should hang level so that the tassels are just clear of the camel's belly.

*Girth—*" Tang "—red webbing, the front girth should be close behind the pad (" idar "), the rear girth as far back as possible, provided it is clear of the penis, both pulled as tight as possible and only loosened for watering.

*Saddle Cover—*" Gaddi "—Large enough to cover the whole saddle, made of leather with red cotton buttons.

*Nose String.—*Fixed with loops on to wooden pegs driven through the nostrils.

(b) Field Service Order :—The " Kodala," " Gorband," " Mora," and " Loomba " are all removed.

*Saddle Bags.—*Brown leather, one on each side, fixed on to the rib of the saddle under the front seat.

" *Chaguls* " or *water tins* strapped on to the rib, under the rear seat.

*Saddle Cover* removed and blankets and waterproof sheet substituted.

*Kit Bag* on rear seat, or behind it, if required to mount a second man.

*Saddle.—*Of the double-seated Bikanir pattern, to carry two men. Three iron arches, 12, 14, and 16 inches wide, attached to wooden ribs, leather seat stretched across the arches. Pads, leather covered, stuffed with camel's hair. Weight of saddle cushions and pads about 60 lbs. The man rides astride, using stirrups.

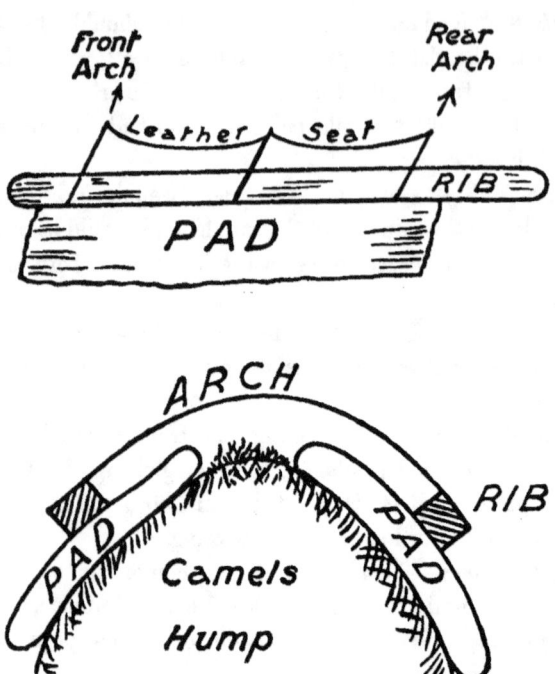

*Saddling.*—The camel should first be well groomed, the saddle-cloth ("mailkoori") is then put over the hump, so that the front ends lie along the shoulders, two cotton cushions ("gaddi") in front of the hump and one behind are placed on triangularly, so that the points meet on the hump. The saddle is now put on so that the centre arch is over the middle of the hump, the front pads ("thara") should rest over the point of the shoulder, the rear pad just in front of the hipbone. In tightening girths, the saddle should be shaken, so that it sits well down on the cushions.

Captain W. G. Walker, V.C., Indian Army, who commanded the corps in Somaliland,[*] made the following observations:—

---

[*] Captains E. M. Hughes, H. E. Browne and G. W. Rawlins, Indian Army, also served with the corps.

## Composition of Corps in Somaliland.

| | From— | |
|---|---|---|
| | Obbia. | Berbera. |
| | Number. | Number. |
| British officers | 3 | 3 |
| Native officers | 9 | 9 |
| Hospital assistants | 1 | 1 |
| Havildars | 12 | 12 |
| Naicks | 9 | 10 |
| Buglers | 4 | 5 |
| Armourer | 1 | 1 |
| Salutri | 1 | 1 |
| Ward orderly | 1 | .. |
| Sowars | 180 | 176 |
| Camels | 245 | 270 |

Organized in two companies.

## Equipment.

| | Kit taken from Obbia. | | Kit taken from Berbera. | |
|---|---|---|---|---|
| | Number. | Weight. | Number. | Weight. |
| | | Lbs. ozs. | | Lbs. ozs. |
| *Clothing*— | | | | |
| Waterproof sheet | 1 | 3 0 | 1 | 3 0 |
| Blanket | 1 | 4 4 | 2 | 8 8 |
| Great coat | 1 | 11 0 | .. | .. |
| Native suits | 2 | 8 0 | 1 | 4 0 |
| Socks ..  pairs | 1 | 0 4 | 1 | 0 4 |
| Native shoes  pairs | 1 | 1 0 | 1 | 1 0 |
| Khaki suit | 1 | 5 0 | .. | .. |
| Khaki pugree | 1 | 2 0 | .. | .. |
| Khaki putties  pairs | 1 | 0 8 | .. | .. |
| Cardigan jacket | .. | .. | 1 | 1 8 |
| Cape, great coat | .. | .. | 1 | 2 0 |
| Total | .. | 35 0 | .. | 20 4 |

The second scale (Berbera) was most suitable—a great coat was not required, except on the Golis Range. A second blanket and cardigan are preferable for cold weather season.

*Accoutrements.*—The "Mackenzie" equipment of belts, braces, and pouches was brought from India. This was mostly unserviceable at the end of the first phase, and was replaced by bandoliers.

During the fourth expedition each man carried one shoulder bandolier (50 rounds) and one waist bandolier (40 rounds and bayonet); 50 rounds extra were carried in pocket and haversack in action, and the balance of 400 rounds was carried on the camel in a canvas bag.

*Line Gear.*—Nil.

*Saddlery.*—The Bikanir pattern double-seated saddle was used throughout. The following articles were carried on saddle :—

Kit.
Two saddle bags (leather) holding 40 lbs. of grain.
Three days' men's rations.
Reserve ammunition—300 rounds.
Entrenching tool or axe.
Picketing rope.
Chaguls—two to four—2 gallon water tins would be preferable.
Bucket—20 p.c.

Riding weight just under four maunds.

*Camp Equipage.*—The usual Indian equipment of 80 lbs. and 160 lbs. general service tents were brought from India, but never taken beyond the base—tents were not necessary, except in the hills.

### *Training.*

In the bush, file or single file was the only possible march formation. In the vicinity of enemy, animals were closed up, men dismounted and extended on the front and flanks; No. 3's led camels. When halted, square was formed, and animals were tied down—one man looking after eight camels. In open country, a line of section or half company columns in single file was found to be the best formation to move in, generally at close interval (10 paces), opening out to deploying intervals when coming under fire.

It would not be advisable to bring camels within 1,500 yards of aimed fire, unless the ground was favourable. Firing off the camel could, I am sure, be used with effect on occasions when it would be inadvisable to dismount—good shooting was made at head and shoulder targets up to 300 yards.

*Followers.*—The strength of the followers was 38. When moving fast, no followers were taken—they came along with the baggage.

The corps landed with 25 per cent. spare animals. The casualties during the third expedition amounted to nearly 50 per cent. This may be considered exceptionally heavy, but owing to the incessant work, poor grazing, want of veterinary supervision, and to the fact that all animals thrown out of work had to be destroyed for supply reasons, the losses were not excessive. During the fourth expedition, the casualties were about 25 per cent.

Lieut.-Colonel P. A. Kenna, who commanded the Mounted Troops submitted the following remarks about the equipment, organization, training, &c., of the Mounted Infantry which served under him in Somaliland:—

*Equipment.*

The equipment for man and horse and first line transport as laid down by me for the previous phase of this campaign and embodied in Sections II, III, and IV of attached Standing Orders,* printed in July, 1903, answered well. I have nothing to alter, and little to add.

*Men's Clothing.*—During actual operations, men of mounted troops are generally without any kit beyond that on their horses, and this must be, and has been kept down to lowest limits. The khaki coat is therefore superfluous, and is generally left with the baggage, so is the man's blanket, and everything else except change of underclothing and a thick jersey or sweater.

*Shirts.*—The man's shirt should, therefore, be of stout material — "greybacks" do well—and should have two large breast-pockets, with buttons and flaps.

*Blankets.*—The saddle-blanket should be longer; its present length does not cover a man, and it is very often his only bedding.

*Combined Pants and Leggings.*—The latest regulation combined pants and loose leggings, with buckle and strap at knee, but with an ordinary seam instead of buttons, *i.e.*, an ordinary pair of trousers, looser from knee to waist, and tighter from below knee to ankle, with knee straps, is the most serviceable, comfortable, and lasting kit for all-round work of mounted men in the field. The adjustable strap at the knee enables these trousers to be used as pants and leggings, or pants and puttees, or as ordinary "slacks." Even the ordinary thin khaki trousers, without any strap, are preferred to pants and leggings, or pants and puttees, by many officers and men for long jaunts on which for days and nights together they cannot change their clothes. These trousers should be of best stout material.

*Spurs.*—Spurs should be issued to all men, and taken away from those who abuse, or cannot use them properly. They are an assistance, and often a necessity, in the field.

*Bit.*—The ordinary Mounted Infantry reversible bit does well, but I prefer the bar fixed, and the upper arm of cheek-piece shorter. The curb-chain, like the spur, is an assistance, and often a necessity; its abuse can be easily obviated by adjusting it and putting the rein on the cheek-piece, upper or lower bar.

*Trotting Camels v. Mules as First Line Transport.*—I still most strongly advocate trotting camels as first line transport to mounted troops in Somaliland everywhere but in the hills, and our hill work has hitherto been limited to lines of communication.

Mules carrying the regulation two maunds in addition to saddle, equipment, and food, led in strings of three by a mounted man and driven along by yet another mounted man, are 20 per cent. slower than mounted troops moving at their most economical pace over the long stretches of waterless

---
* See page 439.

country that have to be continually crossed in Somaliland. I have tested and verified this, even on the best of roads, such as that from Sheikh to Burao, and thence on to Bohotle, in the best of weather.

I know that these loaded mules can cover great distances in their own time, and at their own pace, and with less wastage than horses; also that good mules, even the tiny Abyssinian, ridden by a fair weight, will accompany mounted troops at pace described in VI, 3 (Standing Orders, page 441), for any distance. But the ordinarily loaded and led mules cannot keep with mounted troops on these marches; trotting camels can.

Under "Mobility," I have noted some of the best examples of it, but in all the instances quoted, the first line transport of mounted troops was nil, or limited to Bikanir or other trotting camels, and a very few picked mules carrying one maund, and led singly.

*Bayonet or Substitute.*—I consider the bayonet at the end of a rifle in the hands of a mounted man more dangerous to himself than to his enemy at close quarters, besides entailing the dropping and probable loss of many rifles. This is supported by the trials of the King's Royal Rifles, than whom no regiment has had more experience of Mounted Infantry work. If Mounted Infantry are to have a weapon for hand-to-hand work mounted, a light pointing sword or rapier seems indicated. The ordinary cavalry sword has the following disadvantages:—On prolonged operations, scabbard and sword drop off the saddle wholesale; many swords cannot be drawn through wet and dirt in scabbards; the edge of sword gets too blunt to be hurtful; the sword requires far more skill to wield than is generally available, for it is at best a clumsy weapon.

*Saddle.*—The "General Service" or "Universal pattern" saddle continues to be the most satisfactory. Its little extra weight is of small consequence, provided proper attention is paid to the weight of the rider. The seat should be flatter and not too short.

*Chaguls.*—Chaguls soon wear out; their average life is two months in open country, and one in the bush. Renewals should, therefore, be kept at advanced depôts. The bottle-shaped pattern, to tie at neck, is best.

*Girths.*—Only leather girths should be issued to mounted troops.

*Revolvers.*—Revolvers were issued to the best and most experienced Mounted Infantry company in Somaliland, and on one occasion did good work. But it is difficult to confine their danger to the enemy. In theory, they are excellent; in practice, except in the coolest and most experienced hands, they are risky.

*Mess Tins.*—The British Mounted Infantry had infantry mess tins; they seem as useful and popular as the cavalry tins, though the latter ride better on the saddle. Both are good, one or the other indispensable, rendering each man independent.

*Indian Mounted Infantry want Individual Cooking Kit.*—The Indian Mounted Infantry urgently require some kind of cooking utensil to be carried and used by each man while away from the baggage. Until they are less wedded to their present cumbersome cooking paraphernalia they will be as much handicapped as mounted troops on really active operations. At present, the men risk unnecessary and avoidable deprivations, and hence their efficiency.

Each man of the Bikanir Camel Corps carries in his haversack a "dubba," circular in transverse section, with rounded edges, about 7 inches in diameter and 3 inches in depth, with tightly-fitting lid. In this "dubba" he can carry and prepare his day's food at any time, including "chupatties," for which the lid is used, and for which purpose the "dubba" is made of brass, and not of aluminium. This brass "dubba" weighs about 7 ozs., and would be invaluable to Indian Mounted Infantry, provided each man was taught and made to use it, when moving light.

### Organization, Training, Efficiency, &c.

1. *Original Object of Mounted Infantry.*—Mounted Infantry seem to have been originally started to give more mobility to infantry, to enable it to more closely support cavalry, and reap more quickly the fruits of advantages gained by cavalry.

2. *Mounted Infantry during South African War supplements Cavalry.*—In the late South African War the demand for cavalry far exceeded the supply, so large numbers of mounted infantry were hastily raised to supplement the cavalry, and do cavalry work. At a heavy cost in human life horseflesh, and money, this object was gradually attained, and many fine battalions of mounted infantry were produced, capable of doing most or all cavalry work.

3. *Mounted Infantry in Somaliland supersedes Cavalry.*—But now mounted infantry seems to have superseded cavalry. For mounted infantry alone has been sent to Somaliland to do the work of cavalry, though the whole of the British and Indian cavalry was available for this purpose.

4. *Result.*—The result of this was unsatisfactory, and would have been more so, but for the three months secured to most companies between landing and actually taking the field. Advantage was taken of this time by keen and generally capable officers to better prepare their men for the many duties of trained horsemen, *i.e.*, of cavalry in the field.

5. *Composite Companies.*—(a) Moreover, all companies but one of this mounted infantry were composed of many fragments of various infantry regiments. The men of these companies, therefore, met one another and most of their officers for the first time just before starting for Somaliland—a severe handicap to all ranks, especially in the case of Indian troops.

The disadvantages of these composite companies are so many and so obvious, that recapitulation of them seems unnecessary. Discipline, *esprit de corps*, cohesion—system, in fact, everything on which the efficiency of a unit depends—is adversely affected by them; the difficulties of promotion, which is only temporary in mixed companies, keep away good men; the work of pay and correspondence is complicated and increased.

(b) Many of the men sent with these mounted infantry companies were apparently selected without any consideration as to how or when they had gone through the training of a mounted infantry school; some had evidently forgotten what little they had learnt; while others had as evidently never learnt anything of mounted infantry work.

(c) The establishment of officers, non-commissioned officers, farriers, salutris, saddlers, &c., varied in companies, and only one had a non-commissioned officer to correspond to the Squadron-Quartermaster-sergeant-major of cavalry—a most necessary person.

(d) One, if not the only, advantage of composite companies, is the better opportunity they afford of picking light men. But, while much time and ingenuity is devoted to lightening our military saddles a pound or two, little thought is given to a difference of two or three stone in the weight of the rider. I had a man of the 2nd British Mounted Infantry weighed at the conclusion of a forced march soon after their arrival in Somaliland. His kit consisted of what he stood in, plus a change of socks and a shirt, no blanket or great coat. With saddle and bridle complete, he turned the scale at 17 stone 3 lbs. Both nose-bags (two) and chagul were empty, and his day and a half rations eaten; therefore this man had started at the nice steadying weight of over 19 stone on an Indian countrybred.

6. To obviate these drawbacks:—

(a) Mounted infantry should not be called upon to perform all the duties of cavalry while the latter are available.

(b) When mounted infantry must be used, and selection is possible, preference should be given to light efficient soldiers who can ride, or at least remain in the saddle at a trot and gallop; this desirable accomplishment was by no means universal among the mounted infantry when first landed. They should know the rudimentary principles of stable management, watering, feeding, saddling, knee-haltering, "ringing," or otherwise securing detached horses, &c.; they should be able to mount and dismount quickly on either side, and they should know how to cook and otherwise look after themselves in the field (*vide* Standing Orders, Section 1).

(c) The question of weight is, if possible, of more importance in Somaliland than elsewhere; for the scarcity and uncertainty of water practically compel every horseman to start on almost every occasion with at least one canvas chagul, containing 1 to 1½ gallons of water; this means an extra 10 to 15 lbs. Again, the country produces no grain; horses have, therefore, to carry their own for the days they are to be away from supplies.

(d) *Mounted Infantry to come from One Regiment or Battalion, and not from Many.*—Composite companies should not exist. As mounted infantry is becoming so popular and so essential, each infantry battalion should be ready to supply one mounted infantry company at any moment. The staff of farriers, shoeing smiths, &c., might be provided from the nearest mounted infantry school, where they could always be kept ready and up-to-date.

(e) *Proposed Establishment of Mounted Infantry Companies.*—The establishment of a mounted infantry company taking the field should be the same as that of a squadron of cavalry, British or Indian, according to which Army it belongs, though I would increase the actual number of rank and file by about 10 per cent. to counteract the inevitable initial wastage.

Colonel Kenna remarked further:—

In spite of the many disadvantages mentioned, and which were chiefly in evidence when these mounted infantry landed, a high state of efficiency was eventually attained by them. In proof of this, I may quote a few examples :—

(a) On 18th April, 1903, every available man of British, Burgher and Indian Mounted Infantry marched from Galadi to Gumburu, 48 miles through bush, in 12 hours, without a man or horse falling out ; no water *en route*, and intense heat during last four or five hours.

(b) Between 4 P.M. 17th, and 9 A.M. 19th December, 1903, 200 British and Indian Mounted Infantry, with 50 Bikanirs and 200 Tribal Horse, marched from Badwein to Jidbali, 38 miles, engaged the enemy for five hours at latter place, and returned to Badwein ; distance covered, apart from reconnoitring and five hours' desultory fighting, 76 miles in 41 hours, without any water for horses.

(c) Between 6 P.M. 30th April, and 8 A.M. 2nd May, 1904, some 250 British and Indian Mounted Infantry, with 150 Bikanirs and 40 irregular (Somali) horsemen, marched from Biliyu to Kheman and back to Biliyu, thus covering 100 miles of waterless country (the Northern Haud) in 38 hours on one gallon of water per man and none for horses. About one-third of these men and horses had done 60 miles in the two previous nights, and thus covered 160 miles in 3 days 14 hours. None of these horses were in more than moderate condition, having been in the field from 6 to 12 months.

## The Somali.*

*The Somali as a Fighting Man.*—The Somali, in some form or other, is absolutely necessary to troops operating in Somaliland. For hard fighting he is unreliable, being peculiarly excitable and subject to panic ; for scouting, rounding up stock, or following up an enemy whose resistance has been completely broken, he is invaluable.

*As a Guide.*—For guiding he is indispensable. Much of the country has never been mapped or traversed by white men, while the difficulty of finding one's way about that which is supposed to be known, is proved by the number of officers and men who have strayed or lost themselves, out of the very few who have ventured any distance from the known roads without a Somali.

*His Qualifications as an Irregular Light Horseman.*—The Somali's intelligence and endurance, his light weight and natural horsemanship, combined with all the keen senses of the wild man in his own country admirably fit him for the work of an irregular horseman in conjunction with regular troops.

*Mobility.*—I fix the greatest mobility of mounted infantry moving in this country, independent of any other source of supply, at two days' marching, *i.e.*, about 90 miles from one water and supply depôt to another

---

* See also page 322.

or 45 miles out and 45 back to the same depôt, though I have actually done 50 out and 50 back, with 250 horsemen, in less than 40 hours. These rates could not be kept up indefinitely, and would be only occasional efforts. But, apart from the question of supply, I consider that 40 miles a day can be maintained for at least four days; 100 of my mounted infantry recently covered 160 miles in less than four days. But, after the first two days, the mobility of the mounted infantry depends, in this country, on that of the supplies presumably coming up behind it. In March, 1903, during the advance from Obbia, I moved out with the mounted infantry from Bera, some 10 hours before the main body and supplies, for Galadi. I made latter place direct, about 75 miles, but had to live there nearly two days on half a biscuit per man and some captured sheep, while the horses had nothing but camel mats to eat, there being no grain and not a blade of grass near Galadi at that time. This illustrates the difficulty mounted infantry have in subsisting in this country away from their own supplies, and how dependent their mobility is on that of their supplies after two days. As regards pace, I fix the greatest mobility of mounted infantry at 50 miles in 12 hours. On the 18th April, 1903, the mounted infantry with me did from Galadi to Gumburu, 48 miles, in 12 hours, in great heat, without a man or horse falling out. But in all these examples of mobility the first line transport was nil, or done by Bikanirs or a very few picked mules lightly loaded and led singly.

The Bikanirs have frequently rendered invaluable aid to mounted infantry by carrying half a maund per camel of supplies for men and horses of the mounted infantry.

With less heavily equipped men and camels, such as Arabs, who are small, on Arab or other trotting camels, with Arab saddles and canvas saddle bags, and each man leading a second loaded camel, supplies would be pushed on 40 miles a day, and the present mobility of mounted infantry doubled or trebled.

An escort of Bikanirs, carrying their own supplies for six or eight days, would render such a convoy very independent and detachable, especially if the camel men were fighting men, such as Arabs, and armed.

*Followers*, other than syces to look after spare and sick animals, are out of place with mounted troops on active operations in Somaliland. Salutris, Nalbunds, and all other such skilled Indian workmen should be fighting men; many at present are not.

*Watering Horses.*—Horses on service in Somaliland are fortunate if they get one full drink every day, and do well on that. Even at Bihendula last hot weather I always had at least one-fourth the animals drinking only once a day. Horses thus watered drink nearly two gallons less per diem than if watered two or three times; this does not seem to affect their appetite or condition, while it prepares them to better undergo the strain of watering after working 48 hours or longer in great heat without water or even damp grazing.

The following standing orders and instructions were issued to the Mounted Troops by Lieut.-Colonel P. A. Kenna :—

## I.—Care of Horses.

1. *Feeding, Watering, Fitting of Blankets and Saddles, Care of Feet and Backs*, are the chief points to be attended to on service. The actual grooming on the line of march can be limited to removing ticks and other vermin, and promptly treating wounds or skin diseases, such as ringworm and mange.

2. *Saddle Blanket.*—Knowledge and application of various ways of folding the blanket will save much horseflesh.

3. *Saddlery.*—Horses on service, especially if they start on the big side, soon alter the shape of the back. However well saddles fit at the start, they need constant watching, alteration of blanket or stuffing, or changing from one horse to another, as work tells.

4. *Feet.*—When a horse loses a shoe that cannot be at once replaced, the wall of the hoof must be lowered to the outside level of the sole at the first opportunity, and the ground-edge rounded off with a rasp. This will enable the foot to stand much work without a shoe. At least one man per section should carry a rasp, and know how to use it.

5. *Head Collar and Bridle.*—The combined head collar and bridle, with head rope, will always be used in the field, and the General Service pattern saddle in preference to Colonial or Yeomanry. The ordinary stable or line head collar will not be carried.

6. *Rifle Bucket.*—Rifle buckets will be carried, but only as a support for the rifle, which must not be used as a prop or rest for the rider—a cause of sore backs.

7. *Line of March.*—On the line of march, men will dismount at every opportunity, off-saddle and graze whenever practicable, and as soon as possible after reaching camp. Even on the move, every opportunity should be given to horses to pick up what they can. Grass should be gathered and brought into the lines for all horses at night and for those confined to camp during the day. When off-saddled, horses should be given every opportunity to lie down and roll.

8. *Grazing.*—While grazing, all horses must invariably be knee-haltered, and at least half the armed escort should be mounted, or ready to mount at a moment's notice. The grazing ground should be selected by an officer as soon as practicable after halting. Horses grazing must be given plenty of room, moved as grass is eaten, and not kept crowded in one spot. Animals out grazing are not to be linked together.

9. *Watering.*—Fit horses in easy work and in standing camp will be watered once a day, between noon and evening, the nearer sundown the better. On the line of march they will be watered as opportunity offers, and always in the evening, if possible. When on an allowance of water, half the ration may be given earlier in the day if horses are too thirsty to graze. When water is short, and horses thirsty, the grain being damped will assist their eating it.

10. *Salt.*—Salt, in any form, up to 1 or $1\frac{1}{4}$ ozs. a day, will be given when procurable.

11. *Grains.*—All horses should be accustomed to eat oats, chunna (gram) or jowari, any one of which may be the only food procurable on occasions.

12. *Shoeing.*—Except in special cases, at the discretion of officers commanding units, horses will be shod all round, and a spare pair of fore shoes will be carried in the men's kits on transport.

13. *Spare Horses.*—At least 15 per cent. spare horses should start with units or detachments for prolonged operations and parties going out independently for the day on long patrols, &c., should take at least 5 per cent. spare. A spare horse should be a fit one, with bridle, head-rope and nose-bag on neck, and may carry a saddle, provided the animal is not turned into a pack horse.

## II.—*Man and Horse.*

1. *Man.*—Every man should be able to cook his own meal, load or unload camels or mules, knee-halter a horse, mount or dismount quickly on either side, and destroy a horse in a humane manner.

2. *Horse.*—Every horse and mule should leave the ranks freely, stand the fire of the man on or beside him, sight and smell of camels everywhere, and should lead freely with man on foot or mounted.

3. *Passing Infantry and Loaded Camels.*—In passing infantry, mounted men must avoid going through, hustling, or over-riding infantry, or passing close to windward of them, which often smothers them in dust. These precautions apply still more to loaded camels, which are peculiarly liable to stampede. Mounted men, if obliged to pass close to them, should do so at a walk.

## III.—*Equipment, &c.*

1. *Equipment and Provisions.*—Each mounted man will always have with him on the line of march 100 rounds of ammunition on himself, and 50 on his horse carried in a third bandolier; at least one day's food for man and horse—tea, sugar, &c., being carried in small bags of calico, or some such material, and which will fit into mess tin or "billy"; one small axe and chaguls, to be full at the discretion of officer commanding unit; two nose-bags, blanket under saddle, whatever pattern, head rope and single rein to bridle; magazine charged, cut-off closed and chamber empty, unless action is imminent—the magazine spring can be rested by half-charging or emptying half rifles at intervals, under the direction of officer commanding unit.

2. *Wallets.*—Wallets will not be carried while a saddle-bag, or spare nose-bag is available. Heel rope and heel peg will not be carried; only a light coat or water proof will be on front of saddle.

3. *Line-Ropes.*—In the rocky or sandy ground prevailing in Somaliland where, moreover, troops and parties are usually concentrated at night, line ropes are better than the made-up ropes; the former may be carried on mules, the latter on horses or mules.

## IV.—*Regimental Transport.*

1. The following will be carried on regimental mule or trotting camel transport, and will accompany units, unless ordered to the contrary :—

*Reserve Ammunition.*—250 rounds per rifle.

*Watering Gear and Entrenching Tools* on two mules, including six leather buckets, 40 fathoms of 1½-inch rope, at least two canvas troughs without woodwork, six spades, four picks, 20 "kurpas," if procurable, for cutting grass, one hospital and one veterinary pannier.

2. *Trotting Camels (better than Mules).*—For carrying the above, a trotting camel will be reckoned as of the same capacity as a mule, *i.e.*, two maunds. But when mounted troops have to move any distance at a rate of over 3¼ miles per hour, including halts, say, 40 miles in 12 hours, or even 20 in six hours, fully loaded mules are out of the question. Trotting camels must be used, or mules dropped behind with an escort. The latter course is inadvisable in an enemy's country, with a small force.

### V.—*Reconnaissance.*

1. On reconnaissance, every precaution must be taken to see without being seen; showing up on ridges or heights must be avoided, and every advantage taken of cover from ground when operating against the enemy. All detached parties will take precautions for their own immediate safety.

In thick bush country, detached parties of regular troops should close in to view of their own centre and main body.

2. *Losing Way.*—If lost, men will best regain the main body by retracing their steps, mounting a tree or eminence, and not by wandering aimlessly about the bush.

The main body will assist those lost by similar methods, by firing shots, lighting fires on high ground, fixing a light on a tree by night, &c.

3. *Sun.*—It is very difficult to work directions by the sun from about 11 A.M. to 1 P.M. in these latitudes, especially in the bush. If uncertain of the road and direction, and the sun is the only guide, it is better to halt between these hours.

4. *Guides.*—In bush country, no regular troops will go far from the main body or camp without a Somali guide, until they know the locality or tracks. All ranks are warned against ill-treating or unduly hustling guides or other natives employed with the troops.

### VI.—*Pace. Marching.*

1. *General Rule.*—As a rule, it is waste of time for men of cavalry or mounted infantry to be in the saddle, unless moving faster than they could march on foot over the same ground. When tied to infantry or baggage, they should cover at least half the march on foot, by alternate periods of walking and riding.

2. *Halts.*—On the march there will be a halt of four to five minutes half an hour after starting and at every ensuing hour. If the first halt ends within 20 minutes of the hour, the second halt may be deferred to the next hour.

3. *Long Marches.*—In long marches, the most economic and telling pace for mounted troops moving without infantry or baggage animals, other

than trotting camels or pack horses, is a slow trot, jog, "pace," "crawl," "tripple," &c., which enables troops to keep together and cover regularly five to six miles an hour, including a halt of four or five minutes at each hour, without exhausting the animals. This pace would be modified during the heat of the day, bad going, or other adverse circumstances. Even in open bush country and fair going, 50 miles can thus be covered comfortably in 12 hours, including an hour's off-saddle, if men and horses are in fair condition, without efficiency being impaired.

4. *Pace increases from Front to Rear.*—Even with a column of 100 men, two abreast, the pace set in front becomes at least two miles faster in the rear. When practicable, troops will, therefore, march on a front of mounted infantry "sections" and gaps will be kept between companies or units. But in thick bush, even by day, on narrow front, all must keep closed up unless units can move independently, each with a reliable guide.

5. *Detached Parties.*—Detached parties going out to take up position, such as advanced or flank patrol, will move at a quicker pace than the main body, but men will not go full speed, except in cases of the greatest emergency, and then only for a few hundred yards.

## VII.—*Tactical.*

1. *Long-range Firing.*—Long-range firing is to be avoided; it is waste of ammunition against our present enemy.

2. *Pursuit.*—In pursuing an enemy leaving stock behind him, it must be borne in mind that the stock first met can be picked up later, and that the enemy, with probably much more, is ahead. The strength of the pursuit should not be wasted by detaching parties till the mian object has been reached, or the limit of pursuit decided.

3. *Inlying Picquet.*—In standing camp, if the inlying picquet is not required, each unit will leave at least one horse in the lines ready to start at two minutes' notice.

4. *Patrols.*—Daily patrols from standing camp should vary the hour of departure and return, as well as the route taken.

## VIII.—*Zaribas.*

1. Troops forming camp will zariba, unless ordered to the contrary; men in front of their horses and sleeping on the spot they would occupy in case of alarm or attack.

If more than one zariba is formed, the second and third should be "diamonded" on to the first, thus :—

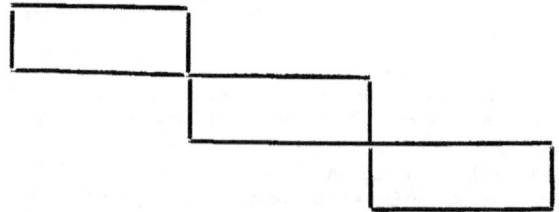

Each will then avoid firing into its neighbour, and will assist it by flanking fire.

The thorn fence of the zariba should not be higher than necessary to stop man or beast; it can hardly be made too wide, but should be low enough to admit of defenders firing over rather than through it.

2. In elaborate zaribas, the cover of the defenders from front fire is best obtained from earth taken from where the thorn fence of the zariba will rest, if ground admits of digging and stones are not plentiful.

## IX.—*Wells.*

1. On approaching wells, sentries will be posted on the most important, and water drawn under the direction of the officer or non-commissioned officer in command. When men go down wells to clear them, or reclaim buckets, &c., a spare strong rope and party should be ready to assist in case of accidents, suffocation from fumes, &c.

## X.—*Night Marching.*

1. *Lights and Passing Orders.*—No smoking or lights allowed; no talking beyond that necessary to conduct the march, orders being passed up or down the column in a low tone of voice when it is impracticable for any one with orders to pass along the narrow tortuous bush paths blocked by troops.

2. *Position of Officer Commanding.*—The officer commanding will move at the head of the main body of the leading unit.

3. *Halts.*—There will be the usual halt at the end of the first half hour and at each ensuing hour, as by day.

4. *Touch.*—Absolute touch must be kept from *rear to front;* if the pace is too fast in front, or an extra halt is required, the word must be sent up quickly but quietly to head of column.

5. *Pace.*—On dark nights, in bush country, the pace can seldom exceed $3\frac{1}{2}$ miles an hour for mounted troops. Touch once lost is then most difficult to regain, and stray parties in the bush without Somalis are even more helpless by night than by day. When possible, there should be at least one guide to every 150 men. A large column compelled to move in single file on one bush track becomes impossible to handle; it should be divided into parties of 150 to 200. These parties, with their guides, can march at intervals of 5 or 10 minutes.

6. *Position of Officers.*—An officer, when available, will ride in rear of each unit or company, and the last of these officers will, at each halt, move up along the column to its head, and report to the officer commanding. In addition, an officer will occasionally move along the column under orders from the officer commanding.

7. *Advanced Guards.*—Apart from native scouts working independently, the only advanced guard practicable in bush, on dark nights, is a few men strung out in file or single file, but in close touch with one another. This

means that they are generally part of the main body, and in same formation. Flankers are out of the question. In fairly open country, on bright or moonlight nights, the advanced guard will be slightly more advanced, with greater distances between links of connecting chain, and the " point " will be strengthened; a few flankers can also be put out, but all must keep in sight, or touch, of next link towards main body, closing in on approaching bush, &c.

## CHAPTER XIII.

### ARTILLERY.

THE small force of regular artillery employed in Somaliland was represented by a section of the 28th (Lahore) Mountain Battery and the King's African Rifle Camel Battery. The following report of Lieutenant H. E. Henderson, R.A., who commanded the section of this Battery, gives an account of the part taken by the section in the operations and of its organization and equipment :—

From the 4th July, 1903, till the end of December, 1903, the Section Operations. No. 28 Mountain Battery remained in posts on the lines of communication, moving from Upper Sheikh to Berbera to refit at the end of August, 1903, and proceeding to Eil Dab in January, 1904, to join the 2nd Brigade, Somaliland Field Force, of which it formed part during the operations in the Nogal, January and February, 1904. The section also formed part of the Las Dureh Column, March and April, 1904.

The engagement at Jidbali on 10th January, 1904, was the only occasion on which the guns came into action. On this day the section formed part of the infantry square. When the square halted facing east near the enemy's position, the guns were moved out a few yards ahead of the front face and came into action at a range of 1,600 yards on a group of huts. Between these huts and the position of the guns was a slight depression formed by the "balli" running north and south, from which the ground sloped up gradually to the position of the square. On the west side of the "balli" was a belt of bushes extending to within about 500 yards of the square.

When fire was opened the enemy advancing through the belt of bushes disclosed their position, and the fire was changed on to them at 800 yards. This was continued at various ranges from 500 to 1,500 yards as opportunities occurred. At this time the enemy were well extended, took cover carefully, and did not offer a good target. The best opportunities were given when they attempted to screen themselves in small groups behind bushes.

About twenty-five minutes from the time of opening fire the enemy broke and took to flight. Streaming across the open plain on the west of the "balli" they offered a better target, and several rounds were fired at them up to 2,200 yards until the guns had to cease fire in order not to hamper the pursuit by the mounted troops,

Altogether 63 rounds were fired. The casualties in the section were two men killed and one camel wounded.

Owing to the fact that the enemy offered no target on which continuous fire could be directed, it was impossible to ascertain exactly the effect of the fire. On examining the ground after the action, however, I came to the conclusion that about 30 men were killed or severely wounded by the effect of gun fire; this is excluding wounded men who escaped from the field, of whose numbers it is impossible to form an estimate.

At the commencement of the action the fire of the guns apparently had the effect of making the enemy disclose their position.

The section was armed with two 7-pr. guns of 200 lbs.

*Material.* The following is number and description of rounds per gun carried:—

| | |
|---|---|
| Common shell | 20 rounds. |
| Shrapnel ,, | 93 ,, |
| Star ,, | 6 ,, |
| Case shot | 20 ,, |

Fuzes T. and P. Number 56 were used.

The extra proportion of case was carried in case of fighting in bush country; the charges for these rounds were increased 30 per cent. There were no missfires, prematures, or blinds.

*Personnel.* Besides the usual proportion of followers, the establishment of the section consisted of:—

2 British officers.
1 native officer
1 trumpeter
32 gunner ranks } Indians, Sikhs, and Punjabi Mussalman.
5 drivers (mule)
1 assistant salutri
1 Somali interpreter.
22   ,,   (camel drivers).
5 mules.
22 Somali camels.

The mules were employed as follows:—

1 per gun for drawing it in draught.
1   ,,   ,,   ammunition.
1 spare.

Of the 22 camels, 4 were spare.

The Somali camel drivers were sometimes a little difficult to manage when halted at or near the base; on the march they did their work sufficiently well. In action they were unsteady.

*Equipment.* The camel saddlery sent from India consisted of:—

(a) Pads for carriage of ammunition.
(b) Cradles and pads for guns, carriage, and wheels.

(a) The former were leather pads with serge lining, stuffed with cocoanut fibre. The two sides were joined at the top by leather; the pads were fitted with leather girths, breast-piece and crupper. They were apparently intended for a different pattern of box to the mule pack ammunition box carried, but when fitted with hooks for the latter, they proved satisfactory. The pads were in two sizes, large and small; the former were too large for Somali camels.

(b) For the carriage of gun, &c., a plain leather pad was used, connected over the top by leather as before. On this the wooden cradle rested, to which the girths, breast-piece and crupper were attached. The cradle was not attached to the pad in any way. The saddles were not quite satisfactory, as the cradles rocked considerably on their pads when the marching was at all fast. This could be minimised if the pads were separate—not connected over the camel's back—and if they were attached to the cradles by straps, as in mule saddlery.

The pads should also be fitted with pockets for facilitating stuffing. The cradles were not sufficiently rigid, and worked loose at the joints.

The guns were provided with draught equipment as an alternative to being carried in pack by camels. This was advisable owing to the timidity of the Somali camel, which might have prevented the guns being brought rapidly into action in an emergency. In the vicinity of the enemy the guns were drawn in draught. The draught equipment was made up locally, and answered its purpose.

Special limbers made in India were not used, as they were too heavy to be carried in pack over country impossible to wheel transport.

### The King's African Rifle Camel Battery.

The camel battery used in Somaliland was commanded by Lieutenant J. A. Ballard, R.F.A., and consisted of the six 7-pr. R.M.L. (180 lbs.) guns and equipment lent by the Indian Government, and despatched from Aden to the Protectorate for their local expeditions against the Mullah. The battery was formerly known as the "Aden Camel Battery," the guns, &c., being periodically taken out for drill by one of the garrison companies stationed at Aden, the camels and drivers being lent by the Supply and Transport Corps. While at Aden the camel battery had, on several occasions, done useful work against the tribes in the hinterland. No men were, however, sent to Somaliland with the guns, which were manned by Somalis trained by the Protectorate officers.

At the beginning of General Manning's expedition the Somali gunners were disbanded, and only a section of the battery was retained for movable column work, the remaining four guns being sent to strengthen the various posts on the lines of communication. The movable section was then called the "King's African Rifle Camel Battery." Twenty-one men, including a havildar from the Sikh Company B.C.A., were selected to form the detachments, the camel drivers being Somalis. The Sikhs made excellent gunners, and remained with the battery until the end of the campaign.

Organization.
A havildar acted as section commander. A detachment of ten Sikhs with a Naick was detailed for each gun. Ten Somali drivers, including a havildar, took charge of the ten camels of the sub-section. Three camels carried the wheels, carriage and gun in the order named, followed by four ammunition camels, and three others with the stores, waterproofs, tools, spare parts and draught equipment. The detachment marched "in order of march." In action, the camels were made to sit, the gun carriage, &c., put together, the ammunition boxes taken off, and the empty camels taken to the rear. Shells were brought up to the guns in leather carriers.

Establishment.
For the two movable guns the establishment was :—
    1 British officer.
    21 Sikh gunners (including one havildar).
    18 Somali drivers.
    2 Somali havildars (drivers) (one per sub-section).
    1 Somali interpreter.
    1 Somali blacksmith.
    1 Somali saddle-maker.

Pay.
The Sikhs were paid through their company. The following rates were paid to the Somalis by the Protectorate paymaster :—

| | |
|---|---|
| Drivers | 15 Rs. per month. |
| Havildars | 18 Rs. ,, |
| Somali Interpreter | 60 Rs. ,, |
| Blacksmith | 40 Rs. ,, |
| Saddlemaker | 40 Rs. ,, |

Equipment.
The carriage was of steel, weight about 200 lbs.; the wheels of wood, weight about 140 lbs.; the elevating gear

PLATE 24.

Sketch of Draught Equipment made for K.A.R. Camel Battery.

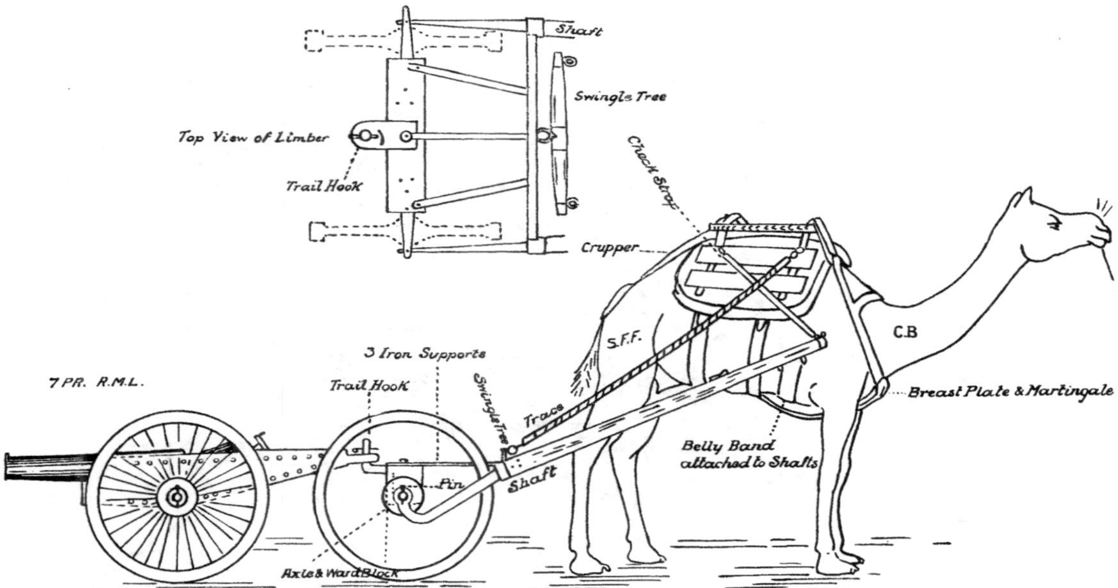

*Top View of Limber*

- Shaft
- Swingle Tree
- Check Strap
- Crupper
- Trail Hook

- Breast Plate & Martingale
- C.B.
- Belly Band attached to Shafts
- S.F.F.
- Trace
- SwingleTree
- Shaft
- Pin
- Axle & Ward Bush
- Trail Hook
- 3 Iron Supports

7 PR. R.M.L.

Weight  Draught Equipment complete 241 lbs.

|  |  |
|---|---|
| 2 Wheels | 142 lbs. |
| Body | 65 " |
| 2 Shafts | 34 " |

(8027 A).—(To face page 448.)

Sketch of Draught Equipment, Complete on One Camel. K.A.R. Camel Battery.

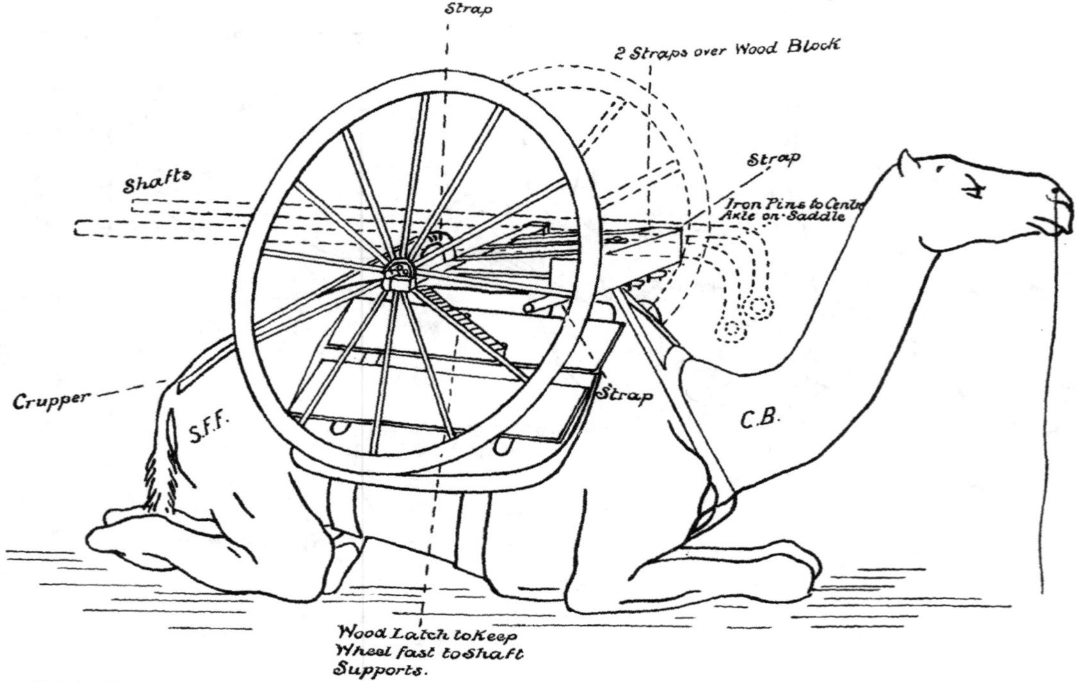

PLATE 25.

(8027 A) —(To follow Plate 24.)

## K.A.R. CAMEL BATTERY.

PLATE 26.

### Camel in Draught.

### Camel Loaded.

*(To follow Plate 25.)*

## K.A.R. CAMEL BATTERY.

### Section ready to March.

### Section on the March.

(*To follow Plate 26.*)

PLATE 28.

## K.A.R. CAMEL BATTERY.

Camel in Draught.

Camels Kneeling for "Action."

(*To follow Plate* 27.)

## K.A.R. CAMEL BATTERY.

### In Action.

*(To follow Plate 28.)*

was a wooden block under breech and wheel in rear; the whole being strapped to wooden cradles on the saddles and carried by three camels.

Two ammunition boxes, each containing 10 rounds, were carried by each ammunition camel, the weight being about 200 lbs. including saddle.

The gun was quite suitable for the country. It was simple, accurate, and could not easily get out of order. Its range was not great, but the country in which the enemy generally attacked being dense bush, this shortcoming was unimportant. With well-trained detachments, from the command "Halt-Action" to the first shot, less than one minute elapsed and a fire of four or five rounds a minute could be maintained.

The gun was provided with two sets of sights for the double shell with reduced charge, and for the ordinary charge. Two clinometers were also carried.

The saddles and ammunition boxes supplied originally were extremely heavy, being intended for Indian camels. This defect was overcome by exchanging the old heavy leather saddles of the ammunition camels for the light Egyptian pattern, which weighed about 20 lbs., and are easily restuffed and repaired. The cumbersome and heavy wooden ammunition boxes were also exchanged for the light leather mountain artillery boxes, each holding 10 shell and cartridges. These two modifications reduced the weight and increased mobility. On the two spare camels per sub-section, light tarpaulins, spare parts, stores, tools, &c., were carried.

The guns were supplied from Aden with double, common, shrapnel, star shell, and case shot. The double and common shell were not carried with the battery, being left with the guns at the posts.

Ammunition.

The ammunition was in good condition, and a reserve was kept at Bohotle. The brass T. and P. No. 56 fuzes were new and burnt well. The cartridges consisted of 12 oz. black pebble powder and gave accurate shooting. All shells were carried fuzed and set for 50 yards range. Forty rounds per gun of reserve ammunition was carried by the columns, the small arm ammunition of 50 rounds per man being carried in bandoliers. The following ammunition was carried by each sub-section :—

|  |  |
|---|---|
| Shrapnel | 60 |
| Case | 15 |
| Star | 5 |
|  | 80 rounds per gun. |

Transport.    Picked Somali camels only were used. These were found to be sufficiently strong for the lighter equipment, and they possessed the advantage of being able to live on the bush only when forage ran short. The Somali camel being generally very nervous and wild, it was necessary to have a driver for each animal.

The kits of the detachments were carried by the various camel transport cadres, not by the battery camels.

By changing the loads daily, watering about every four days and covering them at night, the animals were kept in excellent condition. Casualties in camels were replaced from any Camel Transport Cadre which the guns might be accompanying.

The establishment of transport for the two guns was :—

|  |  |
|---|---|
| 2 guns | 2 camels. |
| 2 sets gun-wheels | 2 ,, |
| 2 gun carriages | 2 ,, |
| Ammunition | 8 ,, |
| 2 draught equipments | 2 ,, |
| Stores and spare parts | 4 ,, |
|  | 20 camels. |

Draught equipment.    One riding camel and one riding pony were issued to the officer commanding.

Owing to the thick, dense bush, the columns were sometimes obliged to march in Indian file formation, so the length of two guns and camels covered a distance of over 150 yards. As the enemy generally made a point of attacking in this sort of bush, the chance of getting the guns together was remote, and thus all control and command was lost. To avoid being surprised in this manner, a draught equipment was constructed, so that if the enemy attacked at close quarters the gun could be put together and drawn as a field gun by a camel, which, when not performing this work, carried the light limber, thus allowing all guns to be kept together when required. A pocket containing four rounds was carried on the limber when used.

The light limber consisted of a pair of shafts and a swingletree attached to a light wooden structure with a hook fixed in the rear for the eye of the gun trail. The wheels were similar to the gun wheels and could be used as spare ones, and the total weight of this construction was 240 lbs. (see Plates 24 and 25).

The advantages of the draught equipment were :—

Instant action.

Guns closer and under better command.

More guns could be used and less space occupied in column.

## CHAPTER XIV.

### SERVICES AND DEPARTMENTS.

#### 1.—ENGINEER SERVICES, INCLUDING WATER SUPPLY.

Organization. No organized Engineer services existed under Colonel Swayne. A company (No. 17) of Sappers and Miners arrived in January, 1903, under Captain W. B. Lesslie, who was then appointed Commanding Royal Engineer to the force. This company was chiefly employed in road-making, perfecting arrangements for water supply and in defensive measures for camps. Nearly all the company was with the Obbia force.

A large increase to the Engineer services took place in July, 1903, and another company of Sappers and Miners (No. 19) joined the force from India. Major R. F. Allen, R.E., was appointed Commanding Royal Engineer to the force, with a Commanding Royal Engineer, Lines of Communication, and seventeen other Royal Engineer officers, excluding the telegraph and survey services and the deep boring party. The 107th Pioneers were also largely employed on Royal Engineer works.

The Royal Engineer officers and the men of the Sappers and Miners and Pioneers were employed on three principal services :—

Water supply and storage.
Defensible posts.
Roads and miscellaneous.

#### WATER SUPPLY.

Importance. In Somaliland the provision of water supply and storage was of peculiar importance, as operations carried out during the season of drought, between October and April held out the best hopes of a decisive result. During that season the movements of the Mullah could be restricted by suitable dispositions to certain tracts of country within striking distance of the British forces, thus diminishing his mobility.

Consequently, an ample storage of water along our main lines of communication so as to admit of the collection of supplies for the concentration of troops prior to any advance, and efficient arrangements for watering troops and animals during operations, were the primary objects to be attained in view of the general strategical situation.

During the operations under Colonel Swayne and Brig.-General Manning, water was generally carried on transport animals in tins or in copper tanks called fantasses. Their capacity was 12½ gallons, but it was not safe to reckon on more than 10 gallons. Each tank when full weighed about 2 maunds (160 lbs.). These tanks were also made use of during General Egerton's operations. *Transport of water.*

Regarded from the point of view of the water supply question, the lines of communication during 1903-1904 may be divided into four main sections, as follows :— *Sources of water supply on lines of communication.*

Berbera to Upper Sheikh.
Upper Sheikh to Elkadalanleh.
Elkadalanleh to Kirrit.
Kirrit to Eil Dab and Bohotle.

*Berbera to Upper Sheikh.*—In this section the supply was chiefly from springs. At Berbera there was a large supply brought in pipes from the deep and warm springs at Dubar. A reservoir was also made at Adhoo Sheikh close to Dubar. (For details of water supply see table, page 460.)

*Upper Sheikh to Elkadalanleh.*—In this section the water was obtained from wells sunk in the bed of the Tug Der.

Gololi was the only place that ran completely dry after months of heavy calls on its resources. This took place in December, 1903, but early in March, 1904, the supply was revived by an opportune downfall of rain. (For details see table, page 460.)

*Elkadalanleh to Kirrit.*—In this section there was a waterless stretch of over 40 miles. Trial borings were made at Der Keinleh without success. Water was found at Idoweina, but this was 6 or 7 miles from the road. At Little Bohotle, 9 miles from Kirrit, a well 66 feet deep was sunk, but no water was obtained. There were in this section a few ballis, pans, or depressions which would fill with water in the rains.

*Kirrit to Eil Dab.*—In this section the supply was from wells in the gypsum formation which extends right into the Nogal. The Kirrit supply failed on September 1st, 1903, and in consequence the advanced depôt was moved to Eil Dab and the demand on the Kirrit wells lessened. By unremitting labour the supply was afterwards restored and its quality improved.

Between Wadamago and Bohotle there was no water except such as might collect in ballis during the rainy season. (For details regarding the water supply in the Nogal and on the Berbera-Las Dureh lines of communication, see table, pages 466 and 468.)

*Water storage on lines of communication.*
The first points to be determined were the amount of water storage capacity required at each post on the lines of communication and the method of storage to be adopted. The decision on these points would naturally govern the quantity and class of stores to be procured for water storage in addition to any provision for active operations. Certain general considerations also stood out. Such were :—

    The source of supply and its probable permanence at each post.

    The garrisons allotted to each post.

    The possibility of a congestion of transport at different places.

    The average daily consumption of infantry brigades and mounted troops excluding transport animals, which worked out as follows :—

Mounted troops .. .. 18,000 gallons daily
1st Brigade (with S.M.I.) 8,000 ,, ,,
2nd Brigade ,, 8,000 ,, ,,

The water required for convoys.

The presence or absence of a civil population drawing from the same sources.

The time available and probable duration of the operations.

The fact that practically all food materials and tools had to be brought up from the base.

Labour was locally unobtainable, thus entailing importation from Aden. Military working parties had to be kept down in strength so as to admit of the accumulation of reserve supplies.

The abnormal strain brought on the water supply by the Field Force.

The necessity for rapid watering of troops and convoys.

The capacity for storing water provided after considering all the above factors is given below with the actual amount of water stored daily.

|  | | Actual Daily Storage | |
|---|---|---|---|
| Place. | Capacity. | From— | To— |
| | Gallons. | Gallons. | Gallons. |
| Upper Sheikh | 265,000 | 70,000 | 250,000 |
| Dubbar | 140,000 | 10,000 | 50,000 |
| Goloii | 50,000 | .. | 50,000 |
| Waran | 30,000 | .. | 30,000 |
| Burao | 255,000 | 170,000 | 250,000 |
| Ber | 24,000 | 20,000 | 24,000 |
| Elkadalanleh | 56,000 | 6,000 | 45,000 |
| Kirrit | 144,000 | 3,000 | 15,000 |
| Olesan | 115,800 | 1,000 | 90,000 |
| Wadamago | 167,000 | 60,000 | 110,000 |
| Ain Abo | 63,000 | 40,000 | 60,000 |
| Eil;Dab | 150,000 | 100,000 | 150,000 |
| Bohotle | 35,000 | 10,000 | 20,000 |
| Beyi | 45,000 | 20,000 | 45,000 |
| Hagal' | 30,000 | 20,000 | 30,000 |
| Las Dureh | 52,000 | 40,000 | 52,000 |
| Las Adey | 15,000 | .. | 15,000 |
| Las Khorai | 50,000 | 30,000 | 50,000 |
| Badwein | 30,000 | .. | .. |
| Yagnri | 30,000 | .. | .. |

**Methods of storage.**

Generally tarpaulin or sailcloths were used for the lining to the reservoir tanks, which were in some places excavated in the ground and in others built of dry stone masonry. Whenever possible the lining was laid in a double layer with the tarpaulin underneath the sailcloth. Each tank had a capacity of from 8,000 to 9,000 gallons to fit in with the dimensions of the sailcloth (30 feet by 30 feet). The average durability of a sailcloth or tarpaulin was about 1½ months. Many of the tanks were grouped so as to be filled from one end by syphoning. Tanks of 6,000 gallons capacity sent from England were also used for permanent reservoirs at posts, but some of these tanks were rendered useless for a time owing to their being painted with lead paints. Evaporation caused some loss of water but was checked by grass mats laid on wire across the tanks.

**Special storage works.**

At Upper Sheikh a masonry dam was constructed with a capacity of 170,000 gallons. It eventually held a daily

PLATE 30.

## Dam at Upper Sheikh.

(*To face page* 456.)

PLATE 31.

## Dam at Upper Sheikh.

(*To follow Plate 30.*)

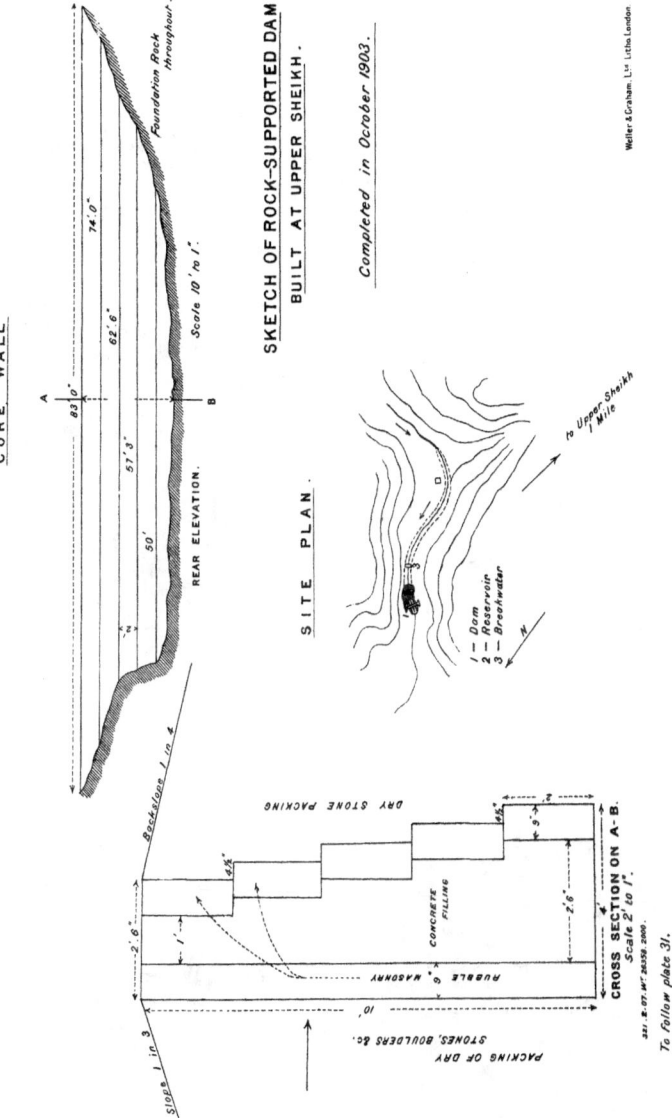

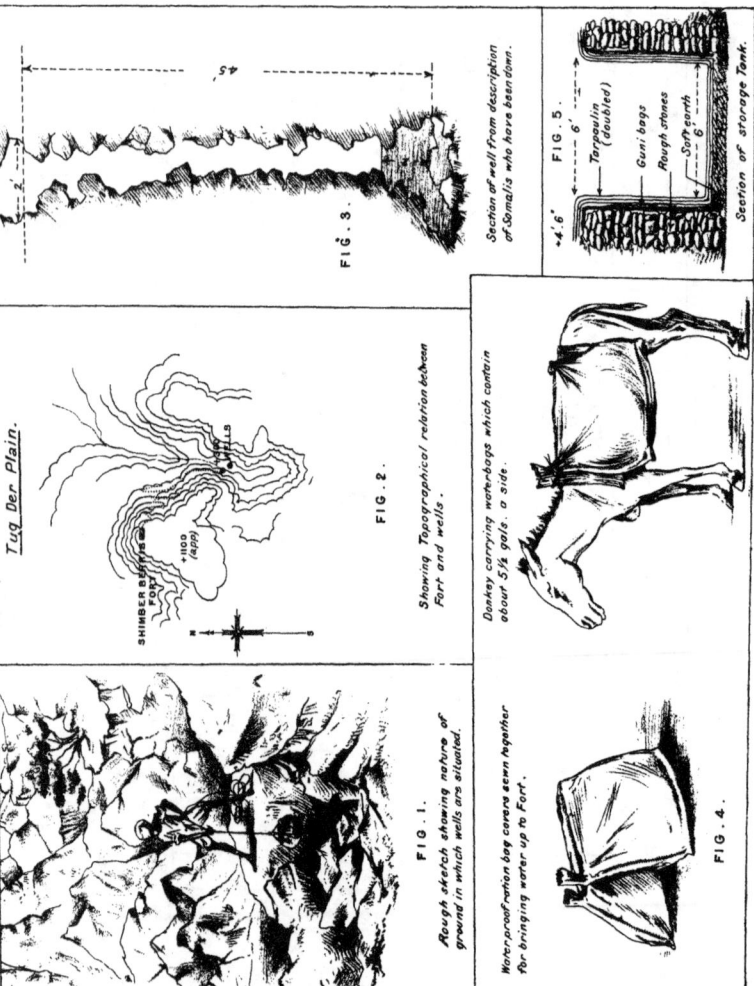

average of 80,000 gallons. Photographs and a plan of the dam are given in Plates 30, 31 and 32.

At Eil Dab a 50,000 gallon reservoir was constructed with sailcloths and tarpaulins. But it had the disadvantage that in case of leakage repair was difficult.

At Kirrit an embankment was made to retain 80,000 gallons, but this was never filled.

At Elkadalanleh about 100,000 gallons were held up by the earth excavated from the trench wells.

Plans of the wells at Shimber Berris and of the well and system of water supply at Wadamago are given in Plates 33, 34 and 35.

The storage at each post was reported by telegram daily to Officer Commanding, Lines of Communication, to the C.R.E., and to the C.R.E., Lines of Communication. *Report of storage.*

From the main storage reservoirs the issues were made to expense tanks and to troughs either by pumps or more generally by syphoning. The scale of allowance was generally as follows :— *System of distribution.*

Men : 2 to 10 gallons per day, or more if water was abundant.

Horses and Mules : 6 to 8 gallons per day.

Indian Camels : 10 gallons every 4th day.

Somali Camels : 8 gallons every 4th day.

But this scale was intended only as a general guide. The actual quantity required on any given day was estimated from the number of men and animals due to arrive, the number of water tins to be filled, and the period elapsed since the last watering in the case of camels, since these last drink more than 8 or 10 gallons per animal if deprived of water for longer than 4 days.

Two kinds of pump were principally used* :— *Pumps.*

The Bastier pump, for depths of over 50 feet.

The lift and force pump for 20 to 25 feet depths.

---

* The Obbia force had also Norton tube wells and rotary pumps, but these proved of little use owing to scarcity of water and the excessive lift which was necessary in most cases.

At Burao there was a windmill pump (ærmotor), but it was necessarily desultory in its action. The lift and force pumps were the more generally used, and delivered from 500 to 600 gallons per hour. They were considered indispensable and the only defect was some trouble in connection with the hose which sometimes became choked.*

On the march. While on the march a sapper detachment either went ahead or marched with the advanced guard so as to put in hand without loss of time the water supply arrangements in camp or on the line of march. With each brigade, two lift and force pumps with hose, some sailcloths specially cut to 30 feet by 20 feet, portable troughs, buckets, rope, &c., were carried on mules.

A large number of pumps were taken with the various operating columns so that in the event of scarcity every source of water might be utilised at halts or in camps so as not only to secure a sufficient supply, but also to ensure that watering might be completed before sunset.

Labour. Labour for pumping was provided generally by fatigue parties from the troops, but this was supplemented by local labour from Aden. The Somali was not to be depended on for such work.

Deep boring operations. During 1903-4 boring operations were carried on at Hope Springs, Elkadalanleh, Der Keinleh and Kirrit. The work, which was under the supervision of Major Joly de Lotbinière, R.E., was carried on by a special party of sappers and by two experts who were specially brought from America and England.

The object of the operations was to discover if an artesian supply of water could be tapped so as to assist the normal supply.

In the four places where boring operations were carried out practically no water was found, but Major de Lotbinière was of opinion that the geological formation was favourable to the existence of an artesian supply of water over a considerable portion of the high tableland of Somaliland. He,

---

*The working parts of these pumps, being of soft metal, deteriorated rapidly, especially when the water carried sand and grit.

however, considered that a drop drill only was suitable for the operations, and that the drop drill used was not big enough. As it was decided not to incur the extra expense of purchasing and installing a larger drill, the operations ceased.

The details of the operations are as follows :—

At *Hope Springs* the boring was carried to 388 feet depth. No bedrock or water was met with. The drill employed was the Calyx Rotary and time taken 36 days.

Nature of soil : surface soil and secondary deposits of clays, marls, sands and conglomerates.

*Elkadalanleh.*—Boring carried to 464 feet depth. No water met with. Drill employed, Calyx Rotary. Time taken, 62 days. Abandoned as shot crowns wore out.

Nature of soil : 70 feet surface soil and clay, 394 feet bedrock limestone with breaks.

*Der Keinleh.*—Boring carried to 258 feet. No water met with. Drill employed, Columbia No. 1 Drop Drill. Time taken, 27 days. Abandoned as drill was too small.

Nature of soil : 4 feet surface soil ; 254 feet bedrock limestone with breaks.

*Kirrit.*—Boring carried to 400 feet. Small quantity of water met with in gypsum. Drill employed, Columbia No. 1 Drop Drill and Rotary Drill. Time taken, 23 days. Abandoned on conclusion of operations.

Nature of soil, 66 feet bedrock gypsum ; 334 feet blue clay with bands of shale and hard limestone.

## ABSTRACT OF WATER

N.B.—Dry seasons October to April. This Table was prepared

### 1. MAIN LINES OF

| Place. | Nature of Supply. | Depth of well to water surface. | Depth of water before use. | Average Yield. |
|---|---|---|---|---|
| 1 | 2 | 3 | 4 | 5 |
| Berbera | (i) Piped from Dubar (ii) 3 wells | See (a) (b) (c) 8 ft. 9 ft. 9 ft. | Dubar. (a) (b) (c) 2 ft. 2 ft. 1½ ft. | (a) 300 gals. per hour (b) 400 ,, (c) 200 ,, |
| Dubar | Springs | At surface | | 4,400 gals. per hour |
| Kalgumrah | 2 wells in bed of river. | 27 ft. to 30 ft. | 2 ft. 6 in. | Ordinarily 100 to 200 gals. per hour from each well, after flood 3 or 4 times the above yield. |
| Bihendula | Springs | At surface | | Abundant |
| Upper Sheikh | (i) From wells in east nullah. (ii) From stream in Sama Sabdha nullah. | (i) 12 ft. (ii) Pool at intervals. | (i) 3 ft. (ii) 1 ft. to 2 ft. in pools. | (i) 2,000 to 5,000 gals. per day in dry season. (ii) This is a stream with a copious supply. |
| Dubbar | Wells in the river bed sunk at various points in pockets. | 4 ft. to 10 ft., and even over 20 ft. in some cases. | 2 ft. to 4 ft. | 300 gals. an hour from each well after rains but will fall to 500 gallons a day under constant use. See remarks opposite Gololi. Yield dependent on number of pockets opened out. |

# SUPPLY DATA.

## from observations between September 1903 and April 1904.
COMMUNICATION.

| Accessibility, best method of drawing. | Quality. | Permanency. | Remarks. |
|---|---|---|---|
| 6 | 7 | 8 | 9 |
| Easy of access | Good | Permanent | Three wells were dug at Berbera as water supply for animals, they are trench wells from 30 to 60 ft. long. |
| Easy of access. Water is collected in settling tanks. | Slightly aperient. | Permanent | Water from these springs is at a temperature of 104°. |
| Wells may fill up after flood and require re-excavation. Bastier pumps or buckets. | Good | After months of use water level fell in April, 1904. Semi-permanent supply dependent on rain. | About 1½ miles up the river running S.W. from Kalgumrah there is a large pool of water in the bed. |
| Easy of access, buckets | Good | Permanent | This is a stream. |
| Easy of access, L and F pumps. | Good | (i) Permanent, but liable to considerable fluctuations in yield. (ii) During drought water sinks into the bed and is obtained by excavating the sand when pools are found. | In rains supply is abundant. |
| L and F pumps. Wells or pits must be dug in the pockets and these will fill after freshets and require to be dug | Good | Precarious, liable to exhaustion. | |

| Place. | Nature of Supply. | Depth of well to water surface. | Depth of water before use. | Average yield. |
|---|---|---|---|---|
| 1 | 2 | 3 | 4 | 5 |
| Gololi | Wells in the river bed sunk at various points in pockets. | 4 ft. to 10 ft. or 15 ft. | 2 ft. to 4 ft. | From 3 or 4 wells 3,000 gals. per diem down to nil per diem. Yield depends on number of pockets opened out. |
| Waran | Wells in the river bed sunk at various points in pockets. | 4 ft. to 10 ft., or 15 ft. | 2 ft. to 4 ft. | 5,000 gals. daily from 5 or 6 wells. Yield depends on number of pockets opened out. |
| Burao | 40 wells in a promontory at bend of river. | 50 ft. to 60 ft., after rains 30 ft. | 2 ft. to 10 ft. | 600 to 800 gals. per day per well up to 3,000 gals. per day per well. |
| Elbadalanleh | (i) 25 wells in the river bed in pockets. (ii) one well on bank. | (i) 4 ft. to 10 ft., even 35 ft., according to time of year. (ii) 50 ft. | 2 ft. 4 ft. | From all wells 1,500 gals. to 8,000 gals. per day after rains, but in drought about 40 to 100 gals. per day from all wells. |
| Ber | Wells in river bed. | 20 ft. to 30 ft. | 1 ft. to 3 ft. | Dependent on number of wells used, varies from 200 to 2,000 gals. per day per well. |
| Olesan | Wells in river bed. About 1 mile down stream there is a pool containing about 5,000 gals. after floods. | 10 ft. to 20 ft. | 2 ft. to 3 ft. | Dependent on number of wells used, varies from 200 to 1,000 gals. per day, after floods 4,000 to 6,000 gals. per day from all wells. |

| Accessibility, best method of drawing. | Quality. | Permanency. | Remarks. |
|---|---|---|---|
| 6 | 7 | 8 | 9 |
| out. In drought, when it is necessary to deepen the pits, the subsoil may be found very stiff. | Good | Precarious, liable to exhaustion. | (1) At Dubbar and at Gololi pits or shallow wells used for tapping the water, which is apparently held up in pockets, as it can only be obtained at particular spots independent of and in no discoverable relation to each other. Pockets vary greatly in their yield. During the dry season the yield from these pockets diminishes rapidly, and is liable to fail altogether, especially if subjected to a heavy drain. (2) The Waran supply is similar, but the pockets are much more extensive. (3) Burao has never been known to fail absolutely, but water may fall very low, involving repeated clearing and deepening of wells. (4) At Elkadula le·, supply is similar to Dubbar and Gololi. (5) All these places are dependent for the replenishment of their supply on the freshets in the river. When yield becomes markedly less, new wells should be sunk to strike other pockets and existing wells deepened. In time all pockets would be exhausted. |
| L. and F. pumps. Wells or pits must be dug in the pockets, and these will fill after freshets and require to be dug out again. In drought, when it is necessary to deepen the pits, the subsoil may be found very stiff. | Good | Permanent, but liable to fluctuation. | |
| Easy of access, bastier pumps or Somali wadans (buckets), wells can be cleared out by Somalis with ease. | Good, but slightly aperient. | Permanent, but liable to fluctuations; never yet failed completely. | |
| L. and F. pumps. (See remarks opposite Gololi). | Good, but aperient. | Precarious, liable to exhaustion. | |
| L. and F. pumps. (See remarks opposite Gololi). | Fair, aperient | Precarious, liable to exhaustion. | Remarks relative to Dubbar-Gololi apply. |
| L. and F. pumps. Wells must be dug for a supply from the river bed. | Fair, aperient | Precarious, liable to exhaustion. | In operations of 1903-4, water was obtained at Olesan by a system of intercepting tanks which filled when it rained in the immediate vicinity. Rains in the hills will cause the river to flood, and water can then be obtained from pockets as at Dubbur and Gololi, and in large quantities. |

| Place. | Nature of Supply. | Depth of well to water surface. | Depth of water before use. | Average yield. |
|---|---|---|---|---|
| 1 | 2 | 3 | 4 | 5 |
| Shimber-Berris | 2 wells 800 ft. below camp. | 43 ft. to 45 ft. | 2 ft. | 250 gals. per day from both wells. |
| Kirrit | (i) 2 cave wells at foot of hill at which is defensible post. | (i) 15 ft. to 20 ft. | 2 ft. | (i) 300 to 1,000 gals. per diem. |
| | (ii) 2 ordinary wells called new wells about ½ mile west of post. | (ii) 25 ft. | 2 ft. | (ii) 300 gals. per diem. |
| | (iii) Cave well (called sweet water well) 100 yds. N.W. of new wells. These are in the gypsum formation. | (iii) 20 ft. | 2 ft. | (iii) 50 gals. per diem. |
| Wadamago | 1 well in gypsum formation. | 55 ft. to 60 ft. | 1½ ft. to 2 ft. | 12,000 gals. per day |
| Garrero | 30 wells in gypsum formation. | 30 ft. | 6 in. to 1 ft. 6 in. | 200 gals. per day from all wells. |
| Bohotle | 400 wells in gypsum formation. | 4 ft. to 30 ft. | Very variable in dry season, 1 ft. to 1½ ft. | After rain, there is a large quantity of water, but after long drought yield may be only 2,000 gals. per day by using all those deep wells. |
| Ain Abo | 1 cave well | 30 ft. | 2 ft. to 3 ft. | 6,000 gals. per day |

| Accessibility, best method of drawing. | Quality. | Permanency. | Remarks. |
|---|---|---|---|
| 6 | 7 | 8 | 9 |
| Somali buckets, *i.e.*, wadans. Well is very narrow and can only be cleaned by letting down a small boy. | Fair, aperient, somewhat coloured. | Permanent .... | These wells have never been subjected to a heavy drain. |
| L. and F. pumps. The cave well as indicated by the name, is a cavern with narrow passages leading under the gypsum. Descent into the passages is easy. | (i) Impregnated with sulphuretted hydrogen. (ii) Fair, palatable. (iii) Fair, palatable. | Precarious, liable to exhaustion. | After rain, the cave wells would fill up and the yield would be trebled or quadrupled. In fact, as the cave well forms a subterranean reservoir, yield would depend on number of pumps used until level reduced. It would then gradually diminish to vanishing point in the dry season. By constant cleaning of the passages, a small supply was kept up during the dry season. The impregnation with sulphuretted hydrogen is probably due to camel droppings having been swept in during former watering by Somalis. By cleaning, the water becomes much better in quality. |
| L. and F. pumps in treble, lift easy of access, water is in a large pit. | Good .... | Permanent, it is possible that this water comes from an underground river. | A copious supply. |
| L. and F. pumps or wadans, easy of access. | Fair .... | Precarious, liable to exhaustion. | In the dry season only 2 or 3 of the wells contain water. In rains, there would be a large quantity of water held up in a hollow in the gypsum formation which is filled with sand. |
| L. and F. pumps and buckets, easy of access. | Fair .... | Semi-permanent. | These wells are in a basin, which after heavy rain forms a lake. In dry season, only the deep wells give water. |
| L. and F. pumps, the cave well can be entered by the existing rough ledges of gypsum. | Fair .... | Permanent. | |

| Place. | Nature of Supply. | Depth of well to water surface. | Depth of water before use. | Average yield. |
|---|---|---|---|---|
| 1 | 2 | 3 | 4 | 5 |
| Eil Dab | 2 wells of the class of cave well. | 20 ft. to 25 ft. | 2 ft. to 3 ft. | 20,000 to 25,000 gals. per day from both wells. |

## II. THE

| Place. | Nature of Supply. | Depth of well to water surface. | Depth of water before use. | Average yield. |
|---|---|---|---|---|
| Badwein | Well and pools. | In well, 20 ft. | 2 ft. to 3 ft. | 2,000 to 5,000 gals. per day. |
| Jidbali | 2 wells | 20 ft. | 1 ft. to 2 ft. | 800 gals. per day from both wells. |
| Adur | 4 wells | 20 ft. | 1 ft. to 2 ft., when not used to 7 ft. depth. | 2 wells, 160 gals. an hour. 2 wells, 40 gals. an hour. |
| Derigobbo | Pools | — | 2 ft. or 3 ft. | Issue of 10,000 gals. made a marked reduction in level. |
| Yaguri | Water lodged in depressions in nullah bed in two sections of nullah about 400 yds. apart and measuring 100 and 50 yds. respectively. | Near surface | Depends on depth of hole dug. | 2,000 gals. to 5,000 gals. per day. |
| Dariali | Several large pools fed apparently by springs. | Near surface | 2 ft. to 3 ft. | Rate of inflow, probably 2,000 to 5,000 gals. per day in main pools. |
| Kurtimo | Water in pools | Near surface | 2 ft. | Doubtful |
| Dawa Dawa | Small pools | Near surface | 2 ft. to 3 ft. | Doubtful |
| Arde Jiffifta | 3 wells | 15 ft. | 2 ft. | Probably 1,500 gals. per hour from best well. |
| Lanle | Well | 15 ft. | 2 ft. | 2,000 gals. per hour |

| Accessibility, best method of drawing. | Quality. | Permanency. | Remarks. |
|---|---|---|---|
| 6 | 7 | 8 | 9 |
| L. and F. pumps; wells can be entered by the existing rough ledges of gypsum. | Fair, aperient, somewhat impregnated with sulphuretted hydrogen. | Permanent | A copious supply. There was a very heavy drain on these wells throughout the operations without any diminution of the level of the wells. |

## NOGAL.

| | | | |
|---|---|---|---|
| L. and F. pumps | Bad | Precarious, liable to exhaustion. | The water is procured from pools and from a well situated in a large pit. |
| L. and F.; wells can be easily entered and cleaned. | Bad | Precarious, liable to exhaustion. | |
| L. and F.; wells can be easily entered and cleaned. | Fair | Probably permanent. | Force halted only a day or two in January, 1904. |
| L. and F. pumps | Fair, some pools, brackish. | Seems to be a spring. | Force only marched through and watered in January, 1904. |
| L. and F. pumps, easy of access by digging. | Good | Liable to dry up up in drought. | |
| Buckets or L. and F. pumps, easy of access. | Good | Permanent | The stay of the force in January, 1904, was not sufficiently prolonged to judge of the permanency of the supply. |
| Buckets, L. and F. pumps, easy of access. | Somewhat brackish. | Seems permanent | ⎫ |
| Buckets L. and F. pumps, easy of access. | Brackish | | ⎬ Force only marched through and watered in January, 1904. |
| L. and F. pumps, easy of access. | Brackish | Seems permanent | |
| L. and F. pumps, easy of access. | Bad | Permanent | ⎭ |

| Place. | Nature of Supply. | Depth of well to water surface. | Depth of water before use. | Average yield. |
|---|---|---|---|---|
| 1 | 2 | 3 | 4 | 5 |
| Gaolo | Large pools in bed of nullah. | At surface | 2 ft. to 3 ft. | Inflow probably 200 to 500 gals. per hour. |
| Halin | Stream | — | — | 3 to 5 gals. per sec. |
| Hudin | In 6 wells in gypsum about 1 mile from post. | 8 ft. | 1 ft. | About 1,500 gals. per hour per well. |

### III. BERBERA—LAS DUREH,

| Place. | Nature of Supply. | Depth of well to water surface. | Depth of water before use. | Average yield. |
|---|---|---|---|---|
| Beyi | In trenches in river bed to the number required. | 8 ft. to 10 ft. | 2 ft. | 400 gals. per diem per well, but after flood probably 3,000 gals. per diem per well. |
| Hagal | In trenches in river bed to the number required. | 4 ft. to 8 ft. | 2 ft. | 400 gals. per diem to 3,000 gals. per diem per well. |
| Las Dureh | In trenches in river bed to the number required. | 1 or 2 ft. to 3 ft. | 2 ft. | 8,000 gals. per day from 6 to 8 pits. |
| Las Adey | Trenches in river bed. | 1 ft. | 2 ft. | 2,000 gals. per day |
| Las Khorai | Pits or trench in nullah bed. | 8 ft. | 2 ft. | 500 gals. per hour |
| Illig | One well on beach. | 12 ft. | 1 ft. | 50 gals. per hour |

| Accessibility, best method of drawing. | Quality. | Permanency. | Remarks. |
|---|---|---|---|
| 6 | 7 | 8 | 9 |
| Buckets or L. and F. pumps, easy of access | Good | Seems permanent. | |
| Buckets or L. and F. pumps, easy of access. | Good | Permanent. | |
| Easy of access, L. and F. pumps. | Bad, very aperient. | Permanent. | |

## LINES OF COMMUNICATION, Etc.

| Accessibility, best method of drawing. | Quality. | Permanency. | Remarks. |
|---|---|---|---|
| Easy of access, L. and F. pumps. | Good, dhall can be cooked. | Permanent | ⎫ |
| Easy of access, L. and F. pumps. | Good | Permanent | ⎬ Floods will fill up the trenches with sand, necessitating re-excavation. |
| Easy of access, L. and F. pumps. | Fair, some of it brackish. | Permanent | ⎭ |
| Easy of access, L. and F. pumps. | Good | Permanent | 50,000 gallons of water were taken out in 4 weeks with reduction of general level by nine inches. There is running water at Iga (Shadid) 18 miles west of Las Adey. |
| L. and F. pumps, easy of access. | Fair | Permanent. | |
| Easy of access, L. and F. pumps. | Slightly brackish. | Seems permanent. | |

## IV. OBBIA LINES

| Place. | Nature of supply | Depth of well to water surface. | Depth of water before use. | Average yield. |
|---|---|---|---|---|
| 1 | 2 | 3 | 4 | 5 |
| Gabarwein | 1 well | 38 ft. | 4 ft. | 1,000 gals. per day |
| Lodobal | Shallow wells | 10 ft. | 4 ft. | Plentiful |
| El Dibber | Wells | — | — | Plentiful |
| Dibit | 4 wells | 8 ft. | 2 ft. | Fair supply |
| Inideenli | 6 wells | — | — | Plentiful |
| Rhakn | (a) 1 open well | — | — | (a) 2,400 gals. a day |
|  | (b) 1 deep well | 25 ft. | — | (b) 300 gals. a day |
|  | (c) 1 well | — | — | (c) 150 gals. a day |
| Wargallo | 1 deep well | 50 ft. | 5 ft. | Limited supply |
| Galkayu | Numerous wells | — | — | Plentiful |
| Bera | 20 wells | 20 ft. | — | Fair supply |
| Rohr | Wells | — | — | Plentiful |
| Badwein | 3 wells | 15 ft. | 2 ft. | Fair supply |
| Dudub | Wells | 20 ft. to 50 ft. | 2 ft. to 6 ft. | Fair supply |
| Galadi | Numerous wells, all of small diameter. | 40 ft. to 80 ft. | 2 ft. to 4 ft. | Plentiful |

| Accessibility, best method of drawing. | Quality. | Permanency. | Remarks. |
|---|---|---|---|
| 6 | 7 | 8 | 9 |

## OF COMMUNICATION.

| Accessibility, best method of drawing. | Quality. | Permanency. | Remarks. |
|---|---|---|---|
| Easy of access, buckets | Good | Likely to fail if much drawn on. | |
| Easy of access, L. and F. pumps. | Good | Seems permanent. | |
| Easy of access | Tainted | Likely to fail if much drawn on. | |
| Easy of access, L. and F. pumps. | Impregnated with sulphuretted hydrogen. | Likely to fail if much drawn on. One does not refill. | |
| Easy of access, L. and F. pumps. | Good | Likely to fail if much drawn on. | |
| (a) Easy of access | Good | Likely to fail if much drawn on. | |
| (b) Requires L. and F. pumps or buckets. | Good | — | |
| (c) Easy of access | Good | — | |
| Buckets or L. and F. pumps. | Inferior | Likely to fail if much drawn on. | This well was large enough to admit of L. and F. pumps being lowered on a staging. |
| Easy of access, L. and F. pumps or buckets. | Impregnated with sulphuretted hydrogen. | Two of these never failed, though much drawn on. | About 2 miles west of Galkayu there is a large crater containing an unlimited supply of excellent water, about 150 ft. below the surface of the ground. Access is difficult, without much labour, since there is only one place whence water can be reached, and there the sides of the crater, which are of sand, are very unsafe. |
| Easy of access, L. and F. pumps and buckets. | Good | Likely to fail if much drawn on. | |
| Easy of access | Good | — | |
| Easy of access, L. and F. pumps and buckets. | Good | Never failed though much drawn on. | |
| Easy of access, L. and F. pumps and buckets. | Good | — | |
| Easy of access, buckets and wadans; impossible to use L. and F. pumps. | Variable | Seems permanent | |

## Defensible Posts on the Lines of Communication.

Defensible posts were constructed at the following places :—

| Name of Post. | Designed for Garrison. | Type. |
|---|---|---|
| | Number. | |
| Berbera | 300 | Special |
| Dubar | 16 | A. |
| Kalgumrah | 10 | A. |
| Bihendula | 25 | A. |
| Lower Sheikh | 25 | A. |
| Upper Sheikh | 150 | D. |
| Dubbar | 25 | D. |
| Gololi | 25 | D. |
| Waran | 25 | D. |
| Burao | 150 | C. |
| Ber | 25 | B. |
| Elkadalanleh | 25 | B. |
| Kirrit | 200 | Special |
| Olesan | 150 | C. |
| Garrero | 100 | Special |
| Wadamago | 100 | C. |
| Ain Abo | 25 | Special |
| Eil Dab | 200 | C. |
| Shimber Berris | 50 | C. |
| Bohotle | 400 | C. |

Types of defences.

A.—Masonry blockhouses roofed if necessary.
B.—Earth redoubts without special flank defence.
C.—Defensible enclosure, rectangular in plan, with flanking bastions.
D.—Non-defensible enclosures for stores, with defence from the flanking bastions only.

The flanking bastions were usually loopholed walls of masonry. The obstacle consisted in a thorn zariba with barbed wire entanglement and fence. The non-defensible enclosure was defined by a thorn zariba.

An example of each type of defence is shown by :—

| | | | |
|---|---|---|---|
| Dubar | A. | Plate. | 37 |
| Ber | B. | ,, | 38 |
| Burao | C. | ,, | 39 and 40 |
| Upper Sheikh | D. | ,, | 41 |

Bohotle Fort. (Destroyed May, 1905.)

(*To face page* 472.)

Plate 37.

## BLOCKHOUSE DUBAR.

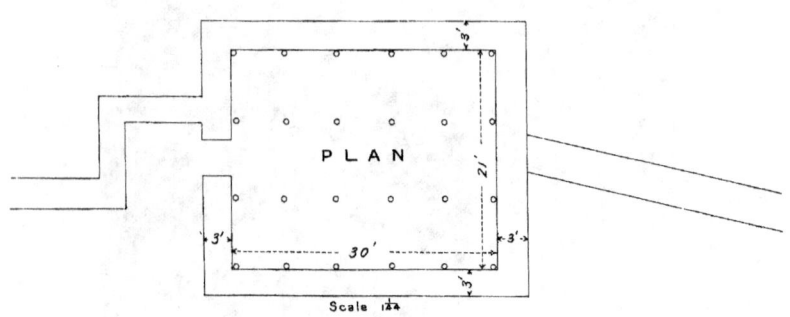

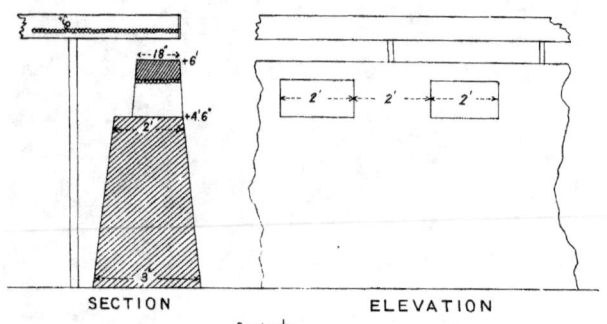

The ground falls slightly from W. to E. making the E. wall 7' high
There are two rows of loopholes in the E. wall and in those
portions of the N. & S. walls inside the garden. one row bottom
of loopholes 4'.6" high, other row 3' high.

To follow plate 36.

Weller & Graham Ltd. Litho. London

Plate 38.

## BER DEFENSIBLE POST

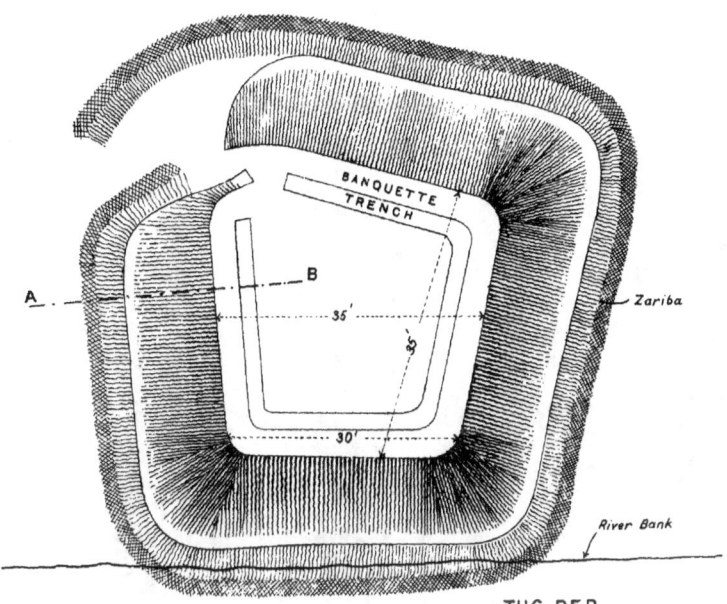

TUG DER.

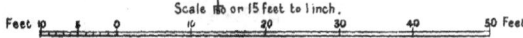

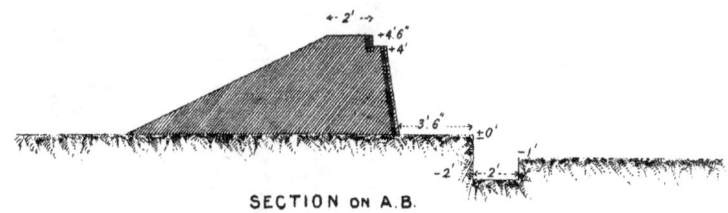

SECTION ON A.B.

BURAO.
25.3.04.
321.2.07.

Scale 5' to 1 inch

To follow plate 37.

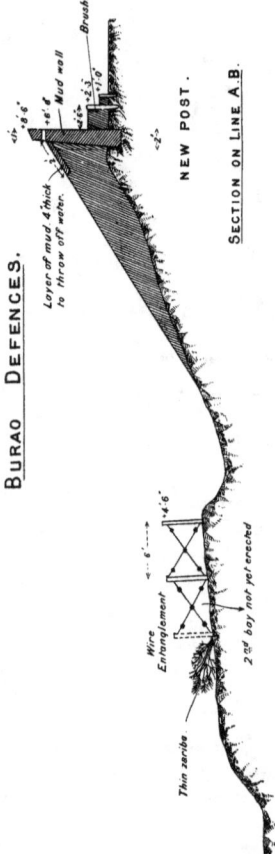
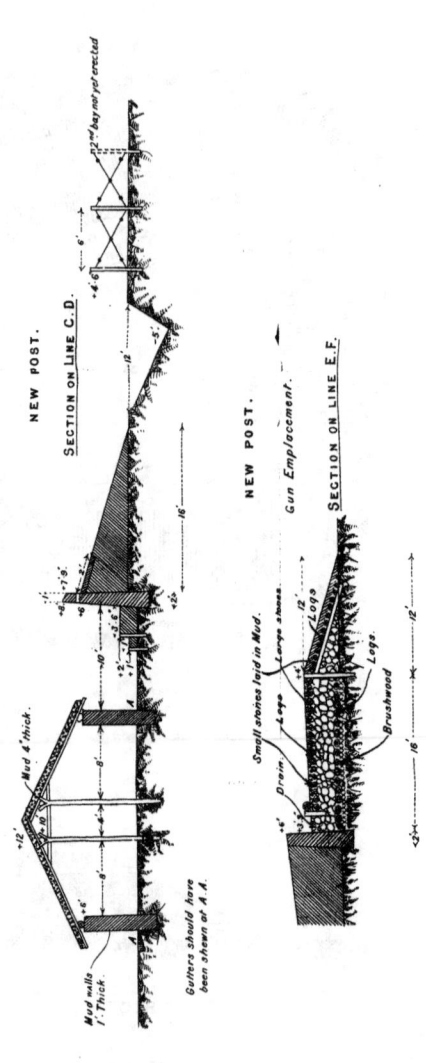

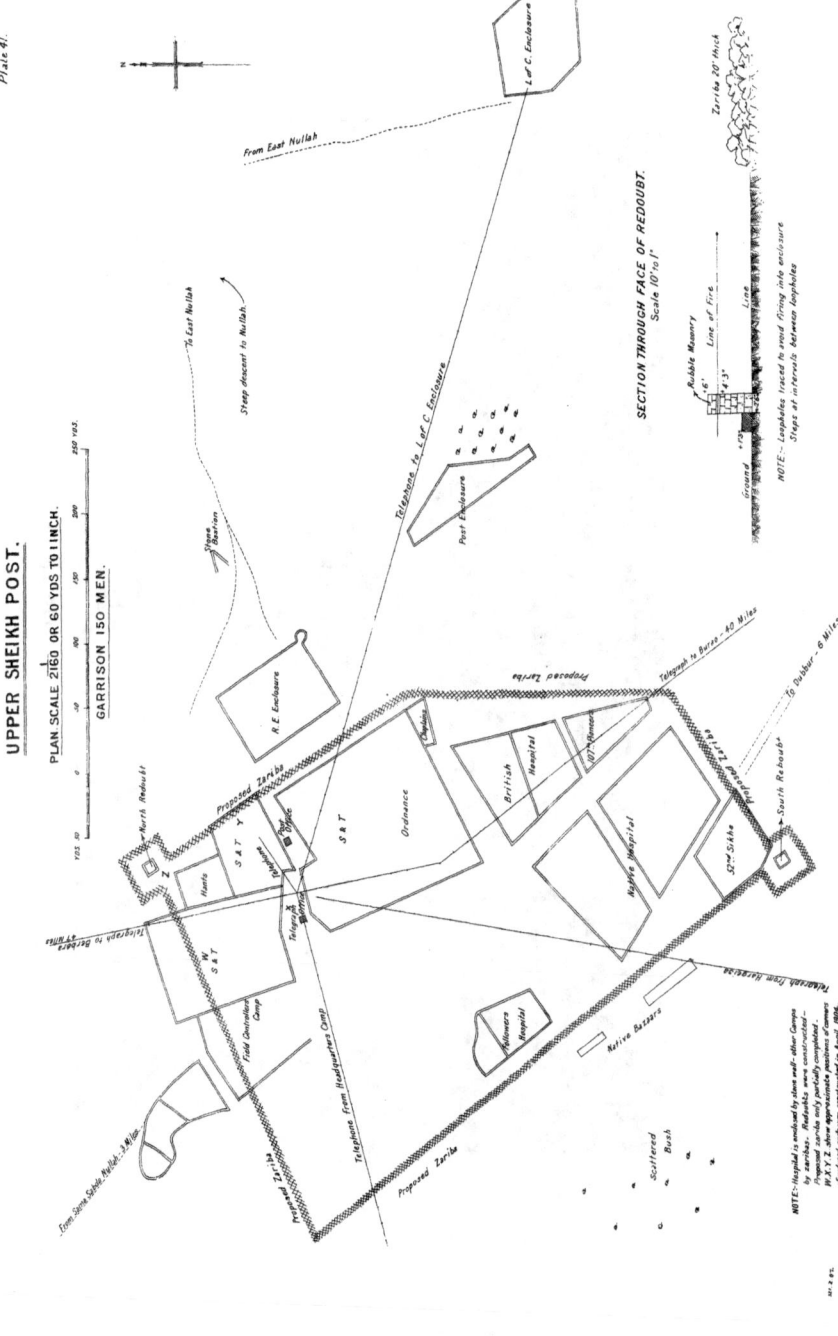

PLATE 42.

Upper Sheikh Redoubt.

(*To face page* 473.)

*Dubar.*—The blockhouse was made of mud masonry and a roof of 6 inches of earth was provided. The walls were of stone laid in mud plaster. The roof was carried on 5-inch posts and rafters on which were laid reeds and mats covered with 6 inches of earth. The blockhouse was surrounded by a barbed wire fence 4 feet high.   Details.

*Ber.*—The parapet was of earth taken from the trench. It was revetted with brushwood. The post was surrounded by a double line of thorn zariba.

*Burao.*—The sketches amply illustrate the defences at this post.

*Upper Sheikh.*—Two masonry redoubts at opposite corners. The special defences were as follows :—

*Berbera.*—The defences were confined to the official quarter known as the Shaab, which is separated by a distance of 1¼ miles of open ground from the native town. In order to reduce the perimeter to be held, detached entrenchments were constructed at certain points along the border of the Shaab to command the surrounding country and to flank each other. A scheme was also devised for the rapid occupation of the line of defence and for loopholing buildings. For details of defence see Plate 43, and the following details :—   Special defences.

*No. 1 Post.*—An earth breastwork 42 feet long with flanks 12 feet long. Revetted with a double row of bhoosa bales on top of cement casks. Parapet, 4 feet high and 2 feet thick on top.

*No. 2 Post.*—Masonry wall, 4 feet 4 inches high, 18 inches thick.

*No. 3 Post.*—Earthwork, 56 feet long. Parapet, 4 feet 6 inches high and similar to No. 1. Had two embrasures for guns 6 feet 6 inches wide.

*No. 4 Post.*—Circular earthwork. 53 feet inside circumference, 4 feet high and revetted with grain bags, thickness as No. 1.

*No. 5 Post.*—Parapet, 170 feet long, similar in section to No. 1. Two embrasures.

*No. 6 Post.*—Similar to No. 2. Wall of masonry 18 inches thick, 6 feet high, with platform on inside 18 inches high.

*No. 7 Post.*—Flat roof of a house 62 feet long, 15 feet high. Low parapet 18 inches high ran all round the roof.

*No. 8 Post.*—Similar to No. 7, 78 feet long.

*No. 9 Post.*—Earthwork in two portions. West portion, 115 feet long, parapet as in No. 1. Eastern portion, 3 feet high, revetted.

*No. 10 Post.*—Circular breastwork of double row of bhoosa bales 4 tiers high. **70 feet circumference.** 4 feet high; 3 feet 6 inches thick.

*Nos. 11 & 12 Posts.*—C. and D. sections of supplies surrounded by a wall of bhoosa 4 tiers high.

*No. 13 Post.*—Breastwork of 2 rows of bhoosa bales as in No. 10.

The post was enclosed by a loopholed wall 250 feet square

Two barbed wire fences were erected as shown in sketch protecting Nos. 1 and 5 works. Standards 15 feet apart and every fourth post was stayed on the outside.

*Kirrit.*—An isolated hill was put in a state of defence by the construction of a masonry parapet wall conforming to the contour of the hill. This wall was flanked by small bastions. The hill commanded the water supply immediately below it, and overlooked the depôt of stores located at its base. For details see Plate 44, and the following details :—

The wall was 2½ feet thick, 4 feet 3 inches high, and had a perimeter of 200 yards.

The whole was surrounded by a double fence of barbed wire.

*Garrero.*—The original fort was a self-contained masonry work on a small rise of ground. A work was added to afford room for huts and, up till November, 1903, the Field Hospital was accommodated there. This post was of small importance.

*Ain Abo.*—The post here consisted of a rectangular stone breastwork. See Plate 45 and following details :—

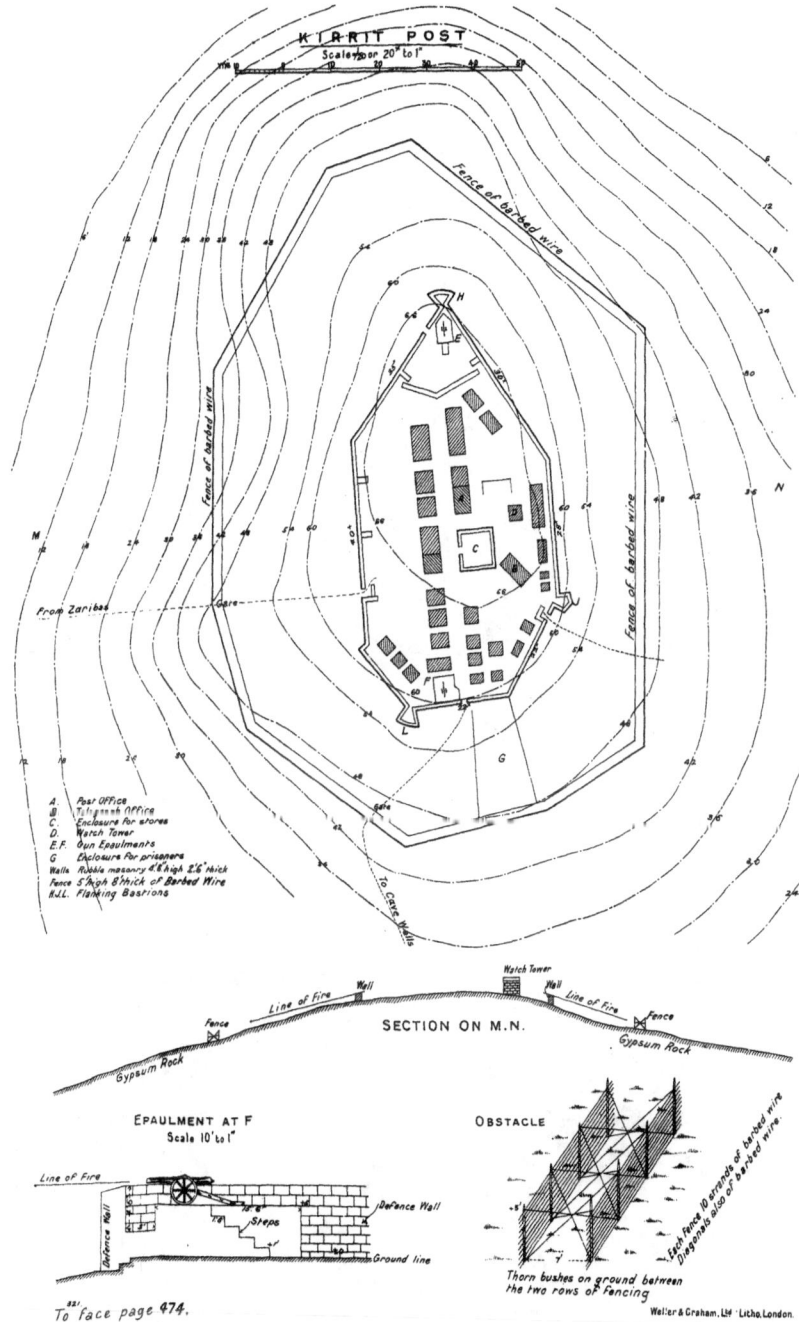

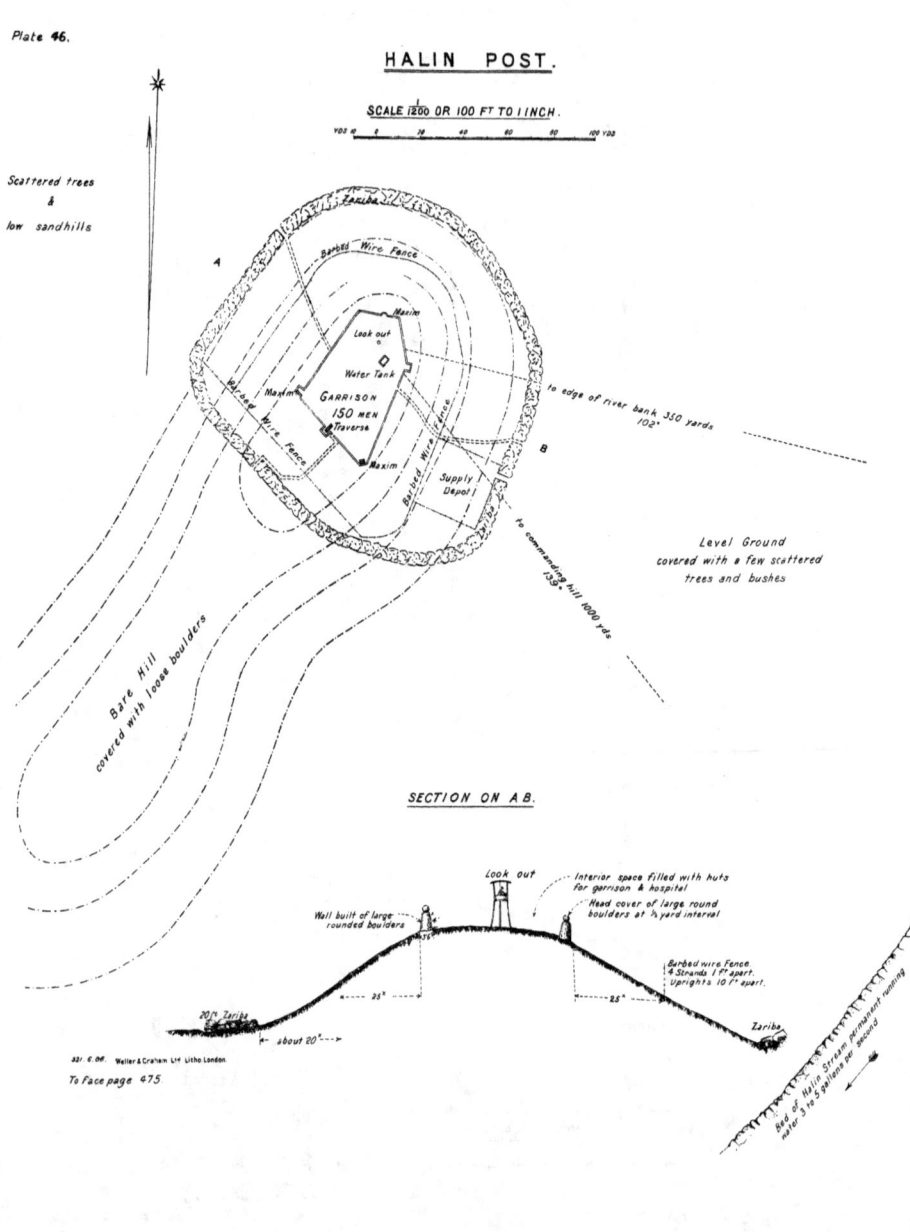

Plate 47.

# LAS KHORAI POST

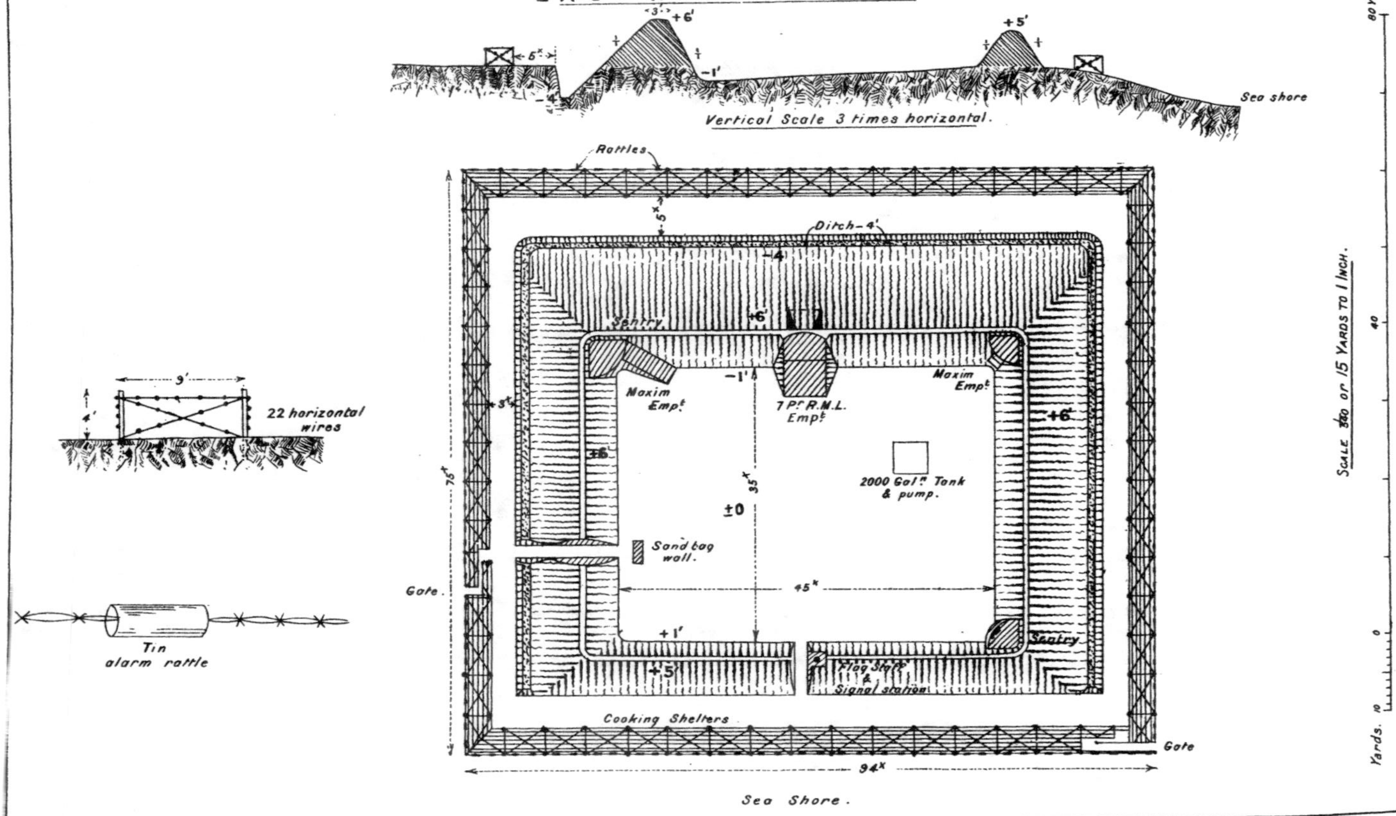


321.2.07.

Weller & Graham, Ltd Litho, London.

To follow plate 46.

Post consisted of a stone breastwork built round two large banyan trees. Breastwork 4½ feet high by 2 feet thick of dry stone masonry.

Defensible posts were also constructed at :—

Other defensible posts.

|  | Designed for Garrison. |
|---|---|
|  | Number. |
| Galadi | .. |
| Badwein | 50 |
| Yaguri | 200 |
| Dariali | 140 |
| Gaolo | 100 |
| Halin | 150 |
| Hudin | .. |
| Las Khorai | 80 |
| Las Adey | 150 |
| Beyi | 25 |

Of the above, plates are given showing the defences at Halin and at Las Khorai, with a sketch plan of the coast at Las Khorai. At Las Khorai the parapets were of sand and unrevetted, but were covered with loose seaweed. A strong wire entanglement was provided and the outer wires were fitted with tin rattles since the sea was so close that a rush could be made on the post in the dark.

### OTHER ENGINEERING WORKS.

Besides the defensible posts and the work on water supply, the work of the Sappers and Miners and Pioneers included the following :—

Roads.—(*a*) The road from Berbera to Lower Sheikh was finished about August, 1903. It was not metalled. The maximum gradient was 1/20 and average width 15-20 feet. (*b*) From Lower Sheikh to Upper Sheikh. This road was opened in October, 1903. Its maximum gradient was 1/15, and width 8-10 feet. (*c*) A road was cut through the jungle from Upper Sheikh to Elkadalanleh, width about 25 feet and with easy grades. And the road from Elkadalanleh to Kirrit

Roads.

was improved. (*d*) Other roads constructed included an alternative route from Upper Sheikh to Burao viâ Waran.

Laying of tram lines and the widening of the pier causeway to Berbera.

Temporary shelters of various kinds.

Mat-walling for E.P. tents at Berbera.

Adaptations of buildings for base offices at Berbera.

The construction of an ice machine house.

Sanitary arrangements.

Breakwater at Las Khorai.

Labour. At Berbera and in the vicinity labour was obtained from a contractor who supplied it at rates slightly exceeding those at Aden. He also supplied coolies for work on lines of communication, if required.

Most of the coolies and native artificers, such as masons, blacksmiths and carpenters, who were employed, came from Aden, but it was found difficult to obtain local labour as the Somali has no liking for engineering work. The men of the Porter Corps were also employed for various works.

The military labour was found by Nos. 17 and 19 Companies, 3rd Sappers and Miners, 107th Pioneers and by working parties from infantry. For native troops, except sappers and miners, the following were the daily rates of working pay :—

|  | Rate of Pay. | |
|---|---|---|
|  | Rs. | a. |
| Subadars .. .. .. .. .. | 0 | 8 |
| Jemadars .. .. .. .. .. | 0 | 6 |
| N.C.O.'s and rank and file .. .. | 0 | 2 |
| British officers .. .. .. .. | 2 | 0 |

The working day was reckoned at eight hours, and to arrive at the amount due, the number of hours the men worked was divided by 8 and a full day's working pay allowed for each of the number of days so arrived at, any balance being paid for as follows :—

| | |
|---|---|
| For less than 2 hours .. .. | Nil. |
| For 2 hours .. .. .. | ¼ day's working pay. |
| From 2 to 4 hours .. .. | ½ day's working pay. |
| From 4 to 6 hours .. .. | ¾ day's working pay. |
| From 6 to 8 hours .. .. | A full day's pay. |

## 2.—Telegraphs, Signalling and Postal Services.
### Telegraphs.

In December, 1902, when it was first decided to send out a telegraph organization, a consultation was held at the War Office with the Officer Commanding 1st Telegraph Company with the object of settling the detail of personnel, stores, &c., for the requirements of the expedition. The Officer Commanding 1st Telegraph Company then drew out an estimate of personnel, stores, &c., required, and it was in accordance with this estimate that the 1st Telegraph Section was despatched. It arrived at Berbera on the 23rd January, 1903, and consisted of :— *Organization.*

2 officers, 58 non-commissioned officers and men with 240 miles air line and 100 miles cable, 8 vibrator and 3 sounder offices, and a small proportion of reserve instruments.

When the force was increased in July, 1903, the above numbers were considered insufficient and more personnel and material were demanded from England. In accordance with this demand, the following personnel and material arrived at Berbera on 18th August, 1903.

1 officer, 50 non-commissioned officers and men, 140 miles air line, 100 miles cable.

The telegraphs were organized under Captain G. B. Roberts, R.E., and were under the orders of the Officer Commanding Lines of Communication.

The first line to be constructed was the line to Bohotle and the following table shows the dates on which offices were opened and the distances from Berbera. *Work.*

|  | Names of Places. | Nature of Line. | Miles from Berbera. | Date of Opening Office. |
|---|---|---|---|---|
| A. Up to July, 1903. | Bihendula | Air | 23 | 3rd February |
|  | Upper Sheikh | ,, | 43½ | 7th February |
|  | Burao | ,, | 83½ | 17th February |
|  | Ber | ,, | 102 | 4th March (subsequently closed and office transferred to Elkadalanleh) |
|  | Olesan | ,, | 142 | 2nd March |
|  | Garrero | ,, | 151 | 6th March |
|  | Bohotle | ,, | 204½ | 8th March |
|  | Damot | Cable (from Bohotle) | 251½ | 14th March (office closed 10th June) |
| B. After 7th July, 1903. | Kirrit | Cable (subsequently air) | 143 | 31st July |
|  | Wadamago | Cable (from Garrero, Air 1st November) | 153 | 16th September |
|  | Shimber Berris | Air | 123 | 18th September |
|  | Gololi | ,, | 61 | 30th September |
|  | Eil Dab | Cable (from Wadamago, Air 1st November) | 170 | 8th October |
|  | Lasakante | Cable |  | 22nd November |
|  | Adadleh | Air |  | 20th November |
|  | Hargeisa | ,, | 90 | 25th November |
|  | Badwein | Cable (air 30th December) |  | 23rd December |
|  | Yaguri | Cable (closed 9th January, re-opened air, 21st January) | 202 | 6th January, 1904 |
|  | Jidbali | Cable |  | 10th January (closed 14th January) |
|  | Adur | ,, |  | 11th January (closed 14th January) |
|  | Dumodleh | ,, |  | 13th January (closed 14th January) |
|  | Dariali | ,, | 243 | 18th January |
|  | Gaolo | ,, | 313 | 27th January (closed 9th February) |
|  | Las Dureh | ,, (afterwards air) | 83 | 28th February |
|  | Beyi | ,, |  | 28th February |
|  | Hagal | ,, |  |  |
|  | Las Adey | ,, | 136 | 13th March |
|  | El Afweina | ,, | 180 | 22nd March |

Total mileages erected and laid were :—
Air line .. .. .. 432 miles.
Cable .. .. .. 504 ,,

479

Average rate of erecting air line    10 miles a day.
Rate of laying or reeling up cable   20    ,,     ,,

Telephones were also installed as shown on attached plates.

Inspectors of the line were appointed who had charge of sections of the line and were responsible for (1) regulation of traffic; (2) control of staff; (3) repair and maintenance of lines and instruments; (4) military discipline of all soldiers employed on Army Telegraphs within their section. *Working of the line.*

As regards the method of working the line, accounting, sending of messages, etc., no special points appear to call for mention, the ordinary rules for working telegraphs in war being followed.

The distribution of personnel and animals for the maintenance of the line was as follows:— *Distribution for maintenance of line.*

|  | Officers | N.C.O.'s and Men. | | | Muleteers | Interpreter | Camolsyce | Riding Camels | Burden Camels | Mules | Water-tins |
|  |  | Clerks | Linemen | Camelmen |  |  |  |  |  |  |  |
|---|---|---|---|---|---|---|---|---|---|---|---|
| Damot        | .. | 2 | 1 | .. | 1  | .. | .. | .. | .. | 1  | .. |
| Bohotle      | .. | 4 | 2 | .. | 3  | .. | .. | .. | .. | 4  | 4  |
| Garrero      | .. | 2 | 6 | 1  | 4  | .. | .. | .. | .. | 10 | 4  |
| Olesan       | .. | 1 | 1 | .. | 1  | .. | .. | .. | .. | 2  | .. |
| Ber          | .. | 1 | 2 | .. | 1  | .. | .. | .. | .. | 2  | .. |
| Burao        | .. | 2 | 2 | .. | 1  | .. | .. | .. | .. | 3  | 1  |
| Sheikh       | .. | 2 | 6 | 1  | 4  | .. | .. | .. | 1  | 10 | 4  |
| Bihendula    | .. | 1 | 3 | 1  | 1  | .. | .. | .. | 3  | 4  | .. |
| Berbera      | 1  | 4 | 5 | .. | 1  | .. | .. | .. | .. | 2  | 2  |
| Working party | 1 | 1 | 12 | .. | 15 | 1 | 1 | 1 | 8 | 17 | .. |

Ber office was closed and an office opened at Elkadalanleh instead. Damot was withdrawn in June.

The above table refers only to the arrangements up to July, 1903, but the same system of distribution was followed after that date.

It was suggested that linemen should be provided with

riding camels, as they could then carry all they wanted for two or three days.

**Interruptions to working of line.**
These were chiefly caused by :—
Natives cutting the wire.
Convoy and other animals knocking down poles or wire.
Broken insulators.

**Remarks on equipment.**
Owing to the nature of the ground hammers and jumpers were practically useless, nearly every hole had to be dug with picks and shovels.

The large wooden stay pegs were eaten by white ants, and had to be replaced by buried stone or steel stay peg anchorages. The white ants, however, attacked few poles, because they were painted, but they did attack the thick double fir poles. Every second pole had to be stayed during the khareef (June to August).

The wire barrows were unnecessarily cumbersome and heavy; their balance when loaded seemed wrong, and they were very awkward over rough ground and through thick bush. Out of 18 barrows about 6 were serviceable at the end of the campaign. These barrows had to be used for laying cable and reeling it up again since cable carts were out of the question. It was suggested that a small barrow, with reeling up gear, capable of being drawn by one mule or being carried, would be of great advantage. The wheel tyres should be at least 4 inches wide.

Contact rods split badly and soon became unserviceable.

Air line and cable stores should be adapted to pack transport. Thus as regards wire for mule transport the drums should have only $\frac{1}{2}$ mile wire, for camels 1 mile.

Creosoted poles were first asked for, but the shipping companies objected to taking them and therefore ordinary poles had to be used.

Telephone and vibrator (lineman's telephone).—The first pattern of instrument provided, that used in South Africa, was generally complained of, but afterwards an improved pattern was supplied.

The working party was generally divided as follows :— **Method of construction.**

| | | |
|---|---|---|
| Hole digging party | .. | 4 to 8 men. |
| Store party | .. .. | 1 to 3 men. |
| Barrow party | .. .. | 1 to 3 men. |
| Strainers | .. .. | 2 men. |
| Builders | .. .. | 2 to 3 men. |

There were as a rule two working parties each under a serjeant whilst the officer supervised the whole.

The method adopted was that No. 1 party started work at the camp while No. 2 went 5 miles up the road and started work there. The officer, after starting No. 1 and giving it the direction, rode after No. 2, and gave it the point to start at and the direction. He then went back to No. 1 to see if it was keeping right and to give it the direction of No. 2's starting point, and then on to No. 2 again, finally going on to settle the location of camp, returning to the parties to finish the work and to show the way to camp. The line was generally placed some 300 to 400 yards from the road.

The serjeant kept in touch with the road, choosing the line where the bush was thick. He had field glasses and a compass, both absolutely indispensable.

*Hole digging party.*—When possible this party worked in pairs. Each pair had a jumping bar and a shovel. Their carbines, water chaguls and haversacks were carried on pack mules.

*Store party.*—This party dealt out poles, insulators, stays, stay pegs, &c. They fixed on the stays, drove in stay pegs and made double poles, &c. They had 2 mules with panniers containing stay wire, pegs, clips, insulators, mallets, &c., and 6 or 7 mules with poles. The poles were carried 8 or 10 a side. If camels are used 32 poles can be carried on each camel, but they must be tied in firm bundles of 16 each. This party also did some clearing. Arms and water carried on pannier mules.

*Barrow party.*—The barrow was harnessed to a mule, which also carried soldering gear. This party had three mules carrying wire, one mule carrying two drums and the other two one each. The first drum used was on the barrow. For remarks *re* drums and barrows see above. This party also had to work putting the wire over the bushes and in a straight line.

*Strainers* worked as usual, arms and water being on the mule with those of the builders.

*Builders.*—This party had a mule with panniers, carrying some spare stores and a short pole, and another with arms and water. Rods, clearing obstacle, would have been useful for this party, but in their place a spare pole was generally used. Every insulator was bound in.

The normal day's work was 5 miles each party, but it varied with the difficulties of the country. The worst delays were caused by stony ground, but the bush, when thick and high, caused a lot of trouble.

As regards animals, mules were preferred for this work. Camels, however, could carry 2 drums full or 10 empty, or 3 sacks of 100 wooden pegs.

Cable laying. A party consisted of 1 non-commissioned officer and 5 or 6 men. The cable was carried on camels, 2 drums to a camel each containing about 1½ miles of cable. The air line barrows were used with a mule harnessed to each. Cable was paid off from the barrow, great care being taken to keep the cable on the ground, and not to let it get up on the low bushes or grass. To ensure this a man held a forked stick between his legs, and kept it dragging along the ground, the cable passing under the fork, he thus forced the bush out of the way as he walked and the cable rested on the ground under the bush and long grass. This was very hard work for the man but was found to be the only way. 15 to 20 miles was the average day's work. The white ants did not attack the cable but it got parched in the sun, and thus it sometimes got leaky when wet.

Attached is a table showing the work done between July, 1903, and March, 1904. Plates 49 and 50 show the telegraph lines in work at two different periods of the expedition.

Summary of Forwarded Messages from 1st July, 1903, to 31st March, 1904.

| Month. | Total Forwarded. | | Free Messages. | | | | Paid Messages. | | | |
|---|---|---|---|---|---|---|---|---|---|---|
| | | | O.H.M.S. | | Reuter's News. | | Private Messages. | | Press Messages. | |
| | Number of Messages. | Number of Words. | Number of Messages. | Number of Words. | Number of Messages. | Number of Words. | Number of Messages. | Number of Words. | Number of Messages. | Number of Words. |
| 1903— | | | | | | | | | | |
| July | 7,236 | 346,090 | 6,828 | 303,039 | 144 | 36,641 | 261 | 6,146 | 3 | 264 |
| August | 9,808 | 493,324 | 9,272 | 400,368 | 351 | 88,724 | 185 | 4,232 | .. | .. |
| September | 11,335 | 589,899 | 10,779 | 498,718 | 370 | 87,354 | 186 | 3,827 | .. | .. |
| October | 13,887 | 667,682 | 13,247 | 564,411 | 370 | 97,787 | 270 | 5,484 | .. | .. |
| November | 14,560 | 687,300 | 13,976 | 594,862 | 324 | 85,705 | 251 | 5,694 | 9 | 1,048 |
| December | 17,190 | 842,732 | 16,399 | 723,643 | 389 | 109,638 | 391 | 8,089 | 11 | 1,362 |
| 1904— | | | | | | | | | | |
| January | 13,795 | 725,726 | 13,344 | 594,210 | 163 | 125,138 | 281 | 5,411 | 7 | 967 |
| February | 10,866 | 566,195 | 10,408 | 430,922 | 158 | 128,838 | 294 | 6,008 | 6 | 427 |
| March | 8,715 | 459,472 | 8,356 | 355,118 | 167 | 100,477 | 192 | 3,877 | .. | .. |
| Total | 107,392 | 5,378,420 | 102,609 | 4,465,291 | 2,436 | 860,302 | 2,311 | 48,768 | 36 | 4,068 |

**Wireless Telegraphy.**

A Marconi installation, under Lieut. Silvertop, R.N., was attached to the Obbia Force in 1903, and attempts were made to utilise it on the lines of communication. Owing, however, to the characteristics of the country, it was found impossible to arrive at any good results, and the attempt to make use of it was abandoned. The party finally left the force in May, 1903.

## SIGNALLING.

**Organization.**

The signalling services in Somaliland during 1903-4 were under a Superintendent of army signalling, who was attached to the Headquarter Staff. When the force was organized into brigades, brigade signalling officers were appointed.

The total personnel available was :—

    21 British
    81 Indian
    6 African
    ―――
    108 Signallers.

**Equipment.**

The equipment carried consisted of 3-inch, 5-inch, and 10-inch heliographs, with flags and lamps. During the latter part of the campaign lamps were discarded as it was found that they were never used.

Some confusion occurred owing to the message forms used in India and those used at home being different. The Superintendent recommended that they should be assimilated.

**Suitability of country for signalling.**

It was considered that all the country traversed by the expeditions under General Egerton was suitable for signalling, but in the Southern Haud, owing to its dense bush, signalling was not practicable. On the Obbia lines of communication signalling could only be used between Obbia and Dibit.

A line of signalling stations could be carried right through from Berbera to Bohotle and from Berbera to the Anane Pass viâ Bur Anod and Dariali. Some notes on visibility of points are given below.

The best time of day for signalling purposes was found to be between 8 A.M. and 11 A.M., and 3.30 P.M. to 5.30 P.M., the mirage in the middle of the day interfering considerably with signalling operations.

Signalling was chiefly made use of :— Work done.

At advanced posts off the line of telegraph.

To keep up communication between the various columns when on the march.

Between picquets.

Permanently for several months between Upper Sheikh and Las Dureh.

To connect up different points in the Nogal, when the telegraph was withdrawn, so as to keep them in touch with the lines of communication at Eil Dab.

After the 20th March, 1904, to keep up communication between the 1st and 2nd Brigades viâ Hudin and El Afweina, by means of two 10-inch helios.

1. The following places were visible from Halin Fort :— Visibility of certain points.

| | Distance. |
|---|---|
| Mid Halin | 7 miles. |
| Lower Halin | 12 ,, |
| *Tagabei | 27 ,, |
| Gaolo | 22 ,, |
| †Gorei | 38 ,, |
| ‡Sorl | 16 ,, |

2. The communication between Hudin and Eil Dab was established viâ a hill on the Bur Anod range 8 miles from Hudin. From this hill, Eil Dab, El Afweina, Dumodleh and Hudin could be seen. Bearings were as follows from this hill :— Signalling possibilities in the Nogal.

---

\* In Dagah Gurgur range, water in valley below.
† In Shilemadu range remote from water.
‡ Pass at the head of Halin Nullah.

|  |  |  |  |
|---|---|---|---|
| To El Afweina | .. | .. | 260 degrees. |
| To Dumodleh .. | .. | .. | 170 ,, |
| To Hudin | .. | .. | 75 ,, |

3. (i) Kabr Ogaden (water at Eil Dab, 2½ miles). From here could be seen :—Mayo Hill (water at Gosawein, 3 miles), 27 miles north-east by east ; Bur Anod (60 miles east-north-east) ; Garab Hill (water at Hoftirro, 4 miles), 20 miles south-east by east ; Samala Hills (water at Samala, 1 mile), 26 miles south-east by east ; Yaguri Hill (39 miles south-east by east).

(ii) Garab Hill ; from here the following places were visible :—Mayo, 21 miles north-east by east ; Bur Anod, 50 miles north-east by north ; Samala, 11 miles south-east by east ; Yaguri Hill, 21 miles south-east by east (water at Yaguri, ¾ mile).

(iii) From Samala :—Mayo, 23 miles north by west ; Bur Anod, 42 miles north-east ; Yaguri Hill, 11 miles south-east by east.

(iv) From Yaguri Hill there was an extensive view over the plains to the north and north-east. To the south-east the hills above the Dehjeuner could be seen, and to the south-south-east the hills near Baran on Southern Haud.

(v) It was believed that a station on the hills south of Tifali could be found, from which both Yaguri Hill and Dariali were visible, but it would probably be necessary to interpolate a second station, probably to west of Odergoeh.

(vi) From Dariali to Halin, communication would probably be as follows :—

A station would be necessary at or near to Arde Jiffifta, and another on the Dagah Gurgur hills. From the latter station Gaolo and the hills immediately over Halin were seen.

(vii) Signalling communication between Dariali and Kallis was more difficult. Most of the water places, such as Gubli, Heli Madu, Beretabli, and Gerrowei lie among the foot hills which shut out any extensive view from west to east. Short of a station well out on the Nogal Plain, from which a view could be obtained to the entrance of the various valleys, stations would be necessary on the top of nearly every ridge. From Gerrowei to Kallis the country is open, and a station on the hills near Gerrowei should be able to get Kallis or some point near it. As Dariali is fairly out in the plain, no intermediate station should be necessary between it and some point near Heli Madu.

(viii) Signalling communication could be carried out from the top of the cliffs which shut in the southern edge of the Nogal, and there are certain prominent points such as the scarp south of Bokh Shanleh, a high peak north-east of Las Elberdali, and the top of the Burhiso Pass, which commands extensive views east and west. All such points would, however, have to draw their water from the valleys below, and would also be dangerous unless strongly held.

(ix) In the Dehjeuner district, Waidat is a prominent peak, which can be seen from all round and might come in useful.

## Postal Services.

Previous to January, 1903, mails were generally sent by camel rider to Berbera, where there was a branch of the Aden Post Office. In January, 1903, a postal staff was sent from India and a base post office was opened at Obbia on 19th January.

*Organization*

The staff consisted of :—

        1 superintendent.
        1 postmaster.
        5 clerks.
        5 followers.

Supplemented on 12th June by :—

        3 clerks.
        4 followers.

A field post office was sent with General Manning's column and mails were despatched from Obbia by ship to Aden and India.

On an average mails were received every four days and were despatched every three days. On 16th April the base office at Obbia was closed and was transferred to Berbera, where up to this time the postal arrangements had been in charge of the base supply and transport officer. On the 9th May a field post office was opened at Bohotle and on 20th June at Sheikh.

The postal service was increased in September by one extra field post office and two spare clerks with one Khalasi, and in October by two clerks and four followers.

Field post offices.

After July, 1903, field post offices were established as follows :—

| Place. | Opened on— | Remarks. |
| --- | --- | --- |
| Berbera .. | April, 1903 | Base post office |
| Behindula | 3rd August | Moved to Wagon's Rust 25th November |
| Upper Sheikh | 20th June | |
| Lower Sheikh | 18th October | Afterwards 2nd Brigade post office |
| Burao | 16th July | |
| Wadamago | 7th December | |
| Eil Dab | 7th January, 1904 | |
| Garrero | 6th July, 1903 | Moved to Kirrit 14th September, and moved to Wadamago 20th January, 1904 |
| Bohotle | 9th May | Afterwards 1st Brigade post office, moved 4th January, 1904 |
| Headquarters | July, 1903 | |
| 1st Brigade | January, 1904 | |
| 2nd Brigade | November, 1903 | |
| Las Dureh | 8th March, 1904 | |

Conveyance of mails.

Mails were conveyed almost entirely by camel riders, except to Las Dureh (before it became an important line) and to Hargeisa, on which services runners were employed. Mules, however, were employed between Wagon's Rust and Burao. The average time for mails between Berbera and Bohotle was 56 hours.

Parcel mails were despatched by convoy, except small parcels, which went by letter mail. The mails were originally sent once a week from Berbera by boats of Messrs. Cowasjie Dinshaw and Co., but on August 5th the service was supple-

mented by two warships—H.M.S. " Merlin " and " Porpoise "
—which plied between Berbera and Aden. On the 14th
October the gunboats were replaced by two R.I.M. ships—
the " Dalhousie " and " Mayo," the latter being taken off on
11th November. On 14th February, 1904, a small boat called
the " Meyun " was chartered specially for mail services, and
took the place of the " Dalhousie."

Money order work was performed at Upper Sheikh, Burao, Money ordeis.
Kirrit, Wadamago, Bohotle, and Berbera.

### 3. Supply and Transport.

Colonel Swayne in his expeditions had to contend with considerable difficulties in the organization of the supply and transport services, especially as a great part of the country was very little known and therefore information as to its resources for water and supply purposes could only be gained from native sources. When General Manning assumed command more information was available and he organized a regular transport service, while supply was placed under a separate head. General Egerton, however, decided to put supply and transport under one head, and on the 9th July, 1903, the entire transport and supply arrangements were placed in charge of an administrative officer of the Supply and Transport Corps (Lieut.-Colonel W. R. Yeilding, C.I.E., D.S.O.).*

It was considered that this was—

The only possible arrangement in this country where supply is so greatly dependent upon transport.

The supply situation would appear to be impossible in Somaliland, unless administered by one officer with the interests of supply and transport equally at heart. (Colonel Yeilding.)

I can only testify to its complete success in the recent operations. The only defect I have noticed is a tendency to allot transport for supply purposes somewhat to the detriment of other departments, such as ordnance or engineering stores. (General Egerton.)

---

* NOTE.—The information contained in this chapter is taken mainly from Colonel Yeilding's report; but conclusions drawn from the experience gained in transport and supply working and duties apply to the whole of the expeditions against the Mullah.

Everything, with the exception of livestock and firewood, had to be carried up from the base to positions occupied by our troops so far distant as 350 miles from the base at Berbera.

**Organization.** The personnel of the supply and transport organization was eventually (*i.e.*, after June, 1903) as follows:—

| | |
|---|---|
| Headquarters .. .. | Director, Supply and Transport.<br>1 Supply and Transport Corps Officer as Assistant for Supply.<br>1 Regimental Officer as Assistant for Transport. |
| With each Brigade .. | 1 Supply and Transport Corps Officer.<br>1 Regimental Officer as Assistant for Transport. |
| At the Base .. .. | 1 Supply and Transport Corps Officer as Base Supply and Transport Officer.<br>1 Regimental Officer as Assistant for Supply.<br>1 Regimental Officer as Base Transport Officer. |
| At the Advanced Base | 1 Supply and Transport Corps Officer.<br>1 Regimental Officer as Assistant. |
| At each Supply Depôt | 1 Regimental Officer in Supply and Transport charge, with the exception of Kirrit, and subsequently Wadamago, where a Supply and Transport Corps Officer was in charge. |
| At each Stage .. .. | A Supply and Transport Corps Warrant or Non-commissioned Officer. |

## TRANSPORT.

**General remarks.** The provision and maintenance of transport for a large expedition into the interior of Somaliland was an undertaking of considerable difficulty.*

After the grazing question, the greatest difficulty was that

---

\* To illustrate the difficulty of supplying long lines of communication, it may be mentioned that it takes a camel to maintain a mule or pony with grain only at Wadamago, 153 miles from Berbera. Thus—a Somali camel carries 240 lbs. Of this he and his attendant eat 94 lbs. between Berbera and Wadamago, to and fro. He therefore delivers only 146 lbs. A mule eats 146 lbs. in 24 days. The actual number of marching days from Berbera to Wadamago and back is 22, so, allowing 2 days' rest at the base, the camel arrives at Wadamago again just in time to re-supply the mule.

of the water supply, and this practically governed the selection of a suitable transport animal.

It is to be noted that there are no permanent running streams in Somaliland. The only water supply is contained in wells. In the rainy season, it is true, water is frequently to be found in "ballis" or depressions in the ground where it would not be found in the dry seasons. But these "ballis" often quickly dry up and cannot be relied on. For all practical purposes, therefore, wells form the sole water supply of a large extent of the country.

For transport work under such conditions as these the camel was the most suitable animal, mules requiring water every day, or at least every other day, while other animals require it still oftener. Much has been written of the tolerance of thirst of the camel, and it is sometimes supposed that camels of all kinds possess equal powers in this respect. Such, however, is not the case. It is largely a question of custom and habit, which are the result of local conditions as to water supply. The native Somali camel, bred in a country where, as above described, the supply of water is difficult to reach, can continue four to seven days (or at a pinch more) without water when working in the dry seasons; but in and immediately after the wet seasons, when the grass is green and full of moisture, and when not worked under military conditions, he requires water only once in 10 days.

One difficulty was that of procuring the Somali camel. It was a matter of difficulty to purchase a large number of Somali camels under any circumstances, and to do so quickly was almost impossible. The main reason of this was the disinclination of the Somali to part with livestock in any form. To the Somali stock represents wealth and position. He has few wants, therefore money has little value in his eyes, except as a means of purchasing more stock. The subject of purchasing and hiring camels in Somaliland is dealt with later.

Another difficulty which transport officers in Somaliland encountered was that of keeping their animals fit for work.

The grazing during the dry season in Somaliland is *very poor indeed*. This shortcoming affects the Somali camel more than other transport animals, for he is *grass*-fed, not *grain*-fed. When in the hands of his tribal owner he subsists entirely on trees, shrubs, and grass. But his owner does not work him continuously, and it is customary, after a comparatively short spell of work (during which, however, the importance of good grazing is never lost sight of), to throw animals out of work to rest and recover their strength. On active military service, however, it is not possible to throw large numbers of animals out of work to rest for any appreciable length of time ; continuous and hard work is the rule, and this the grass-fed Somali camel cannot stand. He rapidly loses condition and becomes unfit. This is more especially the case during the dry months, when the leaves of the shrubs and trees have died and fallen and the grass has either completely died or been eaten down, or is so dry as to afford little nourishment. On active service, too, work, more usually than not, clashes with grazing ; tactical considerations prohibit night marching, and the greater part of the day must therefore be spent on the road, leaving only a few hours available for grazing. The Somali camel will quickly take to eating grain, and a ration of 4 lbs. a day is ample. But it takes a long time to get him into really good condition for continuous hard work, and it was considered that he should be fed on grain for a month before being put into hard work on a campaign in Somaliland. When this cannot be done, the Somali camel wears out in a very short time and but little dependence can be placed on him when put to work under hard military conditions. It must also be borne in mind that, even when a liberal grain ration is issued, a plentiful supply of grass cannot be dispensed with.

The Indian camel, however, though he cannot go without water for such long periods as the Somali camel, is a stronger beast and more accustomed to regular hard work. It was found as a result of the experience of the campaigns that the

Indian camel soon assimilated himself to the conditions of the country, and it was considered by Colonel Yeilding "that the Indian camel saved the situation."

As the result of their experience of both sorts of animals, the general conclusions arrived at by transport officers were as follows :—

That the Indian camel is the better.

That Somali camels are more timid and weaker than the Indian variety, but that they can do without grain or water for longer periods than Indian camels.

That the best Somali camels come from the Hargeisa district.

That the factors which chiefly affect the usefulness of the camel are his age and make, the grazing which he gets, and the care which is taken of him.

That to depend on local resources for transport for an expedition in Somaliland, unless consisting of small numbers only, would be to invite disaster.

Under Colonel Swayne and General Manning the transport on the lines of communication was worked on the convoy system. In the fourth expedition the system of transport adopted was partly the convoy system and partly the staging system, but the former predominated. It was found that losses in stores and supplies while being conveyed on the lines of communication were considerably less when goods were conveyed right through by camel corps on the convoy system,* and stores had to come from such a distance that the force could ill afford to lose any. Complaints were made by the officer commanding the lines of communication of the difficulty of providing water at a post when two large convoys (one going and the other

*Transport system.*

---

\* Colonel J. C. Swann, however, disagreed with the system of base to front convoys, not only on the ground of the difficulty of providing water and escort, but for the reason that the saving effected in supply did not compensate for the wastage in transport.

returning) met at a post. General Egerton, however, considered on the whole that the convoy system was preferable in Somaliland.

**Organization.** During the expeditions previous to 1903 the transport on the lines of communication was all hired, while the transport with the field troops consisted of camels with water tins, two camels per company for cooking, &c., and for reserve ammunition, and officers' camels. All other transport with the field troops was obtained from the local tribes under special arrangements. But when General Manning took over command camels were formed into corps of 200 animals each with drivers at the rate of one to every three camels plus 12 per cent. spare., viz., 75 drivers per corps. These drivers were formed into three squads of 25 men each—each squad being under a headman. The command of the corps was vested in a British officer or British non-commissioned officer who was assisted by one Indian transport assistant (a selected non-commissioned officer detached from one of the units composing the force), and two Somali transport attendants, speaking English or Hindustani, who not only acted as interpreters, but performed general transport duties. It was found impossible to keep these cadres intact and they were broken up, new units being formed. But the principles on which the original cadres had been organized were adhered to. Great difficulty was experienced at this time in obtaining sufficient camels, since most of the camels left over from Colonel Swayne's last expedition were in a very poor condition. In all, 5,108 camels were obtained, of which 3,063 died during the operations. In addition, between 600 and 700 mules were employed, which were obtained from India and South Africa. The mules were formed into two cadres, each cadre being subdivided into four sections. Each cadre consisted of :—

    1 British Non-Commissioned Officer.
    2 Indian Transport Assistants.

With 1 headman or 2 duffadars, 25 to 30 drivers, and 65 to 100 mules per section.

After July, 1903, 11 camel corps and a camel cart train were raised locally. The local supply of camels was much affected by the raiding of camels by the Mullah and by the demands of the expeditions under Colonel Swayne and General Manning, also by the attitude of many of the tribes, who preferred to sit on the fence and watch events rather than really help us in transport matters, perhaps fearing subsequent reprisals by the Mullah. The Ogaden tribes were indeed openly hostile to purchasers in their country. They, however, professed no allegiance to the British Government, and, though they dread the Abyssinians, they resent their authority. The organization of each camel corps is given in the accompanying table :—

*Local camel corps.*

ORGANIZATION of Locally Raised Camel Corps.

| Particulars | | Section. | Half Troop. | Troop. | Sub-Division. | Corps. | Remarks. |
|---|---|---|---|---|---|---|---|
| Lifting power | Mds. | 33 | 132 | 264 | 792 | 1,584 | At 3 maunds* per camel |
| Camels | Number | 12 | 48 | 96 | 294 | 588 | At an average cost not exceeding Rs. 125 per camel, plus Rs. 8 per saddle |
| Riding camels or ponies | ,, | .. | .. | .. | 2 | 4 | 2 per sub-division: for Officers and British Non-commissioned Officers |
| Officers | ,, | .. | .. | .. | .. | 2 | In lieu of Kote-Jemadars |
| British Non-commissioned Officers | ,, | .. | .. | .. | .. | 2 | 2 1st class at Rs. 60 per mensem |
| Jemadars or Transport Assistants | ,, | .. | .. | 1 | 3 | 6 | 2 2nd ,, Rs. 50 ,, <br> 2 3rd ,, Rs. 40 ,, |
| Duffadars | ,, | .. | 1 | 2 | 6 | 12 | At Rs. 20 for mensem each |
| Lance-Naicks (Drivers) | ,, | 1 | 4 | 8 | 24 | 48 | At Rs. 18 for Somalis and Arabs, per mensem each |
| Drivers | ,, | 3 | (a) 13 | (b) 27 | (c) 84 | (d) 168 | At Rs. 15 per mensem each |
| Drivers (Syces) | ,, | .. | .. | .. | .. | 2 | For 4 riding camels or 4 ponies. Pay as for other drivers |
| Transport Vety. Duffadars | ,, | .. | .. | .. | .. | 1 | Indian pay and allowances |
| Palan makers | ,, | .. | .. | 1 | 3 | 6 | At Rs. 20 per month for corps equipped with Aden saddles, none allowed for corps equipped with Herios |

*Maund = 80 lbs.

(a) Includes 1 spare.  (c) Includes 3 spare.
(c) Includes 10 spare.  (d) Includes 20 spare.

Note.—On joining Transport Assistants, Duffadars, Duffadars and Drivers and Syces received clothing as follows:—1 pair native shoes; 1 tobe (or 2 pairs of trousers); 1 blanket; 1 khaki blouse; 1 waterbottle; 1 pair putties (a fez was afterwards added). Each driver also received 1 Somali axe and 2 Chaguls, and to each squad was issued 3 Kerosene oil tins for cooking, and 3 iron plates. The equipment of each camel was 1 saddle with rope 40ft.; 1 loading rope, 60ft.; 1 leading rope, 20ft.; 1 pair hobbles.

As will be seen, each corps had 588 camels with a lifting power of 3 maunds (240 lbs.) per camel. When a local camel corps was formed, each camel was branded with a serial number and the number of the corps as well as the Government mark, thus :—

    On the near side neck    ..  ..  ..  S F F
    On the near flank, corps number, e.g.  ..  4 S C
    On the off flank, serial number in corps, e.g.  37

A roll of transport attendants by troops was kept and the numbers of the 3 camels of each driver were shown opposite his name.

The camel cart train consisted of 100 carts each of which carried 6 maunds in addition to the rations of camel and driver. With two camels per cart 8–10 maunds could be carried on a hard track. The train worked between Sheikh and Burao at first and subsequently between Elkadalanleh and Wadamago. *Arab camel cart train.*

Gelding camels were preferred for cart work, owing to their extra size and weight. The camels received grain and grass and worked best when watered every third day.

The organization of the train was as follows :—

| Particulars. | Section. | Half Troop. | Troop. | Train. | Remarks. |
|---|---|---|---|---|---|
| Lifting Power | 30 | 150 | 300 | 600 | At 6 maunds per cart. |
| Carts | 5 | 25 | 50 | 100 | |
| Camels, draught | 6 | 30 | 60 | (a) 125 | |
| Camels, riding, ponies or mules | — | — | — | 4 | 1 for Officer, 2 for British N.C. Officers, and 1 for Transport Vety. Duffadar. |
| Officer | — | — | — | 1 | |
| British N.C. Officers | — | — | — | 1 | |
| Interpreter | — | — | 1 | 1 | At 40 rs. per mensem. |
| Kote-Duffadars | — | — | 1 | 2 | ,, 40 ,, each, per mensem |
| Naicks | — | — | 2 | 4 | ,, 25 ,, ,, ,, |
| Lance-Naicks (Drivers) | 1 | 5 | 10 | 20 | ,, 18 ,, ,, ,, |
| Drivers | (b) 5 | (c) 25 | (d) 50 | (e) 105 | ,, 15 ,, ,, ,, |
| Syces (Drivers) | — | — | — | 3 | ,, 15 ,, ,, ,, |
| Transport Vety. Duffadar | — | — | — | 1 | Indian pay and allowances |
| Palan makers | — | — | 1 | 2 | ,, ,, |
| Carpenter | — | — | — | 1 | ,, ,, |
| Blacksmith | — | — | — | 1 | ,, ,, |
| Hammerman | — | — | — | 1 | ,, ,, |
| Bellowsboy | — | — | — | 1 | ,, ,, |

(a) One spare camel per section, with 5 added for corps.    (b) Includes 1 spare.
(c) Includes 5 spare.    (d) Includes 10 spare.    (e) Includes 25 spare.

**Indian Silladar camel corps.**

Four Indian Silladar camel corps arrived in July, 1903. They had 2,843 camels which carried 5 maunds each and grain at 6 lbs. per diem for 5 marches in addition to their ordinary loads.

The organization was as follows :—

| Particulars. | Section. | Half Troop. | Troop. | Sub-Div. | Corps. | Remarks. |
|---|---|---|---|---|---|---|
| Carrying Power | 55 | 275 | 550 | 1,100 | 4,400 | 81 sections at 55 Mds. per section. |
| British Officers | — | — | — | — | 1 | |
| Native ,, | — | — | — | 1 | 4 | |
| Quartermaster Duffadar | — | — | — | — | 1 | |
| Kote-Duffadar | — | — | 1 | 2 | 8 | |
| Naicks | — | 1 | 2 | 4 | 16 | |
| Lance-Naicks (surwans) | 1 | 5 | 10 | 20 | 81 | |
| Surwans | 4 | 20 | 40 | 80 | 243 | |
| Syces | — | — | — | — | 7 | For riding ponies. Paid for by supervising establishment. |
| Clerks | — | — | — | — | 2 | |
| Veterinary Assistants | — | — | — | 1 | 4 | |
| Palan makers | — | — | 1 | 2 | 8 | |
| Cooks | — | — | — | — | 3 | |
| Bhisties | — | — | — | — | 3 | |
| Dressers | — | — | — | 1 | 4 | |
| Camels | 12 | 60 | 120 | 240 | 972 | 81 sections of 12 each. |
| Ponies | — | — | — | — | 13 | For Native Officers and Kote-Duffadars. |
| Officers' Chargers | — | — | — | — | 2 | |
| ,, Private Pony | — | — | — | — | 1 | |
| British Officers' Servants | — | — | — | — | 2 | |
| ,, ,, Syces | — | — | — | — | 2 | |
| ,, ,, Grass-cutter | — | — | — | — | 1 | |
| Native Officers' Genl. Servants | — | — | — | — | 2 | |

**Hired camel corps from India.**

One hired camel corps reached Berbera in October, 1903, and consisted of 972 Baluch camels. These animals as they came from cold countries and were long-haired, were not suitable for work in Somaliland.

**Army Service Corps.**

Two companies Army Service Corps, the 15th and 22nd, arrived at Berbera from South Africa on 31st July, 1903. Their strength was :—

      6 officers.
      2 warrant officers.
      60 rank and file.

11 civilian conductors
217 natives (Africans).
46 horses.
900 mules.
80 buck wagons.
4 water carts.

These companies worked between Berbera and Bihendula or Wagon's Rust. Each wagon had 10 mules and carried 4,000 lbs., *i.e.*, 3,000 lbs. stores to be delivered, and 5 days' forage and rations.

The Natal buck wagon was not considered suitable for the country, being found too heavy (1½ tons) and not broad enough in the tyre.

Three Ekka trains were obtained from India in July, 1903. Ekka trains. These trains were not a success as Ekka trains, but most of the ponies were subsequently worked in pack. They were organized as follows :—

| Particulars. | Section. | Half Troop. | Troop. | Sub-Div. | Corps. | Remarks. |
|---|---|---|---|---|---|---|
| Lifting Power ... | 25 | 100 | 200 | 800 | 1,600 | At 5 mds. per Ekka, exclusive of ration for men and ponies and men's kits and water, for 2 days for men. |
| Ekkas ... | 5 | 20 | 40 | 160 | 320 | |
| Ponies ... | 5 | 20 | 40 | 160 | 355 | Includes 32 ponies spare and 3 riding. |
| Brit'sh Officer ... | — | — | — | — | 1 | |
| British N.C.O. ... | — | — | — | — | 1 | |
| Native Officers .. | — | — | — | 1 | 2 | |
| Havildars ... | — | — | 1 | 4 | 8 | |
| Naicks ... | — | 1 | 2 | 8 | 16 | |
| Lance-Naicks (Drivers) | 1 | 4 | 8 | 32 | 64 | |
| Drivers ... | 4 | 16 | 32 | 128 | 288 | Includes 32 spare drivers. |
| Syces ... | — | — | — | — | 3 | |
| Veterinary Assistants | — | — | — | 1 | 2 | |
| Clerk ... | — | — | — | — | 1 | |
| Shoeing-smiths ... | — | — | 1 | 4 | 8 | |
| Saddlers ... | — | — | 1 | 4 | 8 | |
| Carpenters ... | — | — | — | 2 | 4 | |
| Blacksmiths ... | — | — | — | 1 | 2 | |
| Hammermen ... | — | — | — | 1 | 2 | |
| Bellowsboys ... | — | — | — | 1 | 2 | |
| Interpreter ... | — | — | — | — | 1 | |

Generally speaking, wheeled transport was not found suitable for work in Somaliland.

**Porter corps.** A porter corps was raised at Rawal Pindi and arrived at Berbera on the 5th September, 1903. These men worked at Berbera in moving supplies, &c. At this work they were found useful, but not much good at unloading ships. They were also used in well sinking, telegraph line work, grass cutting and as mule attendants. They were principally Punjabi Mahommedans and their organization was :—

     1 British Officer.
     1 Non-commissioned Officer (Supply and Transport Corps).
     2 Jemadars.
     5 Havildars.
  10 Naicks.
  20 Lance-naicks.
460 Coolies.
     1 Clerk.

They were divided into five companies and each company into four sections. Coolies or porters were paid at the rate of 10 rs. 8 a. per month, with rations and clothing.

**Arab coolie corps.** An Arab coolie corps came from Aden and other parts of Arabia. The men were employed at Berbera in unloading ships, unloading cargoes from lighters and in the supply sections.

For one ship the rough estimate was :—

    140 to unload ship.
     50 to unload lighters at pierhead.
    100 to carry goods from pierhead to head of tramway.

The strength of the Corps was :—

| | |
|---|---:|
| Maccadums | 4 |
| Submaccadums | 3 |
| Coolies | 350 |
| | 357 |

under a British officer, divided into 4 gangs. (It was

recommended that 2 British non-commissioned officers should be added).

The rate of pay was :—

15 rs. per month for coolies, with rations but no clothing.
20 rs.   ,,   ,,   submaccadums   ,,   ,,
30 rs.   ,,   ,,   maccadums   ,,   ,,   ,,

The Commandant inflicted only two punishments—fines and dismissal.

On the whole, though the Arab coolie under strict supervision was a better worker than the Indian, the Indian coolie was preferred, being—

The cheaper.

The steadier worker.

More easily managed, and as he was a native of India, officers and non-commissioned officers who understood Hindustani could understand his language and his ways.

Somali coolies were also employed at 12 annas per diem without rations. They worked well on piece work, but were reported to be lazy, undisciplined and undependable. *Somali Coolies.*

Seventy-five pairs of Kajawahs weighing 37 lbs. per pair were made up locally for ambulance work and carried 150 sick. Some camel carts were also provided with hoods and lying down accommodation. *Ambulance transport.*

The Indian transport mules were organized as an Indian mule corps. Some Abyssinian mules were added, and though only $11\frac{1}{2}$ hands high, they carried 2 maunds very well. This mule corps was employed in bringing stores up the Sheikh Pass, thus saving camel transport at that point, where the road was steep. It was not brought south of Burao owing to water difficulties, but it was worked up the steep ascent from Las Khorai to save camel transport. *Indian mule transport.*

A light tramway was laid along the pier at Berbera and eventually linked the landing stage with the various supply sections at the base. It was considered that this was a *Tramway Berbera.*

**Purchase of animals.**

most necessary provision, and that the line should be a double one.

The total purchases of animals during the fourth expedition to the end of March, 1904, were :—

|  | Number. | Average Price. | | |
|---|---|---|---|---|
|  |  | Rs. | a. | p. |
| Camels | 13,245 | 120 | 1 | 2 |
| Donkeys | 117 | 30 | 2 | 7 |
| Pack bullocks | 16 | 50 | 0 | 0 |

The following table refers to camel purchasing only :—

| When Purchased. | Where Purchased. | Number of Camels Purchased. | Average Price Paid. | | |
|---|---|---|---|---|---|
|  |  |  | Rs. | a. | p. |
| 1903— |  |  |  |  |  |
| July | Somaliland | 573 | 103 | 4 | 0 |
| July | Abyssinia | 338 | 85 | 8 | 0 |
| August | Somaliland | 1,062 | 113 | 4 | 0 |
| September | Somaliland | 1,359 | 109 | 4 | 0 |
| October | Somaliland | 1,830 | 118 | 3 | 0 |
| October | Arabia | 321 | 195 | 0 | 0 |
| October | Abyssinia | 154 | 120 | 0 | 0 |
| November | Somaliland | 1,973 | 120 | 10 | 0 |
| November | Arabia | 226 | 190 | 0 | 0 |
| November | Abyssinia | 89 | 120 | 0 | 0 |
| December | Somaliland | 2,014 | 122 | 3 | 11 |
| December | Abyssinia | 108 | 120 | 0 | 0 |
| 1904— |  |  |  |  |  |
| January | Somaliland | 1,383 | 121 | 6 | 1 |
| February | Somaliland | 1,279 | 121 | 14 | 2 |
| March | Somaliland | 536 | 114 | 15 | 11 |

The best district for purchasing was the western area of British Somaliland with the following centres :—

| *Hargeisa District* | .. | .. | Hargeisa. |
|  |  |  | Dallo. |
|  |  |  | Debile. |
| *Bulhar District* | .. | .. | Bulhar. |
| (For Habr Awal.) |  |  | Gondarkar. |
| *Zeila District* | .. | .. | Zeila. |

| | |
|---|---|
| *Ogaden Country* | Sassamine. |
| | Harrardiggit |
| *Burao District* | Burao |
| (For **Musa Abukr**). | Duberin |
| *Coast East of Berbera* | Mait. |

The purchasing officers recommended the following procedure in camel purchasing :—

Agents should be sent in advance to warn the people that camels were required The purchasing officer should divide his area into sections with a centre for each section. On his arrival at the centre the camels should be divided into two or three classes, and a fixed rate should be paid for each class. The purchasing officer must himself divide the camels into classes, and the same system should be adopted in each area for dividing the camels into classes. Centres of purchasing areas should not be too close to one another, as they are in that case liable to interfere with one another. The Somalis are adepts at concealing diseases and weaknesses by making the camels roll in wet mud, by patching old sores over with hair, by blowing out thin camels with water, and by similar devices, therefore each camel must be carefully examined. It was found useful to erect a zariba at each place so that only one camel at a time could be admitted. Payment should always be made at the end of a day's purchases. A good interpreter is a necessity, and when buying near the Abyssinian frontier it is advisable that an official of the Abyssinian Government should accompany the purchasing officer. Grazing guards are also important, and centres should be partly selected on account of facilities for grazing afforded near them. It is well to let the tribes know beforehand that it is no use bringing sickly, weak, or young camels. The brands should be carefully selected, as Somalis copy them easily, and besides branding irons a veterinary chest, headropes, mange dressings and a spring balance and scales should be taken.

The loss in camels was principally caused by exhaustion Losses in camels.

which was produced by conditions which are the inevitable result of endeavours to meet the military situation, and by—

The natural difficulties of the country.

The absence of sufficient grazing at times;

The deficiency in water and the necessity of getting troops at any cost from one waterhole to another in the desert.

The necessity of working the camels at times when the sun was up.

The impossibility of feeding them with grain at great distances from the base.

The impossibility of allowing them sufficient rest.

Carelessness of attendants unless incessantly supervised.

Losses were also caused by poison (principally from the Irgin plant) and pneumonia.

Care of Camels.

The following points represent the result of the experience of the campaign :—

Grooming is unnecessary, but backs may be rubbed when saddles are taken off.

Animals should be unloaded at the first, and loaded at the last possible moment, and should be kept at graze as long as possible. The best hours for camels to graze are between 6 and 11 A.M. and 4 to 7 P.M. The camel is a slow feeder, and should have 5 or 6 hours grazing a day if possible.

On cold nights saddles are best left on, unless blankets are provided.

Grass should be given at night. This can be cut by day or on the march.

Time must be given to transport drivers to cook and sleep. Overworked, underfed drivers means bad transport.

Grazing grounds should be visited by a British officer or by non-commissioned officers, otherwise drivers, to prevent them straying, are apt to tie the camels up or herd them together, thus preventing them grazing.

When grain is given it should be given in the evening: 4 lbs. per diem is enough for Somali camels and 6 lbs. for Indian camels. Grain-fed camels last much longer than those which are merely grazed.

Somali camels should be watered at least every fourth day, Indian camels every other day. Camels should not be watered immediately before marching nor should they be given a big drink on an empty stomach.

When double marches are made the best hours to march are from 4 A.M. to 9 A.M. (say 13 miles) and from 3 P.M. to 5.30 P.M. (say 7 miles). If the march be under 15 miles, it is better to start earlier in the morning and complete the distance in one march. Not more than 3 camels should be tied together in one string.*

All camels should be inspected sitting down once a day, so that their backs can be seen.

---

\* The following extract from Standing Orders is given to show how discipline on the march was maintained :—

*Discipline on the March.*

The success of a march, from a transport point of view, depends on the rapidity with which it is accomplished without animals being overdriven. Every attendant should have it thoroughly impressed on him the danger of delays and of long line. He should be trained to immediately clear to one side should he have to halt.

Transport should move on the very broadest front possible. It is better to have the transport of units mixed up on a broad front than to have it in perfect rotation in a single line.

If it is found necessary to diminish the front this should be done before arriving at the obstacle.

At all difficult points it is the duty of the officer in charge to remain himself, or to detail a competent subordinate, who will remain there until every animal has passed. The officer should go in advance to the obstacle so as to anticipate the action to be taken on the arrival of the leading animal.

The tendency to straggle and tail off must be remedied by all concerned using every endeavour and taking every opportunity to close up. Closing up should not be effected by overdriving animals, but halts and checks should be taken advantage of.

**Hiring of Camels. System.**

A warrant officer and interpreter visited the ground where the hired camels were collected, and took the numbers of the camels presented for hire. The owners came to office about 9 A.M. The names of the head men of the batches of camels, their tribe and destination were registered, as also were the advances (Rs.2 per camel) that were given to them. The owners then left to purchase food, &c., for the journey, and appeared again at 2 P.M. on the convoy ground, where their loads were awaiting them. They loaded up under the supervision of the same warrant officer and interpreter, and marched off with the stores and way-bills.

On their return, and on the production of the receipted duplicate way-bills, the owners, according to the names entered in the register, were paid. The owners, once persuaded to go, carried out their contracts very honestly.

The hired camels were accompanied by baladiers, *i.e.*, armed Somalis, who were provided with arms and ammunition by the Base Supply and Transport Officer.

The scale of baladiers was four per 100 camels, increased for a short period during January and February, 1904, to six per 100 camels, in order to inspire confidence to induce the men to go forward to Wadamago.

Baladiers were paid 8 annas a day, and received free rations.*

---

The driver should be ordered to always get past any animals halted. Obstacles on the road should be removed, if possible, by an advance party of a few men well in front.

The duties of the Transport officers and supervising staff may briefly be summed up as follows :—

(1) Anticipating arrangements for passing obstacles by going on ahead to them.
(2) Maintaining as broad a front as possible.
(3) Closing up at every opportunity.

\* Ba'adiers are a class of Somalis who at all times earn their living by acting as guides and guards to convoys; for instance, a Karia marching from Berbera to the Ogaden would employ baladiers, three or four to 100 camels, and pay them 12 annas per camel. The Consulate lends rifles and ammunition to recognised baladiers..

The total number of camels employed month by month since November, 1902, and also the various rates of hire that prevailed from time to time, were as follows:—

|  | Hired camels obtained |
|---|---|
| **1902.** | |
| November | 986 |
| December | 2,901 |
| **1903.** | |
| January | 3,075 |
| February | 1,929 |
| March | 1,905 |
| April | 1,309 |
| May | 731 |
| June | 229 |
| July | 385 |
| August | 593 |
| September | 533 |
| October | 1,559 |
| November | 1,398 |
| December | 603 |
| **1904.** | |
| January, up to 17th | 317 |

The rates of hire from Berbera that prevailed from time to time were as follows:—

| Garrero. | Rs. |
|---|---|
| November, 1902, to March, 1903 | 15 |
| March, 1903, and on | 17 |

---

A register is maintained in which is recorded the names of the men, tribe, &c., the number of rifles and amount of ammunition given to them, the date on which they start, &c.

Baladiers are allowed pay for the number of days only that are necessary for the performance of the return journey to the place to which they may be sent.

### Bohotle.

| | |
|---|---|
| January, 1903 | 20 |
| January, 1903, to 12th March, 1903 | 22 |
| 12th March, and on | 25 |

### Kirrit.

| | |
|---|---|
| Before August, 1903 | 15 |
| August, 1903, to October, 1903 | 16 |
| October, 1903, and on | 18 |

### Burao.

| | |
|---|---|
| November, 1902, to March, 1903 | 10 |
| March, 1903, to January, 1904 | 12 |
| January, 1904, and on | 14 |

### Sheikh.

| | |
|---|---|
| November, 1902, to April, 1903 | 5 |
| April, 1903, to October, 1903 | 6 |
| October, 1903, and on | 7 |

### Las Dureh.

| | |
|---|---|
| December, 1902, to March, 1903 | 7 |
| March, 1903, to October, 1903 | 8 |
| October, 1903, to November, 1903 | 10 |
| February (Government camels used in interval) | 16 |

### Hargeisa.

| | |
|---|---|
| Up to March, 1903 | 9 |
| Since March, 1903 | 11 |

The natural supply of hired camels, *i.e.*, the supply without any pressure being brought to bear, seems to be governed by the season of the year. A camel owner owns a certain number of burden, milk and eating camels, besides sheep and goats. His wife and children look after his herds.

In the rainy season, when water is abundant, his burden camels, or some of them, are available for hire; he will probably keep enough burden camels to move his hut, &c., and hire the balance. In the dry weather his animals are apparently able to exist on herbage without water, the grass round the permanent water places is soon eaten, and the flocks and herds must move further and further away from such places; the Somali at these times requires his camels to carry water to his family, and he will not then willingly let them out for hire.

The Indian palan (camel saddle) was recommended for use (the Herio or Somali saddle being universally condemned), but Colonel Yeilding was of opinion that the material should be better. viz. :—

<small>Camel Gear.</small>

> That the outer covering should be of goat's hair (jutt).
>
> The inner lining should be of good stout blanket.
>
> The stuffing should be of grass, "punni gas" preferred. If not, Nahr (or wheat straw) grass. Wool and tow are not recommended.
>
> The arches should be of strong elastic wood (shesum, English ash or greenheart).
>
> The side bars, three on each side, should be bamboos, with an extra bar fitted above them. This extra bar should be above the level of the opening for the camel's hump, and should project 6 or 8 inches beyond the others to the front and rear. These bars should always be fixed to saddles required to carry ammunition or other small and heavy boxes.
>
> Ropes should be made of goat's hair or camel's hair, not cotton coir or hemp rope.
>
> The rear arch should be carefully rounded so as to touch the back and sides everywhere, but the front arch should rest on the sides of the withers only and not on the top. Less stuffing is required in the

centre than at the ends. The saddles should not touch the camel's hump. No large seam should be under the saddle. The rear point of the saddle should be 10 to 12 inches above the level of the camel's back and 8 inches above the level of the centre opening of the saddle. In stuffing a saddle, it should be remembered that a camel's motion is fore and aft; the withers and hips naturally resist this motion and tend to keep the saddle in its place, assisted by the hump. If the saddle is fitted throughout to the camel's back, the friction bears upon the ribs, and it is this part of the saddle which should be hollowed out to obviate galls over the ribs. Camel saddles are generally made too long and rub the animals over the hip bones.

*Camel attendants.* Opinions differed as to the personal qualities of the Somali, but it seemed to be generally agreed that, for work in Somaliland he was the best camel attendant. He is a magnificent marcher and easy to feed and water, and is a natural camel man and does not ill-treat his animals. Both he and the Arab require much supervision. The latter is more hardworking and quicker than the Somali, but he often ill-treats his animals, and overdrives them and ties them up when grazing. Not much difficulty was found in obtaining a sufficient number of capable headmen, who had sufficient intelligence and influence to manage their squads and to supervise the animals told off to their squads. Only men who were capable of acting as interpreters were appointed Transport Jemadars or assistants, and they generally proved satisfactory. They spoke Somali and either English or Hindustani. It was considered that all transport attendants should be provided with followers' books on the Indian system.

The rates of pay of Somalis were :—

Jemadars or Transport Assistants—

| | |
|---|---|
| Class I  | 60 rs. per month. |
| „ II  | 50 rs. „ |
| „ III  | 40 rs. „ |
| Duffadars  | 20 rs. „ |
| Lce Naicks  | 18 rs. „ |
| Drivers  | 15 rs. „ |

The annexed table gives the number of casualties among transport animals from July, 1903, to March, 1904 :— *Casualties.*

## CASUALTIES AMONG TRANSPORT ANIMALS.

| Months. | Indian Silladar Camels. | | | | | Hired Camels, Baluch. | | | | | Arab and Somali Camels. | | | | | | Mules. | | | | | Ekka Ponies. | | | | | Donkeys. | | | | |
|---|---|---|---|---|---|---|---|---|---|---|---|---|---|---|---|---|---|---|---|---|---|---|---|---|---|---|---|---|---|---|---|
| | Died. | Destroyed. | Lost or Strayed. | Cast or Sold. | Total. | Died. | Destroyed. | Lost or Strayed. | Cast or Sold. | Total. | Died. | Destroyed. | Lost or Strayed. | Cast or Sold. | Issued as Rations. | Total. | Died. | Destroyed. | Lost or Strayed. | Cast or Sold. | Total. | Died. | Destroyed. | Lost or Strayed. | Cast or Sold. | Total. | Died. | Destroyed. | Lost or Strayed. | Cast or Sold. | Total. |
| July, 1903 | 152 | 4 | | | 156 | | | | | | 19 | 7 | | | | 26 | 27 | 4 | | | 31 | | | | | | | | | | |
| August, 1903 | | | | | | | | | | | 258 | 107 | 10 | 54 | | 429 | 16 | 5 | | | 21 | | | | | | | | | | |
| September, 1903 | 60 | 16 | | | 76 | | | | | | 221 | 133 | 21 | | | 375 | 2 | 4 | | | 6 | | | | | 1 | | | | | 1 |
| October, 1903 | 108 | 12 | | 1 | 120 | 6 | | | | 6 | 403 | 238 | 7 | | | 648 | 5 | 5 | | | 10 | 4 | 7 | | | 10 | 3 | | | | 3 |
| November, 1903 | 131 | 9 | 2 | 1 | 143 | 23 | | | | 23 | 485 | 290 | 35 | | 10 | 820 | 6 | 1 | | | 7 | 19 | 15 | 1 | 9 | 43 | 2 | | | | 2 |
| December, 1903 | 137 | 14 | 5 | | 156 | 34 | 1 | | | 35 | 695 | 452 | 34 | | | 1,181 | 9 | 1 | | | 10 | 48 | 101 | | | 149 | 1 | | | | 1 |
| January, 1904 | 380 | 7 | 3 | | 400 | 48 | 1 | | | 49 | 952 | 302 | 4 | | 113 | 1,371 | 5 | | | | 5 | 5 | 30 | | | 35 | 2 | | 2 | 8 | 30 |
| February, 1904 | 223 | 50 | | | 273 | 133 | 7 | | | 141 | 1,818 | 271 | 8 | | 153 | 2,250 | 6 | 1 | | | 6 | 7 | 26 | | | 33 | 1 | 1 | | 8 | 11 |
| March, 1904 | | | | | | 39 | 59 | | | 98 | 1,339 | 1,072* | 2 | 71 | 64 | 2,548 | 21 | 4 | | | 28 | 14 | 22 | | | 46 | 6 | 6 | | 1 | 13 |

* Includes 43 casualties amongst Somali camels.

The following tables show— *Transport of equipment, baggage, &c.*

(a) How equipment, &c., usually carried on obligatory mules in India was carried with the field force when operating away from the lines of communication between Berbera and Bohotle.

| No. | Item. | How Carried by British and Native Infantry, including Pioneer Regiments. |
|---|---|---|
| 1 | Machine gun section | On mules |
| 2 | Greatcoats if taken | With kits on camels |
| 3 | Ammunition | 80 rounds per rifle on mules<br>200 ,, ,, camels |
| 4 | Entrenching tools | On camels |
| 5 | Kajawahs, mule, S.A. | On mules or camels |
| 6 | Water tanks and water chaguls | On camels |
| 7 | Medical equipment, tentage and baggage of hospital establishment | 1 mule for medical panniers<br>1 mule for water for surgical purposes<br>Remainder on camels |
| 8 | Pioneer equipment | On mules |
| 9 | Signalling equipment | ,, ,, |
| 10 | Cooking pots | On camels |
| 11 | Reserve rations | ,, ,, |

(b) Scale of personal baggage and tentage allowed to the force.

(a) Lines of communication scale.
(b) Operation scale.

| Classification. | (a) Lines of Communication Scale. | | (b) Operation Scale. | Remarks. |
|---|---|---|---|---|
| | Baggage. | Tentage. | Baggage only. | |
| 1. British Commissioned Officers. | 2 Camels (non-Indian) per officer (c). | | 2 officers per camel (c) non-Indian. | |
| 2. Officers ... ... | Normal (d) | Normal (d) | ½ normal scale (d). | |
| 3. British Officers with Honorary Rank. | 80 lbs. (c) | 80 lbs. (c) | 80 lbs. (c) | (c). Includes mess stores, servants' kits and horses' kits in addition to tentage and officers' kits. |
| 4. Warrant Officers and Assistant Surgeons. | 70 lbs. (c) | 40 lbs. (c) | 60 lbs. (c) | |
| 5. British N.C.O.'s, employed as clerks. | 80 lbs. (c) | — | 40 lbs. (c) | |
| 6. Indians employed as clerks. | 40 lbs. (c) | — | 30 lbs. (c) | |
| 7. Storekeepers and Agents. | 40 lbs. (c) | 40 lbs. | 30 lbs. (c) | |
| 8. Native Officers and Hospital Assistants. | 40 lbs. | 40 lbs. | 30 lbs. | |
| 9. British N.C.O.'s and men. | 40 lbs. | 15 per bell tent and 16 per G.S. tent, 160 lbs. | 20 lbs. | Exclusive of cooking pots. |
| 10. Native N.C.O.'s and men. | 30 lbs. | 20 per G.S. tent, 160 lbs. | 15 lbs. | |
| 11. Followers ... ... | 15 lbs. | — | 10 lbs. | Inclusive of cooking pots. |

(d) As per F. S. Equipment Tables, Staff, Section I., Table III.

**Despatch and receipt of stores.** The following was the procedure laid down in Standing Orders regarding the despatch and receipt of stores:—

(1) All way-bills will be marked at the top with the name of despatching depôt and that of destination, for example:—

From Berbera.
For Burao.

(2) All three forms of the way-bills will be signed and dated by consignor immediately below the last article entered on the way-bill.

(3) In handing over stores to convoy officers, the following procedure will be adopted:—Stores to be laid out as found most convenient for loading, and each kind of store separate. Convoy officers will be responsible that the number of packages is correct as way-billed and that bags are intact Convoy officers will hand over stores in a similar manner at destination, and not simply count the number of packages.

(4) Despatching supply and transport, officers are to be most careful that the bags despatched are of full weight; they should weigh a percentage to test them. This is most important so as to prevent a loss of carrying power.

*Despatch of Stores on Government Transport.*—Despatching supply and transport officers will make out way-bills on counterfoil, triplicate, and quadruplicate only.

Convoy officers will sign counterfoil and receive triplicate and quadruplicate forms.

Triplicate forms will be receipted by the consignee and returned by the transport officer to the despatching supply and transport officer, to support the " writes off." The consignee will note on triplicate the decade accounts in which the stores will be found credited. The quadruplicate copy will be handed over by the transport officer to the consignee, and submitted as a voucher in support of the credits. The convoy officer will obtain from the consignee a simple receipt in his note book, quoting number and date to way-bill " contents received correct," or, should there be any loss, the words " with the exception of " added with the loss in detail.

Each receiving supply and transport officer will keep a convoy officer's book, in which should be entered the number and date of each way-bill received (detail of way-bill is not necessary), leaving a column for loss. The convoy officer should sign to all losses, giving a brief explanation of the cause.

The following was considered to be the best method of managing stores on convoy duty :— *Management of stores on convoy duty.*

*For Indian Silladar Camel Corps—*

(1) The Commanding Officer stated the carrying power of the corps after inspection of camels and distributed among the troops. He himself took over the convoy and weighed bags making notes of any damage or shortage.

(2) Each native officer then took over the amount to be carried by his sub-division and handed over to the kote-duffadars, who were assisted by the naicks.

(3) On the arrival of the camels each naick showed the exact amount to be loaded by his half troop, and as each surwan knew the weight his camels had to carry, they loaded up at once. Naicks and lance-naicks were responsible that each camel took its proper load. If possible all packages of the same article were carried by one troop or half troop.

(4) Kote-duffadars had a list of the articles carried by their troop. They and their naicks explained to every man the contents of his package so that on arrival each man could go straight to where his particular load was to be placed.

(5) Lance-naicks were responsible to naicks that the section handed over its loads complete, naicks to kote-duffadars, kote-duffadars to section commanders.

*For Somali Camel Corps—*

(1) The Commanding Officer apportioned the maundage to be carried by each half troop in accordance with the number of 2-maund or 3-maund camels.

(2) The Commanding Officer handed over the stores to be carried by their several commands to the jemadars who handed them over to the duffadars.

(3) The Commanding Officer kept a list of the number of bags and boxes allotted to each half troop.

(4) On arrival at destination each duffadar handed over his loads to the commanding officer or his assistant separately and he was held responsible for deficiencies. Sugar was always carried under the personal charge of a duffadar.

### Supply.

Captain H. de B. Codrington, who was Chief Supply Officer with the Obbia force, arrived at Obbia on the 16th January, 1903. There having been no Supply and Transport Officer present, great confusion existed and some time elapsed before the department was in working order. Three months' supplies had been sent from India for the Indian Contingent, and six months' supplies came with the contingents from South Africa.

The state of affairs at Berbera was very similar. Captain L. M. R. Deas, who arrived at Berbera on the 10th November, 1902, brought with him four months' supplies for half a native battalion, but he had to set about providing supplies for the force on the Berbera–Bohotle lines of communication, and from the 28th March the entire force was supplied from Berbera. This was mainly accomplished by local purchase.

Major-General Egerton, on the 26th October, 1903, authorized the officer commanding lines of communication to deal with routine requirements of the force and required him to maintain a three months' supply. In addition, in a memorandum of the above date he informed him that :—

(1) Demands for requirements other than medical should be addressed to the War Office.
(2) Medical supplies should be demanded from India.

Supplies were obtained from two sources :— *Sources of supply.*

(1) By requisition on the War Office, who gave the necessary orders for the supplies to be sent either from England or India. (Heads of departments notified the officer commanding lines of communication of their requirements so that he was able to give the War Office two months' notice by cable.)
(2) By local purchase. No supplies except grazing, milk, fuel, and animals were available in the interior.

In 1903, three supply depôts were formed on the Obbia lines of communication at Lodobal, Dibit, Galkayu, Bera and Badwein, besides the base depôt at Obbia. On the Berbera–Bohotle lines of communication depôts were formed at Bihendula, Sheikh, Burao, Garrero and Bohotle, besides the base depôt at Berbera. *Supply Depôts.*

The base for supply and transport at Berbera was re-arranged in sections on the Indian system by August, 1903, and supply depôts under officers were formed at :—

| | | | |
|---|---|---|---|
| Wagons Rust | .. | 37 miles south of | Berbera. |
| Sheikh | .. .. | 47 " | Berbera. |
| Burao | .. .. | 87 " | Berbera. |
| Kirrit | .. .. | 143 " | Berbera. (Used up to 31st December, 1903, as an advanced base, and then abandoned, water having failed.) |

| | | | |
|---|---|---|---|
| Wadamago | 153 miles | south of | Berbera. |
| Eil Dab | 170 | ,, | Berbera. |
| Dariali | 243 | ,, | Berbera. |
| Gaolo | 313 | ,, | Berbera. |
| Halin | 320 | ,, | Berbera. |
| Las Khorai | East of Berbera (by sea). | | |

Supply stages were also formed at :—

| | | | |
|---|---|---|---|
| Bihendula | 23½ miles | from | Berbera. |
| Gololi | 61 | ,, | Berbera. |
| Elkadalanleh | 102 | ,, | Berbera. |
| Yaguri | 202 | ,, | Berbera. |
| Bohotle | 206 | ,, | Berbera. |
| Hargeisa | 90 | ,, | Berbera. |
| Aiyu | 23 | ,, | Las Khorai. |

And troops, other than those engaged with the operating force under the direct orders of Major-General Sir C. Egerton, were supplied at :—

| | | | |
|---|---|---|---|
| Las Dureh | 81 miles | from | Berbera. |
| Hope Springs | 67 | ,, | Berbera. |
| Shimber Berris | 123 | ,, | Berbera. |
| Ber | 105 | ,, | Berbera. |
| Galadi | 308 | ,, | Berbera. |
| Waran | 73 | ,, | Berbera. |
| El Afweina | 179 | ,, | Berbera. |
| Baran | 44 | ,, | Las Khorai. |

*Rations.*  During the expeditions under Colonel Swayne, the officers, when with the field force, carried rations for four months under their own arrangements. The men carried 2 lbs. of dates as an emergency ration, and eating camels were driven along with the force. After leaving Burao in May, 1902, till the return of the force to Bohotle in October, the men's rations consisted of meat only, chiefly sheep and camels captured from the enemy. The tribesmen made their own arrangements for water and food, unless captures were made. On the lines of communication, rice and dates and grain for riding camels were sent up by hired transport from Berbera. These articles were bought at Berbera, where a reserve was kept. When the field force returned to Bohotle, rations for all were sent up from Berbera.

The following scale of daily rations applies to the periods under Generals Manning and Egerton.

<small>Scale of daily rations during 3rd and 4th Expeditions.</small>

### British Troops.

| | |
|---|---|
| Flour, bread or biscuits | 1 lb. |
| Meat | 1 ,, |
| Potatoes | 4 ozs. |
| Onions | 4 ,, |
| Jam | 4 ,, |
| Tea, coffee, or chocolate | $1\frac{1}{7}$ ,, |
| Sugar | $2\frac{2}{7}$ ,, |
| Rice | $4\frac{4}{7}$ ,, |
| Salt | $\frac{2}{7}$ ,, |
| Pepper | $\frac{1}{7}$ ,, |
| Dal | $4\frac{4}{7}$ ,, |
| Candle | (1 for officers only) |
| Dried fruit | $2\frac{2}{7}$ ozs. |
| Firewood | 10 lbs. for officers |
| ,, | 4 lbs. for men |
| Worcestershire sauce | 1 bottle for 10 days |

NOTE.—(a) When fractional quantities of jam were indented for, a full tin was issued for fractions of ½ lb. or more, but none for fractions less than ½ lb.

Coffee and chocolate were issued only when available.

(b) Worcestershire sauce and dried fruits were issued only when available.

(c) Candles were issued to officers only.

### Indian Troops and Followers.

| | |
|---|---|
| Atta or rice | 1 lb. 8 ozs. |
| Dal | 4 " |
| Ghi | 2 " |
| Salt | ½ " |
| Gur | 1 " |
| Meat | 28 ozs. a week |

Men who did not eat meat received gur instead, on the scale of 4½ ozs. a week.

| | |
|---|---|
| Potatoes | 2 ozs. |
| or | |
| Onions or other vegetables | 4 " |
| or | |
| Dried fruit | 2 " |
| Tea | ⅓ " |
| Chillies | ⅙ " |
| Turmeric | ⅙ " |
| Garlic | ⅙ " |
| Ginger | ⅓ " |

### Extras.

Rum, ½ dram, 25 U. P., as an extra, was issued on medical recommendation.

Limejuice, 2 ozs. per man per week  } On medical
Gur, ¼ oz. for each ½ oz. limejuice } recommendation.

### African and Somali Troops and Followers.

| | |
|---|---|
| Rice | 1 lb. |
| Dates | 8 ozs. |
| Onions | 4 " |
| Meat (thrice a week in lieu of 8 ozs. rice) | 1 lb. |
| Ghi | 2 ozs. |
| Salt | ⅛ oz. |
| Potatoes (at the coast only) | 2 ozs. |

South African Natives with Army Service Corps.

| | |
|---|---|
| Biscuit or flour | 1 lb. |
| Meat | 1 ,, |
| Coffee | ⅓ oz. |
| Sugar | 2 ozs. |
| Salt | ½ oz. |
| Pepper | 1/16 ,, |
| Onions (if available) | 4 ozs. |

Bi-weekly.

| | |
|---|---|
| Limejuice | ½ oz. |
| Sugar | ¼ ,, |

*Animals.*

### Horses.

| | |
|---|---|
| Grain (gram, oats, or barley) | 6 lbs. |
| Bran | 2 ,, |
| Salt | 1 oz. |
| Hay (if available) | 20 lbs. |

### Mountain Battery Ordnance Mules.

| | |
|---|---|
| Grain (gram or barley) | 4 lbs. |
| Bran | 2 ,, |
| Salt | ⅔ oz. |
| Hay or bhoosa (if available) | 20 lbs. |

Mountain Battery Baggage and A. T.* 1st Class Mules and all Ponies.

| | |
|---|---|
| Grain (for mules, gram or barley; for ponies, gram, oats, or barley) | 6 lbs. |
| Salt | ⅔ oz. |
| Hay or bhoosa (if available) | 15 lbs. |

---

* Army Transport.

### M. B. and A. T. 2nd Class Mules.

| | |
|---|---|
| Grain (gram or barley) .. .. .. | 5 lbs. |
| Salt .. .. .. .. .. .. | ⅔ oz. |
| Hay or bhoosa (if available) .. .. | 13 lbs. |

### Bikanir Camels.

Grain (gram or barley) 6 lbs. or 12 lbs. if no missa bhoosa, or hay was given and grazing was not available; with grazing 8 lbs. might be given.

| | |
|---|---|
| Salt .. .. .. .. .. .. | 1½ ozs. |
| Alum .. .. .. .. .. | 12 ,, |
| Gur .. .. .. .. .. | 1 lb. 8 ozs. |
| Missa bhoosa or hay (if available).. .. | 20 lbs. |

### Indian Camels.

| | |
|---|---|
| Grain (gram or barley) .. .. .. | 6 lbs. |
| Salt .. .. .. .. .. .. | 1½ ozs. |
| Hay (at the base).. .. .. .. | 20 lbs. |

### Riding Camels.

| | |
|---|---|
| Grain (gram or barley) .. .. .. | 6 lbs. |
| Salt .. .. .. .. .. .. | 1½ ozs. |
| Hay (if available) .. .. .. | 20 lbs. |

### Somali and Arab Camels.

| | |
|---|---|
| Grain (gram, jowari, or barley).. .. | 4 lbs. |
| Salt .. .. .. .. .. .. | 1½ ozs. |
| Hay (if available).. .. .. .. | 20 lbs. |

### Donkeys.

| | |
|---|---|
| Grain (gram or barley) .. .. .. | 2 lbs. |
| Salt .. .. .. .. .. .. | ½ oz. |
| Hay (if available) .. .. .. | 13 lbs. |

### Milch Cows.

| | |
|---|---|
| Hay (if available) .. .. .. | 10 lbs. |
| Salt .. .. .. .. .. .. | ½ oz. |

### Army Service Corps Mules.

| | |
|---|---|
| Grain (gram, oats, or barley) .. .. | 8 lbs. |
| Fodder .. .. .. .. .. | 12 ,, |
| Salt .. .. .. .. .. .. | ⅔ oz. |

Firewood was not carried with troops, and the resources Firewood. of the localities where the troops halt was mainly relied on. Troops and followers cut their own firewood, the axes provided being used for this purpose. Firewood was, however, issued at Berbera since it was not locally procurable.

The following table shows the average strength of the Berbera–Bohotle and Obbia forces between January and May, 1903:— The force maintained.

| Particulars. | Number. | | |
|---|---|---|---|
| | Berbera–Bohotle Force. | Obbia Force. | Total. |
| British .. .. .. .. | 198 | 346 | 544 |
| Indians .. .. .. ⎫ African and Somalis .. ⎬ | 2,460 | 1,927 | 4,387 |
| Followers .. .. .. | 1,047 | 1,707 | 2,754 |
| Camels .. .. .. | 1,628 | 1,616 | 3,244 |
| Horses and ponies .. .. | 153 | 722 | 875 |
| Mules and donkeys .. .. | 475 | 761 | 1,236 |

The following shows the daily average numbers of men and animals rationed by the Supply and Transport Corps in Somaliland between 1st July, 1903, and 31st January, 1904:—

| | |
|---|---|
| Fighting men, British, Africans, and Indians .. .. .. .. | 7,522 |
| Followers .. .. .. .. .. | 9,056 |
| Total, men .. | 16,578 |

| | |
|---|---:|
| Camels | 9,382 |
| Horses and Ponies | 2,967 |
| Mules | 2,737 |
| Donkeys | 126 |
| Bullocks | 55 |
| Total, animals | 15,267 |

For the last two months of 1903 and first month of 1904 the average numbers were :—

| | |
|---|---:|
| Fighting men, British, Africans, and Indians | 8,040 |
| Followers | 10,934 |
| Total, men | 18,974 |
| Camels | 11,477 |
| Horses and Ponies | 4,628 |
| Mules | 3,192 |
| Donkeys | 129 |
| Bullocks | 64 |
| Total, animals | 19,490 |

Remarks with regard to rations.

The following suggestions were made by officers with regard to rations :—

1. When animals are driven with the troops they have little fat, therefore 2 oz. ghi per man per day, or tinned lard or suet should be issued to British troops.

2. Preserved meat should be in 1 lb. or ½ lb. tins. More mutton should be issued.

3. Worcester sauce should be eliminated.

4. Dal was found unsuitable in most parts of the country.

5. Limejuice was found to be of little use. (For substitutes recommended by the P.M.O. see " Medical and Sanitary Services ").

6. *Vegetables.*—Dates were issued instead of vegetables but large stocks should not be kept in the very hot weather.

7. *Forage.*—Missa bhoosa is preferred. The oval shaped bale of hay is not recommended, difficult to load and sways when loaded, causing sore backs.

8. The meat supply was principally furnished by sheep for British troops and goats for Indians. Africans received sheep, goats, and Somalis sometimes camels also, as meat rations. Cattle were not often available for rations, except near the base. The sheep averaged 20 lbs. dead weight, and the cattle from 200 to 300 lbs. The Somalis themselves eat camels and keep milch camels to supply them with fresh milk.

In 1903-4 the arrangements for carrying supplies with troops when on the march were as follows:— *Conveyance of supplies on the march.*

All troops and followers carried 1 day's ration on their persons for their own consumption. This was consumed on arrival at destination. *Rations.*

Each corps and unit carried in regimental charge 6 days' rations. The following day's ration was distributed to individuals shortly after their arrival in their new camp from these reserves.

The Brigade Supply Column carried such number of days' supplies as were considered necessary. The regimental reserve was replenished from the brigade supply columns and the latter replenished from the nearest advanced depôt.

Every animal carried for its own consumption one day's grain (except camels which carried 3 days' grain and Army Transport mules which carried 2 days' grain). This one day's grain was ordered to be looked on as an emergency ration, *i.e.*, only to be consumed when local resources failed. *Forage.*

Each brigade supply column carried 5 days' grain for the animals of the brigade.

A canteen was established with branches at Upper Sheikh, Burao, Kirrit and Eil Dab for the sale of *Field Force canteen.*

articles of food supply, etc., over and above those allowed as rations. It proved most useful. The accounts were audited by the Field Controller.

<small>Miscellaneous recommendations with regard to supply and transport.</small>

The following general remarks made by officers regarding the Supply and Transport Service are instructive :—

1. That a Government agency to regulate and effect economy in the shipment of locally purchased stores, supplies, &c., from Aden to Berbera should have been established at Aden.

2. That a most scrupulous check of stores, &c., when put on board vessels at the port of embarkation, was necessary.

3. That a recruiting section of the base transport should have been established through which all men recruited should be passed in order to obviate desertions. Corps commandants should have enlisted their own men, but passed them through the recruiting office. The establishment should have been: 1 warrant officer, 1 sergeant, 1 clerk, 2 specially paid jemadars, and a non-commissioned officer of the local police.

4. That it is desirable in future expeditions that Transport officers should be informed beforehand of the difficulties they are likely to encounter.

STATEMENT showing Important Supplies purchased at Berbera through local suppliers for the Somaliland Field Force during the period from 9th July, 1903, to 31st March, 1904.

| Articles. | | Number or Quantity. | Average Rate Paid. | | | Per— |
|---|---|---|---|---|---|---|
| | | | Rs. | a. | p. | |
| Atta | Md. | 4,969 | 7 | 0 | 0 | 100 lb. |
| Axes, Somali | Number | 14,093 | 0 | 6 | 6 | Each |
| Alum | Md. | 50 | 10 | 0 | 0 | 100 lb. |
| Biscuits | ,, | 225 | 0 | 6 | 0 | Lb. |
| Baking powder | ,, | 45 | 1 | 8 | 0 | ,, |
| Barley | ,, | 3,420 | 5 | 0 | 0 | 100 lb. |
| Bran | ,, | 7,107 | 4 | 2 | 0 | 100 lb. |
| Bootlaces | Pairs | 1,000 | 0 | 2 | 0 | Pair |
| Bags, gunny | Number | 8,000 | 0 | 5 | 6 | Each |
| Chillies | Md. | 290 | 0 | 2 | 6 | Lb. |
| Compressed vegetables | ,, | 168 | 1 | 0 | 0 | ,, |
| Coffee, husk | ,, | 67 | 10 | 0 | 0 | 100 lb. |
| Coffee | ,, | 6 | 0 | 8 | 0 | Lb. |
| Candles | ,, | 193 | 0 | 10 | 0 | ,, |
| Chaguls | Number | 32,376 | 1 | 7 | 10 | Each |
| Cotton seed | Md. | 50 | 5 | 0 | 0 | 100 lb. |
| Cattle | Number | 149 | 56 | 0 | 10 | Each |
| Dates, in— | | | | | | |
| Gosra | Md. | 11,455 | 5 | 0 | 4 | 100 lb. |
| Tins | ,, | 9,024 | 7 | 3 | 0 | 100 lb. |
| Dal | ,, | 699 | 7 | 8 | 0 | 100 lb. |
| Dried fruit | ,, | 218 | 0 | 6 | 0 | Lb. |
| Discs, copper | Number | 3,661 | 0 | 4 | 9 | Each |
| Firewood | Md. | 52,830 | 0 | 13 | 1 | 100 lb. |
| Flour | ,, | 2,112 | 7 | 10 | 0 | 100 lb. |
| Ginger | ,, | 429 | 0 | 6 | 0 | Lb. |
| Garlic | ,, | 435 | 7 | 8 | 0 | 100 lb. |
| Goor | ,, | 2,049 | 11 | 5 | 5¼ | 100 lb. |
| Ghee— | | | | | | |
| Somali | ,, | 2,532 | 45 | 14 | 0 | 100 lb. |
| Indian | ,, | 296 | 45 | 0 | 0 | 100 lb. |
| Gram— | | | | | | |
| Crushed | ,, | 4,700 | 6 | 0 | 0 | 100 lb. |
| Uncrushed | ,, | 117 | 5 | 4 | 0 | 100 lb. |
| Hops | ,, | 3 | 2 | 0 | 0 | Lb. |
| Jam | ,, | 882 | 6 | 12 | 10½ | Dozen |
| Jowari— | | | | | | |
| Crushed | ,, | 42,516 | 5 | 0 | 0 | 100 lb. |
| Whole | ,, | 5,000 | 4 | 12 | 0 | 100 lb. |
| Kajawahs | Pairs | 75 | 15 | 10 | 8 | Pair. |
| Linseed meal | Md. | 216 | 0 | 4 | 0 | Lb. |
| ,, ,, | ,, | 100 | 0 | 2 | 1 | ,, |
| ,, oil | Gallons | 700 | 2 | 12 | 0 | Gallons |
| Loading ropes for— | | | | | | |
| Somali camels | Number | 1,400 | 0 | 12 | 0 | Each |
| Indian camels | ,, | 4,347 | 1 | 15 | 7 | ,, |

STATEMENT showing Important Supplies purchased at Berbera through local suppliers for the Somaliland Field Force during the period from 9th July, 1903, to 31st March, 1904—continued.

| Articles. | | Number or Quantity. | Average Rate Paid. | | | Per— |
|---|---|---|---|---|---|---|
| | | | Rs. | a. | p. | |
| Logline | Yards | 2,000 | 0 | 2 | 0 | Yard |
| Lime juice | Gallons | 500 | 4 | 0 | 0 | Gallon |
| Milk, condensed | Lbs. | 14,967 | 6 | 0 | 0 | Dozen |
| Mussacks, donkey | Number | 319 | 2 | 8 | 0 | Each |
| Onions | Md. | 7,420 | 7 | 0 | 1 | 100 lb. |
| Oil— | | | | | | |
| Kerosene, 125° | Gallons | 1,940 | 0 | 10 | 3 | Gallon |
| Cake | Md. | 18 | 7 | 7 | 0 | 100 lb. |
| Kerosene, 150° | Gallons | 1,280 | 0 | 12 | 0¾ | Gallon |
| Cake, tilseed | Md. | 20 | 10 | 0 | 0 | 100 lb. |
| Potatoes | ,, | 2,592 | 7 | 0 | 2 | 100 lb. |
| Pepper, black | ,, | 38 | 1 | 0 | 0 | Lb. |
| Packhal mules | Pairs | 138 | 34 | 0 | 0 | Pair |
| Rice— | | | | | | |
| Somali | Md. | 22,125 | 7 | 2 | 3 | 100 lb. |
| Indian | ,, | 6,000 | 9 | 0 | 0 | 100 lb. |
| Rum | Gallons | 993 | 5 | 8 | 0 | Gallon |
| Shoes, Somali | Pairs | 8,968 | 4 | 15 | 10½ | Pair |
| Sugar | Md. | 1,160 | 10 | 0 | 0 | 100 lb. |
| Salt | ,, | 2,354 | 1 | 0 | 0 | 100 lb. |
| Sauce | Bottles | 26,016 | 1 | 0 | 0 | Bottle |
| Sickles | Number | 895 | 0 | 12 | 0 | Each |
| Saddles— | | | | | | |
| Donkey, with canvas tops | ,, | 100 | 4 | 0 | 0 | ,, |
| Arab, riding | ,, | 200 | 15 | 0 | 0 | ,, |
| Spring balance | ,, | 6 | 19 | 0 | 0 | ,, |
| Spears | ,, | 1,024 | 1 | 4 | 0 | ,, |
| Scales, Baniah | ,, | 50 | 3 | 8 | 0 | ,, |
| Sheep and goats | ,, | 68,608 | 4 | 6 | 0 | ,, |
| Tea | Md. | 189 | 0 | 8 | 0 | Lb. |
| Turmeric | ,, | 329 | 0 | 2 | 0 | ,, |
| Tobacco— | | | | | | |
| Cavendish | ,, | 86 | 1 | 0 | 0 | ,, |
| Country | ,, | 10 | 0 | 4 | 0 | ,, |
| Tarbooshes, with tassels | Number | 4,340 | 0 | 14 | 0 | Each |
| Tobe, 30-yard piece | ,, | 1,280 | 6 | 8 | 0 | ,, |
| Tobes, red | Yards | 1,200 | 0 | 4 | 0 | Yard |
| Turkish red | ,, | 6,000 | 0 | 4 | 0 | ,, |
| Water bottles, canvas | Number | 9,421 | 1 | 4 | 0 | Each |

NOTE.—Col. Yeilding reported that Mahomed Ibrahim, of the firm of Hajeebhoy, Lalji and Co., of Berbera, rendered the force valuable assistance in procuring supplies at short notice. "He never failed in any emergency."

STATEMENT showing Important Supplies purchased at different places in the country, and the Average Rates paid for the Supplies during the period from July, 1903, to 31st March, 1904.

| Articles. | | Number or Quantity. | Average Rate Paid. | | | Per— |
|---|---|---|---|---|---|---|
| | | | Rs. | a. | p. | |
| Firewood .. .. .. | Mds. .. | 678¾ | 0 | 6 | 0 | Md. |
| Hay .. .. .. | ,, .. | 76,834 | 2 | 3 | 6 | ,, |
| Milk, cow .. | Pints .. | 66,381 | 0 | 5 | 5 | Pint |
| Sheep and goats .. | Number.. | 12,725 | 5 | 12 | 3 | Each |

## 4.—MARINE TRANSPORT—DISEMBARKATIONS AND RE-EMBARKATIONS.

As comparatively little marine transport work was involved in the conduct of the first and second expeditions, the following account of the transport of troops, animals and stores by sea embraces the period covered by the third and fourth expeditions from the time when the troops in the Protectorate were reinforced from England, India and South Africa until the demobilization of the force under Lieut.-General Sir C. Egerton in 1904.

During the period in question, the marine transport service was organized and carried out under arrangements made by the Quartermaster-General's department, War Office, and the Director, Royal Indian Marine, respectively; while the disembarkation of the force at Obbia, which formed an important feature of the third expedition, was conducted under arrangements made by the local Naval authorities. The disembarkation of General Manning's force at Obbia in 1903, although not in chronological order, will be described first, in the form of extracts from Field Force Orders and from the despatch of Captain Hon. A. E. Bethell, Senior Naval Officer, who organized and superintended the landing, assisted by Commander G. S. Hewett, R.I.M., and Lieutenant E. W. Huddleston, R.I.M.

*Organization.*

Extract from Field Force Orders.

The extract from Field Force Orders, dated 7th January, 1903, was to the following effect :—

The following orders by the Senior Naval Officer regarding the disembarkation of troops, &c., are published for information :—

Order of disembarkation will be—
 "1st. Troops.
 "2nd. Officers' and men's baggage.
 "3rd. Stores and ammunition.
 "4th. Animals.

Ships that have camels on board will discharge them into the native boats while the other disembarkation is going on, and every boat, whatever she is loaded with, leaving for the shore, is to tow one horse or mule ashore. When the camels are all landed, the native boats will proceed to assist in the landing of the stores, but troops are only to be landed in ships' boats.

When the weather is unfavourable for landing the animals, the native boats will assist in landing the stores.

The following will be the duties of the under-mentioned officers during the disembarkation of the force at Obbia—

Commander Jones, H.M.S. 'Pomone,' Beach-Master.

He will have under his control all native and ships' boats at the landing place ; regulate the traffic there, and generally order the disembarkation.

He will see that no native boats are used for private purposes without his consent having been obtained, and that everything is done to expedite the disembarkation as much as possible.

He will arrange for the necessary men from H.M.S. 'Pomone' to assist him (troops being applied for to unload the boats), also for a singalman to land with flags.

Letter 'B' commercial is to be hoisted at the landing place if impracticable.

Lieutenant Bevan, H.M.S. 'Pomone,' Assistant Beach-Master.

Commander G. Hewett, Royal Indian Marine, will be on board the Indian transport discharging, and will see that the ship is discharged according to the attached routine, applying for any assistance he may require.

Lieutenant Huddleston, Royal Indian Marine, will assist him, and take his place in the absence of Commander Hewett.

Lieutenant E. S. Carey, H.M.S. 'Naiad,' will act as Executive Officer afloat. He will regulate the order in which the boats are loaded, and generally control them, and arrange for their towage by the steam boats of the squadron ; and also for the meals and reliefs of their crews, signalling to the ships concerned if necessary. He will generally be on board the ship that is discharging. When 'Perseus' arrives, Commander Pears will perform this duty ; Lieutenant Carey doing the duty on board the South African transport assigned to Commander Hewett, Royal Indian Marine, on board the Indian transport. Lieutenant Williams, H.M.S. 'Naiad,' will anchor the transports, and be responsible they are safely berthed.

The despatch of Captain Bethell is instructive as showing the difficulties involved in landing troops under abnormal conditions :— *Despatch of Captain Bethell, R.N.*

H.M.S. " Naiad," at Obbia,
Sir, 17th February, 1903.

I have the honour to report that I left Aden at 10 A.M. on 1st January, having embarked General Manning and his Staff, and proceeded to Obbia, where I arrived at 3 P.M. on 4th January. I found " Perseus " and " Pomone " had cleared the transport I had despatched on 22nd December from Berbera under great difficulties, owing to the bad weather prevailing and the few appliances at their disposal. " Perseus " left at 6 P.M. for Aden. I ordered Commander Pears to complete with coal there, endeavour to hire a steam launch suitable for the work here (General Manning having sanctioned this) and tow her here after the arrival of the mail at Aden on 12th January, proceeding along the south coast of Arabia to Shugra and Makalla, and hoisting on board as many surf boats as he could carry, and to bring their crews.

General Manning landed at 7 A.M. on 5th January, I proceeded to Elhur, a place 28 miles south of Obbia, to examine it, and bring away any surf boats that might be there. I arrived there at 10.30 A.M., and, finding two surf boats, I brought them on board with their crews. Elhur is a far better place for disembarking a force than Obbia.

The anchorage is much the same, though I fancy the water is not quite so rough; but the landing is very good. There is a natural breakwater formed by a barrier reef which runs parallel with the shore, inside of which there is landing for a large number of boats in absolutely smooth water. There is a depth inside the reef of 5 feet at low water and 12 feet at high water. The conditions ashore are just as favourable as Obbia, plenty of excellent grazing and water, and the distance no further from the objective of the expedition. It is a great pity it was not visited when H.M.S. " Pomone " came down to survey Obbia, as there is no question it would have been selected as the base. At Obbia the landing at this time of the year is bad, boats having to pass through the surf to get under the shelter of the reef. I left Elhur at 1.30 P.M. and arrived at Obbia at 5.15 P.M.

At 8.30 A.M. on 8th January the transport " Nowshera " arrived, and about one hour afterwards the Indian marine ship " Canning." Commander Hewett, R.I.M., and Lieutenant Huddleston, R.I.M., came on board to see me, bringing their orders from the Director, Indian Marine.

Lieutenant Huddleston, who had been ordered by the Director of Indian Marine to report himself to the General Officer Commanding for duty on shore, was placed by General Manning under my orders. I directed him to assist Commander Jones as Assistant Beachmaster.

Work was started on " Nowshera " about 10 A.M., and by 6.30 P.M. all the troops (about 1,000) with their kits and baggage and 26 mules had been landed.

9th January all boats were employed clearing " Nowshera " in a rough sea; 10th January still clearing "Nowshera," sea and wind high; at 1 P.M. British Indian steamer from Aden arrived with two Italian attachés, four military officers, a good deal of baggage, some Government stores, three camels and four ponies. As she had to shift berth twice, we did not get to work on her until 4 P.M. She was cleared by 6.30 and sailed for Mombasa.

"Nowshera" was also cleared about the same time, and sailed for Aden by 8 P.M., but as she touched the ground on her way out, she anchored again and sailed at daylight the next morning. She left for Berbera and Aden to ship as many camels as possible and return to Obbia.

11th January we commenced on "Canning"; 80 mules were landed from her and most of her stores.

12th January the Indian transport "Ikhona" arrived at 9 A.M. Being a large steamer she took some time to berth, and it was not until nearly noon that we commenced unloading her. Her troops with their luggage, 78 mules and some stores were landed. "Canning" with her own boats carried on landing her own stores; a good deal of wind and sea.

13th January was a very bad day; wind and sea high. "Canning" carried on landing her stores in her own boats, and finished about 2 P.M. All the remainder of the boats worked on "Ikhona." We were much handicapped by "Canning's" steamboat being under repair. "Pomone's" boat also broke down, and was under repair for about 5 hours. This made the work for the boats very hard, and much time was lost in getting them back after unloading. All the animals were landed (140) and a good deal of stores.

14th January was again a very bad day, and the work of clearing "Ikhona" was much delayed. The two troop barges were got alongside and filled up with stores to expedite the clearing of the steamer. We had again only one steamboat as "Canning's" boat was still under repairs.

15th January was a still worse day. Wind and sea very high. Landing stores was impracticable owing to the high surf. As General Manning was anxious to get "Ikhona" away, I transferred what stores remained to be landed to "Canning." This was completed by 1 P.M., and after the "Canning" had weighed the troop boats astern of her, "Ikhona" sailed for Aden and Berbera at 4 P.M. "Canning" lost her steamboat, it was swamped and sank.

16th January was a very bad day, and landing quite impracticable. "Ranee" arrived from Bombay with Bikanir Camel Corps at 4 P.M.

17th January was another bad day, and landing was quite impossible.

18th January, the weather having moderated, we commenced clearing "Ranee." "Canning" with her boats landed the stores from "Ikhona" that had been put on board her. "Perseus" arrived at 8 A.M. with a tug in tow, hired from Aden. She also brought six surf boats with their crews. Commander Pears, with assistance of tug, laid down moorings close in shore for "Canning's" troop barges.

Thirty-three camels were landed from "Ranee," two were drowned owing to the men not being used to them; a large amount of stores were also landed. Captain of "Caprera" most kindly volunteered the use of his steamboat, and she did most useful work for us during the remainder of the disembarkation, until she was lost on the night of 3rd February.

19th January, boats employed clearing "Ranee" and troop barges of "Ikhona's" stores. An attempt was made to land animals in troop barges, but, owing to the motion, it was found they could not keep their footing if crowded, and not enough could be carried to make it answer. No difficulty was found in landing the animals. They were pushed out of the barge and taken in tow by boats waiting for them. I decided to continue swimming all animals as we had hitherto done, and to use the barges solely for landing stores in. By this means landing of stores is expedited, as the distance to the landing place from the moorings of the barges is short. Altogether 46 mules, 8 horses and 25 camels were landed (one horse and one camel being drowned), and a large quantity of stores. Both "Perseus" and "Pomone's" steamboats gave a lot of trouble and were constantly breaking down.

20th January was the first really fine day we had had, and a good day's work was done in consequence. Altogether 141 camels and a large amount of stores were landed.

21st January, all boats were employed clearing "Ranee." The day was a fine one. The rest of the camels (55) were landed in about two hours. The lighters were found very useful in the smooth water, and were the means of landing a large amount of stores.

22nd January, "Ranee" was cleared by noon, and sailed at 5 P.M. for Bombay.

23rd January, "Canning" sailed at 11 A.M. for Aden and Berbera, where she is to embark camels. "Newark Castle" arrived at 5.30 P.M. from Cape Town.

24th January was a fine day, and we commenced clearing "Newark Castle." 314 animals were landed and some stores. Great difficulty was experienced in slinging the mules who were very vicious. It was necessary to throw some of them in order to get them slung. But for this, well over 400 animals would have been landed. It was found possible in the fine weather to land four animals at a time.

25th January, Italian man-of-war "Caprera" sailed at 3 A.M. for Elhur, as we had received a report that two dhows were landing arms and ammunition for Yusuf Ali. She returned at 3 P.M., stating that no dhows were there, and that she had searched on shore and could find no trace of anything.

248 horses and some stores were landed from "Newark Castle" in a rough sea. "Gaul" arrived from Durban at noon. Her Captain objected to his berth and refused to let my officer place him there, but on my sending for him he went there under protest. I gave him a written understanding that I would take the responsibility of his safety there. It was necessary for him to go there, as he had 365 horses to be swum on shore, and anchored as he insisted on being in 5 fathoms, the distance from the landing place was too great for the animals to swim. We landed 50 British and 25 Boers from "Gaul" to take charge of the horses already landed from "Newark Castle." About 8 P.M. No. 23 Lighter broke from her moorings and drifted

on to the rocks, her cargo was mostly saved. A special report on this has been forwarded.

26th January, weather was improving. Landed all but five sick horses from "Newark Castle" and a few stores, also all troops from "Gaul." Lighter No. 23 was found to be a total wreck. She is over 30 years old I am told, and was too rotten to stand the beating about of the surf. "Pomone's" steamboat, owing to her screw getting foul, drifted on the rocks about 8 A.M., close to No. 23 Lighter; Commander Pears with the tug made four attempts to tow her off, but failed each time.

27th January was a fine day. We landed 227 horses from "Gaul" and a good deal of stores from "Newark Castle." "Pomone's" steamboat was reported to be beyond repair, so I had her boiler and fittings taken out of her. The loss of this boat and the lighter have been much felt.

28th January was a fair day. The rest of "Gaul's" horses (138) and stores from both "Gaul" and "Newark Castle" were landed. "Nowshera" arrived at noon, bringing 193 camels and 42 mules and ponies from Berbera and about 200 tons of stores. "Newark Castle" was shifted at 3 P.M., and "Nowshera" brought into her billet, as General Officer Commanding was anxious to have her discharged as soon as possible. Cavaliere Sola, Italian Consul-General at Aden, arrived in "Nowshera" to effect the arrest of Yusuf Ali and his sons.

29th January, Yusuf Ali and his two sons were arrested and made prisoners on board the Italian man-of-war "Caprera." 195 camels were landed from "Nowshera," and a large amount of stores from "Gaul."

30th January, British India boat from Aden arrived at 9 A.M., bringing mails, some military officers, one camel, four ponies and mules, and a few stores. These were landed and she sailed at noon. The rest of "Nowshera's" animals (40) and stores were landed by 1 P.M. A good day's work was done on "Gaul" landing stores.

31st January, Yusuf Ali and his sons were embarked on board "Nowshera" at 6 A.M., in charge of an Italian guard. They will be handed over to the Resident at Aden until their destination is decided on by the Italian Government. "Nowshera" sailed at 9 A.M. "Gaul" was cleared of all stores and sailed at 4.30 P.M. "Newark Castle" was shifted in for discharging at 2 P.M., and a few stores were landed from her. The wind and sea were bad on this day.

1st February to 5th February, inclusive, were very bad days; a heavy sea running and blowing hard, and landing was impossible. "Ikhona" arrived from Berbera with 600 camels and 26 ponies and mules, and some stores, on 2nd February at noon. No work could be done until 9 A.M. on 6th February, when the surf having subsided, the clearing of "Ikhona" was commenced. Camels suffered too much in the rough sea which prevailed, four being drowned in the first two hours, so they were placed inside the boats with satisfactory results. 153 were landed and some stores.

7th February was again a bad day, but 362 camels and some stores were landed from "Ikhona." The Benadir steamer arrived at 10 A.M.; she brought wireless telegraphy party, 70 tons of coal for " Caprera," and some stores. I lent " Caprera," " Naiad's " sailing pinnace, and three surf boats to assist in transferring her coal. " Pomone " sailed for Aden at 10 P.M.

8th February was again a bad day. The rest of " Ikhona's " camels (87) and 26 ponies and mules were landed, and the ship cleared of stores. She sailed for Bombay at 9 P.M. The Benadir boat was also cleared by 4 P.M. " Canning " arrived at 10 P.M., bringing 300 camels and 200 tons of stores.

9th February was a very bad day, and work had to be suspended at 4 P.M., owing to the heavy surf. One of " Naiad's " cutters and one steel boat were capsized inside the reef. " Canning " landed 191 camels and a good deal of stores were landed from " Newark."

10th February was a very bad day, and landing was most difficult. The rest of " Canning's " camels (109) were landed and stores from both " Canning " and " Newark." At 5.30 P.M. the transport " Sirsa " arrived from Bombay with a complete general hospital and 2,250 tons of stores. She also brought four Madras surf boats with crews for three boats.

11th February was again a very bad day, and boats worked under great difficulties on " Canning " and " Newark."

12th February was so bad that work was stopped, and it was not until 2 P.M. on 13th February that the surf had subsided sufficiently to make it possible to land, when boats worked on " Canning " and " Newark."

14th February, the R.I.M.S. " Hardinge " arrived at 8 A.M.; " Newark " was cleared of all stores required at Obbia at 11 A.M., and sailed for Aden at 4 P.M. " Canning " was also cleared by noon.

15th February the weather had much improved, and the work of clearing " Sirsa " and " Hardinge " was commenced, and good progress made. " Canning " sailed for Bombay at 11.30 A.M.

At 6 P.M. on 16th February " Sirsa " was cleared of all stores requiring to be landed, and that completed the disembarkation.

17th February, " Naiad " and " Hardinge " were employed in embarking stores on board ' Sirsa " and " Hardinge." " Perseus " supplied " Caprera " with 50 tons of coal. " Sirsa " sailed at 5 P.M.

In carrying out the disembarkation, we have had the following disadvantages to contend against:—

 A.—The exposed nature of the anchorage.
 B.—The indifferent landing place and its limited space.
 C.—The few appliances at our disposal. Against these we have had only one advantage, and that has been the practically unlimited labour the General has been able to supply us with for unloading the boats.

A.—The anchorage, though fairly good holding ground, is most exposed. At all times a heavy swell sets in, which, when the wind freshens, causes a breaking sea, very bad for boats. At this time of the year (probably the worst of the season) the wind is strong, and is particularly so at the full and change of the moon, a three to five days' blow, during which landing is dangerous, taking place with great regularity. After this is over the wind gradually subsides, veering sometimes as much as to E.S.E. when it practically dies away for a couple of days. It then backs again, sometimes as far as to north, and gradually freshens up till at full or change of the moon, it culminates in a moderate gale.

B.—The landing place is a bad one. It is formed by a natural breakwater, which runs to the north-east, and is consequently exposed to the swell which sets in with this monsoon. It is, however, partially protected by some off-lying rocks. A passage is possible through the rocks, close to the breakwater. This causes the swell to affect the landing place, and at high water and in bad weather, the sea breaks inside the rocks. There is also a passage round the rocks, but at anything below half tide and always in bad weather the sea breaks, and boats have to pass through the surf.

The usual practice has been for boats going in to go round, and those coming out, through the rocks.

Two boats at half tide are able to go alongside the breakwater, where, with careful attention, they can be unloaded; others, by anchoring and veering in, can be unloaded by men wading out to them, but the space being limited, not more than three or four boats can be unloaded in this manner at the same time.

There is so little water inside the rocks that only boats of very light draught can be used; the 30 feet sailing pinnace belonging to "Naiad" has frequently grounded and been unable to work at low water.

C.—For the greater part of the time, in fact until 18th January, when "Perseus" arrived with a steam tug and six small surf boats with crews, we have been entirely dependent on the ships' cutters, assisted by five small surf boats. These latter for some time could not be got to work, owing to the obstruction of the Sultan Yusuf Ali, and at all times only worked intermittently.

The boats available until 18th January were:—

"Naiad"—
    One 30-ft. pinnace, not always able to work
    One 27-ft. cutter.
    One 25-ft. cutter.

"Pomone"—
    Two 30-ft. cutters.
    One 27-ft. cutter.

"Canning"—
    Two 30-ft. cutters, and occasionally a third one, and five small surf boats.

After arrival of "Perseus," "Canning" left for Berbera to fetch camels, and "Perseus" supplied the same boats as "Pomone." The crews belonging to the surf boats brought by "Perseus," the boats having been found to be useless, were utilised in manning four boats belonging to the transports. After arrival of "Nowshera" on 28th January with 100 Aden boatmen, we were able to man more transport boats, and from that time had as many boats working as could be usefully employed. After the arrival of the tug, we were able to make use of the two troop barges brought from Bombay by "Canning." They were filled up with stores and towed to moorings just outside the rocks, and cleared by the surf boats from them. One of these broke adrift on the night of the 25th January, and was wrecked on the rocks. Our greatest want has been capable steamboats. "Naiad's" 32-ft. steamboat has done remarkably well, but "Canning's" "Perseus's" and "Pomone's," being smaller boats, have been a constant source of trouble. Their fires have frequently been put out by the sea, and they have constantly had to lay up for repairs. "Canning's" boat was swamped and sank on 15th January, and "Pomone's" boat was wrecked on the rocks on 26th January.

The Italian man-of-war "Caprera" most kindly lent us his steamboat, which, despite her small size, did very valuable service in towing, until she sunk on the night of 3rd February. After the arrival of the tug on 18th January the want of steamboats was not so much felt.

A strong tide sets along the coast, and as all transports were berthed well to windward to enable boats to fetch, in pulling in, great delay was caused when steamboats were not available to tow the boats back. In moderate weather even they were unable generally to get back by pulling.

The landing of the animals was our chief difficulty at first. Mules and horses had to be swum, towed astern of the boats, and it was not found possible, until the boats got used to the work, to take more than one animal at a time. Even then some were drowned, and the rate of landing was not more than about 80 per day. Later it was found two could be taken, and by the time the South African transports arrived with, between them, 1,165 mules and horses, the boats were able to take four with ease and safety. This I think is about the limit, as with more the men cannot pull the oars, and the animals first hoisted out are kept waiting too long for the others. Our best day was 314; this would have been probably increased to over 400 had not the mules been so difficult to manage on board the transports. Some took over ten minutes to sling, and had to be thrown before the sling could be got round them, and several cases of bites and kicks occurred amongst the men engaged in slinging them.

The best way of handling the animals in the water was found to be with a rope round their necks, arranged so that it could not slip over their heads and at the same time could not be drawn tight enough to choke them. A line being attached to the nose band of head-stall to keep their noses out of the water. The swimming powers of both horses and mules is remarkable. Several at times got adrift and were swimming about for some time—one, in particular, was 51 minutes before he was caught, and must have been nearly $1\frac{1}{2}$ hours in the water; no animal got drowned under these circumstances, the loss of animals was generally due to their being choked or else their noses being allowed to get under water.

Had it been possible to make a lane to the beach by means of large grass hawsers or bamboos lashed to a light grass rope, mules and horses could have been put overboard from the transports and left to swim ashore alone. The slightest thing in the water will turn them, and with anything to guide them they would swim straight to the beach. The risk here, owing to the presence of rocks, was too great, but had the beach been a clear one, undoubtedly it would have been the easiest and quickest method of landing the animals.

Camels at first were landed in the surf boats, being tied up so that they could not move. This method, though a safe one, was very slow, as with five boats not more than 50 a day could have been landed at the outside. The Indian camels were too heavy, and surf boats refused to take them.

Recourse was therefore had to putting them in the water in tow of the boats. As the camel is a most helpless animal and will not try to swim, they were slung to the boats by two ropes passing under their bodies, a neck rope being used to keep their heads out of the water. In this manner they were landed quite easily. Latterly camels have been landed inside the boats. This was tried on account of the rough weather in which the camels from the "Ikhona" had to be landed. By taking out two thwarts from the steel boats belonging to the Indian transports, it was found possible to put as many as nine camels in some of the boats and five in others. In the ships' boats a pile of herios was made in the stern sheets, and two, and in the larger boats three camels placed on the top of them. No difficulty was experienced in getting the camels out, as they were too unwieldy and heavy, but with the smaller Somali camel, it is undoubtedly the best and quickest way to land them, as they are fit for service much sooner after landing. The journey in the water takes a lot out of them. 362 camels were landed in this manner in one day in a rough sea, and with four boats away clearing the Benadir steamer.

Though the strain on the personnel has been very great, my chief anxiety has been whether the material would hold out. Everything has suffered great damage, and the ships' boats have only been kept going by constant repairs by the carpenters, who, on occasions, have had to work on them for the greater part of the night. Very few of the boats will be worth repairing.

Three lighters (two at Obbia) and three steamboats have been lost. Two of the lighters may possibly be recovered.

The men have stood the strain well. They have left the ship at 5.30 A.M., not returning before 7 P.M.; and on occasions later had no regular meal hours and been wet through all day.

I think great praise is due to them for their cheerful and willing endurance under these most uncomfortable and trying circumstances.

Commander Eugenio Finzi, Commanding His Italian Majesty's Ship "Caprera," has assisted me in every way in his power. On 18th January he volunteered the use of his steamboat for towing, and though I demurred greatly at accepting the offer, as the boat I was afraid was too small to stand the weather, he insisted in sending her until she was unfortunately swamped and sank when made fast astern of "Caprera" on the night of 3rd February. She did most valuable service, in fact at times "Caprera's" and "Naiad's" steamboats were the only ones available, the others having broken down.

The health of the ships' companies has been very good throughout, the sick being chiefly composed of cuts and bruises.

I have, &c.,

A. E. BETHELL,

*Captain and Senior Naval Officer, Obbia.*

Rear-Admiral Sir Charles C. Drury, K.C.S.I.,
Commander-in-Chief, East Indies.

The following letter was sent by General Manning to Captain Bethell on completion of the landing :—

Sir,                               Obbia, 18th February, 1903.

Now that the work of disembarkation from transports has been completed of men, animals and stores for the Somaliland Field Force, I desire to place upon record my appreciation of the good services rendered by the officers, petty officers and men of His Majesty's ships employed in the work of disembarkation.

I am aware that, owing to the violence of the monsoon, the work undertaken was arduous in the extreme, and it has been to me a source of great pleasure to observe the cheerful way in which both officers, petty officers and men of His Majesty's ships have carried out their duties, in spite of the fact that they have been employed for the past six weeks from morning to night in transporting in open boats, men and stores in a rough sea, which necessitated their being continually drenched with water.

The small losses in stores and animals is a proof of the careful and skilful way in which these duties have been performed.

I am indebted to you, yourself, for the excellent arrangements made for the disembarkation which has been carried out so efficiently under conditions which, as regards difficulties, are probably without parallel in the history of the disembarkation of an expeditionary force.

I trust that you will be able to bring to the notice of officers, petty officers and men my appreciation of the services they have rendered.

In conclusion, I request that you will bring to my notice the names of any officers, petty officers or men who, in your opinion, are deserving of mention for the duties performed by them in the course of the disembarkation.

*Report of Lieut. Huddleston, R.I.M.*

Lieutenant E. W. Huddleston, who was Marine Transport Officer during General Manning's expedition, also rendered a report of the marine transport work at Obbia, from the date of arrival of the detachment there on 8th January, 1903, until the closing of that base on 17th April, 1903, and, as far as the records obtainable at Berbera admit, of the work up to the 3rd July at that port, of which the following are extracts :—

The actual number of troops, animals and stores landed and embarked at Obbia and Berbera has been tabulated by me for easy reference, together with a list of the vessels employed, and is herewith attached (see pages 554, etc.).

| | |
|---|---|
| Obbia. | In lat. 5° 19′ 30″ N., long. 48° 30′ E., is an open roadstead. The anchorage for large ships, though entirely open to the sea, has fairly good holding ground, the ships lying from ½ to ¾ mile off shore.
There is a small village, consisting of some native huts and three storehouses and forts, which belonged to the Sheikh Yusuf Ali. |
| Landing. | Landing could be effected at all states of the tide by ships pulling boats and very small native craft. The place for landing being behind a small r' o of sandstone rock, jutting out from the mainland to the north, which, t¹ ,ugh it did not entirely break the force of the heavy sea that was running during the whole of the north-east monsoon, enabled boats to lie in comparative shelter when once through the dangerous surf which marked the entrance to the landing place. |
| Labour. | Labour was absolutely unobtainable, with the exception of six small surf boats, which were propelled by six native oarsmen, and capable of carrying from four to six passengers or 4 to 5 cwt. of stores. This amount of labour was even difficult to obtain, and until the removal of the Sultan, Sheikh Yusuf Ali, from Obbia, was uncertain, the boatmen being entirely in his power. |
| Weather. | The weather at Obbia during January, February, and until the latter end of March was decidedly bad, and on many days landing was impossible. It was observed that the wind was always strongest at full and change of the moon, the wind veering between north and N.N.E., and the regularity of the wind, which with the run of the sea caused a heavy surf at the entrance to the landing place, making it absolutely impracticable for boats to pull through it. |
| Method of landing, &c. | The method of landing men, animals and stores was by ships pulling boats, which were at first towed by the steam launches of the different men-of-war in port, near to the landing-place breakers. H.M.S "Naiad," "Pomone" and "Perseus," each supplying three boats, and the R.I.M.S. "Canning" and "Hardinge," during the time they were in port, also supplying a like number. Besides these boats, four steel boats were taken out of the hired transport "Ranee," and four from the hired transport "Ikhona," and permanently attached to the department, the men to man the boats being Arabs, who were brought from Aden at my request for this purpose. Six Massulah surf boats were also sent from Madras by the Director of the Royal Indian Marine to assist in the disembarkation.
Horses and mules were lowered over the side in a sling; they were then made fast to the boat's stern or gunwale with a short rope tied on to the headstall, the rest of the body being entirely free. By this means two and even three horses were towed on shore by one boat, the largest number landed in one day being close on 200 horses, and the total number landed being 1,744.
Camels were at first landed in a similar manner, but it was found that, not only was this a tedious method of landing the animals, but the percentage of losses was very high. The steel boats mentioned as taken from the hired transports "Ranee" and "Ikhona" were fitted with air tanks; these tanks were cut out and the thwarts for the men to sit on to row were also made movable. The camels' forelegs were then tied up underneath the body, and |

the animals were lowered into the boats alongside the ship. On their arrival ashore the boats were turned over on their side and the lashings on the camels' legs being cut, the animals were pulled out of the boats. By this method as many as 10 camels were placed in one steel boat and safely brought ashore, 365 camels being landed in one day, and no casualties were recorded after this method of landing was tried. Another advantage to this form of landing being that long immersion in the sea water was found hurtful to the animals and was thus avoided.

When embarking horses at Obbia, Massulah boats were turned on their side, the horses were then walked in, and, as soon as two horses were on the side of the boat, it was uprighted. By this means the 42 horses and mules that had to be shipped were safely embarked without any casualties.

In addition to the boats already mentioned, two iron lighters were chartered by the Royal Navy from Aden, but the extremely heavy weather experienced rendered these craft of little use. Two wooden troop barges were also brought by me from Bombay, but they could only be used to tranship stores into, so as to give the boats less distance to pull, it being possible to anchor them closer to the rocks than the ships could possibly come; but, it being impossible to bring the barges through the surf, the stores had again to be re-shipped into the boats when the barge was anchored.

The tug "Dolphin" was chartered from Aden to tow the boats to and from the shore, and proved extremely useful, as it was possible to tow by this means seven or eight full boats at a time close into the landing place, thus lessening the heavy labour for the men pulling in the boats, and enabling the landing of stores to be carried on far more expeditiously.

The two iron lighters chartered by the Royal Navy were both lost, one Casualties to at Obbia and one in being towed down to Obbia, but I have no record as craft. to dates.

One of the troop barges brought by me from India carried away her moorings during a gale of wind on the night of the 25th January, 1903, and drifting on to the rocks at the landing place became a total wreck. She was full of stores at the time, but a greater portion of them were recovered.

A steam cutter belonging to H.M.S. "Pomone," having fouled her propeller by a rope with which she was towing a ship's boat off to the ship drifted on to the rocks and became a total wreck.

A steam cutter belonging to the R.I.M.S. "Canning," laying astern of that vessel was filled by a heavy sea and sunk, and the same fate occurred to a steam cutter belonging to the Italian gunboat "Caprera," which had been assisting in the towing of boats to and from the shore.

One of the steel boats taken from the hired transport "Ikhona," whilst making the entrance to the landing place during a gale, and when there was a heavy surf running, touched the rocks and sank immediately, and one Arab boatman was drowned. Every effort was made to try and raise the boat, and divers were sent down in search of her, but without being successful in finding her; but I am of opinion that by reason of the strong undercurrent and the shifting of the sand, the boat was swept out to seaward, no trace of her ever being found, although she sank in only 2 fathoms of water.

| | |
|---|---|
| Casualties, troops, animals, and stores. | Notwithstanding the very heavy sea and the dangerous surf through which the boats had to be sent to effect a landing, I am happy to be able to report not a single serious accident occurred to any of the troops. The losses to animals was far less than was at first anticipated, and was confined to less than 1 per cent. of horses, mules, &c., and 8 per cent. of camels, out of a total of 1,744 horses landed and 1,355 camels.<br><br>There were no serious casualties on board the ships to either men or animals from the time of their embarkation to the time of their disembarkation at Obbia.<br><br>The base at Obbia was finally closed at noon the 17th April, 1903. |
| Berbera. | The records kept at Berbera on marine transport work until the arrival of the department on 21st April, 1903, do not permit of a full statement of troops, animals and stores being tabulated, as in the case of troops landed at Obbia, but as far as possible, from the records obtained, this has been done, and is herewith attached. (See pages 554, 555).<br><br>The harbour of Berbera is protected from all winds except the south-west, and though small there is good anchorage for three or four large transports. |
| Landing. | There is a small T-shaped pier, constructed of wood on screw piles, at the landing place, alongside of which small vessels of from 300 to 400 tons can be berthed. The pier, however, is small, and, owing to the silting of the sand at the sides of the pier, boats cannot be brought alongside there, there being practically no water at the sides at low water.<br><br>Another small pier, composed of bamboos, with two empty 500-gallon water tanks to make a floating pontoon at the end, was built by me shortly after the arrival of the department to relieve the strain on the larger pier, and also to enable animals to be walked straight into the boats when embarking, the floating pontoons being so constructed as to be on a level with the side of the country craft when alongside. |
| Labour. | Country craft, capable of carrying from 10 to 15 tons of stores, are obtainable at a price which varies from 10 to 20 rupees a day, according to the size of the boat. Coolies are also obtainable up to about 300 or 400 per diem, but labour is expensive, and the work done in proportion to the number of men employed far from satisfactory. |
| Weather. | During the north-east monsoon, from October till the latter end of May, the weather is very fine, light variable winds blowing throughout the day and night. At the end of May till the middle of September, or during the south-west monsoon, the wind blows with tremendous force from the south-west, the wind commencing about midnight and lasting till noon of the following day; and during these hours it is practically impossible with the craft obtainable to do any work afloat. |
| Method of landing, &c. | Men, animals and stores were landed in the craft obtainable at the port. The horses and camels were lowered over the side into the boats, the boats were then towed or sailed ashore near to the pier, and the craft having masts, a line was attached to the masthead and the boats pulled over on to their side and the animals walked out. |
| Casualties. | There were no serious casualties at Berbera, either to men, animals, or craft. |

Money to meet the expenses of the department has been obtained by me from the Field Paymaster, and my accounts rendered direct to the Examiner of Marine Accounts, Bombay.

Lieutenant Huddleston also rendered the following report regarding the Marine Transport work at Las Khorai :—

9th June, 1904.

In accordance with your orders, I have the honour to submit the following report on marine transport work at Las Khorai from the date of my arrival there on the 23rd March, 1904, until the final closing of Las Khorai as a base on the 21st May, 1904 :—

On my arrival at Las Khorai, Captain Grant, R.E., who was in command of the post, had commenced building a breakwater for embarkation purposes, the idea then being to build a bamboo pier on the lee side of the breakwater thus formed. This idea, however, was found impracticable, as the breakwater was continually being washed away. Finally a pier was constructed of sandstone rock blasted from the beach, strengthened with bamboos and sandbags, and projecting about 120 feet from the beach.

The depth of water at the end of the pier was just sufficient to float buggalows at half flood tide.

Las Khorai is an open roadstead open to all winds from east to west through north.

The anchorage for large vessels is from 600 to 800 yards from the beach in about 8½ to 9½ fathoms of water.

The beach itself is slightly shelving (about 1 foot in 40) right out into deep water, and dhows had to anchor about 300 feet to be in 6 feet of water at low water springs.

*Weather.*—The weather during April and up till the 18th May was invariably fine, with light breezes from all points of the compass.

On the 18th May the first signs of the Khareef was felt, a heavy swell rolled in all day, and though the wind was not strong the sea was too rough for work to be satisfactorily carried out, and no work was done till high water.

The pier was considerably damaged and washed away in parts, and had the weather not moderated the pier could not have stood another day.

I attach herewith a rough sketch* of the pier, by Captain Grant, R.E., the depth of water at the extreme end being 4 feet at half flood tide and 6 inches at low water springs.

*Method of Embarkation and Disembarkation.*—The disembarkation of mules was comparatively an easy matter, the dhows sent by you from Berbera being used for this purpose. The mules were lowered into the dhows, and on the dhows reaching the beach they were hauled over on their side, and the mules made to jump out. One casualty occurred in landing the mules and that was caused by a mule trying to jump out of

---

\* Not reproduced.

the boat before the boat was hauled over on its side; the animal broke its leg and had to be shot.

The embarkation was more difficult on account of there not being sufficient water at the end of the pier at either low water springs or neaps, and only between half flood and half ebb tides.

The method of embarking camels was as follows :—

The camels were brought to the end of the pier and their forelegs then tied by a piece of rope on each foot. The dhows for camels were then placed alongside the end of the pier, and a few sandbags placed in the bottom of the dhow. The men then pulled on the ropes attached to the camel's feet, and its legs consequently slipped off the pier into the boat.

No causalties occurred in getting the camels into the boats, and as three boats were used at the same time, the average rate of embarkation was about 30 camels an hour.

To expedite the shipping of camels, by my request, Captain Grant, R.E., constructed three small ramps of stone, sufficiently long to allow the steel boats that were sent by you to be brought alongside, the object of these ramps being to allow of work being commenced before half flood tide, and before the large dhows could be brought alongside. The camels were then made to walk up the ramp and into the steel boats. One accident occurred to a camel in getting into the boat, caused by the camel missing its footing and falling into the bottom of the boat, its shoulder being broken.

The troop lighter sent by you from Berbera was used for the embarkation of camels, and materially expedited the embarkation. With the troop barge and using the dhows and steel boats, 398 camels and 600 men, with their baggage, were embarked in eight hours.

The embarkation of mules and horses was carried out in a different manner. The mules being much lighter, it was possible to sling them into the dhows from the end of the pier, the tackle used for slinging being made fast half way up the mast of the dhow.

No casualties occurred in the embarkation of mules or horses. Six hundred mules being shipped in eight hours, or at an average speed of 75 an hour.

I attach herewith a tabulated statement showing the number of men, animals, and stores embarked and disembarked at Las Khorai, together with a list of the ships that were employed (see Table IV, Disembarkations, and V, Re-embarkations).

Las Khorai was finally closed as a base at midnight on the 21st May, when under orders from the C.R.E., Captain Grant having undermined the pier with 50 lbs. of guncotton, it was blown to pieces, nothing remaining except a few broken pieces of wood and a large mass of rocks.

I returned here in the last ship, the R.I.M.S. "Clive," under your orders, bringing in tow the troop barge and dhows.

No casualties occurred to craft.

Since writing the above Lieutenant Huddleston added the following further observations :—

If Berbera is used again as a base for military operations on a large scale, I would recommend that the officer in charge of marine transport arrangements should be provided with:—

   (1) A good steam tug.
   (2) A steam cutter for communication with the transports.
   (3) Two good lighters of not less than 300 tons carrying capacity in which ramps could be constructed for horses, and two smaller lighters of 100 tons capacity.
   (4) A corps of 500 Arab coolies enlisted at Aden.

The lighters and tug should be bought outright by the Government (as was done in the China Expedition of 1900) and not hired.

In support of my suggestion I would point out that in the Somaliland Expedition—

|  | £ |
|---|---|
| The tug "Dolphin" cost for the 3 months' hire, roughly | 720 |
| „ "Midge" „ „ 10 „ „ | 2,200 |
| Total | £2,920 |

Further, it is only necessary to point out that the detention of transports, loading or unloading, costs anything from £150 to £200 per diem, to show the necessity of having good plant for landing, &c., as often there were three or even four transports in the harbour awaiting discharge at one time.

Should Obbia or, indeed, any open roadstead on the east coast have to be utilised again as a base, at least 20 Madras massulah boats and their crews would, I consider, be most useful, as they were found to be the very best boats for cargo work, being able to take a fair amount of cargo, and also being most seaworthy and adapted for surf work for which they are built.

Commander C. J. C. Kendall, R.I.M., Marine Transport Officer, Somaliland Field Force, reported:— *Report of Commander Kendall, R.I.M.*

Berbera, 11th April, 1904.

From 4th to 8th July, the work of the department was carried out by Lieutenant E. W. Huddleston, R.I.M.

I arrived in Berbera on the 9th July in the R.I.M.S. "Hardinge," and assumed charge of the department.

I found the following establishment and craft available:—

      1 Officer, Lieutenant E. W. Huddleston, R.I.M.
      1 Warrant Officer, Mr. C. Perrett, Clerk R.I.M.
      11 marine lascars.
      36 Madras surf boatmen.
      1 Arab interpreter.

Craft:—
      3 steel life boats.
      1 steam cutter.

Also about 20 sambooks (small open dhows) capable of carrying from 40 to 350 bales, or from 3 to 7 animals, and engaged on daily hire.

**Madras boatmen.** As the Massulah boats employed at Obbia had been returned to Aden and Bombay as unsuitable in Berbera, the men were no longer required here, and under instructions from the Director of the Royal Indian Marine were returned to India, leaving Berbera on the 11th July.

The actual number of troops, animals and stores landed and embarked at Berbera and other coast ports has been tabulated for easy reference, together with a list of the ships employed, and is attached herewith (see Tables).

**Harbour.** Berbera harbour is formed by a narrow sandy spit running parallel to the coast, thus forming a narrow harbour 1¼ miles long, running east by north and west by south, the navigable channel varying in breadth from 4 cables at the entrance to 1½ cables opposite the Shaab pier, to the eastward of which only small vessels should be berthed. The harbour is capable of berthing four large ships and two smaller ones, and is well protected from all winds, except those from the westward, which blow directly into the harbour. The anchorage is safe for steamers, but native craft frequently drive ashore. During the Khareef the only safe anchorage for native craft being under the lee of the Shaab pier.

**Local labour.** Only a limited amount of Somali labour is available during the Khareef, but is obtainable in considerable numbers during the north-east monsoon. The Somali, however, makes a very indifferent labourer, being lazy, unreliable and expensive; he is quite unsuitable for ship's work.

**Landing facilities.** Were very limited and quite insufficient to cope with the traffic.

**The foreshore.** Is flat and shelving and quite unsuitable for landing stores owing to the long distance which such stores would have to be carried to a place of safety above high water.

**Shaab Pier.** For all practical purposes is the only suitable landing place, it is a small T-headed wooden pier with a frontage of 60 feet, situated on the south side of the harbour, connected with the high-water line by a narrow causeway. Built during the Egyptian occupation about 1880, this pier has been much neglected and is in a very indifferent state of repair; this and the causeway were the only places where stores could be stacked after landing; the former was unable to bear the strain thrown on it and broke down several times, but was repaired and strengthened by the field engineer. The local steamers, vessels of about 300 tons and drawing 8 or 9 feet, are able to come alongside and load, but are aground at the low-water springs. This pier is silting up very rapidly and even ship's boats are unable to land at the sides until half flood.

It was found necessary to refuse permission for Messrs. Cowasjee, Dinshaw and Brothers' steamers to come alongside when transports were in harbour, as they blocked the pier and all work ceased.

**Customs Pier.** A stone causeway, jutting out into the harbour from the Custom-House, and dries at low-water springs. Owing to the exposed position of this pier it was only available for a very few hours daily during the Khareef; also, owing to the lack of stacking space in its vicinity and to the distance which all stores landed would have to be transported, this pier was little used by Government; it was, however, very useful on the few occasions when heavy weights had to be landed.

This small pier was constructed under the direction of Lieutenant E. W. Bamboo Pier. Huddleston, and was useful for landing and embarking men in ships' boats. The hospital ship, R.I.M.S. "Hardinge" frequently embarked sick and details at this pier, which has now been dismantled for use at Las Khorai.

During the Khareef the number of native boats is limited to those owned Local craft. locally (about 30), but in the fine weather large numbers enter the port from all parts of the coast, and these are ready and willing to accept work on my terms. My remarks concerning the local labour refer equally to the local boatmen and owners, who are lazy, worthless and most unreliable.

The usual Venice Convention Regulations were in force, but shortly after Quarantine. my arrival the time was reduced from 10 to 8 days, and later was cancelled altogether, except in the case of infected or suspected ships, of which there has only been one, the R.I.M.S. "Canning." However, the necessary precautions were invariably taken, and no communication was permitted until a medical inspection had taken place and practique had been given.

Were not obtainable in Berbera and had to be brought from Aden, and Coal and as the freight charged by Messrs. Cowasjee, Dinshaw and Brothers was very water heavy, sanction was obtained from the Resident at Aden for coal to be sent supplies. over in the R.I.M.S. "Mayo." One hundred tons was brought and formed a nucleus for a coal depôt, and the supply of coal was augmented from time to time from Aden, and also from hired transports. This depôt has successfully complied with all demands from the various military departments, and has supplied the launch and tug employed later by this department, also the chartered vessel "Meyun," and on one occasion the Italian corvette "Galileo," thus enabling her to proceed down the coast with urgent despatches.

Water is laid on at the end of the Shaab Pier, about 600 or 800 gallons being obtainable per diem, but as this was insufficient to meet the demands of the craft of this department, water has to be carried down from the wells.

The coaling and watering of large transports was carried out when necessary by the Government Agents, Messrs. Luke Thomas and Company, at Aden, and the bills for the same submitted to the Marine Transport Officer, Aden, under arrangements made by me.

There are no skilled mechanics or carpenters in Berbera, and I am in- Skilled debted to His Majesty's ships, the ships of the Royal Indian Marine, and the labour. hired transports for their assistance, which enabled me to keep my craft in working condition.

The only means of signalling on my arrival was by men lent from the Signal staff. various ships for that purpose, and as communication with the ships was frequently required, sanction was obtained for the increase of my establishment by three signalmen, who arrived from India on the 3rd October, since which date a signal station has been maintained and has proved of great

**Communication.**
**(a) Mails.\***

value, messages continually being sent by the military authorities to the naval ships, and *vice versâ*, and also in connection with signals to transports, &c.

There is no telegraphic communication between Aden and Somaliland.

In normal times communication is maintained by the steamers of Messrs. Cowasjee, Dinshaw and Brothers, Aden, which, under an existing agreement with the Somaliland Protectorate, leave Aden with the English mails every Monday, arriving in Berbera on Tuesday, and proceeding thence to Bulhar and Zeila, returning to Berbera on Friday, and thence to Aden with the mails, thus entailing a delay of one week for all letters to England and the Continent, which to connect at Aden should leave Berbera not later than Wednesday during the south-west monsoon, and Tuesday during the northeast monsoon. To keep this connection and also to bring over the Indian mails without undue delay, one of His Majesty's ships of war was placed at the disposal of the G.O.C., her primary duty being to leave Berbera on Wednesday with the English mails and returning on Friday with the Indian mails. She was, however, continually employed carrying despatches to and from Aden and Berbera.

**(b) Stores.**

All stores were brought over in Messrs. Cowasjee, Dinshaw and Brothers' vessels, but, owing to the very large quantity of stores requiring conveyance from Aden, the weekly mail was augmented, and frequently as many as three of these vessels arrived in one week. Under the terms of their agreement with the civil authorities, all Protectorate stores brought over were charged for at special rates, which were on an average four times the rate charged to local traders; these rates seem to have been accepted by the Somaliland Field Force. In my opinion these rates are unreasonably high, I therefore drew attention to the matter and pointed out that the work could be better and more economically carried out by a R.I.M. vessel, or if no R.I.M. vessel was available, by chartering a suitable vessel for the purpose, which in addition to carrying stores would also be available for the duties then carried out by His Majesty's ships in the event of their being withdrawn. Sanction having been obtained, the R.I.M.S. "Mayo" arrived here on 18th October and was replaced by the R.I.M.S. "Dalhousie," which was in her turn withdrawn and replaced by the hired transport "Meyun," a small steamer belonging to the Perim Coal Company, which was chartered on the 13th February, 1904, for Rs. 8,000 per mensem, inclusive of all charges, except coal and water.

**Weather.**

During the north-east monsoon, from 15th September to 15th May, the weather is uniformly good and marine transport work can, if required, be carried out day and night. South-west monsoon, from 15th May to 15th September, is the bad weather season, and the winds locally known as Khareef blow with great force and are accompanied by blinding clouds of dust. These winds blow with great regularity, commencing about 8 P.M., blow hard all night, increasing to a whole gale about 6 A.M., moderating again about 10 A.M., then quickly falling light and drawing out from seaward.

---

\* See also Chapter XIV, 2.

During this season work afloat can only be carried out between about 2 P.M. and 8. P.M.

Men, animals and stores were landed in sambooks. The animals were lowered into these boats, which were towed or sailed ashore near the pier, the boat was then hauled over on her bilge with the assistance of a masthead tackle, and the animals made to jump out. This method was continued until the arrival of the lighters, which were fitted with ramps, and towed alongside the pier, and the animals were walked out. *Method of landing.*

No casualties to troops occurred during the disembarkation or embarkation, and only one animal was killed in disembarking. *Casualties to troops and animals.*

Considering the fact that most of the camels were brought from India during the south-west monsoon, the casualties to animals were very slight, and only amounted to four.

On the arrival of the hired transport "Sofala," her master reported the coal in No. 4 hold on fire. At the time labour was practically unobtainable here, but with the assistance of a crew from the R.I.M.S. "Canning," which ship was in port at the time, the fire was eventually put out and no damage was done. No other casualties occurred to craft.

As will be seen from the foregoing remarks, the conditions on my arrival were wholly unfavourable for work afloat. The Khareef was blowing in full force, and on an average not more than six hours' work could be put in daily, of which only four hours were in daylight. The absence of a launch of sufficient power to tow dhows to and from the ships was very urgently felt. The labour was most unsatisfactory, and the plant at my disposal wholly inadequate. I represented this to the G.O.C., and sanction was requested—

(1) To hire or purchase a tug and two lighters;
(2) To engage a gang of Arab stevedores (skilled ship's labourers) from Aden;
(3) To increase my establishment by three signalmen;
(4) To reclaim land in the vicinity of the pier and causeway for stacking stores;
(5) For a tramway to be constructed from the pier to the high-water line.

On the 18th July, sanction having been obtained, I ordered Lieutenant E. W. Huddleston to proceed to Aden and make the necessary arrangements for the hire of a tug and lighters, and to engage 250 Arab stevedores, also to arrange with the Marine Transport Officer for the Government barge No. 22 to be sent over as soon as possible, and also to visit the heads of the various firms with a view to obtaining information regarding the resources of the port. Lieutenant Huddleston returned on the 28th July, having satisfactorily concluded these arrangements.

The tug "Dolphin" was chartered from the Aden Port Trust at a monthly hire of £241 inclusive of all charges, except coal and water. She arrived in Berbera on the 24th July.

Two large iron lighters, each capable of carrying 140 tons of stores, were chartered from the Perim Coal Company, at Rs. 10,000 for the first month and Rs. 6,000 for succeeding months, the company taking all risks of the voyage to and from Berbera and whilst within harbour limits at Berbera. These also arrived on the 24th July from Perim.

On the 28th July the R.I.M.S. "Mayo" arrived with 150 Arab stevedores (the Resident at Aden having refused to allow more than this number to leave the port) as follows:—

        1 head maccadum, at Rs. 40 per mensem.
        3 assistant maccadum, at Rs. 20 per mensem.
        146 coolies, at Rs. 15 per mensem.

The department now for the first time became self-supporting, and I was able to deal with the local labour and boats. The local labour was almost entirely discontinued, only small gangs being occasionally engaged to relieve the congestion on the pier. Up to this time work has been very seriously delayed, owing to the unsatisfactory behaviour of the boatmen. I was now able to alter the conditions of service, and, instead of daily hire, I instituted piece work; a good deal of trouble was experienced from the local boatmen, who refused to accept these terms, but with the means now at my disposal and also by engaging the few foreign boats in the harbour and also assisting with ships' boats, I was able to carry on the work satisfactorily, and sent notice down the coast and also to the Red Sea and the Arab Coast, informing all that I was willing to employ all who wanted work. Foreign boats soon began to arrive in small numbers, and as the weather improved, in increasing numbers, until I was quite independent of all locally owned boats, none of which have been engaged for several months. I am greatly indebted to Mr. O'Byrne, the Chief of Customs, for his assistance in forwarding these notices and also in drawing up a tariff based on his knowledge of rates in peace time.

The only cause of delay now was the lack of stacking space near the pier, and, owing to the continuous pressure of work, it was not possible to begin reclaiming until early in September, since which time every opportunity has been taken of the lull in the work to continue the reclamation, until now there is sufficient space in the vicinity of the pier and causeway to unload at least three vessels without congestion. The whole of this work has been carried out by the Arab Coolie Corps.

On the 12th September the Port Trust, Aden, notified the withdrawal of the tug "Dolphin"; I again ordered Lieutenant Huddleston to proceed to Aden and arrange for the charter of a suitable tug to replace her. The tug "Midge" was chartered from the Perim Coal Company for Rs. 3,000 per mensem, inclusive of all charges, except coal and water. She arrived on the 18th September, and the tug "Dolphin" left for Aden the same day in charge of Mr. Craig, Aden pilot, who was sent over to navigate her. The same day the R.I.M.S. "Dalhousie" arrived with Government Troop Barge No. 22 in tow; this barge had been employed at Obbia, but, owing to the strain caused by towing and to the severity of the weather at Obbia, she had to undergo extensive repairs at Aden, so was not available for service earlier.

The R.I.M.S. "Hardinge" was fitted in Bombay as a hospital ship, and  Hospital ship. has carried from here the main portion of the sick to Bombay. From 23rd September, 1903, to 14th January, 1904, she was required by the Government of India for his Excellency the Viceroy's tour in the Persian Gulf and during this time the R.I.M.S. "Dalhousie" was lent for hospital duties.

The accommodation for sick on the R.I.M.S. "Dalhousie" being very much smaller than that of the R.I.M.S. "Hardinge," 40 spare cots were sent to Berbera, and these were fitted by me in the hired transport "Islanda"; a certain portion of the medical staff of the R.I.M.S. "Dalhousie" were also turned over to the "Islanda," and she was used as a hospital ship for two voyages to India. The R.I.M.S. "Dalhousie" in the meantime being used to take invalids to Aden.

It has been necessary from time to time to despatch small bodies of  Coast ports. troops, stores and specie to Bulhar and Zeila, and arrangements have accordingly been made by me for the charter of local native craft for this purpose whenever required.

It being found necessary to transport camels by sea from Hais to this port, the hired transport "Ranee" was ordered to proceed there with five small dhows in tow, and Lieutenant Huddleston was sent by me to arrange the embarkation; his report on Hais as a place of embarkation has already been forwarded to you under cover of my No. 953, of 23rd October, 1903.

At time of writing, Las Khorai is being used as a base for the 2nd Brigade, and 700 animals have already been landed there, besides a considerable quantity of stores. As the work of embarkation at Las Khorai is not completed, I propose dealing with this in a supplementary report on completion.

The Arab coolies have been a great success, and indeed without them the  Arab coolies. landing of stores would have been greatly delayed; they are indefatigable workers, besides being excellent stevedores.

To meet the expenses of my department, money has been obtained by me  Money. from the Field Controller and my accounts rendered direct to the Examiner, Marine Accounts, Bombay.

In the event of Berbera harbour becoming a base for further operations  Suggestions. or a trade centre for Abyssinia and Somaliland, the facilities for landing and forwarding stores, machinery and merchandise should be very considerably improved, and should, in my opinion, consist of a wharf or wharves on the northern side of the harbour capable of berthing at least two ships, with a railway round the village of Berbera to a terminus situated in some suitable position on the Shaab. The contour of the bottom lends itself to the construction of wharves at a moderate cost. Also the Shaab Pier should be extended and improved.

Should, however, future operations be of a temporary nature only, I would suggest that the Shaab Pier be strengthened and the reclamation now in hand be completed and the banks faced with stone as a protection against the wind and tide. All plant at present available should be purchased outright (the purchase value of the tug and two lighters has already been paid in hire). The launch should be maintained and another boat purchased; the want of an additional boat has been greatly felt.

Navigation.  The leading lights as at present situated are too close together, and it would be a great improvement and assistance to navigation if the front light was placed on the end of the Customs Pier hoisted on a pole, and the rear light altered to a suitable bearing.

The beacon as at present situated is very misleading to strangers; a new and more conspicuous beacon should be erected at the west extreme of the spit.

I have now completed a survey of Berbera Harbour on a scale of 6 inches to 1 land mile. The original, with triangulation sheet and all necessary data, will be forwarded to the Hydrographer, Admiralty, for publication.

To the Officer Commanding
 Lines of Communication, Sheikh.

### Commander Kendall reported further with regard to the embarkations and disembarkations at Las Khorai :—

In continuation of my Report No. 147, dated 11th April, 1904, I have the honour to forward the following report on marine transport work at Las Khorai, and also on the embarkation of troops, animals, and stores at Berbera.

On 12th March, I ordered Lieutenant Huddleston to proceed to Las Khorai and arrange for the disembarkation and embarkation of troops, animals, and stores at that place.

Lieutenant Huddleston reported to me that the place was an open roadstead and that the work would be comparatively easy in fine weather but quite impossible for animals (at any rate) in bad weather; also that there were no facilities in the place. I therefore arranged for 12 local sambooks to leave here, some under sail and some in tow, and also sent a large party of Arab coolies to work on the ships and on shore. Later on, on his reporting that he was experiencing great difficulty in shipping camels, I sent troop barge No. 22 and a steam launch.

His report on the embarkation is forwarded herewith for your information. The embarkation was considerably delayed owing to the transport asked for not arriving in time. The R.I.M.S. "Hardinge" assisted by R.I.M.S. "Clive," doing nearly all the work.

Transports for the embarkation of the Somaliland Field Force were engaged by the War Office and by the Director of the Royal Indian Marine Bombay, under orders from the Government of India.

A tabulated form showing the total numbers embarked and disembarked is attached herewith. (See Disembarkations IV and Re-embarkation V.)

Remarks of G.O.C.  With reference to the above reports, General Egerton remarked :—

The Marine Transport Officer's duties have been very heavy and continuous throughout the operations. At the time of my arrival the facilities for landing troops and stores, and more especially of clearing them away when landed, were primitive in the extreme. The report shows how the machinery was gradually got into working order, but the defects in the earlier stages were productive of delay and increased expense. The present system works perfectly.

Since this report was submitted, the marine transport have done further excellent work in embarking a column of troops of all arms and several thousand animals at Las Khorai, working against time in the face of an imminently threatening monsoon.

## Disembarkations.

The following tables, numbered I to VI, deal with the landing of troops, animals and stores at Berbera, Obbia and other ports on the Somaliland coast during the course of the third and fourth expeditions.

**554**

**L.**

**DETAIL of Troops, &c., disembarked at Berbera from 22nd October, 1902, to 13th June, 1903, under Indian Marine Transport arrangements.**

| Transport No. Name | Left Port | Left Date | Date arrived Berbera | British Officers | Native Officers | Warrant Officers | British (R&F) | Native (R&F) | Followers | Horses | Ponies | Mules | Camels | Approximate Stores | Casualties Horses | Casualties Ponies | Casualties Mules | Casualties Camels | Departure Date | Departure Port |
|---|---|---|---|---|---|---|---|---|---|---|---|---|---|---|---|---|---|---|---|---|
| "Falcon" | Bombay | — | 1902. Oct. 22 | 5 | 1 | — | — | 295 | 41 | — | — | — | — | No record. | — | — | — | — | No record. | No record. |
| "Bancoora" | — | — | Nov. 4 | 6 | 1 | — | — | 12 | — | — | — | — | — | | — | — | — | — | | |
| "Mayo" | — | — | Nov. 9 | 3 | 3 | — | — | 200 | 23 | — | — | — | — | | — | — | — | — | | |
| "Falcon" | — | — | Nov. 10 | 8 | — | — | — | — | — | — | — | — | — | | — | — | — | — | | |
| "Falcon" | — | — | Nov. 11 | 5 | — | — | — | — | — | — | — | — | — | | — | — | — | — | | |
| | — | — | Nov. 25 | 3 | — | — | — | — | — | — | — | — | — | | — | — | — | — | | |
| | — | — | Nov. 27 | 2 | — | — | — | — | — | — | — | — | — | | — | — | — | — | | |
| "Bundesrath" | — | — | Nov. 28 | 17 | — | — | — | 709 | 40 | — | — | — | — | | — | — | — | — | | |
| "Mayo" | — | — | Dec. 3 | 2 | 6 | — | — | 144 | 6 | — | — | — | — | | — | — | — | — | | |
| | — | — | Dec. 9 | 7 | 1 | — | — | — | — | — | — | — | — | | — | — | — | — | | |
| | — | — | Dec. 16 | 1 | 1 | — | — | 3 | 1 | — | — | — | — | | — | — | — | — | | |
| "Falcon" | — | — | Dec. 30 | — | 1 | — | — | — | 5 | — | — | — | — | | — | — | — | — | | |
| "Falcon" | — | — | Dec. 31 | — | 17 | — | 1 | 705 | 3 | — | — | — | — | | — | — | — | — | | |
| "Hardinge" | — | — | 9 | 9 | — | — | — | — | 84 | — | — | — | — | | — | — | — | — | | |
| "Palitana" | — | — | 1903. Jan. 4 | 2 | 3 | — | 1 | 4 | 97 | — | — | — | — | | — | — | — | — | | |
| "Woodcock" | — | — | Jan. 6 | 2 | 1 | — | — | 2 | — | — | — | — | — | | — | — | — | — | | |
| "Hardinge" | — | — | Jan. 20 | 9 | — | 9 | 5 | — | 18 | 3 | — | — | — | | — | — | — | — | | |
| "Woodcock" | — | — | Jan. 23 | 2 | — | 1 | 71 | 18 | 2 | — | 3 | — | — | | — | — | — | — | | |
| "Mayo" | — | — | Feb. 8 | 2 | — | 4 | 5 | 2 | 79 | — | — | — | — | | — | — | — | — | | |
| "Hardinge" | — | — | Feb. 10 | 6 | 18 | — | — | 18 | — | — | — | — | — | | — | — | — | — | | |
| "Hardinge" | — | — | Feb. 22 | — | — | — | — | 16 | — | — | — | — | — | | — | — | — | — | | |
| "Sirsa" | — | — | Feb. 22 | — | 1 | — | — | — | — | — | — | — | — | | — | — | — | — | | |

## 555

| Ship | | Date | Port | | | | | | | | | | | | No record. | No record. | No record. |
|---|---|---|---|---|---|---|---|---|---|---|---|---|---|---|---|---|---|
| "Hardinge" | ... | — | — | | | | | | | | | | | | | | |
| "Falcon" | ... | — | — | | | | | | | | | | | | | | |
| "Palinura" | ... | — | — | | | | | | | | | | | | | | |
| "Falcon" | ... | — | — | | | | | | | | | | 2 | | | | |
| "Nowshera" | ... | — | — | | | 10 | | | | | | | | | | | |
| "Falcon" | ... | — | — | | | | | 3 | | | | | | | | | |
| "Hardinge" | ... | — | — | | 2 | | | | | | | | | | | | |
| "Falcon" | ... | — | — | | | | | | | | | | | | | | |
| "Falcon" | ... | — | — | | 1 | | | | | | | | | | | | |
| "Nowshera" | ... | — | — | | 1 | | | | | | | | | | | | |
| "Hardinge" | ... | Obbia | Apr. 17 | ,, 25 | 2 | | | 3 | | 9 | | | | 600 | 1 | | |
| "Hardinge" | ... | Obbia | ,, 28 | ,, 25 | 1 | | | 2 | | 13 | | | | Nil | | | |
| "Hardinge" | ... | Aden | May 15 | Mar. 3 | | | | 11 | | | | | | 40 | 200 | May 18 | Aden |
| "Falcon" | ... | Aden | ,, — | ,, 8 | 2 | | | | | | 12 | | | 150 | | | |
| "Mayo" | ... | Aden | ,, — | ,, 10 | 1 | | | | 3 | | 10 | | 19 | 30 | | | |
| "Woodcock" | ... | Aden | May 28 | ,, 11 | 1 | | | 3 | 3 | | | 3 | 388 | 170 | 170 | May 21 | Aden |
| "Mayo" | ... | Aden | June 4 | ,, 18 | 2 | | | 2 | | | | | | 50 | | | |
| "Mayo" | ... | Aden | ,, 7 | ,, 24 | 1 | | | | | | | | 109 | 30 | | | |
| "Mayo" | ... | Bombay | ,, 2 | ,, 25 | 15 | 5 | 3 | 1 | | | | | 9 | 80 | 170 | June 8 | Aden |
| "Nerbudda" | ... | Aden | ,, 12 | ,, 31 | 2 | 4 | | | | | | | 50 | 30 | 139 | ,, 12 | Durban |
| "Mayo" | ... | Aden | | Apr. 20 | 1 | 39 | 3 | | | | | | 46 | 80 | | ,, 13 | Aden |
| | | | | ,, 27 | 2 | | 2 | | | | | | 4 | | | | |
| | | | | May 5 | 5 | | 1 | | | | | | 69 | 1 boat | 200 | | |
| | | | | ,, 16 | 1 | | | | | | | | | 140 | | | |
| | | | | ,, 19 | 1 | | | | | | | | | | | | |
| | | | | ,, 29 | | | | | | | | | | | | | |
| | | | | June 5 | | | | | | | | | | | | | |
| | | | | ,, 8 | | | | | | | | | | | | | |
| | | | | ,, 12 | | | | | | | | | | | | | |
| | | | | ,, 13 | | | | | | | | | | | | | |
| Total | ... | | | | 124 | 59 | 40 | 136 | 2,352 | 1,106 | 28 | 3 | 22 | 1,350 | 1,260 | | |

*One elephant.

(Signed) E. W. HUDDLESTON, Lieutenant R.I.M.,
Marine Transport Officer,
Somaliland Expedition.

II.
Detail of Troops, etc.,

| Transport No. | Name. | Left. Port. | Left. Date. | Date arrived Obbia. | British Officers. | Native Officers. | Warrant Officers. | Rank and file. British. | Rank and file. Native. |
|---|---|---|---|---|---|---|---|---|---|
| ... | "Haidari" | Berbera | 23rd December | 25th December | 21 | 12 | ... | ... | 686 |
| 2 | "Nowshera" | Bombay | 2nd January | 8th January | 12 | 17 | 2 | 4 | 702 |
| R.I.M.S. | "Canning" | ,, | 30th December | 8th ,, | 4 | 4 | ... | 2 | 169 |
| 3 | "Ikhona" | ,, | 5th January | 12th ,, | 5 | 2 | 12 | ... | 105 |
| 4 | "Ranee" | ,, | 10th ,, | 16th ,, | 8 | 21 | 1 | ... | 232 |
| Private | "Putiala" | Aden | ... | 10th ,, | 2 | ... | ... | ... | ... |
| H.M. ship | "Perseus" | ,, | ... | 18th ,, | ... | ... | ... | ... | ... |
| Freight | "NewarkCastle" | Cape Town | 10th January | 23rd ,, | 3 | ... | 1 | 5 | 1 |
| ,, | "Gaul" | Durban | 16th ,, | 25th ,, | 16 | ... | 5 | 256 | ... |
| 2 | "Nowshera" | Berbera | 24th ,, | 28th ,, | 13 | ... | 8 | ... | 0 |
| ... | "Fullwell" | Aden | ... | 30th ,, | 1 | ... | 1 | ... | ... |
| ... | "Ikhona" | Berbera | 30th January | 2nd February | 1 | ... | ... | ... | ... |
| ... | "Wissmann" | Aden | ... | 7th ,, | 1 | ... | 1 | 3 | ... |
| R.I.M.S. | "Canning" | Berbera | 4th February | 8th ,, | ... | ... | ... | 2 | ... |
| 6 | "Sirsa" | Bombay | 3rd ,, | 10th ,, | 10 | 13 | ... | 5 | ... |
| H.M. ship | "Cossack" | Aden | ... | 13th ,, | ... | ... | ... | ... | ... |
| R.I.M.S. | "Hardinge" | ,, | 9th February | 14th ,, | 2 | ... | 6 | ... | ... |
| ... | "Wissmann" | ,, | ... | 19th ,, | ... | ... | ... | ... | ... |
| H.M. ship | "Pomone" | ,, | ... | 20th ,, | 2 | ... | ... | ... | ... |
| 1 | "Palitana" | ... | ... | 24th ,, | 6 | 2 | 1 | 2 | ... |
| H.M. ship | "Highflyer" | ... | ... | 27th ,, | ... | ... | ... | ... | ... |
| ,, | "Fox" | ... | ... | 28th ,, | ... | ... | ... | ... | ... |
| R.I.M.S. | "Hardinge" | ... | ... | 3rd March | ... | ... | ... | ... | 15 |
| H.M. ship | "Pomone" | ... | ... | 7th ,, | ... | ... | ... | ... | ... |
| ... | "Wissmann" | ... | ... | 12th ,, | ... | ... | ... | ... | ... |
| 2 | "Nowshera" | Bombay | 23rd February | 15th ,, | 1 | ... | 3 | 3 | ... |
| R.I.M.S. | "Hardinge" | Berbera | March | 19th ,, | 2 | ... | ... | ... | ... |
| ... | ,, | ,, | 30th ,, | 3rd April | ... | ... | ... | ... | ... |
| ... | ,, | Aden | 30th April | 12th ,, | ... | ... | ... | ... | ... |
| | | | | Total | 110 | 71 | 41 | 284 | 920 |

disembarked at Obbia, 1903.

| Followers. | Horses. | Ponies. | Mules. | Camels. | Approximate stores. | Casualties. | | | | Date of departure from Obbia. | |
|---|---|---|---|---|---|---|---|---|---|---|---|
| | | | | | | Horses. | Ponies. | Mules. | Camels. | | |
| | | | | | Tons. | | | | | | |
| 136 | 9 | ... | ... | 6 | 500 | 1 | ... | ... | 1 | ... | |
| 158 | 13 | 113 | 25 | ... | 600 | 1 | ... | 1 | ... | 11th January... | Aden and Berbera. |
| 83 | 8 | ... | 90 | ... | 400 | ... | ... | 1 | ... | 23rd ,, .. | ,, ,, |
| 243 | 7 | ... | 211 | ... | 1,800 | 1 | ... | 3 | ... | 15th ,, .. | ,, ,, |
| 113 | 8 | ... | 46 | 250 | 1,000 | 1 | ... | 2 | 5 | 22nd ,, ... | Bombay. |
| ... | ... | ... | ... | ... | ... | ... | ... | ... | ... | ... | |
| 33 | ... | ... | ... | ... | ... | ... | ... | ... | ... | ... | |
| ... | 398 | ... | 400 | ... | 4,000 | 3 | ... | 2 | ... | 14th February | Aden and London. |
| ... | 355 | ... | ... | ... | 1,200 | 1 | ... | ... | ... | 31st January... | ,, ,, |
| 247 | 6 | ... | 4 | 193 | 300 | ... | ... | ... | 2 | ... | Aden and Bombay. |
| 4 | ... | ... | ... | ... | ... | ... | ... | ... | ... | 30th January. | |
| 208 | 12 | ... | 17 | 596 | 200 | ... | ... | ... | 2 | 8th February... | Bombay. |
| ... | ... | ... | ... | ... | 75 | ... | ... | ... | ... | 8th ,, | |
| 364 | ... | 1 | ... | 299 | 150 | ... | ... | ... | ... | 15th ,, ... | Bombay. |
| 205 | 7 | ... | ... | ... | 1,000 | ... | ... | ... | ... | 17th ,, ... | Berbera and Bombay. |
| ... | ... | ... | ... | ... | ... | ... | ... | ... | ... | 13th ,, | |
| 276 | ... | ... | ... | ... | 500 | ... | ... | ... | ... | 19th ,, ... | Berbera. |
| ... | ... | ... | ... | ... | ... | ... | ... | ... | ... | 19th ,, | |
| ... | ... | ... | ... | ... | 10 | ... | ... | ... | ... | 21st ,, .. | Aden. |
| 23 | 3 | ... | ... | 3 | 50 | ... | ... | ... | ... | 25th ,, | |
| ... | ... | ... | ... | ... | 5 | ... | ... | ... | ... | 1st March. | |
| ... | ... | ... | ... | ... | 2 | ... | ... | ... | ... | 17th April. | |
| ... | ... | ... | ... | 4 | ... | ... | ... | ... | ... | 6th March ... | Berbera. |
| ... | ... | ... | ... | ... | ... | ... | ... | ... | ... | 8th ,, | |
| ... | ... | ... | ... | ... | ... | ... | ... | ... | ... | 15th ,, | |
| 57 | ... | ... | ... | 4 | 250 | ... | ... | ... | ... | 25th ,, | |
| 41 | ... | ... | ... | ... | ... | ... | ... | ... | ... | ... | |
| 3 | ... | ... | ... | ... | ... | ... | ... | ... | ... | 4th April ... | Aden. |
| ... | ... | ... | ... | ... | ... | ... | ... | ... | ... | 17th ,, ... | Berbera. |
| 2,194 | 837 | 114 | 793 | 1,355 | 12,042 | 8 | ... | 9 | 10 | | |

(Signed) E. W. HUDDLESTON, Lieut., R.I.M.,
Marine Transport Officer, Somaliland Expedition.

## III.

**Detail of Troops, &c., disembarked at Berbera from 20th June, 1903, to 31st March, 1904.**

| Transport Number | Name of Transport | Left Port | Left Date | British Officers | Native Officers | Warrant Officers | Assistant Surgeons | N.C.O.s and Men British | N.C.O.s and Men Native | Transport Attendants | Hospital Assistants | Native Stockkeepers | Followers | Horses | Ponies | Mules | Camels | Buck Wagons | Tongas | Dandies | Ekkas | Remarks |
|---|---|---|---|---|---|---|---|---|---|---|---|---|---|---|---|---|---|---|---|---|---|---|
| | R.I.M.S. "Mayo" | Aden | 1903. June 20 | 5 | — | — | — | 300 | — | — | — | — | 17 | 1* | — | — | — | — | — | — | — | 1st Hants Regt. Bde. Sup. Off. Trspt. Cps. Est. |
| | "Upada" | Karachi | ,, 21 | 1 | 2 | — | — | — | — | — | — | — | — | — | — | — | — | — | — | — | — | |
| | R.I.M.S. "Mayo" | Aden | ,, 22 | 2 | 2 | — | — | — | — | 166 | — | — | 2 | — | — | — | 464 | — | — | — | — | 27th Punjab Infy. |
| | "Itria" | Karachi | ,, 22 | 1 | 1 | — | — | — | — | 168 | — | — | — | — | — | — | 412 | — | — | — | — | |
| | "Onda" | ,, | ,, 25 | 1 | 2 | — | — | — | — | 150 | — | — | — | — | — | — | 470 | — | — | — | — | |
| | "Urlada" | ,, | ,, 28 | 1 | 2 | — | — | — | — | 179 | — | — | — | — | — | — | 471 | — | — | — | — | |
| | "Ranee" | ,, | ,, 29 | 1 | 2 | — | — | — | — | 181 | — | — | — | — | — | — | 317 | — | — | — | — | |
| | "Sofala" | ,, | ,, 30 | 1 | 2 | — | 2 | — | 1 | 127 | 2 | 3 | — | — | — | — | — | — | 6 | — | — | |
| | "Clive" | Bombay | July 1 | 7 | 10 | — | — | — | 243 | — | 6 | — | — | — | 7 | — | — | — | 7 | — | — | |
| | | ,, | ,, 2 | 4 | — | — | — | 4 | 9 | — | — | — | — | — | 273 | — | — | — | — | 20 | — | |
| | "Hardinge" | | ,, 3 | 3 | 14 | 1 | — | — | 657 | — | — | 1 | — | — | — | — | — | — | — | — | — | 1 Sec. British Field Hospital. |
| | "Canning" | | ,, 3 | 4 | 2 | — | — | — | 1 | 62 | — | — | — | — | — | — | — | — | — | — | — | 3 Sec. Native Field Hospital. |
| | "Umta" | Karachi | ,, 6 | 1 | 2 | — | — | — | — | 102 | — | — | — | — | 269 | — | 251 | — | 10 | — | — | 27th Punjab Infy. |
| | "Tara"t | Bombay | ,, 6 | 10 | — | 13 | — | 255 | (from South Africa) | — | — | — | 211 | 45 Public | — | 899 | — | 80 | 4 water carts | — | — | 27th Punjab Infy. |
| | "Drayton Grange" | Durban | ,, 16 | 8 | — | — | — | 64 | — | — | — | — | — | — | — | — | — | — | — | — | — | 2 Machine Guns. |

559

| Ship | From | Date | | | | | | | | | | | | | | | | | Remarks |
|---|---|---|---|---|---|---|---|---|---|---|---|---|---|---|---|---|---|---|---|
| "Rance" | Bombay | July 29 | 7 | 4 | — | 2 | — | — | 207 | Pub. Pte.8 | — | — | 90 | — | — | — | — | — |  |
| "Itaura" | London | Aug. 28 | 2 | — | — | 51 | — | 122 | 28 | — | — | — | — | — | — | — | — | — |  |
| "Hardinge" | Bombay | " 11 | 4 | 7 | 5 | — | — | — | 16 | 223 | — | 4 | — | — | — | — | — | — |  |
| "Canning" | " | " 18 | 4 | 8§ | 1 | — | — | — | — | 425 | 7 | 1 | — | — | — | — | — | — | 3 Clerks. |
| "Clive" | " | Sept. 22 | — | 1# | 2 | — | — | — | 966 | 8 | — | — | — | — | — | — | — | — |  |
| "Rance" | " | " 3 | 9 | 10 | — | — | — | 5 | — | 8 | 6 | 2 | — | — | — | — | — | — |  |
| "Dalhousie" | " | " 14 | — | 1 | 2 | — | — | 202 | — | 56 | — | — | — | — | — | — | — | — |  |
| "Shirala" | " | " 25 | 5 | 5 | 1 | — | — | 4 | — | 609 | 3 | 1 | 1 | — | — | — | — | — |  |
| "Uia" | " | Oct. 5 | 3 | 3 | 1 | — | — | 3 | — | — | 24 | — | 303 | — | — | — | 259 | — |  |
| | | | | | | | | 61 | 268 | Pte. 6 | — | — | 680¶ (various) | | | | 83 | |
| "Santhia" | " | " 9 | 1 | 1 | — | — | — | 36 | 139 | — | — | 2 | — | 395 | — | — | — | — |  |
| "Nankin" | " | " 16 | 1 | 1 | — | — | — | 13 | 119 | Pte. 1 | — | — | — | 250 | — | — | — | — |  |
| "Sealda" | " | " 18 | 1 | — | — | — | 2 | 189 | 17 | Pte. 1 | — | — | — | 178 | — | 160 | — | — |  |
| "Islanda" | " | Nov. 10 | 7 | 8 | 2 | — | — | 51 | 16 | — | — | — | — | — | — | — | — | — |  |
| "Sealda" | " | " 16 | — | Clk. | — | — | — | — | 11 | — | — | — | — | — | — | — | — | — |  |
| "Rifors" | " | " 24 | 1 | 1 | 3 | — | — | — | 1 | — | — | — | — | — | — | — | — | — |  |
| "Oriental" | " | Dec. 5 | 1 | 4 | 1 | — | — | — | 12 | — | — | — | — | — | — | — | — | — |  |
| "Novassa" | Durban | " 17 | — | 4 | — | 28 | — | — | — | — | 250 | — | — | — | — | — | — | — |  |
| "Hardinge" | Bombay | 1904. Jan. 14 | 6 | 4 | 3 | 8 | — | 204 | 32 | 2 | — | 4 | — | — | — | — | — | — |  |
| "Hardinge" | Aden | Feb. 6 | 4 | 1 | 2 | 5 | — | — | 3 | 1 | — | — | — | — | — | — | — | — |  |
| "Private vessel" | " | " 14 | 2 | 1 | 1 | — | — | 60 | 4 | — | — | — | — | — | — | — | — | — |  |
| "Private vessel" | " | " 21 | 1 | 1 | — | — | — | — | — | — | — | — | — | — | — | — | — | — |  |
| "Hardinge" | Bombay | Mar. 28 | — | 4 | — | 23 | — | — | 4 | — | — | — | — | — | — | — | — | — |  |
| Totals | | | 113 | 103 | 44 | 2 | 718 | 2 | 1,887 | 17 | 11 | 2,073 | 1,394 | 1,684 | 1,973 | 2,847 | 80 | 27 | 20 | 482 |

\* 2 Coys. Native Mounted Infy.  † 2 Coys. British Mounted Infy.  ‡ 11 Conductors,  § 1 Treasurer,  ∥ Treasurer.  ¶ Various.

(Signed) C. J. KENDALL, Commander R.I.M.,
Marine Transport Officer,
Somaliland Field Force.

## III (A.)

### Detail of Troops, &c., Disembarked at Berbera from April 1, 1904, to July 7, 1904.

| No. | Transport. | Departures. From Port. | Departures. Date. | Date of Arrival at Berbera. | Officers. British | Officers. Native | Officers. Warrant. | Rank and File. British | Rank and File. Native | Camels. | Followers. | Horses. | Sheep. | Mules. | Stores. Tons. | Stores. Packages. | Departures from Berbera. Date. | Departures from Berbera. For Port. |
|---|---|---|---|---|---|---|---|---|---|---|---|---|---|---|---|---|---|---|
| H.T. | Meyun | Aden | March 31 | April 1 | 2 | 3 | — | — | 23 | — | 5 | — | — | — | — | 1,529 | April 3 | Aden |
| R.I.M.S. | Hardinge | Bombay and Aden | 28 | 3 | 1 | — | 2 | — | — | — | 38 | — | — | — | — | 184 | 7 | Las Khorai |
| H.T. | Meyun | Aden | April 4 | 5 | — | 1 | — | — | — | — | — | — | — | — | — | 5 | 5 | Aden |
| R.I.M.S. | Dalhousie | Aden | 5 | 6 | — | — | — | — | — | — | — | — | — | — | — | — | 7 | Las Khorai |
| H.T. | Meyun | Aden | 6 | 7 | 1 | — | — | — | — | — | — | — | — | — | — | 52 | 12 | Aden |
| R.I.M.S. | Dalhousie | Las Khorai | 10 | 11 | 2 | 1 | 2 | 289 | 19 | 1 | 82 | 20 | — | 10 | — | 50 | 12 | Las Khorai and Aden |
| H.T. | Meyun | Aden | 14 | 15 | — | — | — | — | — | — | — | — | — | — | — | — | 16 | Aden |
| H.T. | Meyun | Aden | 18 | 19 | — | — | — | 1 | — | — | 1 | — | — | — | — | 831 | 19 | Aden |
| R.I.M.S. | Hardinge | Las Khorai | 19 | 20 | 6 | — | 1 | — | 49 | — | 156 | — | — | — | — | 274 | 22 | Las Khorai |
| H.T. | Meyun | Aden | 21 | 22 | — | — | — | — | 4 | 3 | 2 | — | — | — | — | — | 22 | Hais |
| H.T. | Meyun | Hais | 23 | 24 | 3 | 1 | 2 | — | 72 | — | 3 | 1 | — | — | — | 1,267 | 26 | Aden |
| R.I.M.S. | Hardinge | Las Khorai | 25 | 26 | — | — | 3 | — | — | — | 114 | — | — | — | — | 1 | 26 | Aden |
| R.I.M.S. | Hardinge | Aden | 28 | 29 | — | — | — | — | — | — | 8 | 1 | — | — | — | — | 29 | Las Khorai |
| H.M.S. | Meyun | Aden | 28 | 29 | 6 | — | — | 100 | 2 | — | — | — | — | — | — | 448 | May 7 | Aden |
| H.M.S. | Fox | Illig | 28 | 29 | 2 | — | — | 27 | 461 | 151 | 146 | — | — | 127 | — | 417 | April 29 | Aden |
| R.I.M.S. | Hardinge | Las Khorai | May 1 | May 2 | 15 | 3 | 3 | 55 | — | — | — | 13 | — | — | — | 276 | 29 | Aden |
| R.I.M.S. | Clive | Bombay | 6 | 7 | 24 | 26 | 2 | 8 | 624 | 1 | 200 | — | — | 682 | — | 800 | May 3 | Aden and Las Khorai |
| R.I.M.S. | Hardinge | Las Khorai | 8 | 9 | 1 | 4 | 2 | — | 115 | 112 | 8 | — | — | 161 | — | 4,094 | 8 | Las Khorai |
| R.I.M.S. | Clive | Las Khorai | 10 | 11 | 3 | 12 | — | 7 | 3 | — | 1 | 3 | — | — | — | 500† | 9 | Aden and Las Khorai |
| H.T. | Meyun | Aden | 12 | 13 | 30 | — | 3 | 102 | 231 | — | 143 | 337 | — | 58 | — | 2,400 | 12 | Las Khorai |
| R.I.M.S. | Hardinge | Las Khorai | 13 | 14 | — | — | — | — | — | — | — | — | — | — | — | 238 | 13 | Aden |
|  |  |  |  |  |  |  |  |  |  |  |  |  |  |  |  | 1,500 | 15 | Las Khorai |

* Specie.  † Two guns.

561

| | Ship | From | Date | | To | Date | | | | | | | | | | | Remarks |
|---|---|---|---|---|---|---|---|---|---|---|---|---|---|---|---|---|---|
| R.I.M.S. | Clive... | ... | May | 14 | ... | May | 15 | 11 | 17 | — | 2 | 475 | 65 | 280 | — | — | Las Khorai |
| H.T. | Meyun | ... | ,, | 15 | ,, | ,, | 16 | — | — | — | — | — | — | 21 | — | — | Aden |
| R.I.M.S. | Hardinge | Las Khorai | ,, | 17 | Las Khorai | ,, | 18 | 3 | — | — | 2 | 56 | 249 | 143 | — | — | Aden and Bombay |
| R.I.M.S. | Clive... | Las Khorai | ,, | 18 | Las Khorai | ,, | 19 | 4 | — | — | 2 | — | 298 | 180 | — | 32 | Las Khorai |
| Freight | Matiana | England | ,, | 18 | ,, | ,, | 19 | — | — | — | — | — | — | — | — | — | Aden |
| H.T. | Meyun | Aden | ,, | 20 | ,, | ,, | 21 | 8 | 2 | — | — | 95 | 84 | 343 | — | 11 | Aden |
| R.I.M.S. | Clive... | Las Khorai | ,, | 22 | ,, | ,, | 23 | 4 | 10 | 6 | — | 166 | 199 | 14 | 812 | 270 | Aden |
| H.T. | Fultala | Las Khorai | ,, | 25 | ,, | ,, | 27 | — | — | 3 | — | — | — | — | — | — | Karachi |
| H.T. | Meyun | Aden | ,, | 27 | ,, | ,, | 28 | 2 | — | — | — | — | — | — | — | — | Aden |
| R.I.M.S. | Clive... | Aden | ,, | 30 | ,, | ,, | 31 | — | — | — | — | — | — | — | — | — | Aden |
| H.T. | Meyun | Aden | June | 2 | June | 3 | — | — | — | — | — | — | — | — | — | — | Aden |
| H.T. | Meyun | Aden | ,, | 10 | ,, | ,, | 11 | — | — | — | — | 5 | — | — | — | — | Aden |
| H.T. | Meyun | Aden | ,, | 18 | ,, | ,, | 19 | — | — | — | — | — | — | — | — | — | Aden |
| H.T. | Meyun | Aden | ,, | 18 | ,, | ,, | 19 | — | — | — | — | — | — | — | — | — | Aden |
| Freight | Goorkha | Aden | ,, | 7 | ,, | ,, | 20 | — | — | — | — | — | — | — | — | — | England |
| H.T. | Surada | Bombay | ,, | | ,, | | | | | | | | | | | | | Aden and Karachi |
| H.T. | Meyun | Aden | July | 24 | July | 25 | — | — | — | — | 27 | — | — | — | — | — | Aden |
| H.T. | Meyun | Aden | ,, | 1 | ,, | 2 | 2 | — | 3 | — | 4 | — | 199 | — | — | 15 | Aden |
| H.T. | Nurani | Bombay | June | 24 | ,, | 3 | — | — | — | — | — | — | — | — | — | — | Aden and Bombay |
| R.I.M.S. | Clive... | Bombay | ... | 25 | ,, | 7 | — | — | — | — | — | — | 2 | — | — | — | Mombassa |

| | | | | | | | | | | | | | | | | |
|---|---|---|---|---|---|---|---|---|---|---|---|---|---|---|---|---|
| Total | ... | ... | ... | ... | ... | 150 | 79 | 32 | 622 | 2,404 | 1,163 | 2,089 | 377 | 812 | 1,128 | 328 |

‡ Boxes ammunition.

(Signed)    C. J. C. KENDALL,

Commander, R.I.M.

## IV.

### SUMMARY of Troops, &c. disembarked at Las Khorai.

| No. | Transport | Departure From Port | Departure Date | Date of Arrival at Las Khorai | Officers British | Officers Native | Officers Warrant | Rank & File British | Rank & File Native | Followers | Horses | Ponies | Mules | Camels | Sheep | Stores Tons | Stores Packages | Departure from Las Khorai Date | For Port |
|---|---|---|---|---|---|---|---|---|---|---|---|---|---|---|---|---|---|---|---|
| R.I.M.S. | "Hardinge" | Berbera | Apr. 7 | Apr. 8 | — | — | — | — | — | — | — | — | — | — | 105 | — | 3,500 | Apr. 14 | Berbera. |
| R.I.M.S. | "Dalhousie" | ,, | ,, 7 | ,, 8 | — | — | — | — | — | — | — | — | — | — | — | — | 700 | ,, 10 | ,, |
| R.I.M.S. | "Dalhousie" | ,, | ,, 12 | ,, 13 | 4 | 1 | — | 2 | 36 | 29 | — | — | 105 | — | — | — | 6,000 | ,, ,, | Aden. |
| R.I.M.S. | "Hardinge" | ,, | ,, 16 | ,, 17 | 5 | 1 | 1 | 1 | 2 | 197 | 8 | — | 539 | — | 1,050 | — | 8,500 | ,, 19 | Berbera. |
| R.I.M.S. | "Hardinge" | ,, | ,, 22 | ,, 23 | 2 | — | 1 | 1 | 11 | 107 | 1 | 2 | 15 | — | — | — | 8,000 | ,, 25 | ,, |
| R.I.M.S. | "Hardinge" | ,, | ,, 29 | ,, 30 | 1 | — | — | — | 4 | 100 | — | — | — | — | — | — | — | May 1 | ,, |
| | Total | ... | ... | ... | 12 | 2 | 2 | 4 | 53 | 433 | 9 | 2 | 798 | — | 1,155 | — | 26,700 | | |

(Signed)   E. W. HUDDLESTON, Lieut., R.I.M.,
Assistant Marine Transport Officer,
Somaliland Field Force.

V.

DATES of arrival of H.M. Ships at Berbera with Details between the 9th July, 1903, and 31st March, 1904.

| Vessel. | Departure | | Date of Arrival at Berbera. | Officers. | | | Rank and File. | | Followers. | Stores, Packages. | Departure. | |
|---|---|---|---|---|---|---|---|---|---|---|---|---|
| | From Port. | Date. | | British. | Native | Warrant. | British. | Native. | | | Date. | For Port. |
| "Porpoise" | Aden | Aug. 11 | Aug. 12 | 1 | — | — | — | — | — | — | Aug. 12 | Aden. |
| "Porpoise" | Aden | Sept. 18 | Sept. 19 | 3 | — | — | — | — | — | — | Sept. 23 | Aden. |
| "Perseus" | Aden | Jan. 25 | Jan. 26 | — | — | — | — | — | — | 18 | Jan. 27 | Coast. |
| "Perseus" | Aden | Mar. — | Mar. 13 | — | — | — | — | — | 2 | 9 | Mar. 14 | Aden. |
| Total | | | | 4 | — | — | — | — | 2 | 27 | | |

(Signed)   C. J. C. KENDALL, Commander, R.I.M.
Marine Transport Officer,
Somaliland Field Force.

## VI.

**DETAIL** of Government Stores discharged from Messrs. Cowasjee, Dinshaw and Brothers' Steamers at Berbera from 1st April, 1904.

| | | | |
|---|---|---|---|
| SS. "Falcon" | April 5 | 17 | packages. |
| SS. "Falcon" | April 12 | 700 | ,, |
| SS. "Falcon" | April 19 | 69 | ,, |
| SS. "Falcon" | April 26 | 3 | ,, |
| SS. "Falcon" | May 3 | 971 | ,, |
| SS. "Falcon" | May 10 | 67 | ,, |
| SS. "Falcon" | May 17 | 3 | ,, |
| SS. "Falcon" | May 24 | 334 | ,, |
| SS. "Falcon" | May 31 | 526 | ,, |
| SS. "Falcon" | June 7 | 52 | ,, |
| SS. "Woodcock" | June 14 | 212 | ,, |
| SS. "Woodcock" | June 21 | 403 | ,, |
| SS. "Wissman" | June 28 | 1,012 | ,, |
| SS. "Falcon" | July 5 | 7 | ,, |
| | Total | 4,376 | packages. |

DETAIL of Government Stores sent to Bulhar by Dhows from 1st April, 1904.

| | | |
|---|---|---|
| 1st May | 144 | packages. |
| 24th May | 125 | ,, |
| 17th June | 21 | ,, |
| Total | 290 | packages |

### *Re-embarkations.*

The following documents, numbered I to VII, relate to the re-embarkation of troops, animals and stores in 1903, on the demobilization of the Field Force in 1904 :—

### I.

EMBARKATION Report, with Embarkation Diary, of Colonel J. C. Swann, Commanding Lines of Communication, 1904.

Berbera.

"Nurani" (1).    The embarkation commenced with the H.T.* "Nurani," which left Berbera on 22nd May, taking the 27th Punjabis, 56th and 57th Silladar Came Corps and the 28th Mountain Battery to Karachi.

---

\* Hired Transport.

The "Hardinge" followed her on the 23rd May, clearing out the rather R.I.M.S. large number of sick accumulated at Berbera. "Hardinge."

The H.T. "Fultala" took the 52nd Sikhs Baluch Camel Corps besides H.T. "Fultala" (1). a small number of other details to Karachi on May 27th.

The R.I.M.S. "Clive" made a preliminary trip to Aden on the 31st May, R.I.M.S. "Clive" (1). with 45 officers, including General Sir C. Egerton and Staff, and Brig.-General Fasken, who were transferred to the P. and O. homeward mail on arrival.

On her return the "Clive" was loaded with the 17th and 19th Companies R.I.M.S. "Clive" (2). Sappers and Miners, the R.E. Field Park, Field Hospitals and numerous other details, but was delayed three days in Berbera in compliance with a telegram detaining her, which arrived from the Government of India within half an hour of her being ready for sea.

The troops, with the exception of the sick, were left on board, and she eventually sailed for Bombay on the 6th June.

On June 8th the "Nurani" embarked a mixed complement of 5th K.A.R., "Nurani" (2). I.C.B.C.A., Baluch, 54th and 55th Camel Corps, Grasscutters and Hospital Kahars for Bombay and put to sea that evening.

The "Fultala," returning from Karachi, took on board the bulk of the H.T. "Fultala." *personnel* of the three Ekka trains, No. 1 N. General Hospital, and other details, and sailed for Bombay on June 11th.

The H.T. "Santhia" arrived on the 11th June, and after embarking H.T. "Santhia." 823 mules and 250 of the Indian Mule Corps, in charge of Captain Ross, and in veterinary care of Veterinary-Captain McGowan, sailed on June 13th. One accident occurred in this embarkation, a sling breaking and the mule suspended in it falling and breaking its back.

The H.T. "Surada" was due at Berbera on the 14th June, but encoun- H.T. "Surada." tered heavy weather, and did not arrive until the 20th instant.

The H.F.S.* "Lalpoora" had arrived on the 19th, and was despatched to H.F.S. "Lalpoora." Durban on the 20th with 200 Cape Boys of the 15th and 22nd Companies A.S.C. under nine conductors, and commanded by Captain O'Hara, A.S.C., with Major Fergusson, R.A.M.C., in medical charge. The accommodation H.T. "Meyun." retained on this ship was insufficient, and the balance of 3 conductors and 42 Cape Boys and 1 sergeant and 5 privates of the 5th Dragoon Guards had to be despatched by the ss. "Meyun" next day, the 21st June, to Aden for passage in the German East Africa liner to Durban.

The H.F.S. "Goorkha" was also got away on the 21st June, having H.F.S. "Goorkha." arrived on the 20th with the British *personnel* of the 15th and 22nd Companies A.S.C. on board.

Work was about to commence of embarking the balance of the Indian mules on the "Surada" when the H.F.S. "Malta" steamed in about noon on the 22nd June.

Work on the "Surada" had to be suspended as all barges and lighters H.F.S. "Malta." were required for the embarkation of the 700 *personnel* of the Hants Regiment, K.R.R.M.I., and No. 2 and 3 Companies Br. Mounted Infantry, which was effected by 6 P.M., when the ship left for England.

---

* Hired Freightship.

H.T. "Surada."

It was then possible to turn attention to the "Surada," on which 501 mules and a few officers' horses were embarked, together with about 550 of the Porter and Mule Corps, No. 2 Company B.M.I., Unit Hospital, No. 3 Field Medical Store Depôt and other details. The ship left for Karachi on the 24th June.

"Nurani" (3).

"The Nurani" was the last transport of the series proceeding to India. On her third voyage she embarked the Bikanir Camel Corps, No. 2 N. General Hospital, and such *personnel* of the various departments as it had been necessary to keep back until the last moment.

No hitch occurred in the embarkation, and no delay other than in the cases of the "Clive" and "Surada" explained on page .

Ships invariably left loaded the day succeeding that on which they arrived. Stores and heavy baggage were loaded immediately on arrival of the transport, horses next day about 2 P.M., and *personnel* commencing about 3 P.M.

The decks of the ship having been previously told off in accordance with the strength of units, the latter were timed to arrive at the pier in such order as would be most convenient for berthing them on board and in parties of such strength as the capacity of the barges and lighters admitted of.

Almost every ship took away a batch of invalids in charge of a medical officer.

The ss. "Meyun" made a weekly trip to Aden, taking away many officers as they became demobilized, and Arab coolies and camel men on discharge.

The Khareef added greatly to the difficulties of this embarkation, as the sea was far too rough for loading and unloading before 2 P.M. each day, and vessels delayed coming in until that hour; thus half the day was wasted.

During the period under consideration, 20 shiploads were embarked, comprising a total of 228 officers, 9,941 of other ranks, British and native, 91 horses and 1,331 mules.

A board of final survey, which included a veterinary officer in the case of the mule ships "Santhia" and "Surada," examined each ship in accordance with King's Regulations previous to her proceeding to sea.

R.I.M.S. 'Clive" (3).

The "Clive" arrived from Bombay and Aden on the 7th July, and after embarking the 1st, 2nd and 3rd K.A.R., proceeded to Mombassa and Chinde on 8th July.

This completed the embarkation.

(Signed)    J. C. SWANN, *Colonel*,
*Commanding Lines of Communication,*
*Somaliland Field Force.*

## I (A).

### EMBARKATION Diary, Berbera, 30th June, 1904.

| Name of Ship. | Date of Sailing. | Officers. | Warrant Officers. | Native Officers, Hospital Assistants and Agents. | British. | Native. | Public Followers. | Private Followers. | Horses, Officers. | Mules and Ponies. |
|---|---|---|---|---|---|---|---|---|---|---|
| H.T. "Nurani" | 1904. May 22 | 11 | — | 25 | — | 684 | 344 | 40 | 11 | 3 |
| R.I.M.S. "Hardinge" | ,, 23 | 31 | — | — | — | 171 | 493 | 55 | 9 | — |
| H.T. "Fultala" | ,, 27 | 13 | 1 | 27 | 5 | 920 | 102 | 54 | — | 3 |
| R.I.M.S. "Clive" | ,, 31 | 45 | — | — | 7 | — | — | — | — | — |
| R.I.M.S. "Clive" | June 6 | 12 | 9 | 33 | — | 374 | 425 | 58 | 8 | — |
| S.S. "Meyun" | ,, | 9 | 3 | 15 | 4 | — | 80 | — | 12 | — |
| H.T. "Nurani" | ,, 11 | 5 | 5 | 26 | 3 | 200 | 773 | 20 | 15 | — |
| H.T. "Fultala" | ,, 13 | 5 | 2 | 5 | 6 | 75 | 818 | 29 | — | — |
| H.T. "Santhia" | ,, 14 | 3 | — | 1 | 1 | — | 250 | 10 | — | 823 |
| S.S. "Meyun" | ,, 17 | 14 | — | — | — | — | 44 | — | — | — |
| S.S. "Falcon" | ,, 20 | 2 | 9 | 4 | — | — | 200 | — | — | 50 |
| H.F.S. "Lalpoora" | ,, 21 | 2 | 4 | — | 6 | — | 55 | 1 | 3 | — |
| S.S. "Meyun" | ,, 21 | 2 | 5 | — | 47 | — | — | — | — | — |
| H.F.S. "Goorkha" | ,, 22 | 13 | 2 | — | 701 | — | — | — | — | — |
| H.F.S. "Malta" | ,, 24 | 28 | 1 | 15 | 13 | 29 | 528 | 27 | 10 | 502 |
| H.T. "Surada" | ,, 28 | 8 | 1 | — | — | — | 29 | — | — | — |
| S.S. "Meyun" | ,, | — | 5 | — | — | — | — | — | — | — |
| H.T. "Nurani" | July 5 | 7 | — | 37 | 25 | 293 | 465 | 54 | 12 | For India |
| S.S. "Meyun" | ,, 5 | 7 | — | — | 2 | — | 211 | 2 | — | For Aden |
| R.I.M.S. "Clive" | ,, 8 | 14 | — | 8 | — | 846 | 100 | — | 11 | ,, |

Berbera,
2nd July, 1904.

(Signed) H. H. F. TURNER, Captain.
Embarkation Staff Officer.

## II.
## Detail of Troops, &c., Embarked at Obbia, 1903.

| Transport No. | Name | Date | British Officers | Native Officers | Warrant Officers | Rank and File British | Rank and File Native | Followers | Horses | Ponies | Mules | Camels | Approximate Stores (Tons) | Italians | Somali men | Women | Children | Remarks |
|---|---|---|---|---|---|---|---|---|---|---|---|---|---|---|---|---|---|---|
| | "Nowshera" | 10th January | 1 | .. | .. | .. | .. | .. | .. | .. | .. | .. | 120 | .. | .. | .. | .. | |
| | "Ikhona" | 15th " | .. | .. | .. | 1 | 1 | .. | 1 | .. | .. | .. | Nil | .. | .. | .. | .. | |
| | "Nowshera" | 30th " | 4 | .. | .. | .. | .. | 16 | .. | .. | .. | .. | 100 | .. | 6 | 7 | .. | |
| | "Ikhona" | 8th February | .. | .. | 1 | 1 | .. | 1 | .. | .. | .. | .. | Nil | 5 | .. | .. | .. | |
| | "Newark Castle" | 15th " | 1 | .. | .. | 1 | .. | .. | .. | .. | .. | .. | Nil | 2 | .. | .. | .. | |
| | "Sirsa" | 17th " | 1 | .. | .. | 3 | 20 | .. | .. | .. | .. | .. | 250 | .. | 28 | .. | .. | |
| | "Hardinge" | 18th " | .. | .. | .. | .. | .. | 1 | .. | .. | .. | .. | 350 | .. | .. | .. | .. | |
| | "Palitana" | 25th " | 2 | .. | 1 | 4 | 6 | 19 | .. | .. | .. | .. | Nil | .. | 6 | 1 | .. | |
| | "Hardinge" | 6th March | 1 | .. | .. | 6 | 3 | 101 | .. | .. | .. | .. | 300 | .. | .. | 9 | 2 | |
| | "Nowshera" | 18th " | 2 | 1 | 4 | 18 | 17 | .. | .. | .. | 21 | .. | 300 | .. | .. | .. | .. | |
| | "Hardinge" | 26th " | 2 | .. | 1 | 6 | 2 | 13 | .. | .. | .. | .. | 550 | .. | .. | .. | .. | |
| | "Nowshera" | 4th April | 2 | .. | .. | .. | .. | .. | .. | .. | .. | .. | 500 | .. | .. | .. | .. | |
| | "Hardinge" | 17th " | 14 | 24 | 10 | 24 | 162 | 380 | 10 | .. | 13 | .. | 600 | .. | .. | .. | .. | |
| Total | | | 28 | 25 | 17 | 63 | 211 | 541 | 11 | .. | 34 | .. | 3,070 | 7 | 40 | 17 | 3 | |

(Signed) E. W. Huddleston, Lieut., R.I.M.
Marine Transport Officer,
Somaliland Expedition.

III.

EMBARKATION of Details, &c., in H.M. Ships between the 9th July, 1903, and 31st March, 1904.

| No. | Vessel | Date | Officers British | Officers Native | Officers Warrant | Rank and File British | Rank and File Native | Followers | Horses | Stores, Packages | Remarks |
|---|---|---|---|---|---|---|---|---|---|---|---|
| | "Merlin" | Aug. 5 | 2 | — | — | — | — | — | — | — | |
| | "Porpoise" | ,, 8 | 2 | — | — | — | — | 2 | — | — | |
| | "Porpoise" | ,, 12 | 4 | — | — | — | — | — | — | — | |
| | "Merlin" | Sept. 9 | 2 | — | — | — | — | — | — | — | |
| | "Porpoise" | ,, 23 | 1 | — | — | 1 | — | — | — | — | |
| | "Merlin" | Oct. 7 | 1 | — | — | 4 | — | — | — | — | |
| | "Porpoise" | Dec. 9 | 1 | — | — | — | 40 | 2 | — | — | |
| | "Mohawk" | Jan. 13 | 1 | — | — | — | 80 | 25 | — | — | |
| | "Perseus" | ,, 27 | 3 | 2 | — | — | 11 | — | — | — | |
| | "Mohawk" | Feb. 27 | 1 | — | — | — | — | — | — | — | |
| | "Hyacinth" | Mar. 2 | — | — | — | — | — | — | — | 67 | |
| | "Pomone" | ,, 15 | — | — | — | — | — | — | — | 92 | |
| | "Mohawk" | ,, 22 | 2 | — | — | — | — | 4 | — | 205 | Somali levies. |
| | Total | | 21 | 2 | — | 5 | 131 | 33 | — | 364 | |

(Signed) C. J. C. KENDALL, Commander, R.I.M.,
Marine Transport Officer,
Somaliland Field Force.

## III (A).

EMBARKATION of Invalids for India in Hospital Ship and Hired Transports between the 9th July, 1903, and 31st March, 1904.

| No. | Vessel. | Date. | Officers. | | | Rank and File. | | Followers. | Horses. | Stores, Packages. | Remarks. |
|---|---|---|---|---|---|---|---|---|---|---|---|
| | | | British. | Native. | Warrant. | British. | Native. | | | | |
| R.I.M.S. | "Hardinge" | July 22 | — | — | — | — | 119 | — | — | — | |
| R.I.M.S. | "Hardinge" | Aug. 18 | 6 | 1 | — | 4 | — | — | — | — | |
| R.I.M.S. | "Hardinge" | „ 28 | — | 4 | 1 | 8 | 137 | 79 | — | — | |
| R.I.M.S. | "Dalhousie" | Oct. 1 | — | 2 | — | 1 | 40 | 41 | — | — | |
| 8 | "Shirala" | „ 9 | — | 1 | — | — | 40 | 7 | — | — | |
| 13 | "Nankin" | „ 27 | — | 1 | — | — | 60 | 29 | — | — | |
| 14 | "Islanda" | „ 30 | — | — | — | — | 26 | 30 | — | — | |
| 15 | "Sealda" | Nov. 2 | — | — | — | — | 73 | 79 | — | — | |
| 14 | "Islanda" | „ 22 | — | — | — | — | 36 | 51 | — | — | |
| R.I.M.S. | "Hardinge" | Jan. 22 | 1 | — | — | 3 | 92 | 174 | 1 | 5 | |
| R.I.M.S. | "Hardinge" | Feb. 20 | 1 | 1 | 3 | 9 | 92 | 172 | — | 92 | |
| R.I.M.S. | "Hardinge" | Mar. 8 | 4 | — | — | — | 8 | 133 | — | 70 | |
| R.I.M.S. | "Hardinge" | „ 16 | 1 | — | 1 | — | 103 | 255 | — | 113 | |
| | Total. | .. | 13 | 10 | 5 | 25 | 826 | 1,050 | 1 | 280 | |

(Signed)    C. J. C. KENDALL, Commander, R.I.M.,
Marine Transport Officer,
Somaliland Field Force.

IV.

PROGRAMME of Vessels conveying Troops, &c., from Somaliland, on Demobilization of the Field Force, to Home and Other Ports abroad other than India, 1904, under arrangements made by the Quartermaster-General's Department, War Office.

| Troops to be Conveyed. | Name of Vessel. | Arrived Berbera. | Arrived other Ports. | Left other Ports. | Arrived Port of Destination. | Name of Station to which Troops proceeded. | Remarks. |
|---|---|---|---|---|---|---|---|
| Detachment Telegraph Battalion R.E. | | | | | | Aldershot | The P. & O. steamship "Malta," started from Bombay 14th June with details from India. |
| 3 Companies 1st Hants Regiment Mounted Infantry, 4th King's Royal Rifle Corps Details | P. & O. steamship "Malta" | 22 June, 1904; left 22 June, 1904 | Suez, 27 June, 1904 | Port Said, 29 June, 1904 | Southampton, 9 July, 1904 | Portsmouth. Portsmouth. | |
| 15th and 22nd Companies Army Service Corps. Also 50 mules for Malta. | Freight ship "Goorkha" | 19 June, 1904; left 21 June, 1904 | Malta, 2 July, 1904 | Malta, 2 July, 1904 | London, Royal Albert Docks, 15 July, 1904 | Various. Aldershot. | |
| Conductors and native drivers employed with Army Service Corps in Somaliland. Also 77 buck-wagons | Freight ship "Lalpoora" | 18 June, 1904; left 20 June, 1904 | Delayed by accident at Mombassa, 2 July, 1904 | Mombassa, 11 July, 1904 | Durban, 27 July, 1904 | South Africa. | |
| King's African Rifles for Mombassa. King's African Rifles for Chinde | R.I.M.S. "Olive" | 7 July, 1904; left 8 July, 1904 | Mombassa, 16 July, 1904 | — | Chinde, 31 July, 1904 | — | |

V.

DETAIL of Troops, &c. embarked at Las Khorai for Berbera, 1904.

| No. | Transport. | Date of Departure. | Officers British | Officers Native | Warrant | Rank and File British | Rank and File Native | Followers | Horses | Ponies | Mules | Camels | Sheep | Stores Tons | Stores Maunds | Stores Packages | Remarks |
|---|---|---|---|---|---|---|---|---|---|---|---|---|---|---|---|---|---|
| R.I.M.S. | "Dalhousie" | Apr. 10 | 21 | — | 2 | 289 | 19 | 82 | 20 | — | 10 | 1 | — | — | — | 50 | |
| ,, | "Hardinge" | ,, 14 | 6 | — | 1 | — | — | 156 | — | — | — | — | — | — | — | — | |
| ,, | "Hardinge" | ,, 19 | 3 | — | 2 | — | 49 | 114 | 1 | — | — | 3 | — | — | — | — | |
| ,, | "Hardinge" | ,, 25 | 15 | — | 3 | — | 72 | 146 | 1 | — | 127 | — | — | — | — | — | |
| ,, | "Hardinge" | May 1 | 24 | — | 2 | 55 | 461 | 200 | — | — | 682 | 151 | — | — | — | 800 | |
| ,, | "Hardinge" | ,, 7 | 10 | 26 | 3 | 8 | 624 | 8 | 13 | — | 161 | 1 | — | — | — | 500 | 2 guns. |
| ,, | "Clive" | ,, 10 | 1 | 4 | — | — | 115 | 143 | 3 | — | 58 | 112 | — | — | — | 2,400 | |
| ,, | "Hardinge" | ,, 13 | 30 | 12 | 3 | 102 | 231 | 260 | 337 | — | 90 | [65 | — | — | — | 1,500 | |
| ,, | "Clive" | ,, 14 | 11 | 17 | — | 2 | 475 | 143 | 2 | — | — | 249 | — | — | — | 646 | |
| ,, | "Hardinge" | ,, 17 | 3 | — | — | 2 | 56 | 180 | — | — | — | 298 | — | — | — | 1,677 | |
| ,, | "Clive" | ,, 18 | 4 | — | — | 2 | — | — | — | — | — | — | — | — | — | 911 | |
| H.T. | "Nurani" | ,, 20 | 4 | — | 3 | — | 166 | 14 | — | — | — | 199 | — | 20 | 900 | 7,000 | |
| R.I.M.S. | "Fultala" | ,, 22 | 8 | 10 | 6 | — | 95 | 343 | — | — | — | 84 | 812 | — | 376 | 95 | Boxes ammunition. |
| ,, | "Clive" | ,, 22 | | 2 | | | | | | | | | | | | | 2 guns. |
| | Total | | 130 | 71 | 24 | 460 | 2,363 | 1,789 | 377 | — | 1,128 | 1,163 | 812 | 20 | 1,276 | 15,579 | |

(Signed) E. W. HUDDLESTON, Lieut., R.I.M.,
Asst.-Marine Transport Officer,
Somaliland Field Force.

## VI.

### DETAIL of Troops, &c., embarked at Berbera from 1st April, 1904.

| No. | Transport | Date of Departure | Officers British | Officers Native | Officers Warrant | Rank and File British | Rank and File Native | Followers | Horses | Ponies | Mules | Camels | Sheep | Tons | Packages | Remarks |
|---|---|---|---|---|---|---|---|---|---|---|---|---|---|---|---|---|
| H.T. | "Meyun" | April 5 | 3 | — | — | — | — | 52 | — | — | — | — | — | — | 3 | |
| R.I.M.S. | "Dalhousie" | „ 7 | — | — | — | — | — | — | — | — | — | — | — | — | 700 | |
| R.I.M.S. | "Hardinge" | „ 7 | 2 | — | — | — | — | — | — | — | — | — | 105 | — | 3,500 | |
| H.T. | "Meyun" | „ 12 | 4 | 1 | — | 2 | 5 | 5 | — | — | 105 | — | — | — | — | |
| R.I.M.S. | "Dalhousie" | „ 12 | 5 | 1 | 1 | 1 | 36 | 29 | — | — | 539 | — | 1,050 | — | 6,000 | |
| R.I.M.S. | "Hardinge" | „ 16 | 2 | — | — | 27 | 2 | 197 | 8 | — | — | — | — | — | 8,500 | |
| H.T. | "Meyun" | „ 16 | 6 | — | — | 100 | — | — | — | — | — | — | — | — | 655 | |
| H.M.S. | "Mohawk" | „ 16 | 2 | — | — | — | — | — | — | — | — | — | — | — | 276 | |
| H.M.S. | "Hyacinth" | „ 17 | 2 | — | — | 1 | — | 5 | — | 2 | 154 | — | — | — | 417 | |
| H.T. | "Meyun" | „ 19 | 2 | — | 1 | 1 | 11 | 107 | 1 | — | — | — | — | — | 1,000 | |
| R.I.M.S. | "Hardinge" | „ 22 | — | — | — | — | — | — | — | — | — | — | — | — | 8,000 | |
| H.T. | "Meyun" | „ 22 | — | — | — | — | — | 4 | — | — | — | — | — | — | — | |
| S.S. | "Falcon" | „ 22 | 6 | — | — | — | 4 | 4 | — | — | — | — | — | — | 1,000 | With 1 letter, and a bag of mails. |
| H.T. | "Meyun" | „ 26 | 3 | — | — | 1 | — | 1 | — | — | — | — | — | — | — | |
| R.I.M.S. | "Hardinge" | „ 26 | 1 | — | — | — | — | 100 | — | — | — | — | — | — | — | |
| S.S. | "Falcon" | „ 29 | 1 | — | — | — | 4 | — | — | — | — | — | — | — | — | |
| R.I.M.S. | "Hardinge" | „ 29 | — | — | — | — | 6 | 11 | — | — | — | — | — | — | — | |
| R.I.M.S. | "Dalhousie" | May 2 | — | — | — | — | — | — | — | — | — | — | — | — | — | |
| R.I.M.S. | "Hardinge" | „ 3 | 9 | — | — | 7 | — | — | — | — | — | — | — | — | — | |

DETAIL of Troops, &c., embarked at Berbera from 1st April, 1904—continued.

| No. | Transport. | Date of Departure. | Officers British | Officers Native | Officers Warrant | Rank and File British | Rank and File Native | Followers | Horses | Ponies | Mules | Camels | Sheep | Tons | Packages | Remarks |
|---|---|---|---|---|---|---|---|---|---|---|---|---|---|---|---|---|
| S.S. | "Falcon" | May 6 | 1 | — | — | 5 | — | 1 | — | — | — | — | — | — | — | |
| H.T. | "Meyun" | „ 7 | — | — | — | — | 1 | — | — | — | — | — | — | — | 31 | |
| R.I.M.S. | "Olive" | „ 8 | 8 | — | — | — | — | 2 | — | — | — | — | — | — | — | |
| R.I.M.S. | "Hardinge" | „ 9 | — | — | — | 4 | — | 54 | — | — | — | — | — | — | — | |
| H.T. | "Meyun" | „ 10 | 1 | — | — | — | — | 2 | — | — | — | — | — | — | 2 | |
| R.I.M.S. | "Olive" | „ 12 | — | — | — | — | 47 | — | — | — | — | — | — | — | — | |
| H.T. | "Meyun" | „ 13 | 4 | — | — | 6 | — | 17 | — | — | — | — | — | — | — | |
| R.I.M.S. | "Olive" | „ 15 | — | — | — | — | — | — | — | — | — | — | — | — | — | |
| B.I.M.S. | "Hardinge" | „ 17 | — | — | — | — | — | — | — | — | 4 | — | — | — | — | |
| H.T. | "Meyun" | „ 20 | 11 | 25 | — | — | 684 | 384 | 11 | — | — | — | — | 100 | 1,017 | 27th Punjabis, Camel Corps, &c. Invalids. |
| R.I.M.S. | "Olive" | „ 21 | — | — | — | — | 171 | 532 | — | — | — | — | — | — | — | |
| Freight | "Matiana" | „ 23 | — | — | — | — | — | 85 | — | — | — | — | — | — | — | |
| H.T. | "Nurani" | „ 28 | — | — | — | — | — | 155 | — | — | — | — | — | — | — | |
| R.I.M.S. | "Hardinge" | „ 25 | 31 | — | 8 | — | — | — | — | — | — | — | — | — | — | |
| R.M.I.S. | "Olive" | „ 25 | — | — | — | — | — | — | — | — | — | — | — | — | — | |
| H.T. | "Meyun" | „ 27 | 13 | 27 | 1 | 5 | 960 | — | 19 | — | 3 | — | — | 120 | — | 2 Maxim guns 52nd Sikhs. |
| H.T. | "Fultala" | „ | — | — | — | — | — | — | — | — | — | — | — | — | — | |
| H.T. | "Meyun" | „ 29 | — | — | — | — | — | — | — | — | — | — | — | — | — | |
| R.I.M. | "Olive" | „ 31 | 45 | — | — | — | — | — | — | — | — | — | — | — | — | |

575

| | Ship | Date | | | | | | | | | | | | Remarks |
|---|---|---|---|---|---|---|---|---|---|---|---|---|---|---|
| H.T. | "Meyun" | June 1 | — | — | — | — | — | — | — | — | — | — | 1,052 | Sappers, Ekka Train. |
| S.S. | "Falcon" | " 3 | 1 | — | — | — | — | 1 | — | — | — | — | — | |
| H.T. | "Meyun" | " 3 | 3 | — | — | — | — | — | — | — | — | — | — | |
| R.I.M.S. | "Olive" | " 6 | 12 | 33 | 9 | 7 | — | 8 | 874 | 483 | — | — | — | 2,885 | A.M.S., S. and T., Camel Corps. |
| H.T. | "Meyun" | " 8 | 8 | — | — | — | — | — | — | 86 | — | — | — | — | Ekka Train. |
| H.T. | "Nurani" | " 8 | 8 | 15 | 1 | 5 | — | 12 | 200 | 793 | — | — | — | — | S. and T. Corps. |
| H.T. | "Fultala" | " 11 | 11 | 2 | 26 | 8 | — | 15 | 75 | 847 | — | — | — | — | |
| H.T. | "Santhia" | " 13 | 13 | 5 | 2 | 6 | — | — | — | 260 | 823 | — | 200 | — | |
| H.T. | "Meyun" | " 14 | 14 | — | — | 1 | — | — | — | 44 | — | — | 50 | — | |
| S.S. | "Woodcock" | " 17 | 1 | — | — | — | — | — | — | 1 | — | — | — | — | |
| Freight | "Lalpoora" | " 20 | 2 | — | 9 | — | — | — | 1 | 200 | — | — | 675 | — | A.S.C. conductors and drivers |
| H.T. | "Meyun" | " 21 | 2 | 4 | 4 | 6 | — | — | — | 55 | — | — | — | — | |
| Freight | "Goorkha" | " 21 | 13 | — | 5 | 47 | — | 3 | — | — | 50 | — | 500 | — | 2 Companies A.S.C. M.I. details, detachment Hants Regiment. |
| Freight | "Malta" | " 22 | 28 | — | 1 | 703 | — | — | — | — | — | — | — | — | |
| H.T. | "Surada" | " 24 | 6 | 15 | 4 | 10 | — | 6 | 32 | 567 | 501 | — | — | 1,938 | |
| H.T. | "Meyun" | " 28 | — | — | 1 | — | — | — | — | 29 | — | — | — | — | |
| H.T. | "Nurani" | July 4 | 13 | 46 | 5 | 29 | — | 12 | 295 | 689 | — | — | — | — | Bikanir Camel Corps. |
| H.T. | "Meyun" | " 5 | 2 | — | — | — | — | — | — | 104 | — | — | — | 250 | |
| R.I.M.S. | "Olive" | " 8 | 13 | 8 | — | — | — | 11 | 846 | 79 | — | 106 | — | 4,500 | K.A. Rifles. |
| H.T. | "Meyun" | | — | — | — | — | — | — | — | — | — | — | — | — | |
| | Total | | 282 | 183 | 75 | 981 | 3,760 | 106 | 2 | 2,179 | — | 1,261 | 1,645 | 41,726 | |

(Signed) C. J. KENDALL, Commander, R.I.M.,
Marine Transport Officer,
Somaliland Field Force.

576

## VII.

Summary of Troops, &c., which left Somaliland on Demobilization, extracted from Embarkation and Disembarkation Reports.

| Name of ship. | Embarked at | Date. | Disembarked at | Date. | European Officers. | Warrant Officers. | British N.C.O.'s and Men. | Native Officers and Hospital Assistants. | Native N.C.O.'s and Men. | Followers. | Horses. | Mules and Ponies. | Buck Wagons. | Remarks. |
|---|---|---|---|---|---|---|---|---|---|---|---|---|---|---|
| | | 1904. | | 1904. | | | | | | | | | | |
| H.T. "Nurani" | Berbera | May 22 | Bombay | May 29 | 11 | — | — | 25 | 684 | 353 | 11 | 4 | — | 27th Punjab, Camel Corps, &c. |
| R.I.M.S. "Hardinge" | ,, | ,, 23 | ,, | ,, 30 | 18 | 3 | — | 2 | 168 | 535 | 9 | — | — | Invalids. |
| H.T. "Fulkala" | ,, | ,, 27 | Karachi | June 3 | 10* | 1 | 5 | 27 | 961 | 145 | 19 | 3 | — | 52nd Sikhs. |
| R.I.M.S. "Clive" | ,, | ,, 31 | Aden | — | 13 | — | — | — | — | — | — | — | — | |
| R.I.M.S. "Clive" | ,, | June 6 | Bombay | June 14 | 45† | 11 | 7 | 31 | 374 | 477 | 8 | — | — | Sappers, Ekka Train, &c. |
| S.S. "Meyun" | ,, | ,, 8 | Aden | — | 12 | 2 | — | — | — | 80 | — | — | — | |
| H.T. "Nurani" | ,, | ,, 8 | Bombay | June 15 | 9 | — | 5 | 15 | 199 | 777 | 12 | — | — | A.M.S., S. and T., Camel Corps, &c. |
| H.T. "Fulkala" | ,, | ,, 11 | ,, | ,, 19 | 5 | 2 | 3 | 26 | 66 | 876 | 8 | — | — | 3rd Ekka Train, &c. |
| H.T. "Santhia" | ,, | ,, 13 | ,, | ,, 21 | 2 | 5 | 6 | 5 | — | 258 | — | 825 | — | S. and T. Corps, &c. |
| S.S. "Meyun" | ,, | ,, 14 | Aden | — | 3 | 2 | 1 | 1 | — | 44 | — | — | — | |
| S.S. "Falcon" | ,, | ,, 17 | ,, | — | 14 | — | — | — | — | — | — | — | — | |
| H.F.S. "Lalpoora" | ,, | ,, 20 | Durban | July 27 | 2 | 9 | — | 4 | — | 201 | — | — | 77‡ | A.S.C. Conductors and Drivers |
| S.S. "Meyun" | ,, | ,, 21 | Aden | — | 2 | 4 | 6 | — | — | 55 | — | — | — | |
| H.F.S. "Goorkha" | ,, | ,, 21 | England | July 15 | 8 | 5 | 47 | — | — | — | — | 50§ | — | 2 Companies A.S.C. |
| H.F.S. "Malta" | ,, | ,, 22 | ,, | ,, 9 | 28 | 1703 | — | — | — | — | — | — | — | M.I. Details Hants Regiment. |

577

| Ship | Date | Port | Date | | | | | | | | | | Notes |
|---|---|---|---|---|---|---|---|---|---|---|---|---|---|
| H.T. "Surada" .. | ,, 24 | Bombay | ,, 1 | — | 6 | — | 10 | 15 | 29 | 553 | 6 | 501 | Indian Porter Corps, &c. |
| S.S. "Meyun" .. | ,, 28 | Aden .. | — | — | 1 | — | — | — | 29 | — | — | |
| H.T. "Nurani" .. | July 4 | Bombay | July 12 | 13 | 5 | — | 29 | 46 | 295 | 689 | 12 | — | Bikanir Camel Corps, &c. |
| S.S. "Meyun" .. | ,, 5 | Aden .. | — | — | — | — | — | — | 100 | — | — | |
| R.I.M.S. "Clive" .. | ,, 8 { | Mombassa | July 16 | 6 | — | — | — | 5 | 442 | 47 | 7 | — | } K.A. Rifles. |
| | | Chinde .. | ,, 31 | 7 | — | — | — | 3 | 402 | 35 | 4 | — | |
| Totals | .. | .. | | 216 | 49 | 822 | 205 | 3,619 | 5,254 | 96 | 1,383 | 77 | |

\* Disembarked at Aden for England.    † Transhipping at Aden to P. and O. ss. "Persia," for home.
‡ Not reported on Embarkation Report.    § Mules for Malta.

(8927A)        2 o

## 5.—MEDICAL AND SANITARY SERVICES.

Organization.    During the first expedition under Colonel Swayne the medical staff consisted of 1 officer and 3 hospital assistants, distributed as follows : 1 officer and 1 assistant with the column, 1 assistant at Samala and 1 at Burao. This staff was considered dangerously small. It was afterwards supplemmented, and under General Manning the Medical Service was organized under a Principal Medical Officer (Colonel J. F. Williamson, C.M.G., R.A.M.C.), while other medical officers were allotted as required. Colonel Williamson later became Principal Medical Officer under General Egerton and then had under him a Senior Medical Officer on the lines of communication, a Medical Officer at the Base and other medical officers attached to the various organizations.

During General Manning's expedition the following were the medical units with the force :—

Obbia force—
    1 section British Field Hospital, No. 15.
    No. 69 Native Field Hospital.
    Native General Hospital, 300 beds, with a British section of 32 beds.

Berbera-Bohotle force—
    No. 65 Native Field Hospital.
    Native General Hospital, 200 beds, with a British section of 12 beds.

The hospital ship "Hardinge" alluded to below.

Post hospitals were established on the lines of communication.

On the closing of the Obbia lines of communication the Native General Hospital was moved to Berbera on the "Hardinge," while the field hospitals crossed the Haud with the field force.

After June, 1903, the following medical units formed part of the Field Force :—

    1 Section No. 15 British Field Hospital.

1 Section No. 18 British Field Hospital.
3 Sections No. 58 Native ,, ,,
4 Sections No. 65 ,, ,, ,,
4 Sections No. 69 ,, ,, ,,

No. 1 Native General Hospital, 200 beds, with a British Section of 12 beds.

No. 2 Native General Hospital, 300 beds, with a British Section of 34 beds.

A field medical store depôt at the base.

The field hospitals were distributed among the troops in due proportion to the number in each brigade, force or garrison.

The hospital ship " Hardinge " was equipped on the scale of a 100 bed Native General Hospital, with some additional accommodation for British sick. Its total carrying capacity as a hospital ship was 457 patients (146 cot and 311 convalescent cases). This ship was reported on as a " thoroughly well equipped hospital ship admirably adapted for the purpose."

The general hospitals were located :—
No. 1 at Upper Sheikh
No. 2 at Berbera.

The principal diseases contracted during the Somaliland expeditions were :— *Diseases.*

*Scurvy.*—This accounted for by far the largest number of admissions to hospital. The principal causes of scurvy were—

The absolute impossibility of giving a fresh vegetable ration ;

The necessity of often going without small luxuries, such as spices, &c.

The poor quality of the meat ration at times ;

The properties of the water at many places which made it very difficult or impossible to cook food properly.

In addition to the above some of the troops came from stations such as Aden, where scurvy prevailed, and in the case of followers nostalgia was a cause.

The Principal Medical Officer recommended that in future expeditions vegetable seeds should be supplied by the Supply and Transport Corps. Vegetables could then be grown at posts on the lines of communication.

The actual remedies found effective were fresh milk,* fresh meat, dried fruits and a rum ration bi-weekly. Citrate of potash was also given as a preventative. Lime juice was found to have " practically little or no effect in checking scurvy." The Principal Medical Officer did not recommend its inclusion as a part of the army ration, but preferred tabloids of citrate of calcium or of citrate of potash and calcium chloride, five grains each.

Non-meat eaters suffered more severely than meat eaters.

*Malarial Fevers.*—Many cases were only recrudescences of pre-existing diseases. But malarial fever was met with, in the wet season, at Bohotle, Bihendula and Berbera. At Bohotle and Berbera there have at times been virulent outbreaks among the native population, and during the first expedition under Colonel Swayne there were as many as 271 cases of malarial fever among the troops; nearly all of these came from Berbera.

*Dysentery and Diarrhœa.*—Dysentery was considered to be due to the dust laden atmosphere and foul water.

Diarrhœa was due to similar causes and also to the saline properties of the water; this was specially the case in the Nogal, where violent purgation attended with severe vomiting occurred at certain camps where apparently only clear sparkling water had been drunk.

*Enteric Fever.*—Only some 17 cases were treated. It is little met with in Somaliland and very probably was introduced by some case among the troops from India.

*Conjunctivitis.*—Cases occurred among the African troops who wore the fez which was no protection against the glare.

General remarks.

The Principal Medical Officer considered that many of the

* Dairies were established at Berbera and Upper Sheikh, where there were general hospitals. The cows at Berbera were purchased and those at Sheikh were hired.

followers were too old and were already suffering from chronic diseases. He thought it possible that impersonation took place on a large scale between the place of enlistment and the port of embarkation, and to obviate this he recommended a second medical examination at the port of embarkation.

These were :—(a) Gunshot wounds ; (b) spear wounds.   Wounds.

Surgical wounds healed well and rapidly, but scratches and "field wounds" had a great tendency to suppurate and resist ordinary treatment. Some thorn bushes had poisonous properties and caused wounds which often passed to severe erysipelatous attacks.

Inflammation of the exposed parts of the body such as hands, arms and face were common, due to the intense power of the sun, and often proceeded to ulceration, and an affection resembling the South African veldt sore followed.

In the case of Somalis recovery from bodily injuries was remarkably quick. Even penetrating rifle and spear wounds of the head, chest and abdomen were recovered from rapidly.

The chief difficulty was the disposal of dead animals.  Sanitary.
These were always removed from the vicinity of camps, disembowelled and burnt when possible. Transport officers were enjoined to open up, and, if possible, burn animals which died between posts, dragging them clear away from the road first. In the latter part of the expedition it was not always found possible to cope with the numbers of carcases beyond opening them up.

Incinerators were established at all standing camps for the burning of refuse.

The ordinary trench latrine was used in camps and posts with good effect, as the campaign may be said to have been almost wholly free from enteric, dysentery or camp diarrhœa, except such cases as were caused as stated above under Dysentery and Diarrhœa.

Each unit and transport cadre was responsible in fixed camps for the cleanliness of its lines and for the disposal of any dead animals, and this was found to work well.

One hundred sweepers from India formed the conservancy establishment, supplemented at various points by locally engaged Somalis and by the lower grade of prisoners.

**Water.** Water in Somaliland has such an important effect on the health of the troops that some remarks on the water supply are inserted here (but see also Chapter XIV, 1).

(a) At Berbera.—The water is brought from Dubar at the foot of the hills. The supply is plentiful and the water, though slightly saline, is not unwholesome.

(b) From the Gutihari Pass to the foot of the Sheikh Pass the quality is good and quantity fairly abundant, especially at Bihendula, where there is a large supply of excellent water.

(c) At Upper Sheikh the water supply is from springs in the adjacent nullahs, mainly fed by upland surface drainage.

(d) On the interior plateaux the water supply in the dry season is wholly dependent on wells of a more or less permanent character, of an average depth of from 50 to 60 feet.

In the wells the hardness of the water is excessive. Sulphates of magnesium and calcium are present everywhere in large quantities, and in some places these are associated with sodium sulphate. Where this is the case, as in parts of the Nogal, excessive purgation with severe colic is often experienced. As many as 300 to 400 cases in a day have had to be treated whilst in the Nogal.

The water of many wells in Somaliland contain much sulphuretted hydrogen in solution. This, though at first very unpleasant, disappears to a great extent if there is sufficient time to expose it to light and air, and does not appear to be unwholesome. The best water in the interior plateaux is that got from wells in dry river beds.

**Medical comforts.** The Principal Medical Officer considered the medical comforts to have been "uniformly of good quality." He preferred the "Ideal" tinned milk to the other varieties.

A reserve stock (100 per cent., of medical comforts for field hospitals) was at all times maintained in the advanced depôts of the Supply and Transport Corps.

The main difficulty was the transport of the sick down the long lines of communication to the base. The ambulance transport used consisted of dandies, light double kajawahs for camels, camel carts, ambulance bullocks tongas, mules riding and burden camels. But in the first expedition under Colonel Swayne the sick and wounded were transported on camels by means of a sort of couch constructed of sticks and camel saddles. This means of transportation was not suitable for badly wounded or seriously ill men. <sub>General remarks on the medical service.</sub>

The light kajawahs have been alluded to under "Transport." In 1902 camel litters were sent from Bombay, made of bamboo, but they oscillated violently with every step the camel took, and weighed nearly 100 lbs. Thus it was found that the dandy was the only safe means of transport for really serious cases, but 10 Kahars per dandy were necessary; six Kahars being wholly insufficient. The marches averaged 20 miles per day, and at times heavy men had to be carried.

Generally, the medical equipment was sufficient to deal efficiently with all casualties and sickness met with in the Field Force.

A Dental Surgeon (Mr. Kenneth-Clark) was attached to the Force on September 10th, 1903, and performed a considerable number of operations. He visited all the posts on the lines of communication, spending a few weeks at each. He considered the dental outfit too heavy for camel transport, and in accordance with his suggestions it was subsequently altered. <sub>Dental work.</sub>

### 6.—VETERINARY DEPARTMENT.

The Veterinary Department during the period of General Manning's command was organized under a senior veterinary officer, Major A. F. Appleton, A.V.C., who accompanied the force to Obbia. Another veterinary officer was in charge of <sub>Organization.</sub>

the Berbera–Bohotle lines of communication, and under each officer were one British non-commissioned officer and two to four veterinary assistants. The principal sick depôt at this time was at Bohotle, having been moved from Olesan owing to lack of water.

With the arrival of General Egerton and the increase in establishment, the veterinary service was placed in charge of an Inspecting Veterinary Officer, Major C. B. M. Harris, D.S.O., A.V.C., who had the following establishment under him:—

    5 Veterinary Officers.
    4 Europeans. A Section No. 6 Field Veterinary Hospital.
    2 Salutris. ,, ,,
    1 Tindal. ,, ,,
    1 Lascar. ,, ,,
    3 Syces ,, ,,
    1 Cook. ,, ,,
    1 Bhisti. ,, ,,
    1 Pakhali. ,, ,,
    1 Sweeper. ,, ,,
    1 Clerk. No. 2 Field Veterinary Office.
    1 Veterinary Officer (included above). Base Veterinary Depôt.
    2 Europeans. Base Veterinary Depôt.
    1 Veterinary Officer (included above). Advanced Veterinary Depôt, Wadamago.
    1 Dresser. ,,
    1 Salutri. ,,

The Base Veterinary Depôt was at Berbera. The Field Veterinary Hospital was at Berbera till August 19th, 1903, at Bihendula till the middle of November, 1903, and afterwards at Berbera. The advanced Veterinary Depôt was at Wadamago from November 15th, 1903.

Veterinary officers were appointed to the various movable columns when detached and an inspecting officer was appointed to the lines of communication.

The inspecting veterinary officers urged strongly that all veterinary personnel should be under the Veterinary Department. During the expedition, under the existing Indian regulations, veterinary assistants in the supply and transport corps were solely under the orders of their commandants.

The chief diseases among animals were as follows :— Diseases.

### Horses and Mules.

*Epizootic Lymphangitis.*—12 cases occurred, all of which were imported.

*Strangles,* also imported.

*Mange.*—A few cases. Spread quickly prevented.

*Foot-and-Mouth.*—Among bullocks, probably contracted locally.

*Eye Diseases.*—Acute conjunctivitis and ophthalmia caused loss of sight and was produced by dust and glare. Puncture of the lens also occurred by thorns when grazing.

*Sore Backs.*—Chiefly caused by the inadequate amount of saddlers and of materials for making alterations.

### Camels.

*Strangles.*—A severe outbreak occurred in the Base Veterinary Depôt. It was an acute contagious laryngitis with ulceration of the mucous membrane of the pharynx. If not strangles, it was closely allied to it.

*Mange.*—Very prevalent among camels. To prevent it, it was recommended that mange baths should be constructed at the base and at other veterinary depôts.

*Poisonous Wounds* from thorns in the bush.

*Vegetable Poisoning.*—Especially from the Irgin bush, frequently eaten by camels. It has bunches of long, fleshy, peculiar light green stems, like elongated tallow candles, radiating from a common centre and curving outwards. Usually from 8 to 12 feet high. Poisoning also occurred from the Moh, Boa and Euphorbia.

*Camel Influenza.*—Very infectious.

*Camel Croup.*—Contagious.

*Camel Kud Kud.*—Rather like anthrax, only occurred among Somali camels.

*Camel Laryngitis.*—Very acute. Contagious, not infectious.

*Wry Neck.*—A large dose of Epsom salts (4 lbs.) generally cured this.

*Megrims.*—Animal dashed madly about. It occurred when animals were fat or had over-eaten themselves, especially when exposed to the sun. Yielded to prompt treatment, bleeding, &c.

*Sore Backs.*—Chiefly caused by the local saddle or Herio, which was considered to be cruel and useless, but sore backs were also caused by careless saddling, changing saddles and the shape of the back being altered by loss of condition owing to long and continuous marching. The Inspecting Veterinary Officer suggested as remedies that :—

> The system should allow of the resting of camels. During rests saddles should be refitted.
>
> Saddles should be fitted to an animal, marked with a corresponding number, and not changed.
>
> Palans should not be removed at night.

Attendants. The veterinary hospitals suffered at times from shortness of attendants. One line orderly per 100 sick animals and salutris in the same proportion was recommended.

## 7.—REMOUNT DEPARTMENT.

Organization. The Remount Department was placed in charge of Captain Hon. T. Lister, 10th Hussars, from July 4th, 1903, and after that officer's death, Lieutenant A. E. H. Breslin, 4th Hussars, took over charge of the department.

The Remount Department was under the Headquarters Staff until October 26th, 1903, from which date it was placed under the Officer Commanding Lines of Communication.

The personnel consisted of :—
- 1 officer.
- 1 warrant officer.
- 1 clerk.
- 3 sergeants.
- 1 farrier staff sergeant.
- 1 farrier sergeant.
- 3 privates.
- 8 shoeing smiths.

With the following native establishment :—
- 1 Somali interpreter.
- 1 Duffadar.
- 6 Nalbunds.
- 49 Syces.
- 2 sweepers.

The native attendants were distributed as follows : One Indian syce to three horses ; two Somalis to seven ponies ; two Abyssinians to seven mules. Some men were lent from the Indian Porter Corps and some Mounted Infantry syces were also added.

*Depôts.*—Depôts were located :—First at Bihendula, but in October this depôt was moved to Berbera, where it remained till December, 1903. After that date an advanced depôt was formed at Wadamago, consisting at first of 215 horses, 80 ponies and 105 mules, subsequently increased to 474 horses, 292 ponies and 120 mules ; a small depôt was still maintained at the base. In February, 1904, the advanced depôt was closed and the staff returned to Berbera. In 1904, an establishment from the Indian cavalry was employed to take the remounts from the depôts to the troops in the field.

The following estimates for remount requirements were made in July, 1904, to provide for the contingency of three months' active operations after September, and to meet them 900 remounts were ordered from India, and local purchasing was adopted :— **Estimated requirements.**

*Regular Troops—*
  125 per cent. (horses to mounted men) to be in the ranks by August 31st.
  25 per cent. at the depôt for September issue.
  25 per cent. at the depôt for October issue.
  25 per cent. at the depôt for November issue.

*Levies and Illalos—*
  110 per cent. to be in the ranks by August 31st.
  10 per cent. at the depôt for September issue.
  10 per cent. at the depôt for October issue.
  10 per cent. at the depôt for November issue.

*Officers—*
  One pony per officer throughout the force.

The above calculation was taken from the figures of the previous five months, and aimed at the Regulars having 100 per cent. fit horses after three months' active operations, and the Irregulars 40 per cent. fit after three months' active operations; 50 per cent. still mounted, but horses not fit for further work; 10 per cent. dismounted. As the following table shows, 3,785 animals were required to carry out the arrangement:—

TABLE showing Number of Horses to each Corps or Unit.

| Corps or Unit. | Number. | | | | Reserve Horses. | |
| --- | --- | --- | --- | --- | --- | --- |
| | Officers. | Rank and File. | Horses in Regimental Charge. | Horses Required to complete with 25 per cent. spare. | 25 per cent. for September, October and November. | 10 per cent. for September, October and November. |
| Four companies British Mounted Infantry (including Hants) | 21 | 523 | 410 | 295 | 535 | — |
| Two companies Indian Mounted Infantry | 11 | 262 | 276 | 80 | 273 | — |
| Somali Mounted Infantry | — | — | — | 367 | 448 | — |
| Illalos and Levies | 24 | 1,986 | 1,228 | 1,427 | — | 451 |
| Total | 56 | 2,771 | 1,914 | 2,169 | 1,256 | 451 |
| Horses available from Veterinary Hospital and Remount Depôt | — | — | — | 91 | — | — |
| Total | 56 | 2,771 | 1,914 | 2,078 | 1,256 | 451 |

The actual number of remounts received into the depôt was 4,605, including mules, of which a certain number was handed over to the Director of Supply and Transport, and these were not included in the above estimate.

The estimate made proved correct, and all demands for remounts were complied with.

**Remounts from India. Shipments.**

The remounts from India arrived in three batches, viz. :—
October 14th, steamship "Ula," with 251 remounts.
October 17th, steamship "Santhia," with 394 remounts.
October 24th, steamship "Nankin," with 250 remounts.

Of these 10 per cent. were found useless. Those from the "Ula" were considered best, consisting mostly of Arabs. The price paid to regiments (300 rupees) was found insufficient to get good class Arabs.

**Local purchase.**

Purchases were made at Harrar, Jig Jiga, Hargeisa, Burao, Zeila, Waran and on the Lines of Communication; of these the ponies that came from Harrar and Jig Jiga underwent such hardships on the road that they were practically useless.

**Remarks on Remounts.**

The Officer Commanding the lines of communication made the following observations regarding the remounts :—

1. *Arabs.*—The ideal remount for this country.

2. *Somalis.*—A hard, wiry, little beast, stands a lot of hard work and knocking about. Can travel in most parts without being shod. Can go without water for a day or two. Not used to grain, and thrives on grazing that most other ponies will not look at. Can carry a lot of weight for its size.

3. *South Africans (including a few Argentines).*—They stood the want of grain and irregular intervals of water very well.

4. *Indian Country-breds.* — Mostly indifferent. Chief defects : too big, too long in the back, badly ribbed up and washy. Those sent from India were not representative of the best class of Indian country-bred.

5. *Abyssinian Ponies.*—The majority were no use, badly made, no size and totally unfit to go any distance.

PLATE 51.

Somali Pony.

(*To face page* 590.)

6. *Abyssinian Mules.*—Good. Sound, stout-hearted and full of endurance. Will thrive on grazing where other animals will starve.

It was recommended in case of future operations that all heavy weights should be mounted on Arabs and light weights on Somalis, if procurable, but there was a great dearth of the latter at the close of the operations.

All remounts were shod in front and the larger horses were shod on all four feet. The English shoes were much preferred to the Indian, though rather heavy.

Shoeing.

The scale of rations at Remount Depôts was:—

Rations.

|  | Quantity. | | |
| --- | --- | --- | --- |
|  | Horses. | Ponies. | Mules. |
|  | Lbs. | Lbs. | Lbs. |
| At Bihendula— | | | |
| Gram .. | 6 | 6 | 5 |
| Bran .. | 2 | .. | .. |
| Grass (in addition to grazing) | 10 | 10 | 10 |
| At Berbera— | | | |
| Gram .. | 3 | .. | .. |
| Oats .. | 3 | .. | .. |
| Bran .. | 2 | 1 | .. |
| Grass .. | 20 | 15 | 1 |
| Jowari | .. | 5 | 3 |
| Bhoosa | .. | .. | 13½ |

Except on the march from Elkadalanleh to Kirrit (45 miles without water) remounts did not suffer from want of water on the lines of communication. But from Harrar there was a stretch of 90 miles without water and about 10 per cent. died on the road, and all arrived in a very bad condition.

Water.

The subjoined tables give details regarding the purchase of remounts during the fourth expedition :—

Purchases of remounts.

## I.

STATEMENT showing Animals Purchased in Abyssinia and Somaliland.

| Months. | Class of Animal Purchased. | | | | | |
|---|---|---|---|---|---|---|
| | Horses. | | Ponies. | | Mules. | |
| | Number. | Total Amount. | Number. | Total Amount. | Number. | Total Amount. |
| | | Rs. a. | | Rs. a. | | Rs. a. |
| July, 1903 | — | — | 38 | 9,420 0 | — | — |
| August, 1903 | 6 | 1,750 0 | 90 | 23,441 0 | — | — |
| September, 1903 | 11 | 2,900 0 | 255 | 64,849 0 | — | — |
| October, 1903 | 18 | 4,935 0 | 949 | 2,52,876 0 | 6 | 900 0 |
| November, 1903 | 6 | 1,800 0 | 238 | 64,865 0 | — | — |
| December, 1903 | 4 | 1,120 0 | 10 | 2,425 0 | 1 | 127 8 |
| January, 1904 | 1 | 250 0 | 1 | 250 0 | — | — |
| Total | 46 | 12,755 0 | 1,581 | 4,18,126 0 | 7 | 1,027 8 |
| Average | — | 277 4 | — | 264 7 | — | 146 12 |

## II.

STATEMENT showing Animals Purchased in Abyssinia and Somaliland, in Dollars.

| Months. | Ponies. | | Mules. | |
|---|---|---|---|---|
| | Number. | Amount Expended. | Number. | Amount Expended. |
| | | Dollars. | | Dollars. |
| September, 1903 | 117 | 13,525 | 709 | 63,726 |
| October, 1903 | 176 | 23,804 | 549 | 37,914 |
| Total | 293 | 37,329 | 1,258 | 101,640 |

## III.

STATEMENT showing Total Expenditure.

| Class of Animals. | Number. | Total Amount Expended. | | Average Cost. |
|---|---|---|---|---|
| | | Rs. | a. | Rupees. |
| Horses | 46 | 12,755 | 0 | $255\frac{13}{46}$ |
| Ponies | 1,874 | 4,74,119 | 8 | $252\frac{1871}{1874}$ |
| Mules | 1,265 | 1,53,487 | 8 | $121\frac{422\frac{1}{2}}{1265}$ |

(8927A)

## IV.

STATEMENT showing the Number of Ponies Purchased by Nos. 4 and 5 Companies, Somali Mounted Infantry, out of Protectorate Funds.

| Month of Purchase. | Number of Ponies Purchased. | Amount Expended. | Average Price. | Remarks. |
|---|---|---|---|---|
| | | Rupees. | Rupees. | |
| July, 1903 | 83 | 16,775 | $202\frac{9}{83}$ | |
| August, 1903 | 71 | 19,117 | $269\frac{4}{71}$ | |
| September, 1903 | 27 | 8,055 | $297\frac{4}{27}$ | |
| October, 1903 | 42 | 12,350 | 294 | |
| November, 1903 | 1 | 350 | 350 | |
| Total.. | 224 | 56,647 | $252\frac{199}{224}$ | |

**Camel remount depôt.**

In addition to the work of the Remount Department proper a Camel Remount Depôt was established near Gololi by circular memorandum dated 7th October, 1903, which ran as follows :—

1. Captain E. G. W. Pratt is appointed Commandant of the Camel Remount Depôt, which will be established in the neighbourhood of Gololi, on the Arori plain.

2. The Remount Depôt will receive over, with their own corps attendants in charge, any temporarily unfit camels of Camel Corps working as far south as Burao, and will endeavour to meet the indents of Camel Corps Commandants for replacement of unfit camels. No camels will be received over unless branded with the number of the corps to which they belong and their serial number in the corps. This is necessary to prevent exchanges and confusion in regard to unfit camels. In forwarding indents for camels in replacement, Corps Commandants will intimate the serial numbers to be given to them before issue.

3. Camels suffering from serious ailments, requiring skilled veterinary treatment should be sent to the Base Veterinary Hospital at Berbera as heretofore.

4. Officers in charge of Camel Corps passing up and down the lines of communication should give timely notice to the Camel Remount Officer of any camels which they may wish to send to the Camel Remount Depôt

to graze and rest, and the number of fit camels required in replacement. They will also have to provide attendants to take over the latter.

5. The Camel Remount Officer will, as far as possible, replace the unfit camels from the remount stock purchased by him, or received from Hargeisa and elsewhere. These camels will form part of the corps to which issued, and will be supernumerary to the corps' strength, and will eventually be absorbed in replacement of casualties.

6. The unfit camels sent to the Remount Depôt will, when fit, be sent back to their corps on whose returns they will continue to be borne.

7. The establishment of the Camel Remount Depôt will be as under :—
    1 Officer (Captain E. G. W. Pratt).
    1 transport veterinary dufadar (with a small stock of medicines).
    1 interpreter, 1 headman, 12 Somali drivers, 3 riding camels and attendants.

8. The Supply and Transport Officer, Burao, will afford every assistance to camel corps commandants in getting their camels sent to or brought from the Remount Depôt.

## 8.—ORDNANCE DEPARTMENT.

Major H. A. Anley, Army Ordnance Department, assumed charge of the ordnance service during January, 1903, and until it was handed over to the Indian Ordnance Department the service was conducted entirely in accordance with the system of the Army Ordnance Department There were in January, 1903, two ordnance officers, one, the chief, at Berbera, and another at Obbia. These officers were placed directly under headquarters. The Obbia detachment which had originally come from South Africa with a quantity of stores, moved to Berbera during April, 1903, and a base depôt was formed at Berbera, whilst an advanced depôt was opened at Bohotle on April 18th, 1903.

In July, 1903, the advanced depôt was moved to Kirrit, and a depôt was opened at Sheikh. At this time the strength of the department was :—

*Organization.*

|  | Officers. | Warrant Officers. | Sergeants. | Lance Corporals. | Privates. | Armourer Sergeant. |
|---|---|---|---|---|---|---|
| At— |  |  |  |  |  |  |
| Berbera | 1 | .. | 1 | 5 | 5 | 1 |
| Sheikh | 1 | .. | 1 | 2 | 4 | .. |
| Bohotle (Kirrit) | .. | 1 | 1 | .. | 1 | 1 |
| Aden | .. | .. | 1 | .. | .. | .. |
| On Lines of Communication | .. | .. | .. | .. | .. |  |

This establishment was supplemented by local labour.

The ordnance workshops were at Berbera.

The Indian Ordnance Department took over the ordnance services of the force on October 4th, 1903, and Captain E. P. Carter, R.A., was appointed Principal Ordnance Officer on the Headquarter Staff. He also fulfilled the duties of Ordnance Officer, lines of communication, and while the Headquarter Staff were at the front he was attached to the staff of the Officer Commanding, lines of communication.

The strength of the Department after the Indian Ordnance Department took over was:—

|  | Number. | | |
|---|---|---|---|
|  | First Party. | Reinforcements. | Total Strength. |
| Officers | 2 | .. | 2 |
| Warrant Officers | 4 | 2 | 6 |
| N.C.O.'s | 7 | 2 | 9 |
| Clerks | 4 | .. | 4 |
| Lascars | 44 | 12 | 56 |
| Artificers | 10 | 19 | 29 |
| Servants | 14 | 1 | 15 |
| Total | 85 | 36 | 121 |

also 11 Somali coolies who were employed at 12 annas per diem, and four Somali cooks at 6 annas per diem.

Depôts.   Ordnance Depôts were established at :—
Sheikh.

Kirrit (moved to Wadamago, February 7th, 1904).
Bohotle (closed November 17th, 1903).
Eil Dab.
Yaguri (closed February 3rd, 1904).
Las Dureh (March 8th, 1904, to April 11th, 1904).
Arsenal at Berbera.

All ordinary replacements were demanded through the Officer Commanding, lines of communication, any extraordinary requirements being sanctioned by the General Officer Commanding. System.

The issue of replacements was not large after corps had been refitted in October, 1903, and the equipment lasted without many exchanges or condemnations.

Clothing and necessaries were issued free on certificate by Commanding Officers that the articles were required to replace others worn out, lost or damaged, through no fault of the men on active service.

During the advance from Obbia the scale of S.A. ammunition was 100 rounds in regimental charge and 200 in Brigade Reserve, while 200 rounds were held in charge by the A.O.D. After July, 1903, the scale was 400 rounds in regimental charge and 200 rounds in post charge, reduced in the second phase of the campaign to 300 rounds in regimental charge and 100 rounds in post charge.* Scale of ammunition.

The scale of ammunition carried by artillery was :—

*Per gun.*

|  |  | Rounds. |
|---|---|---|
| With guns { Common shell | .. | 20 |
| Shrapnel | .. | 93 |
| Star .. | .. | 6 |
| Case shot | .. | 20 |
| In post reserve | .. | 70 |
| Carbine ammunition (carried on person) | .. | 100 per carbine. |

---

* See also page 331.

General remarks.

At the beginning of General Manning's campaign sufficient stores were taken from South Africa to meet the requirements of the force for four months, but the conditions of this campaign were so altered by its duration that further provision had to be made after the two depôts at Berbera and Obbia had been established. Gear for camel and mule transport, for which no provision had been made, had to be provided locally in A.O.D. workshops, and a considerable quantity of rope was obtained by local purchase from Aden. Ropes were also urgently required for wells, &c. These were supplied from Aden and from home. Generally there was a sufficiency of stores as supplied from home to meet demands, and local purchases were few as the resources of the country were small.

The following remarks on stores and equipment were made by various officers* :—

Remarks on stores, equipments, &c. P.O.O.

*Packing.*—For Somaliland, packages require to be of a size and weight convenient for pack transport; for this purpose a convenient weight is 80 lbs., or sub-multiples of 80 lbs. Contents of packages should be marked on the outside.

The one-ton vat was considered unsuited for rough usage, and for the country. Woollen clothing, horse rugs, &c., should be packed with some preventive against insects.

*Clothing.*—Boots require screw nails and toe plates. The tins of grease for boots require a better fastening.

*Tents.*—Circular tents and hospital marquees of the English pattern were found to be useless. Two hospital marquees at Upper Sheikh were blown to rags in less than three weeks. At Berbera the khareef wind blew so strongly and continuously that only E.P. tents with sides stiffened with matting could stand it. The Indian 160 lbs. G.S. tent and E.P. tents are the best.

*Troughs, Waterproof, 600 gallons.*—These should be attached to the posts by hooks. The posts should have a

---

\* See also remarks by Lieut.-Colonel Kenna in Chapter XII. Remarks on artillery equipment are given in Chapter XIII.

second loop about one foot below the top one, and should be 3 ft. 6 in. long.

*Pumps, Lifts and Force.*—A length of spare hose should be supplied with each pump and spare parts.

*Saddlery.*—Generally found too big for ponies.

*Covers, Sail Cloth, Waterproof,* 30 *by* 30.—Very useful, but should, if possible, be so treated as to be proof against white ants. The tarpaulins are too heavy for pack transport.

*Tanks, Camel,* 12½ *gallons.*—" An excellent store standing much knocking about." They should be supplied with leather washers, of which a spare supply should be arranged for. Stores should also be supplied for the soldering and repairing of the tanks themselves.

It was recommended that in future expeditions ice machines should be provided.

Two sorts of labels were required, one for public and one for private followers.

It was also suggested that the unit of the Army Ordnance Department should be the section, viz. :—One officer, one warrant officer, one staff sergeant, six sergeants, 17 rank and file.

At Sheikh, specially during the winter months, jerseys, P.M.O. woollen drawers, extra blankets and warm coats were very necessary. As regards headgear for Europeans the Cawnpore pith hat (tent club pattern) was considered by far the best. The S.A. Slasher hats afforded quite inadequate protection to the head.

The most suitable clothing was good milled khaki, the serge coats being too heavy and hot for marching in Somaliland though well adapted for men at posts such as Sheikh, Shimber Berris and Burao in the winter months.

10-inch and 5-inch helios were considered to be the most Signalling suitable for use in Somaliland, but the 10-inch should be equipment. packed in leather cases.

The 4-gallon tins of oil were found unserviceable. Oil Veterinary should be made up in 80-lb. loads. equipment.

The thermometers were reported on as indifferent.

The scalpels wore away easily and the saws for post-mortems were quite useless. The Inspecting Veterinary Officer was strongly of opinion that the contents of the veterinary chest required serious and comprehensive attention, and recommended the inclusion of a microscope and a "Diagnostic." He also considered that a set of hobbles for casting should be included in the equipment of a field veterinary hospital.

Wheel clipping machines were preferred to hand clippers, as the former work much faster and only require a new knife when out of order.

Clerical equipment.
Typewriters were found to be invaluable, and a printing press was considered an important adjunct to the headquarters and lines of communication of an expeditionary force.

## 9.—Accounts Department.

Organization.
The Accounts Department was under a Field Controller belonging to the Indian Military Accounts Department, assisted, after July, 1903, by two paymasters (one belonging to the Indian Military Accounts Department and one to the Army Pay Department) by a Protectorate paymaster and by a Treasury Chest Officer.

A Field Audit Office was first opened at Berbera in February, 1903.

All the accounts, except those concerned with officers of the Imperial forces, went through the Field Controller. The Paymaster of the Army Pay Department was responsible for the pay and accounts of all troops paid at Imperial rates of pay.

Currency.
The currency used was Rupees, except in the case of remount purchases in Abyssinia, for which purpose two consignments of Maria Theresa dollars were obtained. The Field Controller, however, recommended that in future Abyssinian currency should be used for such purposes.

Remarks by C.S.O.
The following remarks were made by the Chief Staff Officer in the fourth expedition :—

## V. Finance.

1. The accounts under the Indian system of audit were at a disadvantage from the outset, in July, 1903, owing to the arrears which had accrued during the previous seven months, both in their preparation and audit. The inelasticity of the system and the labour it entails on staff auditing and accounting establishments are in marked contrast to the home system.

2. Complaints were general by officers accounting under the Indian system of the numerous vouchers and counter-signatures required, of the minute subdivisions of covering orders to be obtained and submitted with their accounts, also of the voluminous objection statements to which they had to reply under all conditions of active service; as the audit was not up to date the objections involved reference to records, generally speaking some months old, which, consequently, had to accompany the officers on the march.

3. A field force order is sufficient authority to pass any expenditure of an exceptional nature that may be incurred, and the military accounts rules provide for a free relaxation of audit to meet the exigencies of war. They lay down no limit to the sanctioning power of the Chief Supply and Transport Officer of the force in respect of supply and transport stores.

4. Except in small matters of ordnance stores, there is no delegation of powers to General officers commanding brigades, to officers in independent command, or to accounting officers, the result being that the accounting officers were required to obtain as vouchers for their accounts multitudinous sanctions by officers in independent commands, which, for purposes of final audit, required covering sanction in field force orders. These various orders testify to the laborious duplication and, in some cases, triplication of work entailed on staff establishments, and reveal a portion only of labour of accounting and audit.

5. The Indian system as compared with the home system undoubtedly tends towards economy up to a certain point, but, as the chief part of the labour involved is in duplication and triplication, and in adjusting small details, it appears that in this respect the economy is false.

6. Absolute accuracy on field service is unattainable and it would appear that by a very small reduction in the percentage of paper accuracy aimed at, a great saving might be effected in the valuable time and energies absorbed, both of the Accounts Department itself and of the staffs, departments and units concerned, and in a corresponding reduction in the establishments, stationery, &c., maintained for accounting purposes.

7. From a non-departmental point of view, it appears that to facilitate a suitable relaxation of audit the following steps are desirable in the interests of true economy :—

   (a) A delegation of sanctioning powers to officers in independent command.
   (b) A delegation of powers to accounting officers to write off unaccounted balances of expenditure up to a certain percentage of the total of each

account. In this case it has been pointed out by the Field Controller, it might be advantageous to vary the percentage according to the officer's rank or position.

(c) A careful elimination of the duplication of work to ensure that one signature to each transaction covers all the responsibility of each officer concerned in that transaction, whether sanctioning, issuing, receiving or demanding.

(d) The auditing officer to be responsible to the General Officer Commanding for the review of unaccounted balances, and for the adjustment of the whole of any such balance as exceeds the authorised percentage.

## VI. Officers.

The difference in the system of payment of special service officers under the Allowance Regulations and of special service or staff officers, paid according to Indian regulations, was found to operate to the disadvantage of officers of the Indian establishment, pending the formal sanction to the scheme of organization of the field force ; no staff pay is available for them till this sanction is received, whereas the grade pay of special service officers of the home establishment is available in whatever position they are employed. The Indian system has the advantage that the rate of staff pay is fixed according to the responsibility and importance of each appointment, but has a great disadvantage in the restriction it imposes on the employment of an officer for various duties according to the exigencies of active service, in that he is liable to suffer pecuniary loss unless he is performing the duties of an appointment already included in the sanctioned establishment of the field force.

This and other anomalies would be avoided were all officers, sent for extra regimental duty, from the Indian establishment, appointed special service officers with graded pay at rates fixed on the analogy of the grading under the allowance regulations.

*Remarks by General Egerton.*

General Egerton remarked on the above :—

Greater latitude should be allowed to general officers in the field as to the employment of staff officers in other capacities than those they are officially filling. The centre of gravity is continually changing, but to shift an officer from a billet in one place under the existing Indian regulations requires not only special sanction of Government, but entails heavy loss of pay on the officer during the interval between his relinquishing one appointment till he takes up another. Such complications are altogether avoided by the graded system, which only needs to be a little elaborated to meet all the requirements of the Indian system.

# CHAPTER XV.

## DEMOBILIZATION.

The substance of General Sir C. Egerton's telegrams of the 9th and 15th April, 1904, to the War Office, recommending the reduction and demobilization of the force, is given in Chapter VI, and on the 18th April the Secretary of State for War stated in the House of Commons that it had been decided to discontinue the military operations and to reduce the field force in Somaliland. The Secretary of State for War had, however, on the 15th April informed General Egerton that previous to the actual demobilization being taken in hand the operations against Illig were to be carried out. Illig, however, was captured and destroyed on the 21st April, and on the 10th May the Secretary of State for War telegraphed to the General Officer Commanding as follows :—

*General arrangements for demobilization.* His Majesty's Government have decided that the whole of the troops now in Somaliland, excepting only local levies, are to be placed under orders to return to their permanent stations, two companies Indian Mounted Infantry and two Indian battalions being, however, temporarily detained to hold the Burao-Bohotle line and the Ain Valley, pending the completion of the necessary arrangements for the organization of local forces. The remainder of the Indian troops will return at once to India ; British troops to be sent home ; African troops to proceed to their own Protectorates. Colonel Swayne is returning to resume civil and military charge of the Protectorate, and organize the future defence arrangements. His arrival will set you free to return to India. Detailed orders as to troops and stores will follow.

On the 18th May the Secretary of State for India informed the Viceroy of India of these arrangements and stated that the selection of the native infantry battalions was left to him, and that the troops and followers who were returning to India were to be moved under his directions, except that the 101st Grenadiers and 107th Pioneers were to remain in Somaliland for not more than four months.

On the 21st May General Egerton reported that arrangements for the transfer to Colonel Swayne of the civil administration and of the temporary garrison and local levies were complete; also those for the demobilization of the Field Force by Colonel Swann. He also stated that the concentration of the troops at Berbera would shortly be concluded. The General therefore requested permission to leave Somaliland and hand over the command temporarily to Colonel Swann. Sanction being given for this course, General Egerton left Berbera on the 2nd June, handing over the demobilization arrangements to Colonel Swann, and the civil administration to Captain Cordeaux, pending the arrival of Colonel Swayne from England.

On the 4th June the Secretary of State for Foreign Affairs telegraphed to Colonel (local Brig.-General) Swayne :—

Plan of concentration of troops.

From the date of your assuming civil and military charge of Somaliland the administration of the troops remaining in the Protectorate will be transferred from the War Office to the Foreign Office, but you are authorized to communicate direct with the War Office on all questions connected with the clearing up of stores surplus of your requirements, and with the Government of India with regard to any minor details as to Indian troops.

Consequent on these instructions, the concentration at Berbera was carried out in accordance with the following plan :—

1. On the 19th April orders were sent to the Officer Commanding 1st Brigade to withdraw from the Nogal by the 8th May and to report to headquarters the route by which he would withdraw.

2. On the 22nd April orders were issued for the disbandment of the Musa Abukr levy under the orders of the Political Officer.

3. On the 25th April orders were issued for the formation of a movable column at Eil Dab.*

4. On the 1st May orders were issued for the movement of the 27th Punjabis and the 52nd Sikhs to Berbera, the posts they were holding being relieved by the 101st Grenadiers and the 107th Pioneers. The posts at Olesan, Garrero, Kirrit and Gerloka were abandoned.

5. On the 16th May it was decided that :—

(1) On the arrival of the 1st Brigade at Eil Dab the whole of the Brigade, except the Somali Mounted Infantry, were to proceed to Berbera for demobilization.

(2) Pending the formation of a movable column, Eil Dab was to be garrisoned by—

    100 rifles, 107th Pioneers.
    2 companies Somali Mounted Infantry.

*Embarkation of troops.*

The actual embarkation† of troops began on the 23rd May by the hired transport "Nurani," which sailed for Karachi on that date, having on board the 27th Punjabis, 28th Mountain Battery, and details. The R.I.M.S. "Hardinge" sailed on the same date with invalids and officers.

The transportation of troops to India was continued by the "Fultala," which sailed on 27th May, by the R.I.M.S. "Clive," sailing on the 6th June, and by the transports "Santhia" and "Surada"; the "Fultala" and "Nurani" doing several voyages to and fro.

The British troops were conveyed home by the transports "Malta" and "Goorkha," which left Berbera on the 22nd June and 21st June respectively.

African troops were moved to Mombassa and Chinde by the R.I.M.S. "Clive" on the 8th July, and South African

---

\* This movable column was eventually organized by Lieut.-Colonel Aplin, in compliance with orders issued on 22nd June, and consisted of 2 companies Indian Mounted Infantry, 300 107th Pioneers, 150 Somali Mounted Infantry, 20 Illalos, 2 maxims.

† See also Chapter XIV. 4.

details to Durban by the freight ship "Lalpoora" on the 20th June.

Thus by the 8th July the demobilization of the force was complete as far as regards personnel.

In Field Force Orders of the 22nd May a provisional scheme was published for the future garrison of Somaliland. The orders also laid down that "the scheme will be carried out under the orders of Officer Commanding Lines of Communication, who will also carry out the demobilization of the remainder of the force in communication with the Officer Commanding 1st Brigade, and General Officer Commanding 2nd Brigade." This scheme is inserted at the end of this chapter.

*Disposal of clothing, stores, &c.*

On the 30th April General Egerton telegraphed to the Secretary of State for War as follows :—

Request instruction by telegraph as to disposal of all clothing, equipment and transport gear supplied by Supply and Transport Corps. Suggest troops and followers being allowed to retain clothing in use, as is custom under Indian Regulations. Clothing, equipment and transport gear in stock being retained for issue to permanent garrison hereafter; unserviceable articles being sold by auction.

The Secretary of State for War replied on the 12th May :—

Your proposals approved. Send in due course priced list in detail of the articles of clothing, equipment and transport gear retained for the permanent garrison, stating to whom articles handed over.

And on the 19th May he telegraphed :—

Arrange for all stores, Protectorate property, to be separated and collected from various posts, to await further instructions as to disposal on arrival of Colonel Swayne. It is understood that Indian troops retained in the country will be left complete with their own supply and transport arrangements.

On the 13th June the Officer Commanding Lines of Communication asked the Secretary of State for War for more definite instructions as to the disposal and handing over of stores, and on the 17th June he was informed in reply :—

The following is the procedure for the disposal of stores and animals :—
(1) Stores, &c., for the use of temporary garrison to be handed over free of charge.

(2) Stores, &c., for the use of the normal Protectorate force to be handed over on payment of their value, after deducting the estimated cost of removal to India or this country. Stores, &c., not worth the cost of removal to be charged to the Protectorate at the price they would fetch in the market locally.

In order to assist in the transfer of stores, &c., to the Foreign Office an Army Service Corps officer was sent to Somaliland in June (see page 609). As a result of his recommendations some stores were taken over by the Protectorate, a few were locally sold, and the remainder (chiefly equipment and ammunition) was sent back to England. The water tanks were taken over by the Egyptian Government.

On the 1st May orders were issued for all engineer stores to be returned to the Engineer Field Park, Berbera, and on the 6th May it was decided that:— *Engineer stores.*

Ordnance establishments, before returning to India, were to return to Ordnance charge all equipment and stores which were— *Ordnance.*

(a) Not of Indian patterns.
(b) Not on Indian equipment tables.

In a similar manner, establishments, before returning to England, the Colonies or Protectorates, were to return stores and complete equipment according to the patterns and equipment tables in force at their destination.

The General Officer Commanding 2nd Brigade, and Officers Commanding 1st Brigade, Lines of Communication and Mounted Troops were to dispose of all cases of lost or damaged stores belonging to units under their respective commands, the value of which did not exceed 100 rs. A Board, other than a Regimental Board, was to be held on all lost or damaged stores, the total value of which exceeded 100 rs., and the decision of the Board, after approval by the officers above mentioned, so far as units under their respective commands were concerned, was to be final.

The above orders also applied to individual officers whose equipment was not borne on the books of any unit or department, and who were to be called upon by the Field Controller to account for such stores as were not returned nor accounted for.

*Disposal of animals.*

As early as the 15th March General Egerton had written (S.A. 2235) to the Secretary of the Army Council submitting proposals as to the disposal of transport animals and vehicles on the demobilization of the Field Force. He suggested that the camels should be disposed of locally, after the requirements of the Protectorate and the Aden garrison had been considered; that the Indian Government should be given the option of purchasing the mules; that the buckwagons should be returned to South Africa; and that the ekkas and ponies should be disposed of at Aden.

On the 7th April the Secretary of State for War telegraphed approving generally of the above suggestions, and after some further correspondence he telegraphed to General Egerton on the 9th May :—

Camels should be disposed of as suggested in your letter No. S.A. 2235 . . . . Bullocks and donkeys disposed of locally. . . . 50 transport ponies should be sold locally. . . .

On the 19th May the Indian Government notified their willingness to take 1,200 to 1,500 selected mules, and finally 1,200 were sent to India, and 50 to Malta, while 500 Abyssinians and 90 Army Service Corps mules were handed over to the Foreign Office, 419 were retained for the temporary garrison and the balance was disposed of locally.

The Bikanir riding camels were sold to the Protectorate at 250 rs. each, and remounts were disposed of locally, the Protectorate being given first offer.

*Disposal of transport animals.*

As regards transport animals, it was decided that all mules, exclusive of Army Service Corps and battery mules, then with the force, but including regimental gun mules with Pioneer battalions, mules with sappers and miners, and mules in remount charge and riding mules, were to be handed over to Supply and Transport Officers of the nearest posts for despatch to the officer in charge of the Indian Mule Transport, Berbera, who was to grant units receipts for mules and mule equipment received by him.

The gear of the mules was to be surveyed by units before being handed over to Supply and Transport Corps, and only gear in serviceable condition and suitable for transport purposes was to be accepted. Unserviceable gear and gear of special pattern peculiar to Pioneer battalions was to be disposed of under the orders of the Principal Ordnance Officer, Somaliland Field Force.

The attendants accompanied their animals, but those attached to the 52nd Sikhs and Sappers and Miners were to return to India with their units.

As regards vehicles, eight buck-wagons were retained for use in the Protectorate, the 90 Army Service Corps mules referred to above being retained for use with these vehicles. The remainder of the wagons (77) were returned to South Africa. *Disposal of vehicles.*

On the 13th May General Egerton telegraphed to the Secretary of State for War suggesting that all surplus articles of supply should be offered to the Egyptian Government at book value. This was approved on the understanding that the Foreign Office, as represented by Brigadier-General Swayne, should first be able to select what they required. General Egerton wished also to dispose of any balance to India and Aden, but neither the Indian Government nor the General Officer Commanding Aden required these supplies, and the correspondence continued with a telegram from the Secretary of State to the Officer Commanding Lines of Communication on 10th June :— *Disposal of supplies.*

Report by post quantity, description commissariat supplies, surplus to requirements, and your recommendations as to disposal, stating if any can be advantageously sold locally.

Finally it was decided to send Major G. Paul, C.M.G., Army Service Corps, to Somaliland, to advise Brig.-General

(8927A) 2 Q

Swayne as to the disposal of surplus stores, supplies, &c., and to represent the War Office. Major Paul arrived at Berbera in July, 1904, and, as a result of his recommendations, some supplies were locally consumed, being handed over to the Protectorate; some (chiefly forage) were sold locally, and others (tobacco, preserved meat and vegetables, &c.) were sent back to England.

*Machine guns.*

There were 21 machine guns in the country when the operations ceased. Of these 15 accompanied corps leaving Somaliland, 2 belonged to the Protectorate, and the other 4 were handed over to the Protectorate for the military occupation of the country.

*Demobilization of A.P.D. and closing of accounts.*

With respect to financial arrangements, General Egerton telegraphed on the 22nd May:—

> Please telegraph instructions up to what date and of what month accounts will be audited by Field Controller. Controller suggests that Bombay Command should undertake audit of establishment bills, supply, transport and all other accounts except those of corps. Accounts of corps to be submitted to commands on which dependent. One officer, Supply and Transport Corps, with necessary establishment, to proceed to Poona, where field audit office should be located and adjust all supply and transport accounts. Instructions also requested regarding payment of troops and establishments forming temporary garrison, and for the demobilization of the Army Pay Department.

These suggestions were sanctioned and the Army Pay Department establishment was sent home as soon as all the troops drawing pay from that source had embarked.

*Staff offices.*

As to the staff offices, it was arranged that on demobilization all permanent records and books of regulations of staff offices were to be handed over to the Base Commandant, while office equipment, stationery, furniture and tents were to be returned to the Ordnance Department at Berbera. These last were subsequently taken over by the Protectorate.

ORGANIZATION OF LOCAL FORCES AFTER DEMOBILIZATION.

*Instructions to General Swayne.*

On the 19th May the Secretary of State for Foreign Affairs informed Brig.-General Swayne that His Majesty's Government desired that he should take charge, civil and military, of the Protectorate, and arm and organize the protected tribes in such a manner as to enable them, after a time, to protect themselves. Lord Lansdowne remarked that the two battalions of Indian troops which it was proposed to retain temporarily would assist in maintaining order while the new arrangements with the tribes were being matured, and added that it was contemplated that a small nucleus of regular troops should remain permanently at Berbera as before the war. It was also pointed out that His Majesty's Government did not desire that any fresh troops should be raised in Somaliland until they knew the cost and had issued instructions.

Lord Lansdowne again telegraphed on the 8th June asking that, before deciding on the manner in which his instructions of the 19th May were to be carried into effect, he might have a report of the conclusions arrived at by General Swayne after inquiry on the spot. He also asked for the proposed distribution of the 1,300 men demanded* and stated that the two Indian battalions left in the country could not remain more than three months. General Swayne was, however, informed that he was at liberty to proceed with the organization and arming of the tribes. In reply to the above General Swayne telegraphed on the 15th June :—

I deprecate departure of regular troops until it becomes clear whether the Mullah is able again to combine the large number of hostile riflemen who are now divided into tribal groups. If the Mullah advances soon in force, the tribes, at present having no cohesion, could not face him, and arms in issue may fall into the Mullah's hands.

The General also stated that he proposed increasing 6th King's African Rifles to a total of 500 mounted men, and raising 800 infantry as temporary troops for one year "to hold strategical posts Berbera to Burao, with posts covering flanks at Las Dureh and Hargeisa, thus supporting

---

* General Swayne had previously estimated that a force of 1,300 men would be required, *i.e.*, 500 Camel Corps (6th King's African Rifles (and Soudanese and 800 infantry (Somalis).

the tribes until they have established cohesion and are in a position to ward off attacks. . . . Our tribes, when furnished with ponies and rifles, would take over Bohotle and Eil Dab on the understanding that we leave four months' supplies for 200 men in each post, and give assistance by subsidy—total, £3,500 a year."

**Increase to 6th K.A.R. authorized.** On the 17th June authority was given for the increase of 6th King's African Rifles to 500 mounted men, to be ultimately employed for the protection of the coast, and the proposal in the last paragraph (above) of General Swayne's despatch, regarding ponies, rifles, supplies and subsidy was also sanctioned.

**Proposals of General Swayne to raise troops.** On the 17th June, General Swayne renewed his proposal to raise 800 infantry, but now proposed that they should be composed of Punjabis from India. He estimated the cost of these troops at £50,000 a year. This proposal was approved, but as the men could not be raised and trained in so short a period as one year, it was finally arranged with the Indian Government that one battalion of native infantry should proceed from India for service in the Protectorate.

### PROVISIONAL SCHEME FOR THE GARRISON OF SOMALILAND ON DEMOBILIZATION OF THE SOMALILAND FIELD FORCE.

**Command.** I. Under orders from His Majesty's Government, His Majesty's Commissioner, Consul-General and Commander-in-Chief of the Somaliland Protectorate will, on arrival, assume military command of the garrison of the Protectorate.

**Garrison.** II. The garrison will consist of:—
  (a) Regular troops, under orders to return to their permanent stations but temporarily detained to hold the Burao–Bohotle line and the Ain valley, pending completion of necessary arrangements for organization of local forces.
  (b) Local levies :—
    6th King's African Rifles, 2 companies of Somali Mounted Infantry.
    Illalos, 60.
    Temporary levy, 20.

**Regular troops.** III. 1. *Command and Staff.*
Commanding—The senior combatant officer.

Deputy Assistant Adjutant and Quartermaster-General.—Captain G. M. Molloy, 34th Poona Horse (Special Service Officer).

Royal Engineers Officers.—(1) To be detailed by Commandant Royal Royal Engineers ; (2) Lieutenant K. E. Edgeworth, Royal Engineers (for special duty with deep boring operations).

Chief Supply and Transport Officer.—Captain E. A. Swinhoe, Supply and Transport Corps.

Assistant Supply Officers.—(1) Captain H. D. Foulkes, Royal Artillery (Special Service Officer) ; (2) Lieutenant J. G. Lyons, 76th Punjabis (Special Service Officer).

Assistant Transport Officer.—Lieutenant J. G. Craik, Seaforth Highlanders (Special Service Officer).

Indian Camel Corps.—Commandant—Lieutenant H. H. Syer, 31st Lancers (Special Service Officer); Assistant Commandant—Lieutenant P. C. Hampe-Vincent, 129th Baluchis (Special Service Officer).

Senior Medical Officer.—Major G. B. Irvine, Indian Medical Staff.

2. *Troops* :—

No. 6 Company, Indian Mounted Infantry (Poona).
No. 7 Company, Indian Mounted Infantry (Umballa).
The 101st Grenadiers.
107th Pioneers.
Section D-18 British Field Hospital.
Sections A, B and C-58 Native Field Hospital.
One section, No. 65 Native Field Hospital.
Native-General Hospital, 100 beds.
Indian Camel Corps.

3. *Subordinate and Clerical Staff.*—The Deputy Assistant Adjutant and Quartermaster-General will take over the Brigade Staff Office of the 2nd Brigade on demobilization, which should be completed in stationery, &c., from the Ordnance Department. Sergeant H. C. Brook, now with the 2nd Brigade Office, will join Captain Molloy.

The Royal Engineer officer will require no clerk, but should indent upon the Ordnance Department for any stationery he requires.

The Chief Supply and Transport Officer will have :—
    4 warrant Officers.
    11 non-commissioned officers.
    13 clerks.
    11 agents.
    Subordinate establishment.
and will complete his stationery requirements.

The Senior Medical Officer will require no special clerical establishment, but should indent for stationery if required.

4. *Ammunition.*—(a) Service ammunition will be maintained in the country at the rate of :—
    600 rounds per rifle.
    30,200 rounds per maxim.

Rifle ammunition will be Mark II, Indian pattern (as far as available). For maxim guns, Mark II, ordinary pattern.

Of the above, 300 rounds per rifle and 12,600 rounds per maxim will accompany units.

The balance will be stored at Berbera in the Fort.

(b) Practice ammunition will be drawn by units at the rates of 250 rounds Mark V per rifle, 1,700 rounds Mark II per maxim.

5. *Equipment.*—(a) Each infantry battalion and company of mounted infantry will obtain sufficient articles of ordnance supply to meet requirements till the end of the year and will complete their other equipment and establishment of followers from the departments of supply.

(b) Each infantry battalion will retain the maxim guns now with them, any weak gun detachment mules being replaced.

(c) Obligatory mules will accompany units and, except during operations, will as heretofore, be employed under the orders of the Chief Supply and Transport Officer.

6. *Medical.*—The necessary orders for the medical arrangements mentioned in para. III (2), and for those required by units will be issued by the Principal Medical Officer, Somaliland Field Force.

Six hospital assistants to be detailed by the Principal Medical Officer.

7. *Veterinary.*—The Officer Commanding Indian Mounted Infantry companies will indent for any requirements of equipment or medicines from the Indian Veterinary Office, Somaliland Field Force.

8. *Remounts.*—The Officer Commanding Indian Mounted Infantry companies will indent on the Remount Officer, Somaliland Field Force, for the necessary remounts to complete requirements, including 15 per cent. spare.

9. *Postal.*—Postal arrangements will be made by the Superintendent of Post Offices, the balance of the present postal staff with the Somaliland Field Force returning to India.

10. *Telegraphs.*—The field telegraph line will be maintained. The Director of Telegraphs will arrange for the necessary staff, the balance of the present staff with the Somaliland Field Force proceeding to England.

11. *Concessions and Privileges.*—Concessions and privileges, such as pay, field service batta, free rations, field service clothing, &c., will be as heretofore.

Distribution.

IV. 1. The garrison will be distributed as follows :—

Bohotle .. { 107th Pioneers, 1½ companies.
{ Illalos, 20 rifles.

Wadamago .. 107th Pioneers, ½ company.

Eil Dab .. { Poona Mounted Infantry, 1 company.
{ Umballa Mounted Infantry, 1 company.
{ 107th Pioneers, 5 companies.
{ 6th King's African Rifles, Somali Mounted Infantry, 2 Companies.
{ Illalos, 20 rifles.

| | | |
|---|---|---|
| Shimber-Berris | } | 107th Pioneers 1 company. |
| Elkadalanleh | | |
| Burao.. | .. | The 101st Grenadiers, 3 companies. |
| Sheikh | .. | The 101st Grenadiers, 2 companies. |
| Hargeisa | .. | The 101st Grenadiers, 1 company. |
| Las Dureh | .. | The 101st Grenadiers, ½ company. |
| Berbera | .. | The 101st Grenadiers, 1½ companies. |

*Various.*—

Detachments from the above for other posts as required.
Illalos, 20 rifles.
Temporary levy, 20 rifles.

2. *Movements in Relief.*—The movements will be carried out under the orders of the Officer Commanding, Lines of Communication, Somaliland Field Force.

Pending the completion of these movements, Eil Dab will only have a garrison of 100 rifles, 107th Pioneers, and the Somali Mounted Infantry.

V. The Chief Supply and Transport Officer will arrange to place supplies Supplies. to the end of the year at posts for the garrisons allotted to each post.

VI. The Chief Supply and Transport Officer will organize and maintain Transport. sufficient transport at Eil-Dab to enable a movable column consisting of :—

  2 companies, Indian Mounted Infantry.
  300 rifles, 107th Pioneers,
  150 rifles, Somali Mounted Infantry,
  20 Illalos,

to move with 10 days' supplies and 1 day's water in tanks for men. He will also maintain at posts what is necessary for water and other duties.

Should the reserve of supplies as in para. V be completed, the Chief Supply and Transport Officer will arrange for the disbandment of the transport other than that mentioned above.

VII. The Royal Engineer Officer will arrange to maintain, where neces- R.E. stores sary, a complement of civil labour at posts. He will also indent upon the and works. Field Park, Somaliland Field Force for the requirements of the force in pumps and other stores, for whose maintenance in repair the necessary civil labour should be entertained.

The Field Park at Berbera will be in the charge of the Protectorate Staff, as also any engineering work required at Berbera, and between Berbera and Lower Sheikh.

The Chief Supply and Transport Officer will indent upon the Director, Supply and Transport, Somaliland Field Force, for his requirements in water tanks, pakhals, &c., both for the posts and movable column.

VIII. 1. *Records.*—The Assistant Quartermaster-General, Intelligence, Intelligence. will place in charge of Captain L. W. D. Everett, 6th King's African Rifles, the Intelligence records which are to be left in the country.

2. *Interpreters.*—The Assistant Quartermaster-General, Intelligence, will arrange for interpreters as follows :—

Deputy Assistant Adjutant and Quartermaster-General 1 interpreter.
Royal Engineer Officer .. .. .. .. .. 1 ,,
Supply and Transport Corps .. .. .. .. 5 interpreters.
Senior Medical Officer .. .. .. .. .. 1 ,,
Mounted Infantry (per company) .. .. .. 1 ,,
Infantry Regiments (per battalion) .. .. .. 1 ,,
Post duties .. .. .. .. .. .. .. 8 ,,

H. E. STANTON, *Major*,
*C.S.O., Somaliland Field Force.*

BERBERA, 20TH MAY, 1904.

# INDEX.

## A.

| | PAGE |
|---|---|
| **Abanabro, Kanyazmach,** commands Abyssinian forces | 85 |
| **Abyssinians,** co-operation of, first expedition | 53, 59, 63, 74, 82 |
| ,, ,, third ,, | 115, 128, 138, 181 |
| ,, ,, fourth ,, | 205, 212, 220, 232, 251 |
| ,, expedition of, against Mullah, 1900 | 50 |
| ,, proposal of, for combined expedition against Mullah | 51 |
| **Abyssinian Somaliland,** area of | 20 |
| **Accounts Department,** demobilization of | 610 |
| ,, ,, organization of | 336, 344, 600 |
| ,, remarks on, by C.S.O. | 600 |
| ,, remarks on, by Lieut.-General Egerton | 602 |
| ,, of Intelligence Officers | 399, 407 |
| **Administration** of British Protectorate | 42 |
| **Agdaldanshe Mountains** | 24 |
| **Aidagalla,** expedition against | 47 |
| **Alexandria,** Convention of (1877) | 45 |
| **Ali Yusuf** | 180, 222, 223 |
| **Allen,** Major | 340, 452 |
| **Ammunition** | 59, 331, 356, 446, 449, 597, 613 |
| **Animals,** disposal of, on demobilization | 608 |
| **Anley,** Major | 337, 595 |
| **Area and Population** of British Protectorate | 7 |
| **Area** of Somaliland | 7 |
| **Arms** | 59, 398 |
| ,, orders regarding, by Lieut.-General Egerton | 330 |
| ,, trade in | 37, 104, 107 |
| **Armourers** | 82 |
| **Army Service Corps** | 498 |
| **Arori Plain** | 15 |
| **Artillery** | 445 |
| **Attendants,** camel | 510 |
| ,, veterinary | 586 |
| **Atkinson-Willes,** Rear-Admiral, co-operation of, fourth expedition | 279 |
| ,, ,, in command of Illig expedition | 280 |
| ,, ,, orders issued by, at Illig | 281 |
| ,, ,, reports to | 271, 272, 276 |

## B.

| | PAGE |
|---|---|
| Baggage, scale of .... .... .... .... .... .... .... | 356, 514 |
| Baladiers .... .... .... .... .... .... .... .... .... | 506 |
| Baliwein, skirmish at .... .... .... .... .... .... | 96 |
| Bandar Gori .... .... .... .... .... .... .... .... | 29 |
| ,, Kasim .... .... .... .... .... .... .... .... | 29 |
| Base depot, military .... .... .... .... .... .... | 366 |
| Base, organization of, first and second expeditions .... .... .... | 347 |
| ,, ,, third expedition .... .... .... .... .... | 348 |
| ,, ,, fourth expedition.... .... .... .... .... | 363 |
| Battery, K.A.R. Camel 117, 150, 154, 222, 224, 228, 247, 249, 263, 342, 445, 447 | |
| Battery, 28th Mountain .... .... 218, 222, 223, 225, 238, 239, 342, 445 | |
| Beazeley, Captain .... .... .... .... .... .... | 340, 416 |
| Benadir Company .... .... .... .... .... .... .... | 43, 46, 113 |
| ,, settlements .... .... .... .... .... .... .... | 122 |
| Berbera .... .... .... .... .... .... .... .... .... | 27 |
| ,, arrival of ships at .... .... .... .... .... .... | 563 |
| ,, base at .... .... .... .... .... .... .... | 217, 364 |
| ,, disembarkations at .... .... .... | 542, 546, 554, 558, 560 |
| ,, embarkations at .... .... .... .... | 567, 570, 571, 573, 574, 576 |
| Berbera-Bohotle force, operations of .... .... .... .... | 146 |
| Bethell, Captain, R.N., report on disembarkations at Obbia .... .... | 531 |
| Bevan, Lieutenant, R.N., capture of dhows by .... .... .... | 269 |
| Bikanir Camel Corps .... .... .... .... .... .... | 135, 425 |
| Blockade of coast .... .... .... .... .... .... | 104, 112, 266 |
| Bohotle, concentration at, third expedition .... .... .... | 187, 192 |
| ,, ,, fourth ,, .... .... .... .... | 222 |
| ,, ,, ,, ,, orders for .... .... .... | 222 |
| ,, return of force to, second expedition .... .... | 107 |
| Bosanquet, Rear-Admiral .... .... .... .... .... .... | 267 |
| Bosaso .... .... .... .... .... .... .... .... | 29 |
| Boring, deep water, operations .... .... .... .... .... | 458 |
| Boundaries of Somaliland.... .... .... .... .... .... | 7 |
| Brigade, 1st .... .... .... .... .... .... .... .... | 218, 341 |
| ,, 2nd .... .... .... .... .... .... .... | 218, 342 |
| British Government, treaty with tribes .... .... .... .... | 45 |
| ,, Protectorate, administration of .... .... .... .... | 42 |
| ,, ,, ,, transferred to Foreign Office .... | 47 |
| ,, ,, area and population .... .... .... .... | 7 |
| ,, ,, defence of .... .... .... .... .... .... | 201 |
| ,, ,, divisions of .... .... .... .... .... .... | 10 |
| ,, ,, establishment of .... .... .... .... .... | 45 |
| ,, ,, land forces in .... .... .... .... .... | 47 |
| ,, tactics .... .... .... .... .... .... .... | 324 |
| Brooke, Major .... .... .... .... .... .... | 141, 142, 150, 254 |

|  | PAGE |
|---|---|
| Bulhar .... .... .... .... .... .... .... .... .... | 26 |
| Burgher Contingent .... .... .... 120, 127, 140, 145, 197, 200, 421 | |
| Burhilli, engagement at, between Abyssinians and Mullah .... .... | 181 |

## C.

| | |
|---|---|
| Cabinet decisions, second expedition .... .... .... .... .... | 89 |
| ,, third ,, .... .... .... .... .... | 118 |
| Cables, submarine .... .... .... .... .... .... .... .... | 33 |
| Cable, telegraph, laying of .... .... .... .... .... | 482 |
| Camel cart train, organization of .... .... ... .... .... | 497 |
| ,, Corps, Bikanir .... .... .... .... .... .... 135, 174, 425 | |
| ,, ,, hired .... .... .... .... .... .... .... .... | 498 |
| ,, ,, Indian Silladar, organization of .... .... .... .... | 498 |
| ,, ,, local, organization of .... .... .... .... .... | 495 |
| ,, saddles .... .... .... .... .... .... .... 429, 509 | |
| Camelry, remarks on, by Brig.-General Manning .... .... .... | 329 |
| Camels, attendants .... .... .... .... .... .... .... .... | 510 |
| Camels, branding of .... .... .... .... .... .... .... | 497 |
| ,, care of .... .... .... .... .... .... .... .... | 504 |
| ,, casualties among .... .... .... .... .... .... .... | 512 |
| ,, diseases of .... .... .... .... .... .... .... .... | 585 |
| ,, embarkation and disembarkation of .... .... 537, 540, 544, 549 | |
| ,, gear .... .... .... .... .... .... .... | 509 |
| ,, hiring of .... .... .... .... .... .... .... | 506 |
| ,, losses in .... .... .... .... .... .... .... | 503 |
| ,, purchasing of .... .... .... .... .... .... | 502 |
| ,, remount depôt for .... .... .... .... .... | 594 |
| ,, want of, at Obbia .... .... .... .... .... | 132 |
| Canteen, Field Force .... .... .... .... .... .... | 525 |
| Captured stock .... .... .... .... .... .... 81, 362 | |
| Carter, Captain .... .... .... .... .... .... 340, 596 | |
| Carter, Lieutenant, awarded Victoria Cross .... .... .... | 234 |
| Casualties of British at Daratoleh .... .... .... .... 177, 178 | |
| ,, ,, Erigo .... .... .... .... .... .... | 106 |
| ,, ,, first expedition .... .... .... .... | 80 |
| ,, ,, Gumburu .... .... .... .... .... | 166 |
| ,, ,, Illig .... .... .... .... .... | 288 |
| ,, ,, Jidbali .... .... .... .... .... | 242 |
| ,, ,, Lieut.-Colonel Kenna's reconnaissance to Jidbali | 234 |
| ,, ,, at Samala .... .... .... .... .... | 68 |
| ,, ,, third expedition .... .... .... .... | 198 |
| ,, of enemy at Daratoleh .... .... .... .... | 178 |
| ,, ,, Erigo .... .... .... .... .... | 106 |
| ,, ,, Ferdiddin .... .... .... .... .... | 78 |
| ,, ,, Gumburu .... .... .... .... 165, 169 | |

|   |   |   | PAGE |
|---|---|---|---|
| **Casualties** of enemy at Illig | | | 287, 295 |
| ,, ,, Jidbali | | | 241 |
| ,, ,, Samala | | | 69 |
| ,, ,, Waylahed | | | 70 |
| ,, in transport animals | | | 503, 511 |
| **Censorship** | | | 415 |
| **Clerical equipment** | | | 600 |
| **Climate** of Somaliland | | | 36 |
| **Coast**, blockade of | | | 104, 112, 266 |
| ,, naval reconnaissance of | | | 114 |
| **Cobbe**, Lieut.-Colonel | | | 93 |
| ,, advance of, from Galadi | | | 152, 154 |
| ,, awarded Victoria Cross | | | 98 |
| ,, instructions to | | | 154 |
| ,, reconnaissances by | | | 133, 139 |
| ,, report by, on action at Gumburu | | | 160 |
| **Cobbold**, Captain, accompanies Abyssinians during first expedition | | | 83 |
| ,, accompanies Abyssinians during third expedition | | | 128 |
| **Comforts**, medical | | | 582 |
| **Commands**, organization of, first and second expeditions | | | 335 |
| ,, ,, third expedition | | | 335 |
| ,, ,, fourth expedition | | | 339 |
| **Communications**, inland | | | 33 |
| **Communication**, lines of, third expedition | | | 134, 137, 141, 190, 336, 337 |
| ,, ,, fourth expedition | | | 219, 342 |
| ,, ,, garrisons of posts | | | 347, 349, 350, 358, 360, 472 |
| ,, ,, Obbia, standing orders | | | 351 |
| ,, ,, organization of first and second expeditions | | | 347 |
| ,, ,, organization of third expedition | | | 348 |
| ,, ,, organization of fourth expedition | | | 357 |
| ,, ,, posts on | | | 347, 349, 357, 359 |
| ,, ,, staff of | | | 348, 349, 359 |
| **Communications** oversea | | | 33 |
| **Concentration** of troops on demobilization, plan of | | | 604 |
| **Convoy duty**, management of stores on | | | 515 |
| **Coolie Corps**, Arab | | | 500, 551 |
| **Coolies**, Somali | | | 501 |
| **Cordeaux, Mr.**, Acting Consul-General | | | 90 |
| **Correspondents**, Press | | | 415 |
| **Courgerod**, first expedition at | | | 74, 78 |
| **Currency** | | | 600 |

### D.

|   |   |
|---|---|
| **Daba Debba Valley** | 15 |
| **Dairies** | 580 |
| **Daldawan Plain** | 15 |

|  | PAGE |
|---|---|
| **Damot**, arrival of Swayne at | 97 |
| **Daratoleh**, action at, report of by Colonel Gough | 173 |
| „ description of | 326 |
| **Darror Valley** | 10, 15 |
| **Defences**, types of | 472 |
| **Defensible posts** | 472, 475 |
| **Demobilization** | 603 |
| „ general arrangements for | 603 |
| „ organization of local forces after | 610 |
| „ provisional scheme for | 612 |
| **Dental work** | 583 |
| **Der Tug** | 16 |
| **Deserters** | 392 |
| **Diary, intelligence** | 395, 405, 409 |
| **Diary, staff**, extracts from | 375, 379, 380, 381, 382 |
| **Diseases** human | 579 |
| „ of animals | 585 |
| **Disembarkations** at Berbera | 542, 546, 554, 558, 560 |
| „ Las Khorai | 543, 552, 562 |
| „ Obbia | 540, 556 |
| „ „ report of Captain Bethell on | 531 |
| **Disembarkations**, orders regarding | 530 |
| **Divisional troops** | 217 |
| **Dolbahanta** tribes | 40, 41, 62, 75, 77, 89, 91, 206, 212 |
| „ tribe, chief of, murdered by Mullah | 50 |
| **Drainage**, lines of, in Somaliland | 8 |
| **Durbo**, landing and action at | 271, 275, 276, 278 |
| **Duties**, staff | 367 |
| **Dureh, Las**, advance of column from | 256 |
| „ concentration of column at | 255 |
| **Dysentery and Diarrhoea** | 580 |

### E.

|  |  |  |  |
|---|---|---|---|
| **Egerton**, Lieut.-General, Sir C., appointment of |  |  | 195 |
| „ | „ | correspondence of, with His Majesty's Government before fourth expedition | 202 |
| „ | „ | recommends cessation of operations | 264 |
| „ | „ | standing orders by, fourth expedition | 330 |
| „ | „ | correspondence of, about demobilization | 603 |
| **Egypt**, connection of, with Somaliland |  |  | 44, 45 |
| **Eil Dab Column** |  |  | 254 |

|  |  | PAGE |
|---|---|---|
| **Ekka trains** | .... .... .... .... .... .... .... .... | 499 |
| **Embarkations** at Berbera .... | .... .... .... 567, 570, 571, 573, 574, | 576 |
| ,, Las Khorai | .... .... .... .... .... 543, 552, | 572 |
| ,, Obbia | .... .... .... .... .... .... .... | 568 |
| **En** .... .... .... .... .... | .... .... .... .... .... .... .... | 32 |
| **Encampments**, orders regarding, by Lieut.-General Egerton, fourth expedition | .... .... .... .... .... .... .... .... | 331 |
| **Engineer Services** .... | .... .... .... .... .... .... .... | 452 |
| **Engineering works** | .... .... .... .... .... .... .... | 475 |
| **Equipment** .... 400, 428, 431, 433, 446, 448, 450, 480, 484, 513, 583, 598, 599, 600, 614 | | |
| **Erigo**, action at | .... .... .... .... .... .... .... .... | 104 |
| **Expedition, first,** | .... .... .... .... .... .... .... .... | 52 |
| ,, casualties in | .... .... .... .... .... .... | 80 |
| ,, final report on by Colonel Swayne | .... .... .... | 80 |
| ,, movement begun | .... .... .... .... .... | 63 |
| ,, organization of base | .... .... .... .... .... | 347 |
| ,, ,, commands and staffs | .... .... | 335 |
| ,, ,, lines of communication | .... .... | 347 |
| ,, plan of operations for | .... .... .... .... | 53 |
| ,, preparations for | .... .... .... .... .... | 56 |
| ,, proposed by Consul-General | .... .... .... .... | 51 |
| ,, strategy of | .... .... .... .... .... .... | 308 |
| ,, termination of | .... .... .... .... .... .... | 79 |
| **Expedition, second** | .... .... .... .... .... .... .... | 89 |
| ,, operations begun | .... .... .... .... .... | 94 |
| ,, organization of base | .... .... .... .... .... | 347 |
| ,, ,, commands and staffs | .... .... | 335 |
| ,, ,, lines of communication | .... . . | 347 |
| ,, plan of operations for | .... .... .... .... | 92 |
| ,, preparations for | .... .... .... .... .... | 90 |
| ,, results of | .... .... .... .... .... .... | 108 |
| ,, return of force to Bohotle | .... .... .... .... | 107 |
| ,, strategy of | .... .... .... .... .... .... | 308 |
| ,, strength of forces in | .... .... .... .... | 94 |
| **Expedition, third** | .... .... .... .... .... .... .... .... | 109 |
| ,, advance from Galkayu | .... .... .... .... | 149 |
| ,, commencement of operations | .... .... .... | 129 |
| ,, Italian co-operation in | .... .... .... .... | 119 |
| ,, organization of base | .... .... .... .... .... | 348 |
| ,, ,, commands and staffs | .... .... | 335 |
| ,, ,, force during | .... .... .... .... | 120 |
| ,, ,, lines of communication | .... .... | 348 |
| ,, plan of operations for | .... .... .... .... | 117, 196 |
| ,, preparations for | .... .... .... .... .... | 109 |
| ,, strategy of | .... .... .... .... .... .... | 309 |

|  | PAGE |
|---|---|
| Expedition, third, strength of forces in | 118, 345 |
| ,, supplies during | 137 |
| ,, termination of | 195 |
| Expedition, fourth | 199 |
| ,, advance to Halin | 244 |
| ,, concentration of force | 234 |
| ,, organization of base | 363 |
| ,, organization of commands and staffs | 339 |
| ,, ,, force | 217 |
| ,, ,, lines of communication | 357 |
| ,, plan of operations 208, 209, 210, 211, 213, 214, 247, 253 | |
| ,, preparations for advance | 231 |
| ,, result of operations | 264 |
| ,, sanction to advance given | 214 |
| ,, strategy of | 314 |
| ,, strength of Field Force | 346 |
| ,, termination of operations | 263, 264 |
| Expeditions, small | 47 |

## F.

|  |  |
|---|---|
| Faf | 32 |
| Fafan Tug | 32 |
| Fasken, General, arrival of, at Galkayu | 148 |
| ,, commands 2nd Brigade, fourth expedition | 218 |
| ,, in command of Las Dureh column | 255 |
| ,, operations of, fourth expedition | 257 |
| Ferdiddin, action at | 75 |
| Fevers | 588 |
| Forage on the march, conveyance of | 525 |
| ,, scale of | 521 |
| Foods, staple, in Somaliland | 38 |
| Forces, local, organization of, after demobilization | 610 |
| ,, reorganization of, before second expedition | 89 |
| ,, ,, ,, third ,, | 116 |
| Foreign Office takes over administration of British Protectorate | 47 |
| Forestier-Walker, Lieut.-Colonel | 335, 339, 390 |
| Formations, march and fighting | 324 |
| France, settlement of boundary with | 46 |
| Friedrichs, Captain, death of | 77 |
| Fuel | 352, 523 |
| ,, in Somaliland | 38 |

## G.

|  |  |
|---|---|
| Gabri, Fitaurari, commands Abyssinian forces, third expedition | 182 |
| Gadabursi Horse | 237, 417, 418 |

|  | PAGE |
|---|---|
| **Galadi,** garrison of, fourth expedition | 228 |
| „ „ „ withdrawal of | 235 |
| „ occupation of | 151 |
| „ withdrawal of Brig.-General Manning to | 159, 171, 184 |
| **Galgudan Plain** | 15 |
| **Galkayu,** arrival at, third expedition | 143 |
| „ „ advance from, third expedition | 149 |
| „ „ of Brig.-General Manning at, after Gumburu | 184 |
| **Gallule River** | 17, 283, 285, 298 |
| **Gardens** | 362, 580 |
| **Gaunt,** Captain, R.N. | 271, 273, 275, 277, 278 |
| **Gear,** camel | 429, 509 |
| **Geledi** | 25 |
| **Geography, physical,** of Somaliland | 8 |
| **Gerolimato, Mr.** | 84, 87 |
| **Gildessa** | 31 |
| **Golis** | 10, 12, 13 |
| **Gor Ali range** | 24 |
| **Gough,** Lieut.-Colonel, despatch of column commanded by | 146 |
| „ operations of | 172 |
| „ report by, of action at Daratoleh | 173 |
| „ return to Bohotle | 181 |
| „ awarded Victoria Cross | 180 |
| **Grenadiers, 101st** | 110, 116, 124, 194, 219, 256, 337, 344, 349, 350, 360 |
| „ 102nd | 110 |
| **Guban** | 10, 11 |
| **Gumburu,** action at | 160 |
| „ arrival of Lieut.-Colonel Cobbe at | 156 |
| „ narrative of action at, by survivors | 169 |
| **Gurgis,** definition of | 31 |

## H.

|  |  |
|---|---|
| **Habi** | 32 |
| **Hais** | 29 |
| **Halin,** movement of Colonel Swayne to | 98, 100 |
| „ advance to, fourth expedition | 244 |
| **Hampshire Regiment** | 201, 218, 222, 223, 236, 238, 239, 241, 242, 247, 256, 280, 286, 287, 289, 290, 291, 292, 293, 294, 342 |
| **Hanbury-Tracy,** Major, appointed to accompany Abyssinians | 63 |
| „ departure for Harrar | 63 |
| „ report of | 83 |
| **Hans,** definition of | 155 |
| **Harakatis Plain** | 15 |
| **Hargeisa** | 32 |

|  | PAGE |
|---|---|
| **Harrar** .... .... .... .... .... .... .... .... .... | 31 |
| ,, **Highlands** .... .... .... .... .... .... .... .... | 20 |
| **Harrington,** Colonel .... .... .... .... 51, 104, 116, 128, 220 | |
| **Harbours,** principal .. . .... .... .... .... .... .... | 25 |
| **Haroun,** definition of .... .... .... .... .... .... .... | 158 |
| **Harris,** Major .... .... .... .... .... .... .... 340, 584 | |
| **Haud, The** .... .... .... .... .... .... .... .... .... 10, 17 | |
| ,, area of .... .... .... .... .... .... .... .... | 18 |
| ,, Northern .... .... .... .... .... .... .... .... | 17 |
| ,, Southern .... .... .... .... .... .... .... .... | 19 |
| **Hayes-Sadler,** Consul-General, estimate by, of Mullah's forces .... | 49 |
| ,, ,, expedition proposed by . .... .:.. | 49 |
| ,, ,, instructions of, to Colonel Swayne .... | 54 |
| ,, ,, proclamation of, before first expedition | 62 |
| **Henderson,** Major .... .... .... .... .... .... .... .... | 340 |
| **Hiring** of camels .... .... .... .... .... .... .... .... | 506 |
| **Hire,** rates of .... .... .... .... .... .... .... .... | 507 |
| **History** of British connection with Somaliland.... .... .... .... | 44 |
| **Hood,** Captain, R.N. .... .... .... .... 285, 286, 287, 288, 289 | |
| **Horse, Gadabursi** .... .... .... .... .... .... .... 237, 417, 418 | |
| ,, **Tribal,** organization of .... .... .... .... 231, 236, 417 | |
| **Horses,** allotment of, to corps and units .... .... .... .... | 589 |
| ,, care of .... .... .... .... .... .... .... .... | 439 |
| ,, diseases of .... .... .... .... .... .... .... .... | 585 |
| **Hospitals** .... .... .... .... .... .... .... .... .... | 578 |
| **Hospital ship** .... .... .... .... .... .... .... 551, 579 | |
| **Huddleston,** Lieutenant, R.I.M., reports of, on marine transport work 539, 543, 545 | |
| **Huguf Plain,** The .... .... .... .... .... .... .... .... | 14 |

## I.

|  |  |
|---|---|
| **Illalos** .... .... .... .... .... .... .... 158, 391, 397, 406 | |
| **Illig** .... .... .... .... .... .... .... .... .... .... | 30 |
| ,, capture of .... .... .... .... .... .... .... .... | 280 |
| ,, ,, as affecting strategy of fourth expedition .... | 320 |
| ,, ,, casualties at .... .... .... .... .... 288, 295 | |
| ,, expedition to .... .... .... .... .... .... .... | 265 |
| ,, fortifications at, destruction of .... .... .... .... | 293 |
| ,, naval demonstration at .... .... .... .... .... | 252 |
| ., ,, reconnaissance of .... .... .... .... .... | 270 |
| ,, notes on .... .... .... .... .... .... .... | 296 |
| ,, proposed occupation of .... .... .... .... .... | 230 |
| ,, orders by Rear-Admiral Atkinson-Willes at .... .... | 281 |
| ,, return of expedition from .... .... .... .... .... | 295 |

2 R

|                                                                                          | PAGE |
|---|---|
| **India,** arrival of contingent from, third expedition | 137 |
| „ despatch „ „ „ | 127 |
| „ „ of transport from, fourth expedition | 216 |
| „ „ „ troops from, fourth expedition | 200, 208 |
| **Indian Government,** correspondence with, on demobilization | 603, 609, 612 |
| **Intelligence** | 59, 61, 332, 388, 615 |
| „ accounts | 399, 407 |
| „ diary | 395, 405, 409 |
| „ officers | 335, 339, 393, 396, 404, 407, 409 |
| „ organization of, fourth expedition | 390 |
| „ returns | 407 |
| **Interpreters** | 401, 616 |
| **Italian Somaliland** | 22 |
| **Italy,** negotiations with, before third expedition | 111 |
| „ „ during fourth „ | 254, 259 |
| „ Protectorate of, establishment of | 46 |

## J.

|   |   |
|---|---|
| **Jackson,** Lieut.-Colonel, account by, of capture of Illig | 291 |
| „ „ in command of Hampshire detachment at Illig | 280 |
| **Jibuti** | 25 |
| „ railway from, to Harrar | 47 |
| **Jidbali,** battle of | 238 |
| „ „ casualties at | 242 |
| „ „ „ of enemy at | 241 |
| „ reasons of Mullah for fighting at | 250 |
| „ result of engagement at | 251 |
| **Juba River** | 38 |

## K.

|   |   |
|---|---|
| **Karias,** definition of | 73 |
| **Kendall,** Commander, reports by, on Marine transport | 545, 552 |
| **Kenna,** Lieut.-Colonel, commands mounted troops, fourth expedition | 217 |
| „ instructions to, at Galadi, fourth expedition | 227 |
| „ „ on proceeding to Obbia | 129 |
| „ operations of, in Darror Valley | 260 |
| „ reconnaissance by, to Jidbali | 233 |
| „ „ „ casualties during | 234 |
| „ remarks by, on mounted troops | 432, 437 |
| „ standing orders by, for mounted troops | 438 |
| **Khansa bush** | 15 |
| **Khorat Las** | 29 |
| „ disembarkations at | 543, 552, 562 |

|  | PAGE |
|---|---|
| Khorai Las, embarkations at | 543, 552, 572 |
| ,, formation of post at | 254 |
| ,, Marine transport work at | 543, 552 |
| ,, naval reconnaissance of | 253 |
| Kob Faradod, burning of | 64 |
| Kurkar range | 15 |

## L.

| Labour | 458, 476, 540, 542, 546 |
|---|---|
| Lansdowne, Lord, correspondence of, with Brig.-General Swayne after conclusion of operations | 604, 611 |
| ,, correspondence of, with Italian Government | 111, 119 |
| Levies, Somali | 56, 57, 80, 91, 108, 231, 323, 417 |
| Lister, Captain | 242, 343, 586 |
| Lovatelli, Count | 133 |

## M.

| McNeill, Captain, appointed to command at Samala | 65 |
|---|---|
| ,, at Ferdiddin | 77 |
| ,, report of | 66 |
| Mails, conveyance of | 33, 488, 548 |
| Manning, General, appointment of, to command third expedition | 111 |
| ,, commands 1st Brigade, fourth expedition | 218 |
| ,, despatches by | 148, 171, 184, 188, 193, 195 |
| ,, final report by, third expedition | 195 |
| ,, instructions to | 126, 144, 149, 187 |
| ,, letter of, to Captain Bethell | 539 |
| ,, march to Galadi, fourth expedition | 224, 226 |
| ,, operations of, in the Nogal | 258 |
| ,, plans of | 144 |
| ,, remarks on camelry by | 329 |
| ,, ,, by, on tactics | 325 |
| ,, return to Bohotle from Galadi | 228 |
| ,, report by, from Galkayu | 143 |
| Maps | 402, 403 |
| Marches in Somaliland | 35 |
| March discipline | 332, 356, 441, 505 |
| ,, formations | 324, 327, 328, 332, 355, 356, 441, 443 |
| Marconi telegraphs | 147, 197, 336, 484 |
| Marehan Plateau | 21 |
| Medical arrangements, landing at Illig | 283 |
| ,, ,, on demobilization | 614 |
| ,, comforts | 582 |

(8927A)

|  |  | PAGE |
|---|---|---|
| Medical services, first expedition.... | | 82, 578 |
| ,, ,, organization of.... | | 336, 578 |
| ,, ,, remarks on | | 583 |
| Melliss, Lieut.-Colonel | | 231, 257, 420 |
| Meteorological | | 383, 540,542, 548 |
| Mijjarten, co-operation of, third expedition | | 113 |
| ,, ,, fourth ,, | | 258, 319 |
| ,, Sultan, treaties with .... | | 46 |
| Mirso, The .... | | 14 |
| Money order work.... | | 489 |
| Mounted infantry, organization of | | 424 |
| Mounted troops | | 420 |
| ,, command of, fourth expedition | | 340 |
| ,, remarks on, by Lieut.-Colonel Kenna | | 432, 437 |
| ,, standing orders for, by Lieut.-Colonel Kenna | | 438 |
| Mudug oasis | 20, 83, 95, 99, 103, 117, 119, 122, 124, 125, 126, 132, 136, 140, 144, 186, 203, 208, 213, 214, 230, 310, 312 | |
| Mudug, wells of | | 19 |
| Mullah, dealings of, with tribes .... | | 41 |
| Mullah, history of .... | | 48 |
| ,, letter from, to the English people | | 191 |
| ,, movements of, first expedition .... | 52, 54, 60, 63, 69, 70, 73, 74, 77 | |
| ,, ,, second ,, | 90, 91, 93, 95, 97, 102, 108 | |
| ,, ,, third ,, | 117, 122, 124, 143, 146, 148, 153, 154, 177, 190, 193, 194, 196, 311 | |
| ,, ,, fourth ,, | 202, 219, 230, 231, 232, 234, 244, 246, 247, 252, 257, 260, 261, 262, 264, 316, 318, 394 | |
| ,, terms offered to, by General Egerton .... | | 253 |
| Munn, Captain, mission of | | 229 |
| Musa Farah, Risaldar Major | | 71, 93, 95, 96 |

## N.

|  |  | |
|---|---|---|
| Naval operations | | 266, 270 |
| Navigation .... | | 552 |
| Negegr plain | | 15 |
| Night marching | | 64, 82, 443 |
| Nogal The, | | 10, 16 |
| ,, Lieut.-General Egerton's advance into | | 203, 204, 244 |
| ,, evacuation of .... | | 604 |
| ,, held by Brig.-General Manning, fourth expedition | | 247, 253, 258 |
| ,, Mullah's retreat into | | 190 |
| ,, Colonel Swayne's advance into | | 100 |
| Nur, Sultan | | 49 |

## O.

| | PAGE |
|---|---|
| **Obbia** .... .... .... .... .... .... .... .... .... | 30 |
| „ advance from, begun .... .... .... .... .... .... | 140 |
| „ disembarkation at .... .... .... .... .... .... | 131, 531 |
| „ disembarkation at, report on by Captain Bethell, R.N. .... | 531 |
| ,. embarkations at .... .... .... .... .... .... .... | 568 |
| „ naval demonstration at .... .... .... .... .... | 229, 270 |
| „ naval reconnaissance of .... .... .... .... .... .... | 270 |
| „ selection of, as landing place, third expedition .... .... .... | 115 |
| **Ogaden country** .... .... .... .... .... .... .... .... | 21 |
| **Ogo** .... .... .... .... .... .... .... .... .... .... | 10, 14 |
| **Ogo Guban** .... .... .... .... .... .... .... .... .... | 10, 13 |
| **Operations,** combined naval and military .... .... .... .... | 266 |
| **Orders,** Field Force, example of .... .... .... .... .... | 384, 386 |
| „ landing .... .... .... .... .... .... .... .... | 281 |
| „ operation .... .... .... .... .... .... 222, 237, 238, 246, 249, 263 |
| „ standing, fourth expedition, by Lieut.-General Egerton .... | 330 |
| „ „ by Colonel Kenna, for mounted troops .... .... | 433 |
| „ „ Obbia lines of communication .... .... .... | 351 |
| **Ordnance** depôts .... .... .... .... .... .... .... | 595, 596 |
| „ services, demobilization of .... .... .... .... .... | 607 |
| „ „ organization of .... .... .... .... | 336, 595 |
| „ „ remarks on .... .... .... .... .... .... | 598 |
| „ system .... .... .... .... .... .... .... .... | 597 |
| **Osborn,** Captain .... .... .... .... .... .... | 94, 95, 99, 101 |
| **Osman Mahmud,** Sultan .... .... .... .... .... .... | 50, 95 |
| „ ,. action of, first expedition .... .... .... | 71 |
| „ ,, „ second „ .... .... .... | 102 |

## P.

| | |
|---|---|
| **Park Field,** R.E. .... .... .... .... .... .... .... | 344, 607 |
| **Passes** principal .... .... .... .... .... .... .... | 34 |
| **Pay,** Army Department .... .... .... .... .... .... | 336, 610 |
| **Pears,** Commander, R.N. .... .... .... .... 267, 271, 272, 274, 276, 278 |
| **Phillips,** Major .... .... .... .... .... 61, 76, 98, 99, 101, 102, 103 |
| **Pioneers** 107th, .... .... 137, 146, 218, 222, 236, 256, 337, 344, 360, 452 |
| **Plunkett,** Colonel .... .... .... .... 147, 149, 152, 153, 163, 164, 179 |
| **Police** .... .... .... .... .... .... .... .... | 364 |
| „ reorganization of .... .... .... .... .... .... | 48 |
| **Political officer** .... .... .... .... .... .... | 363, 374 |
| **Population and area of** British Protectorate .... .... .... | 7 |
| **Porter corps** .... .... .... .... .... .... .... | 500 |
| **Ports** on eastern coast, survey of, before third expedition .... .... | 114 |
| „ principal .... .... .... .... .... .... .... | 25 |

|  | PAGE |
|---|---|
| **Postal services** | 336, 487 |
| **Posts**, defence of | 360, 364, 472, 475 |
| **Post offices**, field, number opened | 488 |
| **Powell**, Lieutenant, R.N., reports of action at Durbo... | 274, 278 |
| **Press correspondents** | 415 |
| **Prisoners of war** | 353, 362 |
| **Protectorate British**, administration of | 42 |
|     ,,    ,, transferred to Foreign Office | 47 |
|     ,, area and population of | 7 |
|     ,, defence of | 201 |
|     ,, divisions of | 10 |
|     ,, establishment of | 45 |
|     ,, land forces in | 47 |
| **Provost Marshal** | 344, 367 |
| **Pumps** | 457 |
| **Punjabis, 27th** 218, 219, 222, 233, 236, 238, 239, 241, 255, 256, 342, 360 | |
| **Purchase** of animals | 502 |
|     ,, remounts | 590, 591 |

## R.

|  |  |
|---|---|
| **Railway**, survey for, from Berbera to Bohotle | 217 |
| **Ranges**, maritime | 12 |
| **Routes**, principal | 35 |
| **Rations** | 518 |
|     ,, remarks with regard to | 524 |
| **Re-embarkations** | 564, 605 |
| **Reinforcements**, third expedition | 110 |
|     ,, fourth ,, | 199, 205 |
| **Remount** department, organization of | 336, 586 |
|     ,, depôts | 587, 594 |
|     ,, requirements, estimates for | 587 |
| **Remounts** from India | 590 |
|     ,, purchase of | 590, 591 |
|     ,, remarks on | 590 |
|     ,, on demobilization | 614 |
| **Rifles, King's African** 1st 110, 117, 123, 129, 134, 140, 145, 149, 150, 152, 154, 160, 163, 166, 172, 184, 193, 195, 218, 222, 224, 244, 245, 263, 336, 342, 350 | |
|   ,,   ,, 2nd 47, 48, 57, 105, 106, 107, 110, 117, 123, 147, 149, 150, 152, 154, 159, 160, 163, 165, 166, 169, 175, 176, 177, 178, 179, 180, 184, 193, 194, 218, 222, 226, 239, 242, 244, 337, 342, 350 | |
|   ,,   ,, 3rd 110, 129, 134, 140, 145, 153, 159, 172, 184, 193, 194, 218, 222, 224, 239, 242, 244, 245, 336, 342, 350 | |

Rifles, King's African, 5th   110, 129, 134, 149, 151, 153, 167, 184, 193,
                              194, 218, 235, 336, 342, 350
  „           „       6th   48, 105, 110, 118, 154, 160, 174, 176, 180,
                              219, 337, 417
Rifles, King's Royal   .... .... .... .... 127, 161, 165, 168, 425, 434
Rifles, 123rd Outram's   .... .... .... .... .... .... .... 110
Roads   .... .... .... .... .... .... .... .... 360, 475
Roberts, Earl, Commander-in-Chief, advice of ....   .... ....   199, 212
  „           „       instructions by, to Brig.-General
                      Manning   .... .... ....   126
  „           „       questions by, addressed to
                      Lieut.-General Egerton   ....   200
Rochfort, Colonel, accompanies Abyssinian forces, third expedition ....   128
  „           „           „       fourth   „   ....   220
  „           report of   .... .... .... .... ....   181
Rodd, Sir R., negotiations by, with Italy   .... .... .... ....   119
Rolland, Captain, awarded Victoria Cross   .... .... .... ....   180

## S.

Saddles, camel   .... .... .... .... .... .... ....   429, 509
Samala, action at ....   .... .... .... .... .... ....   66
  „   advanced base formed at   .... .... .... .... ....   65
Sanak plain ....   .... .... .... .... .... .... ....   15
Sanitation   .... .... .... .... .... .... ....   351, 365, 581
Sappers and Miners   122, 140, 141, 145, 146, 149, 150, 184, 193, 194,
    218, 222, 223, 224, 236, 238, 239, 240, 248, 249, 251, 256, 336, 337, 344, 452
Scouting   .... .... .... .... .... .... .... ....   393
Scurvy   .... .... .... .... .... .... .... ....   579
Services and departments ....   .... .... .... .... ....   452
Settlements, permanent, native ....   .... .... .... .... ....   31
  „   temporary   .... .... .... .... .... .... ....   32
Seyla Ban plain   .... .... .... .... .... .... ....   15
Shaab tank ....   .... .... .... .... .... .... ....   28
Shakerley, Captain....   .... .... .... ....   155, 156, 165, 168
Sharp, Major   .... .... .... .... ....   .... 150, 173, 177
Shebeli Webi   .... .... .... .... .... .... ....   25, 38
Sheikh Upper   .... .... .... .... .... .... ....   32
Shilemale plain   .... .... .... .... .... .... ....   15
Shoeing   .... .... .... .... .... .... .... ....   591
Signalling ....   .... .... .... .... .... ....   82, 340, 355, 484
  „   equipment   .... .... .... .... .... ....   484, 599
Sikhs, 52nd   110, 122, 134, 140, 145, 149, 150, 166, 172, 193, 195, 218,
              222, 223, 236, 247, 248, 255, 256, 336, 342, 350, 360
Smith, Lieutenant, awarded Victoria Cross   .... .... .... ....   241

|   |   | PAGE |
|---|---|---|
| **Somali** as a soldier | | 322, 437 |
| ,, levies | | 56, 57, 80, 91, 108, 231, 323, 417 |
| ,, tactics | | 321 |
| ,, tribes | | 40 |
| ,, ,, disposition of | | 40 |
| ,, warfare | | 320 |
| **Somaliland,** Abyssinian, area of | | 20, 42 |
| ,, area and boundaries | | 7 |
| ,, British connection with, history of | | 44 |
| ,, climate of | | 36 |
| ,, drainage in, lines of | | 8 |
| ,, French, administration of | | 42 |
| ,, fuel in | | 38 |
| ,, garrison of, provisional scheme for, on demobilization | | 612 |
| ,, Italian | | 22, 42, 46 |
| ,, physical geography | | 8 |
| ,, staple foods in | | 38 |
| ,, water in | | 38 |
| ,, wells in | | 39 |
| **South Africa,** despatch of contingent from, third expedition | | 127 |
| **Spies** and secret agents | | 392, 400 |
| **Staff** duties | | 367 |
| ,, diary, extracts from | | 375, 379, 380, 381, 382 |
| ,, offices, equipment of | | 370 |
| ,, organization of | | 368 |
| **Staffs,** organization of, first and second expeditions | | 59, 335 |
| ,, ,, third expedition | | 335 |
| ,, ,, fourth ,, | | 339 |
| **Stanton,** Major | | 339, 368, 616 |
| **States,** field | | 344 |
| **Stores,** despatch and receipt of | | 514 |
| ,, disposal of, on demobilization | | 606 |
| ,, landing of | | 542, 544, 548, 564 |
| ,, on convoy duty, management of | | 515 |
| ,, remarks on | | 598 |
| **Strategy** | | 305 |
| **Strength** of Field Force, third expedition | | 345 |
| ,, ,, fourth ,, | | 346 |
| **Sudi Haji** | | 49 |
| **Suleiman Mountains** | | 24 |
| **Supplies,** conveyance of, on the march | | 525 |
| ,, disposal of, on demobilization | | 609 |
| ,, important purchase of, statement of | | 527 |
| ,, first expedition | | 61 |
| ,, third ,, | | 137, 353, 354 |
| ,, orders regarding, by Lieut.-General Egerton, fourth expedition | | 332 |

|   |   | PAGE |
|---|---|---|
| Supply depots | .... | 354, 517 |
| ,, organization of | .... | 516 |
| ,, sources of | .... | 517 |
| ,, meat | .... | 525 |
| ,, remarks on | .... | 526 |
| ,, and transport, organization of | .... | 336, 489 |
| Survey section | .... | 336, 404, 416 |
| Swann, Colonel, in command of Berbera–Bohotle force | .... | 136, 337, 349 |
| ,, ,, lines of communication, fourth expedition | .... | 342 |
| ,, instructions to, by General Manning | .... | 136 |
| ,, report by, on re-embarkations | .... | 564 |
| Swayne, Colonel, appointed to take charge of Protectorate after operations | .... | 610 |
| ,, appointment of, to command first expedition | .... | 51 |
| ,, ,, ,, ,, second ,, | .... | 90 |
| ,, departure of, to England | .... | 111 |
| ,, final report of, on first expedition | .... | 80 |
| ,, instructions to, by Consul-General | .... | 54 |
| ,, proposals of, for organization of forces after operations | .... | 611 |
| ,, punishes the tribes | .... | 73 |
| ,, report of action at Erigo | .... | 104 |
| ,, ,, October, 1902 | .... | 102 |
| ,, ,, to Consul-General, before first expedition | .... | 56 |

### T.

|   |   | |
|---|---|---|
| Tactics | .... | 320, 442 |
| ,, British | .... | 324 |
| ,, Somali | .... | 321 |
| Tarigas | .... | 31 |
| Telegraph communication opened | .... | 138 |
| ,, cable, laying of | .... | 482 |
| ,, equipment | .... | 480 |
| ,, messages, summary of | .... | 483 |
| ,, line, interruptions to | .... | 363, 480 |
| ,, ,, working of | .... | 479 |
| ,, offices opened | .... | 478 |
| ,, section, R.E. | .... | 138, 223, 337, 344, 477 |
| ,, services | .... | 336, 477 |
| Telegraphs, Marconi | .... | 147, 197, 336, 484 |
| ,, method of construction | .... | 481 |
| ,, fourth expedition | .... | 231 |
| Topography | .... | 402 |

(8927a)      2 s

|   | PAGE |
|---|---|
| **Towns** | 25, 31 |
| **Tramline** at Berbera | 208, 476, 501 |
| **Transport** ambulance | 501, 583 |
| ,, animals, casualties among | 503, 511 |
| ,, land 36, 132, 185, 196, 202, 212, 215, 308, 354, 356, 428, 450, 490, 526 | |
| ,, marine, organization of | 336, 529 |
| ,, ,, remarks of Lieut.-General Egerton on | 552 |
| ,, ,, reports of Commander Kendall on | 545, 552 |
| ,, ,, ,, Lieutenant Huddleston on | 539, 543, 545 |
| **Transport,** mule | 501 |
| ,, on demobilization | 608, 615 |
| ,, orders regarding, by Lieut.-General Egerton, fourth expedition | 333 |
| ,, organization of | 494 |
| ,, system of | 493 |
| ,, water | 36 |
| **Treaties** with Mijjarten Sultan | 46 |
| **Treaty** with tribes by British Government | 45 |
| **Tribal Horse,** organization of | 231, 236, 417 |
| **Tribes, Somali** | 40 |
| ,, disposition of | 40 |

## V.

|   |   |
|---|---|
| **Vehicles,** disposal of, on demobilization | 609 |
| ,, use of, in Somaliland | 499 |
| **Veterinary** attendants | 586 |
| ,, equipment | 599 |
| ,, department, organization of | 336, 583 |
| **Volturno,** captain of, action of | 254 |

## W.

|   |   |
|---|---|
| **Walker,** Captain, awarded Victoria Cross | 180 |
| **Wallace,** Lieut.-Colonel, in command of movable column | 219 |
| ,, reconnaissance by | 232 |
| **War Office,** control of third expedition handed over to | 118 |
| **Warsangli Mountains** | 14 |
| ,, Plateau | 15 |
| **Water** as affecting health of troops | 582 |
| ,, boring, deep | 458 |
| ,, distribution of | 361, 457 |
| ,, in Somaliland | 38 |
| ,, on the march | 458 |
| ,, orders regarding, by Lieut.-General Egerton, fourth expedition | 331 |

|  |  | PAGE |
|---|---|---|
| **Water** storage | .... .... .... .... .... .... | .... 197, 331, 454 |
| ,, supply | .... .... .... .... .... .... | .... 307, 360, 452 |
| ,, ,, during third expedition | .... .... .... .... | 135, 353 |
| ,, ,, ,, fourth ,, | .... .... .... .... | 243, 360 |
| ,, ,, data, abstract of | .... .... .... .... .... | 460 |
| ,, transport of.... | .... .... .... .... .... | .... 332, 353, 453 |
| **Waylahed,** skirmish at | .... .... .... .... .... .... | 69 |
| **Webi Shebeli** | .... .... .... .... .... .... .... | .... 25, 38 |
| **Wells** in Somaliland | .... .... .... .... .... .... | 39 |
| **Williamson,** Colonel | .... .... .... .... .... | .... 335, 340, 578 |
| **Wounds** .... .... | .... . .... .... .... .... .... | .... 581 |

## Y.

| **Yeilding,** Colonel | .... .... .... .... .... .... .... | 340, 489 |
|---|---|---|
| **Yusuf Ali** .... | .... .... .... .... | 46, 71, 112, 129, 132, 133, 189 |

## Z.

| **Zaribas** | .... .... .... .... .... .... .... | .... 325, 351, 442 |
|---|---|---|
| **Zeila**.... | .... .... .... .... .... .... .... .... | .... 26 |
| ,, Plain .... | .... .... .... .... .... .... .... | .... 11 |

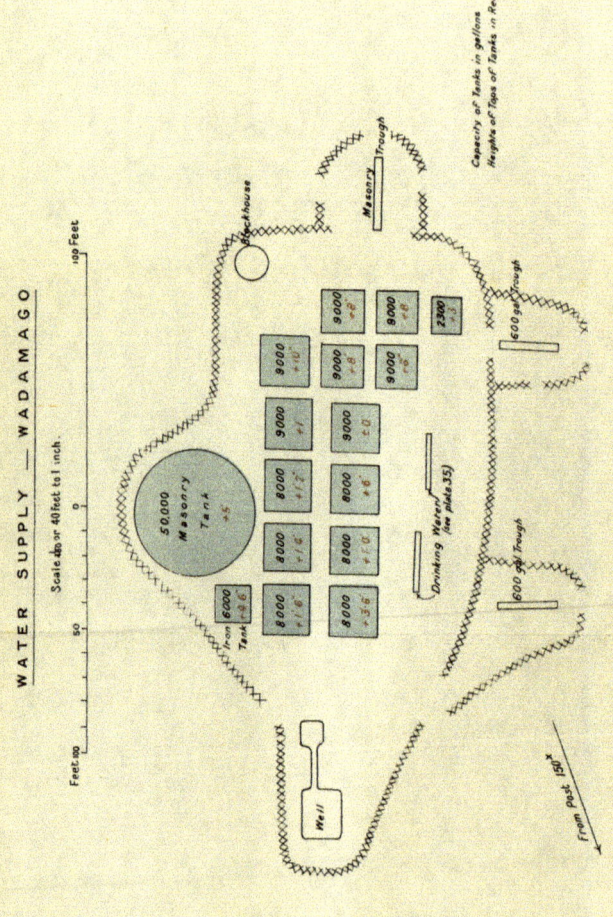

Plate 35.

## SECTION OF WELL AT WADAMAGO

Scale (approx.) about 10 feet to 1 inch.

Feet 0   10   20   30   40   50   60   70 Feet

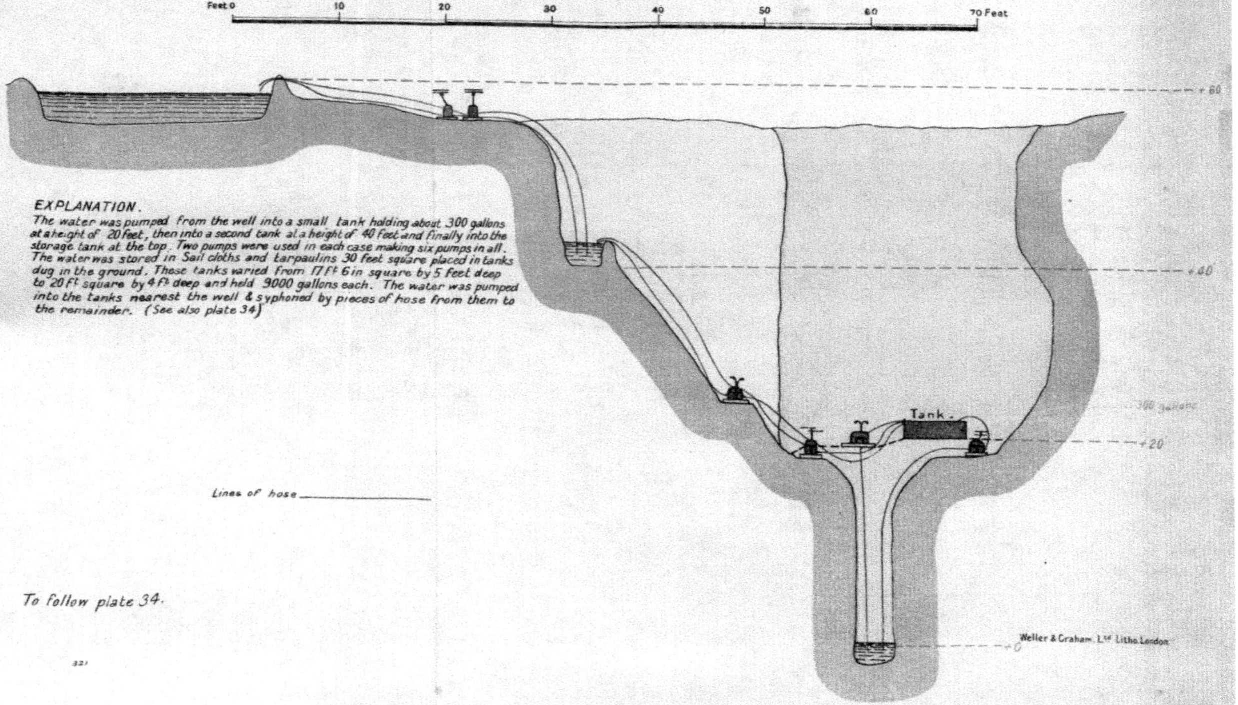

### EXPLANATION.

The water was pumped from the well into a small tank holding about 300 gallons at a height of 20 feet, then into a second tank at a height of 40 feet and finally into the storage tank at the top. Two pumps were used in each case making six pumps in all. The water was stored in Sail cloths and tarpaulins 30 feet square placed in tanks dug in the ground. These tanks varied from 17ft 6in. square by 5 feet deep to 20ft square by 4ft deep and held 9000 gallons each. The water was pumped into the tanks nearest the well & syphoned by pieces of hose from them to the remainder. (See also plate 34).

Lines of hose ————

To follow plate 34.

Weller & Graham, Ltd. Little London

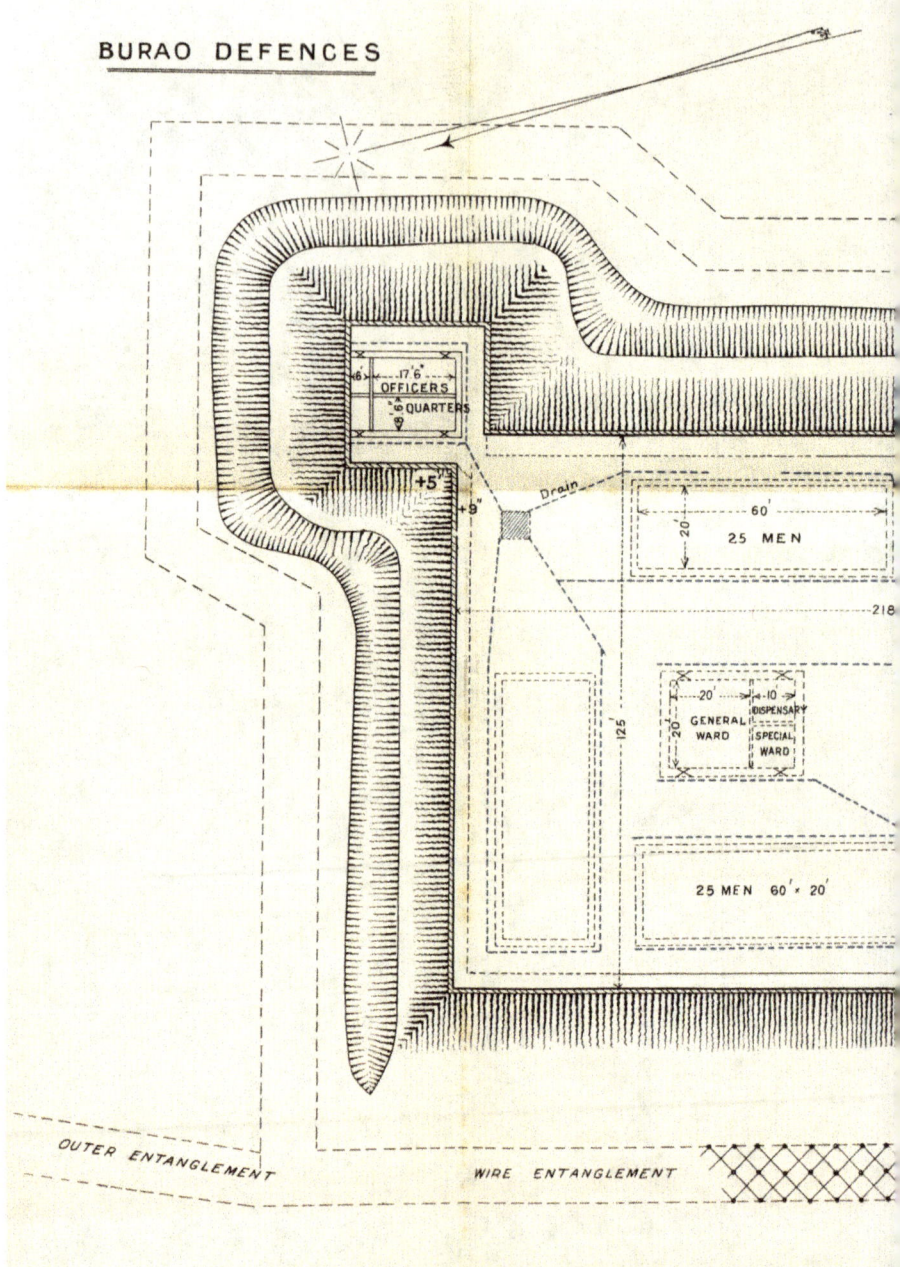

Plate 40.

# NEW POST

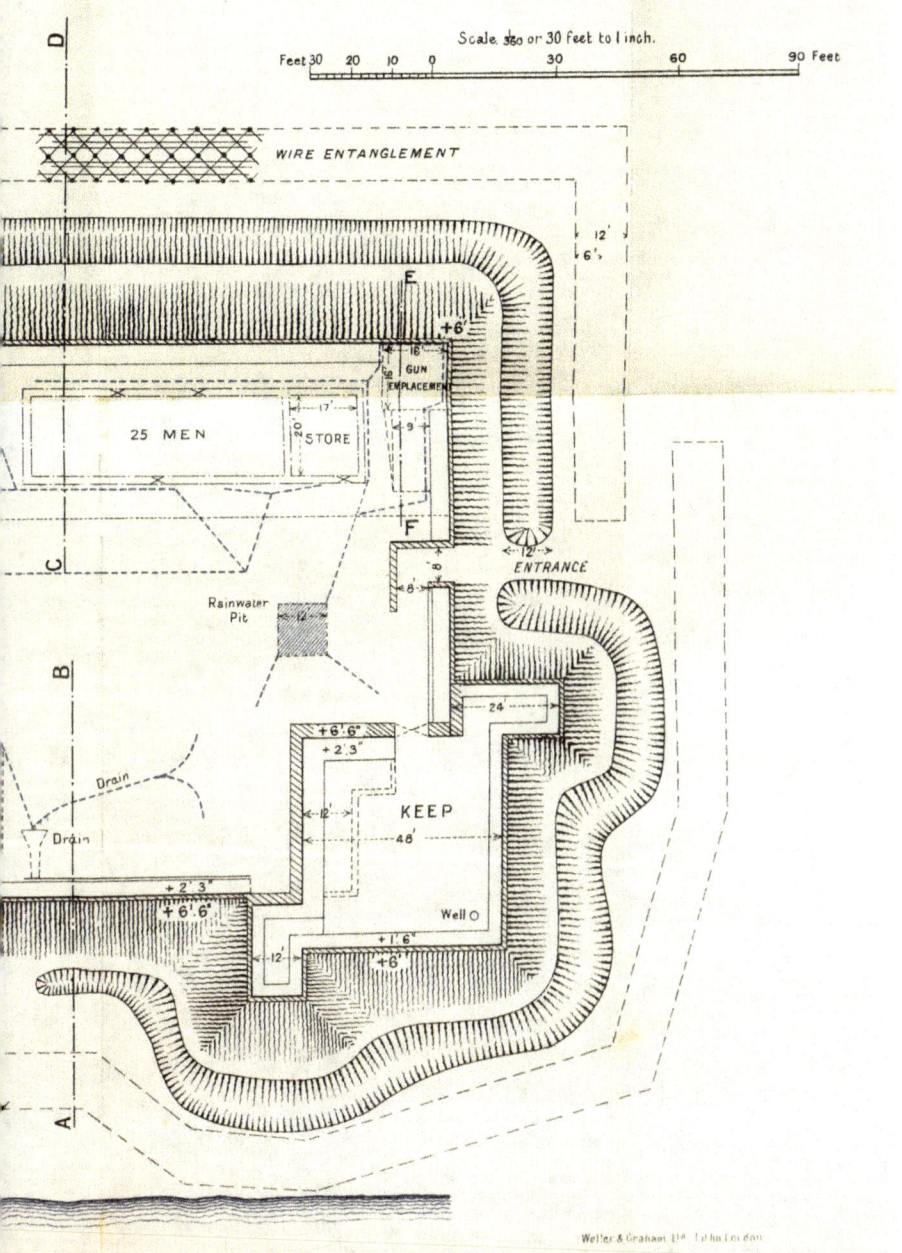

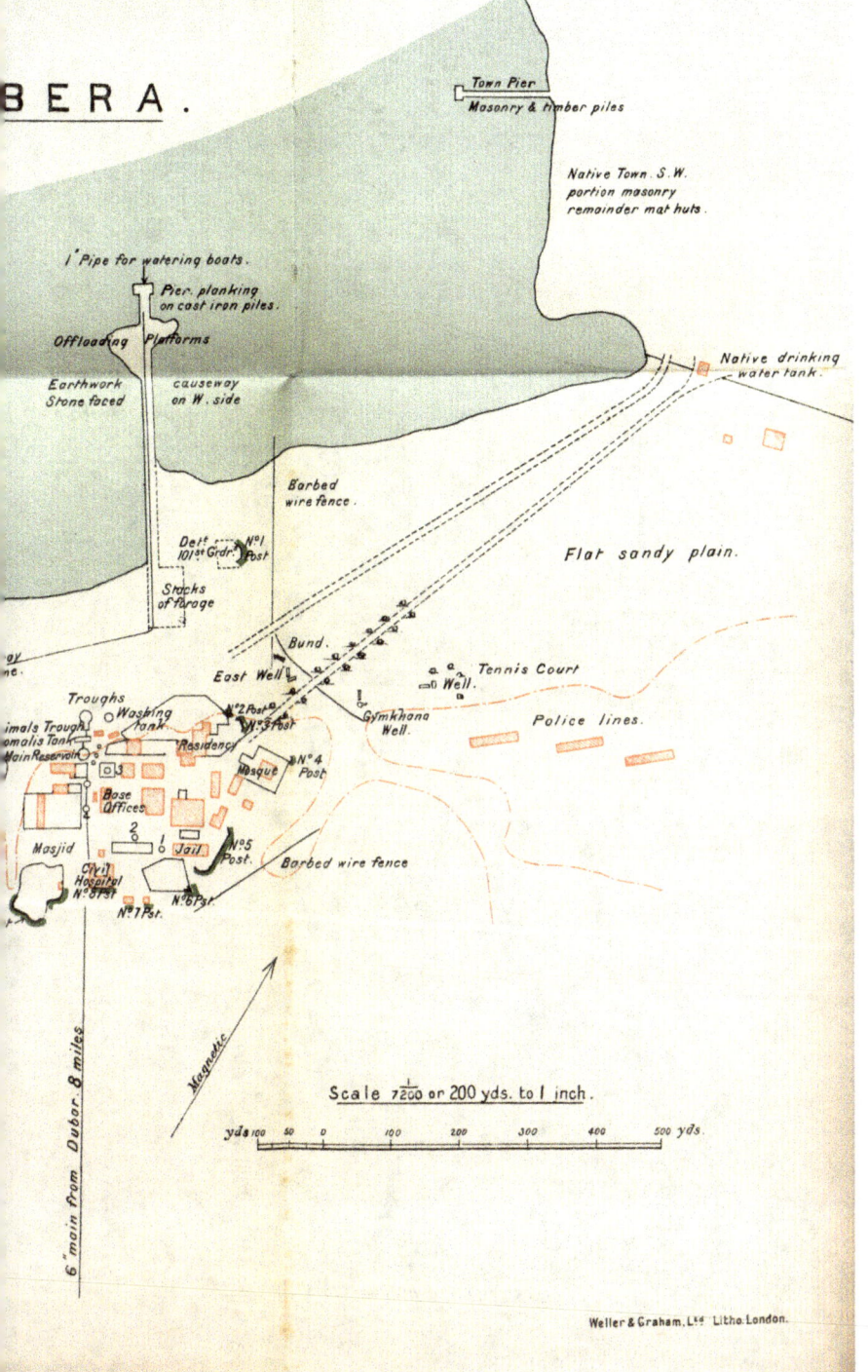

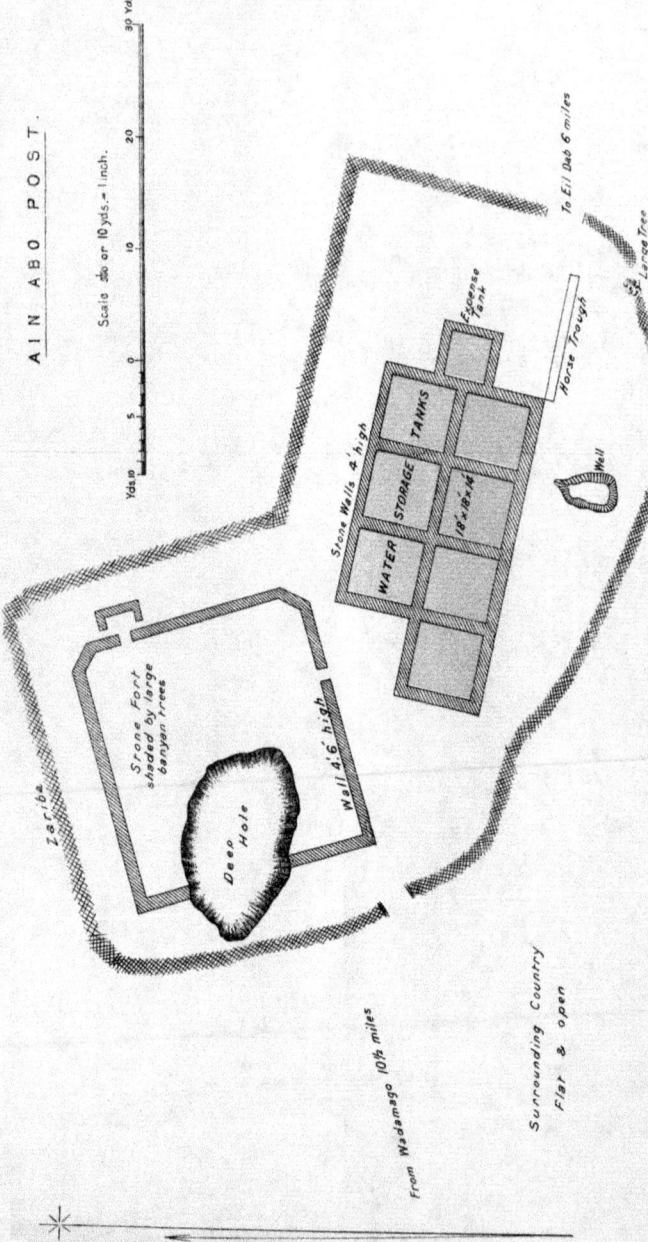

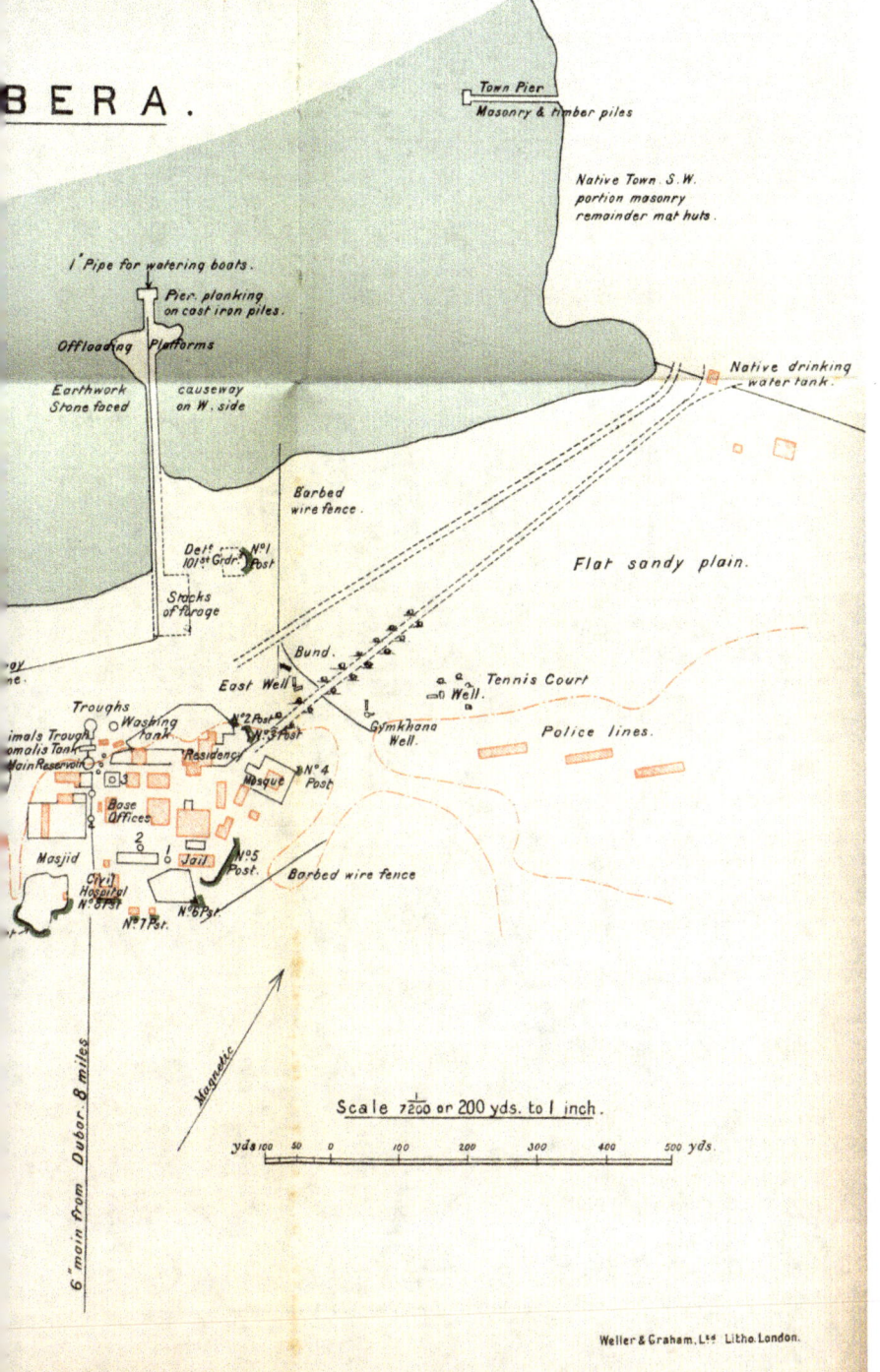

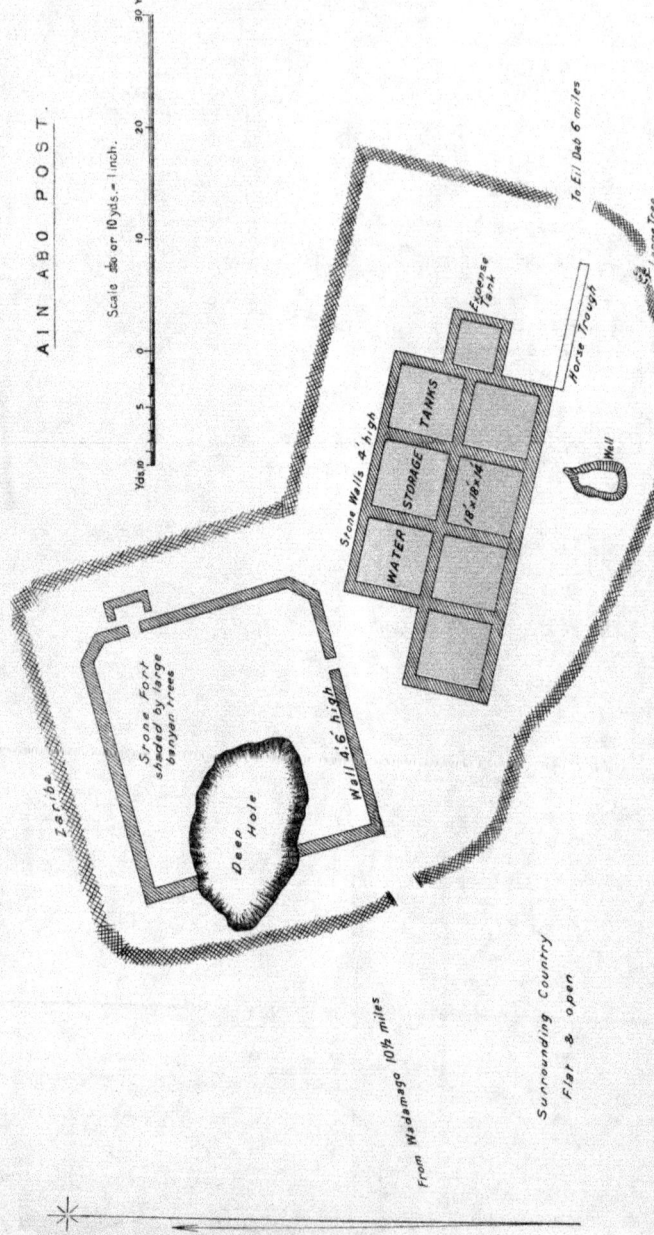

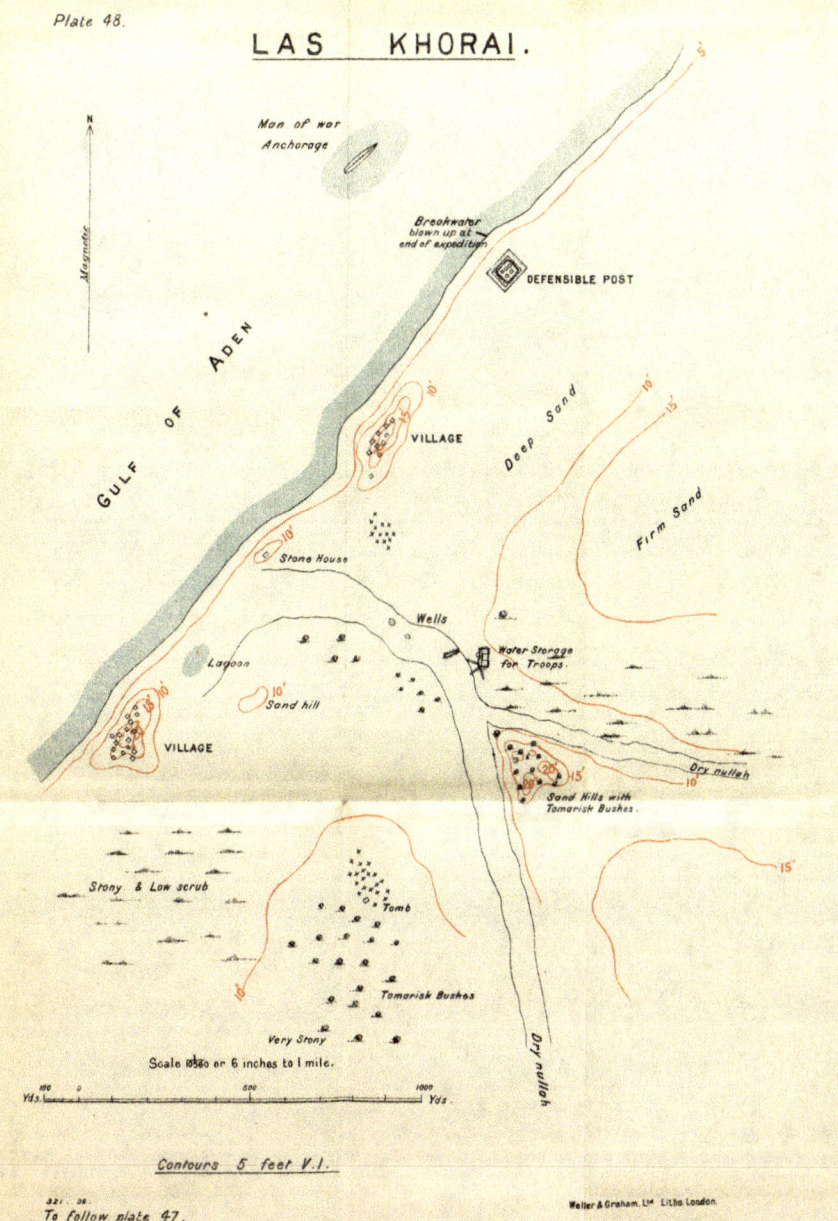

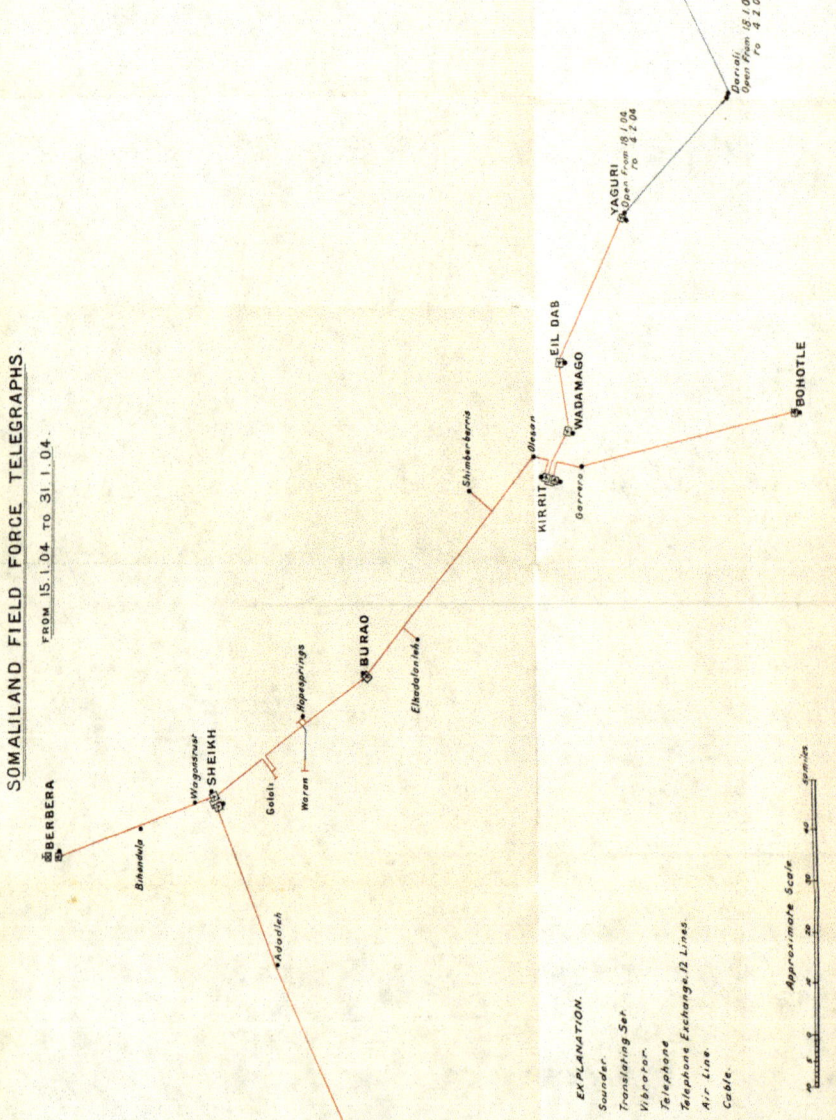

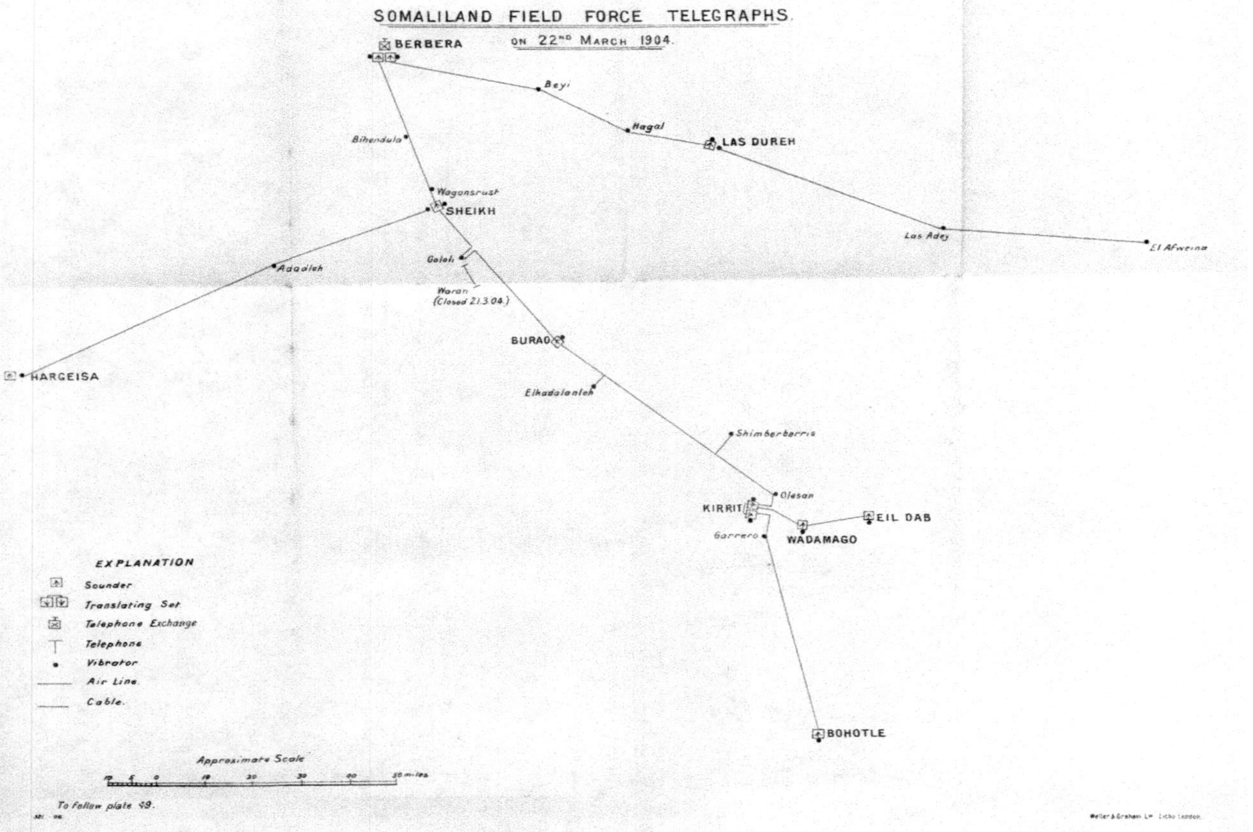

Plate 50.

# SOMALILAND FIELD FORCE TELEGRAPHS.
## ON 22ND MARCH 1904.

EXPLANATION

- Sounder
- Translating Set
- Telephone Exchange
- Telephone
- Vibrator
- Air Line
- Cable

Approximate Scale

To follow plate 49.

www.ingramcontent.com/pod-product-compliance
Lightning Source LLC
Chambersburg PA
CBHW052342230426
43664CB00042B/2662